Japan Business and Economics Series

This series provides a forum for empirical and theoretical work on Japanese business enterprise, Japanese management practices, and the Japanese economy. Japan continues to grow as a major economic world power, and Japanese companies create products and deliver services that compete successfully with those of the best firms around the world. Much can be learned from an understanding of how this has been accomplished and how it is being sustained.

The series aims to balance empirical and theoretical work, always in search of a deeper understanding of the Japanese phenomenon. It also implicitly takes for granted that there are significant differences between Japan and other countries and that these differences are worth knowing about. The series editors expect books published in the series to present a broad range of work on social, cultural, economic, and political institutions. If, as some have predicted, the twenty-first century sees the rise of Asia as the largest economic region in the world, the rest of the world needs to understand the country that is, and will continue to be, one of the major players in this region.

Editorial Board

Japanese Multinationals Abroad

Individual and Organizational Learning

Edited by Schon L. Beechler and Allan Bird

New York   Oxford
Oxford University Press
1999

Oxford University Press

Oxford   New York
Athens   Auckland   Bangkok   Bogotá   Buenos Aires   Calcutta
Cape Town   Chennai   Dar es Salaam   Delhi   Florence   Hong Kong   Istanbul
Karachi   Kuala Lumpur   Madrid   Melbourne   Mexico City   Mumbai
Nairobi   Paris   São Paulo   Singapore   Taipei   Tokyo   Toronto   Warsaw

and associated companies in
Berlin   Ibadan

Library of Congress Cataloging-in-Publication Data
Japanese multinationals abroad: individual and organizational
learning / edited by Schon L. Beechler and Allan Bird.
p.   cm.—(Japan business and economics series)
Includes bibliographical references and index.
ISBN 0-19-511925-8
1. Corporations, Japanese—Management.   2. International business
enterprises.   3. Industrial management—Japan.   I. Beechler, Schon,
1959–   .   II. Bird, Allan.   III. Series.
HD2907.J348   1998   98-20135
658'.049'0952—dc21

1 3 5 7 9 8 6 4 2

Printed in the United States of America
on acid-free paper

Preface

This book is the culmination of the first 10 years of a journey that has taken us across continents and time zones more times than we can count in an effort to better understand the nature of Japanese management abroad and the processes of organizational and individual learning. From our perspective as editors, this book is an important milestone in that journey because it brings together, in one volume, new and important empirical contributions from authors whom we have come to know and respect as experts in the field of Japanese management overseas.

The first step in realizing the vision for this book was afforded at the Annual Conference of the Association of Japanese Business Studies, held in Ann Arbor, Michigan in June 1995. We invited all the authors to submit original papers to the AJBS conference and organized a two-day discussion seminar to discuss the individual papers and the volume as a whole immediately before the conference. Each author provided valuable feedback to the other chapter writers and participated in discussions that will long be a highlight of our own individual and collective learning.

This book could not have been possible without the generous cooperation and valuable insights from the hundreds of managers interviewed for the research reported in this volume. Because their identities must remain confidential, we cannot thank them by name but want them to know that our gratitude is enormous.

We would like to express our appreciation to the editors and staff at Oxford University Press. In particular, Herb Addison, Vice President and Executive Editor, Tamara Destine, Editorial Assistant, and Robert Milks, Production Editor, all showed the highest levels of professionalism, as well as patience, in every stage of the publication process.

Finally, we would like to thank our families. Allan would like to thank his wife, Diane, for her unfailing support and encouragement. His four children, Kyle, Allyson, Jared, and Campbell, also warrant heartfelt gratitude for their willingness to forgive him the missed birthday, school concert, or camping trip while he was on the road in pursuit of "one more company, one more interview." Finally, he dedicates this book to his father, A. Dee Bird, who taught him that ideas matter.

Schon would like to thank her husband, Eric Ernst, for being an understanding husband and loyal friend who "always knew" we would publish this book. Although her daughter can't read yet, Schon would also like to thank Jamisen for being such a good kid that her mother was able to spend the time necessary to finish a project begun before her conception.

Finally, she dedicates this book to her mother, Lois Griffin, who taught her from an early age that she should always do those things that make her happy. It was good advice, Mom.

Contents

Contributors

Schon Beechler
Columbia University

Allan Bird
California Polytechnic State University

Mary Yoko Brannen
University of Michigan

Mauricio Bustos
El Colegio de la Frontera Norte

Oscar Contreras
University of Sonora

Martin Kenney
University of California, Davis

John Kidd
Aston University

Jill Kleinberg
University of Kansas

Rochelle Kopp
Japan Intercultural Consulting

David Methé
Kobe University

Joan Penner-Hahn
University of Michigan

Vladimir Pucik
IMD

Jairo Romero
University of California, Davis

Jane Salk
Groupe ESSEC

Noriya Sumihara
Tenri University

Sully Taylor
Portland State University

D. Eleanor Westney
Massachusetts Institute of Technology

PART I

INTRODUCTION

ALLAN BIRD & SCHON BEECHLER

The End of Innocence
Japanese Multinationals Abroad

From 1979 to 1989 the world witnessed the arrival of a global economic superpower. During this 10-year period Japanese foreign direct investment totaled $67.5 billion (Organization for Economic Cooperation and Development, 1991), and by 1993 Japanese firms had been so successful that 281 of *Business Week's* Global 1,000 were Japanese (July 12, 1993). Of all Japanese investment overseas, nearly 50% went to the United States. In Tennessee alone, Japanese multinational corporations (MNCs) established over 500 affiliate operations.

In light of these developments, one might anticipate a well-developed interest in Japanese overseas affiliates among management scholars. Yet an analysis of the leading U.S. journals in this field (*Administrative Science Quarterly, Strategic Management Journal, Academy of Management Journal, Academy of Management Review, Organizational Dynamics, Human Resource Management Journal*, and the *Journal of International Business Studies*) reveals a dramatically different story. From 1980 through 1994 only a handful of articles on the management of Japanese operations abroad appeared.

At first blush an observer might conclude that management scholars are guilty of neglect. A closer examination reveals a more optimistic picture. In Japan, Europe, and North America a growing number of researchers—from several disciplines and employing disparate theories and methodologies—have been piecing together a picture of how Japanese MNCs manage their overseas affiliates. This volume represents a first attempt at pulling together in one place some of their observations.

The audience for this volume includes the broad community of international business researchers as well as the more focused community of Japanese management specialists. This work builds upon an expanding body of research in addressing a set of increasingly critical issues for both groups. Although international business researchers have been drawn to the success of Japanese MNCs, their attention has focused more on strategic aspects of how Japanese MNCs compete in the international arena. Much less research has been directed toward how those strategies are actually implemented, toward the management processes, within Japanese overseas affiliates. Similarly, Japanese management specialists have tended to focus on what Japanese firms are doing within Japan, viewing the overseas affiliate as an extension of the parent confronted with unique challenges, but not dramatically different from domestic operations.

As the writers in this volume will demonstrate, how Japanese MNCs manage the people in their overseas operations has wide-ranging implications for MNC performance as well as the performance of the local economies in which they operate. Moreover, the recent experience of Japanese firms is informative for MNCs headquartered in other countries that are currently facing internationalization challenges as well as for government administrators charged with attracting and monitoring Japanese foreign direct investment.

The works assembled here possess two notable and mutually supportive characteristics. First, the contributors present a *diversity* of perspectives. The source of this diversity is multifaceted. It begins with the nationality of the authors, which spans three geographic regions—Japan, North America, and Europe—and extends to their disciplinary backgrounds, which include anthropology, psychology, sociology, and management science. The nature of the phenomena studied and how and where they were studied also vary dramatically. Several authors focus on events within a single firm, whereas others compare experiences across a number of firms. Among the multifirm studies, several contributions are restricted to a single industry; others contrast management practices across industries. Research sites stretch from Italy to Indonesia and cover the major economic centers of North America, Asia, and Western Europe.

The second and perhaps somewhat paradoxical attribute of this collection is found in the *complementarity* of the authors' findings. Despite differences in research focus, disciplines, methodologies, or contexts, when taken as a whole a number of unifying themes emerge and consensus emerges around several observations. The end result is somewhat analogous to what happens when sight is given to the fabled six blind men grasping an elephant. In the original tale, each blind man grabs hold of the elephant in a different place—one a leg, one the tail, one the trunk, and so on. The result is a confused and contradictory description of an elephant. In the case of this volume, sight makes all the difference. Although each writer focuses on a single aspect of managing the Japanese overseas affiliate—cross-cultural interaction, knowledge flows and control, organizational learning, and so forth—what emerges reflects and informs the whole.

Following this introductory chapter, Eleanor Westney provides an important historical context for the research found in this volume by analyzing the evolution of research on multinational enterprises in general and Japanese MNCs in particular. The remainder of the volume is divided into three parts, with chapters in each part grouped around common levels of analysis. In the first part, the contributors address the individual- and group-level impact of Japanese management practices. To do so, they apply an anthropological perspective that analyzes interactions between Japanese expatriates and local employees as an ongoing dynamic leading to negotiated "hybrid" or "third" cultures. The focus is on the process by which variations in cultural assumptions and values interact with corporate cultures and contexts as both Japanese and local employees try to resolve difficulties resulting from cultural differences. The second part of this book moves up to the business unit level and examines various issues related to implementing management policies and systems in overseas affiliates. To this end, the authors focus on topics such as how Japanese firms attempt to transfer or substantially modify home country management philosophies, policies, and practices in order to fit the local affiliate. The final part addresses issues at the corporate level. The primary concern here is with the impact of subsidiary management activities on the organization as a whole. In this part, the contributors address various aspects of organizational learning related to the transfer of managerial knowledge from subsidiary to parent or from one overseas affiliate to another.

Throughout this volume the contributors emphasize the "MNC" in Japanese MNCs rather than focus on their "Japanese-ness." The authors are concerned not only with understanding the experience of Japanese MNCs but also in placing that experience within the larger context of MNCs as a form of organization with unique characteristics. Consequently, wherever the attention is directed—on negotiated cultures, the development of organizational capabilities, or organizational learning, to name a few of the issues addressed—great care is taken to frame the discussion in ways that clearly link the Japanese experience to that of MNCs with other national origins.

We would like to briefly describe the individual chapters and explain how they relate to each other and the volume as a whole. The stage is set by Eleanor Westney's chapter, "Changing Perspectives on the Organization of Japanese Multinational Companies." Westney provides an important historical context for the subsequent chapters in this volume by examining the evolution of the analysis of multinational enterprises and the impact on that analysis of the internationalization of Japanese firms. Westney begins with a brief overview of the prevailing views of authors writing about the internationalization of Japanese firms in the 1970s and describes a number of the reasons why some of the pronouncements that appear odd today were based both on prevailing assumptions and methodologies employed at the time. As echoed by Vladimir Pucik later, Westney notes that a number of criticisms leveled against Japanese MNCs during this early period still sound familiar today.

In reviewing work done in the 1980s, Westney notes that a shift in the international paradigm used by researchers to analyze multinational operations may underlie the seeming paradoxes of Japanese management that became accepted knowledge during this period. She explores the idea that the weaknesses were not necessarily in the Japanese firms themselves, but in the models that academics used to analyze them. Westney then identifies two important trends in the study of Japanese MNCs in the 1990s: the first is a move away from simply identifying problems and barriers faced by Japanese firms as they internationalize, and the second is a move away from an undifferentiated model of "the Japanese MNC" to an examination of differences between Japanese firms. Finally, the chapter looks to the future of Japanese MNCs and some of the current trends that will likely shape their future evolution.

Putting Japanese and Local Nationals Together: Creating Third Cultures

The three chapters in part II focus on the emergent cultures created when Japanese expatriate managers and local employees interact. In chapter 3, "When Japanese and Other Nationals Create Something New: A Comparative Study of Negotiated Work

Culture in Germany and the United States," authors Mary Yoko Brannen and Jane Salk employ parallel theoretical perspectives to focus on how organizational actors use their various cultural identities and affiliations to participate in and influence a new work setting. Positioning their analysis at the nexus of research on managing multinational organizations, research on international joint ventures, and research on cultural differences, they compare the experience of one Japanese multinational's efforts to manage two overseas affiliates, one a wholly owned subsidiary in western Massachusetts and the other a joint venture in Durren, Germany.

Their interview and archival data gleaned from a 4½-year effort provide fertile soil for examining the processes of negotiating new cultures in these sites. Brannen and Salk argue that the outcomes of the negotiations they studied led to cultures that were not Japanese, German, or American, nor a combination of Japanese *and* host country cultures. Rather, they were unique to a specific time and place. Their findings also highlight the impossibility of predicting in advance what type of "negotiated" culture will result in a given multinational setting.

In chapter 4, "Negotiated Understandings: Organizational Implications of a Cross-National Business Negotiation," Jill Kleinberg changes venue and gives the notion of negotiated culture an interesting twist by studying actual negotiations between Japanese and American executives involving the buyout of a company. She extends her previous work on "sketch maps" by constructing the "text" of negotiation interactions. She does so by employing an ethnographic approach in the study of 20 hours of "formal" negotiations spread over four separate sessions. This is supplemented by interviews with persons on both sides of the bargaining table regarding their perceptions and interpretations of the unfolding drama. "Unofficial" agendas temper interactions while unconscious agendas insinuate themselves into the discussions. The outcomes negotiated ultimately transcend the specific terms of the buyout, creating culture in the process. As a consequence, aspects of existing organizational cultures in the two companies are both reinforced and reshaped. Simultaneously, new elements of organizational culture take root.

Noriya Sumihara builds on these themes in chapter 5, "Roles of Knowledge and 'Cross-Knowledge' in Creating a Third Culture: An Example of Performance Appraisal in a Japanese Corporation in New York." Drawing on Giddens's notions of tacit and discursive knowledge, Sumihara explores how cross-cultural interactions give rise to conflicts that, in turn, force organizational members to make explicit their understandings of how and why actions should be taken. These attempts at explanation and understanding, however, are influenced by individuals' knowledge of the other culture. Inherently rich with expressed and implied meanings, the performance appraisal is an ideal setting for his study. Indeed, Sumihara finds that, as both large and small conflicts surface, members' attempts to explain them are strongly influenced by their knowledge of the other culture's expectations as well as their ability to explain their own culture's expectations. He concludes by noting that the recursive nature of cross-knowledge sharing leads to the evolution of a third culture, one that continues to evolve and adapt in response to the incessant onslaught of ever new conflicts.

In the final chapter in this part Rochelle Kopp takes a different tack from that of the previous authors and explores the nature of conflict between Japanese and local employees in Japanese subsidiaries based in the United States. In "The Rice-Paper Ceiling in Japanese Companies: Why It Exists and Persists," she explores a variety of different organizational practices and managerial behaviors, unearthing the causes of misunderstanding and conflict. Kopp insightfully notes that many of the conflicts that U.S. employees confront arise not from a failure to transplant, but from success in transplanting Japanese human resource management (HRM) systems to their U.S. operations. She points out that within Japan the traditional HRM system is two-tiered and makes an important distinction between *seishain,* regular full-time employees, and non-*seishain.* Problems arise in the United States because local employees are familiar with the *seishain* elements of the system but are classified as being part of the non-*seishain* tier. Kopp closes with a number of practical suggestions for managers on how to address these challenges.

Transplanting and Transforming HRM: Philosophies, Policies, and Practices at the Subsidiary Level

Part III focuses on the overseas affiliate as the unit of analysis. Chapter 7 by Sully Taylor, "National Origin and the Development of Organizational Capabilities: The Case of International Human Resource Management in Two Japanese MNCs," compares the experiences of two Japanese subsidiaries in Spain. Her specific interest is in identifying the extent to which these two MNCs are able to develop or enhance organizational capabilities essential to international competition within their Spanish subsidiaries. She identifies four capabilities: (1) the ability to disperse creative activities throughout the firm, (2) the ability to establish knowledge transfer mechanisms within the firm's network, (3) the ability to disperse authority to utilize transfer mechanisms, (4) the ability of top management to recognize and respect expertise wherever it may arise from within the firm. Findings from field interviews reveal that the two firms are developing capabilities at quite different rates and in different ways, thereby suggesting that, although superficially similar in that both employ "Japanese" management systems, they are strikingly different in how they go about adapting to new contexts.

In chapter 8, "Labor-Management Relations in the Japanese Consumer Electronics Maquiladoras," Martin Kenney, Jairo Romero, Oscar Contreras, and Mauricio Bustos address a question that has been debated for at least the last 20 years, "Can the Japanese production management system be transplanted overseas?" Because it is the largest non-Asian, newly industrializing country, they chose Mexico as the venue for exploring this question. Reviewing findings from interviews and surveys, these authors conclude that Japanese management systems are being transferred but in a superficial way. In contrast to Fruin's (1997) thesis that Japanese manufacturing facilities constitute "knowledge works" or learning institutions, Kenney and his coauthors find that Japanese maquiladoras appear to be straightforward reproductions of a basic Japanese production management system that has been modified only to the extent necessary to remain efficient in a Mexican context.

In chapter 9, "When Performance Does Not Matter: Human Resource Management in Japanese-owned U.S. Affiliates," Vladimir Pucik draws on extensive research he has conducted on Japanese affiliates operating in the United States to show that relatively little has changed over the past decade, and indeed since the 1970s, in the way Japanese companies manage their white-collar human resources, despite the available learning opportunities. According to Pucik, the mantra "think globally, act locally" is translated into "they do the thinking, and we do the acting."

In this chapter, the author proposes that Japanese MNCs have not learned because, although their current systems may not be optimal, they are well known to Japanese managers and are therefore familiar. In addition, Pucik argues that dynamics in Japan and the expatriate orientation of Japanese multinational firms create barriers to change and management effectiveness. In an argument parallel to Kopp's description of the *seishain* and non-*seishain* classes of workers, Pucik asserts that the maximization of managerial employment in Japan remains the hidden but paramount corporate objective that inhibits organizational change in overseas white-collar HRM practices and ultimately undermines Japanese MNCs' global competitiveness.

Organizational Learning and the Parent-Subsidiary Connection

The final part addresses Japanese MNCs and their overseas subsidiaries from the standpoint of the firm as a whole and the relationship between subsidiary and parent. A central theme running through the three chapters in this part is organizational learning. Perhaps this should not be too surprising. Although part II focuses on person-to-person interaction, the notion of a negotiated culture carries a powerful undercurrent of adaptive learning. Similarly, the focus in part III on the transfer of management systems and the refinement of organizational capabilities also contains within it an implicit sense of learning, albeit learning in which the subsidiary is under the tutelage of the parent. In this final part, although the issue of directionality of learning is addressed, the primary concern is with the nature of organizational learning and the impact of learning processes for *both* the subsidiary and the parent.

David Methé and Joan Penner-Hahn lead off in chapter 10, "Globalization of Pharmaceutical Research and Development in Japanese Companies: Organizational Learning and the Parent-Subsidiary Relationship." They begin by noting that Japanese firms are often held up as examples of learning organizations, but that there have been few studies of this learning in the context of extended international operations. Drawing on data from the experiences of 10 Japanese pharmaceutical companies, these authors examine the process of globalization for research and development (R & D) activities. The firms studied have structured relationships so that learning occurs in one of three ways. Some set up "dual-channel integrated" systems through which parent learning can be transferred to the subsidiary and vice versa in a way that includes the entire organization. Still others establish "dual-channel disjointed" systems that allow for learning that is isolated between the parent and a specific subsidiary, with little, if any, transference to other areas of the firm. Finally, some firms institute "single channel" mechanisms that allow for learning flows to move in only one direction, either from parent to subsidiary or vice versa. These three types of mechanisms relate to three different types of learning, with dual-channel integrated approaches yielding deutero learning, while dual-channel disjointed and single channel approaches result in double-loop and single-loop learning, respectively. They conclude that the type of learning most appropriate for a given organization is a function of the firm's resources, capabilities, and overall strategic approach. Moreover, the critical determinants affecting learning in any of these approaches are the availability and utilization of human resources. In this regard, each Japanese MNC's configuration of human capital becomes the deciding factor in determining both how and what can be learned.

In "Working Together, But How?" John Kidd addresses the issue of learning in the parent-subsidiary relationship but from a very different perspective than that of Methé and Penner-Hahn. His concern is with the culture-influenced mental maps that employees bring to the task of managing the parent-subsidiary relationship. Invoking Hofstede's (1991) work-related cultural dimensions of power distance, uncertainty avoidance, individualism, and masculinity, as well as Hall's notion of high versus low context culture, Kidd discusses the ways in which cultural norms and expectations affect individual managers' abilities to work with and learn from one another. He draws on Nonaka and Takeuchi's notions of knowledge creation to delineate the way in which individual experience is translated into organizational learning. Returning to the cultural variations he finds in the myriad subsidiaries of Japanese firms throughout Western Europe, he concludes that what individual managers, and by extension their firms, are able to learn is heavily influenced by the mix of cultures in which they operate.

In the final chapter of the book, "Organizational Learning in Japanese Overseas Affiliates," Allan Bird, Sully Taylor, and Schon Beechler pull together data from field interviews and questionnaire surveys conducted in 147 Japanese overseas affiliates distributed across the United States, Mexico, the United Kingdom, Spain, Indonesia, Malaysia, the Philippines, Singapore, and Thailand. Their specific interest is in the establishment of the overseas affiliate as an occasion for learning by both the parent and the subsidiary. Employing an *enactment→selection→retention* model of learning, these authors identify four learning types that emerge through the decisions Japanese MNCs make as they move forward with the establishment of the affiliate. What at first appear to be tactical decisions take on strategic significance as their impact reverberates through subsequent decisions.

Read individually, each of the chapters illuminates our understanding of Japanese firms and their experiences as they extend their operations out into the world community. Taken as a whole, this collection provides an integrated picture of how Japanese organizations, Japanese managers, and local employees learn in ways that enable them to adapt and prosper.

Finally, although this volume focuses exclusively on Japanese firms and the people who work within them, the message it carries is one that appears applicable to all MNCs regardless of their national origin. The successes and failures described in this volume are recognizable to all who operate in the international arena; their responses, though on occasion unique, carry understandable rationales. In this sense, the volume reflects and embodies the experience of the Japanese MNCs on which it is based. The authors, despite coming from different disciplines and cultural backgrounds and focusing on different phenomena and levels of analysis in different industries and countries, nevertheless identify a body of common experience and a consonant set of concepts and themes to explain the recent experience of Japanese MNCs abroad.

References

Business Week. 12 July 1993. "The Business Week Global 1000."

Fruin, M. 1997. *Knowledge Works.* New York: Oxford University Press.

Hall, E. T. 1959. *The Silent Language.* New York: Doubleday.

Hofstede, G. 1991. *Cultures and Organizations: Software of the Mind.* London: McGraw-Hill.

Nonaka, I., & Takeuchi, H. 1995. *The Knowledge-Creating Company.* New York: Oxford University Press.

Organization for Economic Cooperation and Development. 1991. *OECD Economic Surveys: Japan.* New York: OECD.

D. ELEANOR WESTNEY

Changing Perspectives on the Organization of Japanese Multinational Companies

As an empirical phenomenon, multinational corporations (MNCs) have existed at least since the nineteenth century, and some would argue for an even longer history (Wilkins, 1970). Serious academic studies of the MNC as an organizational form, however, and even the widespread use of the terms "multinational enterprise" or "multinational corporation," date from the early 1960s (Jones, 1996). The postwar internationalization of Japanese firms began later that same decade,[1] and although early analysts of Japanese MNCs identified certain distinctive features in their patterns of internationalization, by and large they fitted the experience of Japanese firms into the theories of the MNC that had been developed on the basis of Western, and especially United States, companies (Abo, 1989). In what has become a recurring theme in writing on Japanese MNCs, however, these early analyses predicted that Japanese firms would face formidable challenges in internationalizing their organizations. But few could have predicted that the internationalization of Japanese firms would pose equally formidable challenges to the theories and analyses of the MNC, exposing inadequacies in existing theories and raising new questions, becoming in the process central to the evolving field of international management.

As the editors of this volume indicate in their introduction, the authors represented here address issues of MNC management and organization in the context of Japanese firms, rather than issues of Japanese-style management in the context of internationalization. This chapter surveys earlier work on Japanese MNCs and its relationship to the changing models of the international management field, in order to provide a historical context for the other chapters and a base for understanding their contribution to the study of the MNC.

11

The Study of the Internationalization of Japanese Firms in the 1970s

In the 1960s and 1970s, definitions of the MNC exhibited a great deal of variety, but the one element common to virtually all was that "it engages in international production and operates plants in a number of countries" (Dymsza, 1972: 6). The internationalization of production was the core of the phenomenon, as it was defined in these decades, and the question of why a firm would set up manufacturing operations in a foreign country was the focus of the early theories of the MNC. The answer, which with variations became the touchstone of international business right up to the present, involved two sets of factors. One set concerned location factors: that is, the relative comparative advantage of the firm's home country and the host country in which it set up production. The other involved the firm-specific factors that constituted the company's competitive advantage, developed in the company's home base—usually a particular product or set of products—whose attractiveness to customers beyond its borders more than compensated for the disadvantages of setting up operations in a foreign business environment (a line of approach that began with Hymer, 1960). Ray Vernon's widely influential product life cycle theory of internationalization (1966) made the stages in this process more specific: a firm's products found export markets after its position in its home market was established, and the firm eventually set up its own production operations abroad in order to defend those markets against the emergence of local competitors. As markets in the home country matured, the main locus of production shifted to those offshore plants, as the home country operations moved on to new product generations. Given that in the 1980s one of the distinctive features of Japanese MNCs was widely seen to be their reluctance to internationalize (see, for example, Trevor, 1983), Vernon's view of internationalization as primarily defensive in nature, a view based on the development patterns of U.S. MNCs, is worth emphasizing. A quotation in 1972 from General Electric's Chairman, Fred J. Borch, illustrates this more dramatically: "Most U.S. companies have as their basic orientation the U.S. market. They would prefer to participate in world markets by export, but tariffs and, increasingly, nontariff barriers have forced them to establish plants within foreign borders in order to participate there" (Bradley & Bursk, 1972: 40–41). But the question of how MNCs were organized and managed, as opposed to why they existed or what political and economic impact they had on host countries, received theoretically grounded analysis much more slowly. In contrast to economics, for which the MNC was an important anomaly that demanded theoretically based explanation, or to development studies, in which economists, political scientists, and sociologists were concerned with analyzing the impact of MNCs on developing countries, organization theory did not identify the MNC as a significant phenomenon (Evans, 1981; Ghoshal & Westney, 1993). Much of the discussion of MNC organization and management in the 1960s, therefore, followed the managerially oriented, functional approach of business schools, looking separately at finance, marketing, HRM, and strategic planning in the context of the MNC. The lack of attention from organization theorists was not the only handicap in developing more systematic analyses; data on MNCs as organizations were extremely hard to obtain. Ironically, the United States, which was the home base of the overwhelming majority of large MNCs in the 1960s and the main center of academic theory on the subject, probably had less firm-level data on outward foreign direct investment than most other countries in the world. Its relative lack of regulation of the flows of investment across its borders meant an absence of a central government system for monitoring (and thereby providing data on) the foreign activities of U.S. MNCs at the firm level.

Developing such data was a laborious process, and it was first addressed in a major project at Harvard under the direction of Ray Vernon: the Harvard Multinational Enterprise Project, begun in 1965 and funded by the Ford Foundation. This project had a major impact on the organizational analysis of MNCs in general and an even greater impact on the study of Japanese MNCs, stimulating the first major publications on the topic in both English and Japanese. The project's initial focus was on U.S. firms, and its working definition of an MNC was a large firm (operationalized by presence in the 1967 Fortune 500 list of the largest U.S. industrial companies) with manufacturing subsidiaries in six or more countries (Vernon, 1971: 7–11). The project produced the first major empirical analyses of MNCs as organizations, providing data on the sequence of internationalization, the geographic distribution of the activities of the 187 firms in the database, and the kinds of industries in which MNCs clustered. It also took research on the MNC into the realm of organizational structure, examining coordination and control in the form of ownership patterns (the percentage of parent ownership in local subsidiaries) and the administrative structure (specifically, whether international activities were covered by an international division, a geographic or worldwide product division structure, or a matrix). It was a landmark in the study of MNCs: when its final report was written in 1975, it listed 17 books, 151 articles, and 28 doctoral dissertations that grew out of or were closely associated with it (Vernon, 1994: 224).

The original database did not include Japanese firms, and therefore the earliest and most influential publications—Vernon's *Sovereignty at Bay* (1971) and Stopford and Wells's *Managing the Multinational Enterprise* (1972)—were based exclusively on the data for the original 187 American MNCs. In later data collection, the firms in the Fortune 200 1970 list of the largest non-U.S. firms with manufacturing subsidiaries in six countries or more were also included. Although the project did not originally include Japanese firms, the first two major academic analyses of Japanese MNCs in English were both inspired by and associated with the Harvard project, as were several studies in Japanese.[2] The two English-language studies were both published in 1976: Michael Yoshino's *Japan's Multinational Enterprises* and Yoshi Tsurumi's *The Japanese Are Coming*.[3] Although neither strictly followed the methodology of the Harvard project (that had to wait until Hideki Yoshihara's study, published in Japanese in 1979), both took their key themes from it—the target locations of foreign direct investment (FDI), the industries represented, ownership patterns, and administrative structure—and it provided an explicit base for comparison. Hideki Yoshihara's study adopted the methodology of the Harvard project as well as its framework, analyzing the large Japanese companies (in the list of the 500 largest Japanese industrial firms) with manufacturing operations in five or more countries. But in an interesting addition to the Harvard methodology, Yoshihara also examined what he called "export-centered companies": large firms with sales subsidiaries in five or more countries. Of the 500 largest Japanese industrial firms in 1975, only 33 qualified as multinational companies and 48 as export-centered companies.

The dominant patterns of foreign production in Japanese companies revealed in these early studies contrasted significantly with those of the U.S. firms in the Harvard database. Japanese manufacturing operations abroad were concentrated in the developing countries (85% of the manufacturing subsidiaries in 1973, according to Yoshihara's database), especially in Asia. Moreover, as both Yoshino and Tsurumi pointed out, much of Japan's FDI in manufacturing was initiated by small- and medium-scale Japanese firms rather than by the largest companies.[4] Indeed, one early Japanese discussion questioned whether such ventures even deserved to be called multinationals, since in the view of the authors MNCs were companies that exemplified advanced modern management, and these firms, relatively small in scale and often family-owned, were "pre-modern" in terms of their management systems (Nihon Keizai Chosa Kyogikai, 1976: 7–12). The industries with the highest levels of FDI in manufacturing were textiles and the mature segments of the consumer electronics industries; significant Japanese FDI was also observable in the resource-based industries, including mining and agricultural and forest products. Indeed, Tsurumi went so far as to assert his conviction that "by 1980 over two-thirds of the total direct investments of Japanese abroad will be of the resource-oriented type" (1976: 37).

Although the patterns of Japanese FDI differed from U.S. patterns, they nevertheless fit comfortably into existing theories of FDI based on comparative advantage and the product life cycle: Japanese firms went abroad seeking low-wage labor that was increasingly scarce in the high-growth Japanese economy (textiles), seeking natural resources, or following the product life cycle into Asian markets, where products whose markets had already matured in Japan were finding eager customers, and then producing locally to maintain those markets in the face of rising tariffs and import restrictions (Kojima, 1978; Ozawa, 1979). But while the economic side of Japanese FDI fit easily into existing frameworks, the organizational patterns of Japanese firms expanding their activities to other countries exhibited some interesting anomalies.

One that was immediately obvious was the role of the trading company. Trading companies had offices and maintained staff in offices throughout the world—but these were not manufacturing operations, and therefore this did not qualify them as MNCs, in the formal definition of the term (even though they faced most or indeed all of the organizational and managerial challenges of the MNC). They had equity positions in a number of production operations: they were often joint venture partners in large natural resource projects, for example, and Tsurumi found that in 1971, 25% of the foreign manufacturing subsidiaries of small firms and nearly 40% of those of large firms were jointly established with a Japanese trading company (1976: 79). But these investments, while perhaps formally qualifying the trading companies as MNCs, were clearly not the main focus of their international activities. Another anomaly was noted by Tsurumi and explored more systematically by Yoshihara: the strong propensity of Japanese firms to invest in sales and service subsidiaries in the developed countries of North America and Western Europe, whose markets they served not by the local manufacturing plants in an integrated country subsidiary envisioned in the MNC model, but by exports from Japan (Yoshihara's "export-oriented companies"). Japan's trading companies and these export-oriented companies illustrated in dramatic fashion the inadequacy of a definition of the MNC that centered on manufacturing alone.

Other differences between the organization and behavior of Japanese firms and the model derived from the U.S. experience led the analysts of the 1970s to assess the prospects for Japanese MNCs in ways that make startling reading from the perspective of the mid-1990s. It is unfair to an otherwise extremely insightful analysis to single out Yoshino's prediction for the future competitiveness of Japanese MNCs, but it is illustrative of the limitations of the models of the 1960s and 1970s that the Japanese case did so much to expose:

> Japan's inability to generate major innovative technologies will almost certainly limit the multinational spread of her industries and will particularly inhibit large-scale entry of Japanese manufacturing activities into the U.S. market. For the foreseeable future, then, Japanese enterprise will scarcely challenge the dominance of U.S.-based multinational enterprises. (Yoshino, 1976: 90)

Given the overwhelming emphasis in MNC theory in the 1960s and 1970s on product innovation as the key firm-specific advantage on which a company could build a multinational presence, Yoshino's assessment should not surprise us. Process innovations and competitive advantages based on the organization of work were not on the conceptual screen of analysts of international business until the burgeoning international presence of Japanese firms put them there in the decade after Yoshino's pronouncement. Interesting enough, Yoshino did note the production advantage of Japanese manufacturing companies, but like many others even as late as the 1980s, he attributed it to advantages of scale rather than to fundamental improvements in the organization of the factory (Yoshino, 1976: 132).

Tsurumi and Yoshihara both sounded another chord that rings strangely in the ears today, after more than a decade in which Japanese companies have been held up as exemplars of integrated global strategies. In a comparison of Japanese and U.S. MNCs, Tsurumi described the "parent's control over subsidiary" as "close" in U.S. companies and "loose" in Japanese. Even more surprising to readers today, he characterized parent-subsidiary relations as "globally integrated" in U.S. MNCs and "disjointed—local market oriented" in Japanese (Tsurumi, 1976: 4). This perception is echoed at the end of the decade by Yoshihara: "One reason why a global structure has not been adopted in Japanese MNCs is that they have not yet developed a truly global strategy" (Yoshihara, 1979: 204, translated from Japanese).

One reason for this perception was the strong local market orientation of the Japanese manufacturing plants in Asia, which had much the same potential disadvantages as the proliferation of local market-oriented plants in European multinationals as they faced competition from U.S. firms like IBM and Procter & Gamble, which had developed more "global logistics" (see for example Dymsza, 1972, ch. 6). But another factor was the perceived lack of an integrated global strategy. Japanese firms seemed to follow an incremental strategy driven by a desire to increase exports, often relying on initiatives from midlevel managers. Richard Pascale's analysis of Honda's penetration of the U.S. market reflects this perception: he portrays it as a process of incremental, trial-and-error learning processes by midlevel managers involved in the United States, rather than the top-down "global strategy" depicted by the 1980s business press (Pascale, 1984). But whether the expansion patterns of Japanese firms merely reflected the real processes of strategy in most companies—what James Brian Quinn dubbed "logical incrementalism"—or whether they reflected a real difference in the behavior of U.S. and Japanese firms was not a matter of debate in the 1970s: Japanese firms were widely seen as less global than their American counterparts, in strategy as well as organization.

This perception was powerfully reinforced by differences in coordination and control patterns, and here the analysis of Japanese multinationals anticipated the research emphasis of the 1980s on HRM and managerial processes as central to the organizational study of the MNC (a growing emphasis charted by Martinez & Jarillo, 1989). In the Harvard study, in accordance with the highly influential paradigm of strategy and structure developed by Alfred Chandler, the key organizational variable was administrative structure: in the case of the MNC, whether international activities were administered by an international division, a global product structure, a geographic structure, or a matrix. John Stopford found that firms with high levels of product divers-ification and of international activity tended to adopt matrix structures, and by exten-sion other analysts quickly came to see the matrix as the most advanced organization for the MNC of the 1970s (Stopford & Wells, 1972). No Japanese firm had adopted a matrix form in the 1970s, and Yoshihara found only one with a global product divi-sion structure; all the rest of the firms in his study were still in the "initial stage" of having international activities administered by an international division. This reinforced the perception of Japanese firms as lacking a global approach.

Although the 1970s studies of Japanese MNCs paid due attention to the struc-tural variable so emphasized in Western research of the time, they also broadened their organizational discussion to include three variables that were to become cen-tral in the next decade's analyses of MNCs: decision-making patterns, the cross-border flows of personnel, and the balance of home and host country "managerial culture." One of the reasons for this apparent prescience was the background of these early researchers on Japanese MNCs. Michael Yoshino came to the study of Japa-nese MNCs not from international business but from the analysis of the managerial and organizational systems of large Japanese enterprises in Japan (Yoshino, 1968). Yoshi Tsurumi had addressed in previous research a topic central to international business—cross-border technology transfer—but in his focus on Japan's introduc-tion and enhancement of Western technology in the postwar era he had paid close attention to firm-level management and strategic processes (Tsurumi, 1968). Both men brought to the topic a strong anchoring in the broader organizational and manage-rial processes of the firm. But we should note that these broader issues were raised not in the context of a critique of existing models of the MNC, but in terms of the distinctive challenges facing the Japanese firm as it expanded overseas.

The studies of the 1970s found that Japanese MNCs in Southeast Asia faced criti-cisms that sound familiar to this day:

1. They had a very high proportion of expatriate managers, higher than U.S. or European firms in the region;

2. Local managers felt excluded from decision-making processes both within the local subsidiary and in the interactions between parent and subsidiary;
3. Japanese firms had a tendency to create "Little Japans": in Tsurumi's words, "Little change is made in the production procedures from the Japanese source (parent plant) to the overseas plant(s)" (Tsurumi, 1976: 194).

The hostile reaction to these patterns raised two questions. Why did they arouse so much criticism? And what caused them?

Clearly, one of the major sources of criticism was the frustration of local managers, whose expectations of their roles and of their prospects for upward mobility were thwarted by the apparent monopolization of influence by Japanese expatriate managers and whose aspirations for the local adaptation of organizational patterns were constrained by the tight coupling to the patterns of Japanese production sites. And in an era of mounting concern over the political and economic impact of MNCs, host governments in Asia were eager to make MNC subsidiaries as responsive to local interests as possible, and the number of expatriate managers joined ownership as a focus of official concern. But both Tsurumi and Yoshihara argued that in addition, local governments and employees in Asia had higher expectations of the local responsiveness of an Asian MNC, expectations that aroused disproportionate resentment when they were not met (an analogous factor in North America and Western Europe in the 1980s was the high level of expectations of Japanese subsidiaries induced by the highly favorable press coverage of "Japanese-style management"). And both authors also argued that criticism of Japanese MNCs was encouraged and exaggerated by local Western expatriates and by local elites with strong ties to incumbent Western MNCs, who resented the competition from the newer Japanese subsidiaries (Tsurumi, 1976: 257; Yoshihara, 1979: 258–70). In other words, Japanese MNC patterns both violated the expectations of MNC organizational behavior that had been set up by Western MNCs and changed the nature of competition in local markets. We can see in retrospect that there were clearly grounds here both for a reassessment of the prevailing models of the MNC and for seeing the Japanese as developing an alternate model—but this reassessment did not begin until the next decade.

Another factor intensified the attention paid to the Japanese MNC in Asia. Japanese firms tended to take the pattern of "oligopolistic matching" that characterized their competitive behavior in their home market into their geographic patterns of international expansion. In other words, when a Japanese firm set up operations in a country, its rivals tended to follow suit, creating a sudden surge in Japanese investment that gave it a much higher degree of visibility.

This kind of "home country effect" leads us to the answers given to the second question raised by the apparently distinctive organizational patterns of the emerging Japanese MNCs: what caused them? One set of explanations involved *life cycle effects*: that is, Japanese firms had only recently begun to expand internationally, and in these early stages of technology and organization transfer inevitably relied on a high level of expatriate management and home country involvement. This was quite possibly temporary and might plausibly have been observable in Western MNCs had they been studied at a comparable stage of development. Another set of explanations involved home country effects: that is, the distinctive patterns observed in Japanese MNCs were the product of distinctive organizational systems that had developed in the home country and were deeply institutionalized in Japanese firms; these were therefore unlikely to change over time without major changes in the organization and management of the Japanese firm in Japan itself. Even though the analysts of the 1970s (like those of the 1980s) believed that both sets of factors were operating, they assigned more importance to the latter.

The home country patterns portrayed in these early analyses as integral to the distinctive patterns of Japanese subsidiaries were remarkably similar to those that the researchers here see as key points of stress in Japanese subsidiaries today (see especially the chapters in the first part):

- Decision making that involved the careful building of agreement among all those managers whose activities would be affected by the decision, as much through informal networking as through formal decision-making procedures;
- Managerial roles defined in very broad terms and dependent on the initiatives of the incumbent for effectiveness and a high level of reliance on middle managers;
- Priority of work over other sectors of life: as Yoshino put it, "emotional commitment to the organization by employees at every level" (Yoshino, 1976: 166);
- Heavy reliance on experience-based tacit know-how and learning by doing (Yoshino, 1976: 167–68; Tsurumi, 1976: 193).

The causal links between these patterns at home and the high proportion of expatriate managers and the other distinctive organizational features of Japanese MNCs drawn by the analysts of the 1970s have considerable continuity with the approach followed in the ensuing decades. Michael Yoshino explained the link in terms that later institutional theorists would have labeled as *cognitive isomorphism* (Meyer & Scott, 1983), that is, the taking for granted of a certain way of doing things and a virtually automatic transfer of that way across arenas of activity: "The Japanese manager who must head the foreign subsidiary is so wedded to the traditional managerial systems of his country that he would find it impossible to manage an organization without the support of subordinates who share the same work style" (Yoshino, 1976: 168). In other words, Japanese expatriate managers carried their mode of managing and decision making into their subsidiaries, because it was the only way of managing that they knew, and the difficulties of transferring this distinctive management system to local managers were so great (because such a transfer required such lengthy socialization into the system and the organizational networks) that they continued to rely on their own managers.

The implications of this analysis were clearly spelled out by both Yoshino and Tsurumi: Japanese firms would not be able to internationalize successfully until they changed their management systems at home. To quote Yoshino again, "In order to undertake major expansion internationally, the Japanese must bring about basic changes in their management system—changes that will not be easy to achieve. And in the process, they may well sacrifice those elements that have made their system so effective internally" (1976: 178). Tsurumi went even further, extending the backwash of multinationalization beyond the management system to the society as a whole:

> The moment literally hundreds of Japanese firms each made the incremental decision to go multinational, they unknowingly destined Japan to its present situation. That is to say, industrial structures, government-business relations, diplomatic stances, and even corporate culture, that Japan has cultivated at home for over a century, have now become exposed to external forces to change. In short, a societal change of no less colossal magnitude than that which Japan faced in 1868 and again in 1945 is now a crisis Japan is experiencing. (Tsurumi, 1976: 304)

In other words, building a Japanese MNC was as much a matter of organizational evolution and learning at home as it was abroad.

Few people thought at this time to ask why, if this were true for Japanese firms, it was not equally true of all firms. Howard Perlmutter and others had argued that becoming a "true" multinational required a major shift in managerial mindsets, from ethnocentric to polycentric to geocentric (Perlmutter, 1969), and Stopford and Wells had argued that the administrative structures for international activities had to be increasingly integrated with the overall organizational structure over time. But the hypothesis that a corporation's management system as a whole would have to evolve at home as well as in the foreign subsidiary was only raised in the 1980s, as a new model of the MNC emerged, and it has yet to receive the sustained research attention it deserves.

Reassessing Japanese MNCS: The 1980s and 1990s

During the 1980s, the rapidly expanding international presence of Japanese companies, especially in the American market, moved the study of Japanese firms into the mainstream of management research in strategy, technology and production management, marketing—and of course, international business. Contrary to Yoshino's 1976 prediction, during the 1980s the United States became the major destination of Japanese manufacturing investment abroad, and in the latter part of the decade Western Europe began to experience rapidly rising levels of Japanese FDI. It was increasingly clear, however, that the Japanese firms were continuing to exhibit distinctive features in the organization and management of their operations abroad. By the middle of the 1980s, a growing number of analysts began to view Japanese MNCs not as inadequate versions of a single, Western-based model of the MNC but as constituting an alternative model, both in terms of strategy and organization: the "global" MNC. By the late 1980s and early 1990s, however, the global MNC fell out of favor as a management model, as the international management field focused increasingly on a new "advanced" normative model of the MNC—the "transnational"—against which Japanese MNCs once again fell short.

The global model of the MNC was succinctly described by Michael Porter, who turned his attention to international strategy and the MNC in the mid-1980s (1986a,

1986b): "The purest global strategy is to concentrate as many activities as possible in one country, serve the market from this home base, and tightly coordinate those activities that must inherently be performed near the buyer. This is the pattern adopted by many Japanese firms in the 1960s and 1970s, such as Toyota" (Porter, 1986a: 18). By focusing attention not on the location of manufacturing, but on the geographic dispersion of each of the elements of the value chain, Porter and others working in the 1980s broadened the definition of the MNC beyond the production focus of the previous decade. By the 1990s, the prevailing definition of the MNC had shifted to "a company that owns or controls value-adding activities in more than one country" (Dunning, 1993: 3).

The new global form of MNC, which the Japanese firms exemplified, was made possible by changes in the international business environment—falling tariff barriers, growing convergence of per capita GNP among a growing number of highly industrialized countries, and rising consumption levels in the developing countries—and by technological changes that rapidly lowered the costs of cross-border transport and communication (see the discussion in Bartlett, 1986, for a more extended analysis). Japanese firms were not unique in their recourse to the global model, but they were often portrayed as uniquely effective in exploiting it, not only because the timing of their internationalization coincided with the maturation of the economic, political, and technological forces leading to the "global economy," but also because of the interaction of these "period effects" (as sociologists would dub them) with the country effects on their management systems (Bartlett, 1986: 373–74). The model of the global MNC took many of the features that in the previous decade had been seen as signs of the immaturity of Japanese MNCs—tight coupling of the activities of offshore subsidiaries with those of the home country organization, dense communications between local (expatriate) managers and their Japanese counterparts and superiors, close coordination between local and central decision making—and recast them in terms of a new organizational form.

For a brief period in the early and mid-1980s, the Japanese MNC enjoyed the status of a new management model, which was held up to Western managers for emulation (Gluck, 1983; Hamel & Prahalad, 1985; Hout, Porter, & Rudden, 1982; Porter, 1986b). But this period of glory was much briefer for the Japanese MNC than for the Japanese firm in general, which continued to enjoy "model" status (though it was far from uncontested) until the collapse of the bubble economy in the early 1990s. By the second half of the 1980s, Japanese MNCs were increasingly portrayed on both sides of the Pacific as struggling to develop more appropriate organizations for effective internationalization (Bartlett & Yoshihara, 1988; DeNero, 1990; Okumura, 1989a). Indeed, a voracious reader able to keep pace with the rapidly expanding academic literature on Japanese management in Japan and the smaller but still substantial literature on the strategy and organization of Japanese MNCs would, if he or she tried to integrate the two literatures, have discovered some rather puzzling paradoxes:

1. The Japanese management system has been a key source of Japan's competitive advantage, especially its decision-making processes, which acted to encourage extensive information sharing and knowledge creation, and its HRM system (see, for example, Aoki, 1988; Nonaka 1988).

The Japanese management system has been a key weakness of Japan's MNCs, especially its decision-making processes, which weakened information sharing across borders, and its HRM system (Bartlett & Yoshihara, 1988; Lifson, 1992).

2. Japanese firms have exhibited a remarkable capacity for learning from other countries (Cole, 1989; Rosenberg & Steinmueller, 1988).

   Japanese MNCs have exhibited a notable incapacity for learning from their subsidiaries in other countries (DeNero, 1990; Okumura, 1989b).

3. Japanese firms have been models of effective linkage between strategy and organization, in terms of developing dynamic core capabilities (Prahalad & Hamel, 1990).

   Japanese MNCs are struggling to build organizations and organizational capabilities to match their international strategies (Bartlett & Ghoshal, 1989).

These paradoxes are perhaps more apparent than real. Like the rapid fall from glory of the global model of the Japanese MNC, they owe much to shifts in the paradigms that came to dominate the analysis of the strategy and organization of multinational enterprise from the mid-1980s.

From the late 1970s on, a group associated with the Harvard Business School (notably C. K. Prahalad, Yves Doz, and Christopher Bartlett) had been building a framework for analyzing the MNC that portrayed it as dealing with two sets of forces: those pulling it toward responsiveness to the demands of the various local environments in which it operated and those pulling it toward integrating its activities across borders and toward the standardization that facilitated such integration. Seeing MNCs as torn between local demands and pulls toward centralization was not novel: it was a view that had loomed large in discussions of the MNC since the 1960s. The innovation was that, instead of portraying these forces as two ends of a single continuum, the "Integration-Responsiveness," or "I-R," framework identified them as two potentially orthogonal sets of variables, creating a more complex conceptual space for developing models of the MNC.[5] Although the framework was originally developed with little reference to Japanese firms (the focus was instead on European and U.S. MNCs), the Japanese case fit extremely well into one of the three models derived from the framework, which from the mid-1980s have become standard in the MNC literature, although considerable variation in labeling has persisted. The Japanese MNCs typified the global MNC, high on cross-border integration and low on local responsiveness. The classic MNC—often labeled "multidomestic"—was seen as responding strongly to the forces for local responsiveness, putting most of the value chain into its country subsidiaries, which over time developed considerable autonomy (at the cost of cross-border integration). And in some industries, MNCs were portrayed as trying to develop a model that combined high levels of local responsiveness and of cross-border integration—variously called the transnational (Bartlett, 1986; Bartlett & Ghoshal, 1989), the heterarchy (Hedlund, 1986), or the multifocal firm (Prahalad & Doz, 1987).

In the early 1980s, none of the three models was seen as inherently superior; the industry was the key factor determining which of these strategies was most appropriate. In a number of industries, particularly those in which the Japanese firms excelled, such as autos and consumer electronics, the forces for local responsiveness were relatively weak, while the rewards for integration and standardization were large, whereas in other industries, such as packaged food, the reverse was true. Only in a few industries were the forces seen as equally demanding. But by the mid-1980s, the advocates of the I-R framework had come to believe that international business environments in general were moving rapidly in the direction of escalating pressures on both dimensions, making both the global and multidomestic strategies and organizations less sustainable (Bartlett, 1986; Bartlett and Ghoshal, 1989). They asserted that most companies faced strong pressures to converge on the new model combining high levels of local responsiveness with cross-border integration and increasing geographic dispersion of capabilities, in which the home country organization becomes one subsidiary within an interdependent multinational network.

An important factor in the development of this convergence approach has been the recognition that the MNC's dispersion and internal diversity constitute a potential source of innovation and learning well beyond what is accessible to a purely domestic company. No longer is the MNC seen as simply exploiting advantages developed in its home market; instead, it is able to monitor developments in key markets around the world, call upon innovating capabilities in any or all of a range of locations, and introduce new products and processes wherever the benefits to its competitiveness warrant (see, for example, Vernon, 1979, for a very early statement of this perspective, and Bartlett & Ghoshal, 1986 and 1989, for detailed development). In the words of Gunnar Hedlund, "Global reach in itself constitutes a competitive and innovative advantage, the development and exploitation of which require non-hierarchical control structures and other aspects of heterarchy" (Hedlund, 1993b: 130). But if geographically dispersed capabilities coordinated through networks of interdependence are the fundamental condition for transnational learning, then global MNCs (like the Japanese, which still have most of their capabilities concentrated in their home country and have built up their organizations abroad relatively slowly) are at a significant disadvantage compared to MNCs whose value-adding capabilities are much more widely dispersed. The rapidly growing acceptance of the "transnational" perspective on the MNC goes a long way toward explaining the paradoxes noted here in terms of the evaluation of the Japanese MNC compared to that of the Japanese firm in general. As in the 1970s, the international management field has come to focus on an "advanced" model of the MNC against which Japanese MNCs fell short.[6]

As in the late 1970s, even those who share this perception of the inadequacies of Japanese MNCs often disagree on the reasons. Life cycle effects continue to be a plausible explanation: Nigel Campbell has only recently asserted that a set of studies of Japanese MNCs show clearly that "Japanese multinationals are still at an early stage in evolving their management strategies." (Campbell, 1994). And in comparison with the many decades of evolution of such widely praised transnationals as IBM, ABB, Unilever, or Ford, most leading Japanese MNCs, who set up their first foreign manufacturing operations only in the 1970s or 1980s, are still very young indeed.

Other analysts have pointed out, as they did in the 1970s, that life cycle effects alone do not account for the Japanese patterns of internationalization, which bear the strong imprint of the "country effects" that have shaped their management systems at home. The 1980s demonstrated that Japanese factory organization could be transferred to plants abroad and that close working relationships could be developed between factories in Japan and their "sister plants" abroad. But the ability of Japanese MNCs to transfer patterns from their home base factories to their foreign subsidiaries, so admired by the Western business press, resonates more with the older model of the MNC as leveraging its home-based knowledge internationally than with the "interdependent" model of two-way, interactive learning that characterizes the new model of the MNC. And the much vaunted success of Japanese MNCs in integrating blue-collar workers at home and abroad into a cross-border production network has little significance for the management-centered transnational model, which sees managers, not blue-collar workers, as the key players in the development of the new form (see the discussion of the central importance of "matrixing the minds of the managers" in Bartlett and Ghoshal, 1989). If the "typically Japanese" decision-making processes that involve dense, informal horizontal communications among middle-level managers—what Nonaka (1988) has called "middle-up-down management"—are to stretch across borders, they require the participation of managers outside Japan who "speak the language" both literally, in terms of Japanese, and figuratively, in terms of an understanding of the norms, the participants, and basic assumptions of that particular company's network of communication and decision making (for an insightful discussion of this issue, see Lifson, 1992). And in principle, for most Japanese companies, the key actors in this network have continued to be Japanese expatriate managers in the offshore subsidiaries, rather than the "geocentric" mix of home country, local, and third-country managers that is the ideal of the transnational model (see Pucik et al., 1989). Finally, the established learning patterns of Japanese firms, in which information has been sought abroad and brought back to Japan for knowledge creation, might well be seen as a barrier to the distributed knowledge creation that has become the hallmark of the transnational (see the discussion of the "central-for-global" innovation pattern of Japanese MNCs in Bartlett and Ghoshal, 1989 and 1990, and the discussion by Methé and Penner-Hahn, chapter 10).

Therefore, since the end of the 1980s—as at the end of the 1970s—Japanese MNCs have been widely seen, among both Japanese and Western analysts of the MNC, as facing the need to change their management systems at home if they are to succeed in building effective multinational corporations. Bartlett and Yoshihara put this in terms that echoed Yoshino's 1976 assessment when they concluded that "[h]aving used their highly cohesive centralized organizations as the means to penetrate world export markets, many Japanese companies are now faced with the challenge of dismantling the very engine that drove their success and rebuilding it in a different form" (1988: 40).

But there is at least one important difference between the late 1970s perception of the need for change in Japanese companies and that of the late 1980s: by the latter period, Japanese companies are no longer seen as unique in facing major organizational changes at home if they are to deal with the challenges of the evolving international business environment. The transnational model means changes at home for virtually all companies, not just Japanese firms. Different writers have emphasized different aspects of these changes. Bartlett and Ghoshal, for example, have focused on the development of a more specialized and interdependent role for the home country operations, which in the new model would become one country operation among many, with the corporate headquarters separated from the home base subsidiary. Gunnar Hedlund emphasized the move away from hierarchical control systems to heterarchical coordination systems—a major change in management structures and processes (Hedlund, 1986, 1993a). Prahalad and Doz (Doz & Prahalad, 1984; Prahalad & Doz, 1987) discussed the need for a major redesign of administrative systems, from planning and budgeting to career management systems. And virtually all the writers on the "new" MNC, managers as well as academics, have strongly emphasized the centrality of HRM in the transformation processes: the need to redesign the processes by which managers are recruited, trained, evaluated, assigned, and promoted.

Since the end of the 1980s, therefore, it has been clear that the move to the new model of the MNC demands major changes in the home country organization not only for Japanese MNCs but also for Western MNCs. But will these changes involve convergence toward a single, dominant model of a transnational or heterarchical MNC, with perhaps minor variations in form across countries? Or will Japanese MNCs follow a different evolutionary path towards the "learning-oriented, network MNC," produced by complex and distinctive interactions of home country effects, period effects, and industry effects? The theory and models of the international management field have gravitated over the last decade toward an implicitly convergent model of MNC evolution, and this model has had a strong impact on the analysis of Japanese MNCs. But analyses of Japanese firms and the Japanese business system have over the same period rejected convergence models in favor of the concept of interacting but separate and distinctive evolutionary trajectories for Western and Japanese business systems (see, for example, Aoki, 1988; Dore, 1987; Imai and Komiya, 1994). This difference explains the contradictory assessments of organization and management in Japanese firms and Japanese MNCs noted earlier in this section. Addressing these contradictions involves the longstanding issue of convergence versus distinctive evolutionary trajectories, an issue once again emerging as a key in research on Japanese MNCs.

The 1990s and Beyond

One approach to the convergence issue is to focus on finely grained empirical analysis of structure and process in Japanese MNCs, rather than on the model building that tended to dominate much of the writings on the subject in the 1980s. We in the 1990s have seen a rapid expansion in empirically based studies of Japanese MNCs, much of it by younger scholars on both sides of the Pacific, trained in both the analysis of the Japanese business system and in the paradigms of social science and management disciplines. Many of these researchers are represented in this volume, and the chapters here exemplify two very important and welcome trends.

The first trend is the move beyond simply identifying the problems and barriers faced by Japanese firms as they internationalize, problems that bear striking resemblances in the 1990s to those identified in the 1970s. Many of the chapters in this volume take such problems as a starting point and proceed with careful empirical analysis of the processes by which companies are dealing with problems and of the consequent evolution of their organizations, primarily abroad but also, to some extent, at home. And this analysis is increasingly grounded in the evolving paradigms in social science and management that focus on the dynamic analysis of organizational culture (the chapters in the first part of this book) and capabilities and evolutionary models of the firm (the chapters in the second and third parts).

The second trend is the move from an undifferentiated model of the "Japanese MNC" to an examination of differences across industries, across firms, and across locations. Several of the chapters in this volume show that there are far more differences in how Japanese companies in the 1990s are approaching the challenges of building local capabilities and integrating across borders than anyone would guess from reading the earlier literature on Japanese MNCs. Identifying these differences is a key task and will allow scholars to develop much more accurate assessments of the role of country effects on Japanese MNCs, effects that were perhaps exaggerated in the 1970s and 1980s. More accurately, the chapters in this volume strongly suggest that the interaction of country effects, industry effects, and company effects is much more complex than earlier models would lead us to believe.

The value of these trends is all the greater given that the effects of internationalization on the company at home as well as abroad have finally been recognized as a general rather than a Japanese issue. But there are several reasons why Japanese firms may be extremely well suited to the study of this crucial issue. One of course is the life cycle factor: they are at an earlier stage of internationalization than many U.S. and European MNCs, and therefore the processes can be analyzed "in real time," as opposed to retrospectively. But another factor is that Japanese companies are currently going through a period of what sociologists would call deinstitutionalization, the questioning of the value of patterns previously taken for granted. The continuing domestic recession has posed an array of problems for Japanese firms. Perhaps the most serious is the skewed company demography produced by the orgy of new graduate hires in the bubble years of the late 1980s and early 1990s (when the main labor market story in Japan was the acute shortage of new graduates, especially in technical fields), followed by the dramatic contraction of hiring in the unexpectedly long recession. The resulting demographic profile—of the "Bubble Bulge" resting on the slender cohorts of the recession years—poses a major threat to the seniority-based HRM systems that, as the analyses of the 1980s so persuasively argued, are fundamental to the Japanese system (see, for example, the chapters in Imai & Komiya, 1994). The lack of major new "hit" products, despite a decade of accelerated spending on R & D, has also evoked a profound uneasiness about the corporate, and indeed the national, technology system. And the unexpectedly vigorous revival of U.S. competitiveness, especially in the multimedia and information industries, has sent many Japanese businessmen racing to the bookstores for handbooks on "re-engineering, American-style." This period of deinstitutionalization coincides with renewed pressures to become more global in strategy and organization. And in the discussions of the need for major change in Japanese management and Japanese companies, the awareness of the potential role of internationalization and globalization looms much larger than was the case during the restructuring of U.S. firms during the last decade. The future evolution of Japanese firms and the Japanese business system is likely to be closely bound up with the processes of evolution of the country's MNCs.

To take just one aspect of the interaction between internationalization and the evolution of the firm: since the very earliest stages of their internationalization, Japanese MNCs have been criticized for their heavy reliance on expatriate middle-level managers to act as the key cross-border integrators. And yet in the late 1980s, Steve Kobrin laid out clearly the problems with the opposite approach, adopted by many U.S. companies: relying on moving local managers into the home country operations for training and development and then dispatching them back to their own country subsidiaries to act as key cross-border integrators. Kobrin (1988) pointed out that this meant that fewer home country managers received the extended experience of managing in other contexts and the awareness of international management issues that such experience can bring—with a potential problem for the next generation of top company managers, who would thus be less likely to have extended international experience. One can argue that the Japanese pattern of dispatching large numbers of midlevel managers abroad is likely, over time, to have an impact on the attitudes and organization of the home country operations far greater than the U.S. pattern that Kobrin describes.

One further effect of the deinstitutionalization of the Japanese business system is likely to be increasing variation across Japanese companies, both at home and abroad. We are therefore likely to see even more divergence in the kinds of multinational enterprises based in Japan. It will be harder and harder to bracket all Japanese MNCs into a single category, and this will enable analysts to become more precise about looking at the impact of home country, of industry, and of company-specific factors in the development of the organizational patterns of MNCs. This means that the relevance of the experience of Japanese MNCs for both academic analysts of the MNC and for managers of non-Japanese MNCs is likely to increase significantly.

In the mid-1980s, Abegglen and Stalk, in their analysis of Japanese companies, outlined the various difficulties that Japanese firms faced in internationalization, but nevertheless concluded that "the process of becoming multinational will be difficult and costly, but it will take place"(1985: 286). The research on Japanese MNCs represented in this book is itself a major landmark of research into this process, but, equally important, it provides an excellent base for future research into the increasingly varied patterns of evolution of Japanese MNCs.

Notes

1. A number of Japanese firms developed extensive operations in Japan's colonies before the end of World War II, but these were confiscated at the war's end.

2. This chapter focuses on the organizational analyses of Japanese MNCs and therefore does not include a discussion of several other books written later in this decade from the economic perspective, notably Kojima (1978) and Ozawa (1979).

3. Ray Vernon himself wrote the introduction for Yoshino's book, placing it in the context of the Harvard project, and Tsurumi in his introduction to his book positioned it as "an integral part of the Multinational Enterprise Project" (Tsurumi, 1976: xx).

4. It is far from clear whether this was in fact a difference between U.S. and Japanese patterns, or an artifact of the different databases available in the two countries. Japan's

legacy of Ministry of International Trade and Industry control of foreign direct investment has produced an excellent record of all offshore investments by Japanese firms and therefore tracks the activities of small- and medium-sized firms in a way that has not been possible in the United States, where databases have been built on the more accessible information about very large firms.

5. The parallels with the integration-differentiation framework developed by Lawrence and Lorsch are striking and have been acknowledged by Chris Bartlett (1986: 400). The I-R framework has proved much more influential and enduring in international management than in organization theory.

6. Although we should note that even some of its most noted advocates are uncomfortable viewing the transnational as a model toward which MNCs must converge: Chris Bartlett, for example, asserts that "[t]he transnational is not so much a type of structural configuration as a management mentality" (1986: 399).

References

Abegglen, J. C., & Stalk, G. 1985. *Kaisha: The Japanese Corporation.* New York: Basic Books.

Abo, T. 1989. "The Emergence of Japanese Multinational Enterprises and the Theory of Foreign Direct Investment." In Shibagaki, K., M. Trevor, M., & Abo, T. (eds.), *Japanese and European Management: Their International Adaptability.* Tokyo: University of Tokyo Press. 3–17.

Aoki, M. 1988. *Information, Incentives, and Bargaining in the Japanese Economy.* New York: Cambridge University Press.

Bartlett, C. A. 1986. "Building and Managing the Transnational: The New Organizational Challenge." In Porter, M. E. (ed.), *Competition in Global Industries.* Boston: Harvard Business School Press. 367–404.

Bartlett, C. A., & Ghoshal, S. 1986. "Tap Your Subsidiaries for Global Reach." *Harvard Business Review.* 64 (4): 87–94.

Bartlett, C. A., & Ghoshal, S. 1989. *Managing Across Borders: The Transnational Solution.* Boston: Harvard Business School Press.

Bartlett, C. A., & Ghoshal, S. 1990. "Managing Innovation in the Transnational Corporation." In Bartlett, C. A., Doz, Y., & Hedlund, G. (eds.), *Managing the Global Firm.* London: Routledge.

Bartlett, C. A., & Yoshihara, H. 1988. "New Challenges for Japanese Multinationals: Is Organization Adaptation their Achilles Heel?" *Human Resource Management.* 27 (1): 19–43.

Bradley, G. E., & Bursk, E. C. 1972. "Multinationalism and the 29th Day." *Harvard Business Review.* 50 (1): 37–47.

Campbell, N. 1994. "Introduction." In Campbell, N., & Burton, F. (eds.), *Japanese Multinationals: Strategies and Management in the Global Kaisha.* London: Routledge. 1–8.

Cole, R. E. 1989. *Strategies for Learning: Small-group Activities in American, Japanese, and Swedish Industry.* Berkeley: University of California Press.

DeNero, H. 1990. "Creating the 'Hyphenated' Corporation." *McKinsey Quarterly* (4): 153–173.

Dore, R. P. 1987. *Taking Japan Seriously.* London: Athlone Press.

Doz, Y., & Prahalad, C. K. 1984. "Patterns of Strategic Control in Multinational Corporations." *Journal of Internal Business Studies.* 15 (2): 55–72.

Dunning, J. H. 1993. *Multinational Enterprises and the Global Economy.* Wokingham, UK: Addison-Wesley Publishing Co.

Dymsza, W. A. 1972. *Multinational Business Strategy*. New York: McGraw-Hill.

Evans, P. B. 1981. "Recent Research on Multinational Corporations." *Annual Review of Sociology*. 7: 199–223.

Ghoshal, S., & Westney, D. E. 1993. "Introduction." In Ghoshal, S., & Westney, D. E. (eds.). *Organization Theory and the Multinational Corporation*. London: Macmillan. 1–23.

Gluck, F. 1983. "Global Competition in the 1980s." *Journal of Business Strategy*. 3 (4): 22–27.

Hamel, G., & Prahalad, C. K. 1985. "Do You Really Have a Global Strategy?" *Harvard Business Review*. 63 (5): 139–148.

Hedlund, G. 1986. "The Hypermodern MNC: A Heterarchy?" *Human Resource Management*. 25: 9–35.

Hedlund, G. 1993a. "Assumptions of Hierarchy and Heterarchy, with Application to the Management of the Multinational Corporation." In Ghoshal, S. & Westney, D. E. (eds.), *Organization Theory and the Multinational Corporation*. London: Macmillan. 211–236.

Hedlund, G. 1993b. "Organization and Management of Transnational Corporations in Practice and Research." In UNCTAD Division on Transnational Corporations and Investment (ed.), *Transnational Corporations and World Development*. London: International Thomson Business Press. 123–141.

Hout, T., Porter, M. E., & Rudden, E. 1982. "How Global Companies Win Out." *Harvard Business Review*. 60 (5): 98–108.

Hymer, S. 1960. *The International Operations of National Firms: A Study of Direct Investment*. Unpublished doctoral dissertation, MIT.

Imai, K., & Komiya, R. 1994. *Business Enterprise in Japan: Views of Leading Japanese Economists* (Trans. and ed. by Ronald Dore and Hugh Whittaker). Cambridge, MA: MIT Press.

Jones, G. 1996. "Transnational Corporations—A Historical Perspective." In UNCTAD Division on Transnational Corporations and Investment (ed.), *Transnational Corporations and World Development*. London: International Thomson Business Press. 3–26.

Kobrin, S. J. 1988. "Expatriate Reduction and Strategic Control in American Multinational Corporations." *Human Resource Management*. 27 (1): 63–75.

Kojima, K. 1978. *Japanese Foreign Direct Investment*. Tokyo: Charles E. Tuttle Co.

Lifson, T. B. 1992. "The Managerial Integration of Japanese Business in America." In Kumon, S. & Rosovsky, H. (eds.), *The Political Economy of Japan, Vol. 3: Cultural and Social Dynamics*. Stanford: Stanford University Press. 231–266.

Martinez, J. I., & Jarillo, J. C. 1989. "The Evolution of Research on Coordination Mechanisms in Multinational Corporations." *Journal of International Business Studies*. 20 (3): 489–514.

Meyer, J. W., & Scott, W. R. 1983. *Organizational Environments: Ritual and Reality*. Beverly Hills, CA: Sage Publications.

Nihon Keizai Chosa Kyogikai (ed.). 1976. *Takokuseki Kigyo no Keiei—Nihon Kigyo e no shinshin (The Management of Multinational Enterprise—A Guide for Japanese Companies)*. Tokyo: Diamond-sha.

Nonaka, I. 1988. "Toward Middle-Up-Down Management: Accelerating Information Creation." *Sloan Management Review*. 29 (3): 9–18.

Okumura, A. 1989a. "The Globalization of Japanese Companies." In Shibayaki, K., Trevor, M., & Abo, T. (eds.), *Japanese and European Management: Their International Adaptability*. Tokyo: University of Tokyo Press. 31–40.

Okumura, A. 1989b. "Guro-barize-shon to Nihonteki Keiei no Shinka." In Okumura, A., & Kato, M. (eds.), *Guro-baru Kiko to Kaigai Shinshutsu Butai: Takokuseki Kigyo to Kokusai Soshiki*. Tokyo: Tokyo Daiichi Hoki Shuppan KK. 15: 318–331.

Ozawa, T. 1979. *Multinationalism, Japanese Style*. Princeton: Princeton University Press.

Pascale, R. T. 1984. "Perspectives on Strategy: The Real Story behind Honda's Success. *California Management Review*. 26 (3): 47–72.

Perlmutter, H. 1969. "The Tortuous Evolution of the Multinational Corporation." *Columbia Journal of World Business*. 5 (1): 9–18.

Porter, M. E. 1986a. "Changing Patterns of International Competition." *California Management Review*. 28 (2): 9–40.

Porter, M. E. (ed.). 1986b. *Competition in Global Industries*. Boston, MA: Harvard Business School Press.

Prahalad, C. K., & Doz, Y. 1987. *The Multinational Mission: Balancing Local Demands and Global Vision*. New York: Free Press.

Prahalad, C. K., & Hamel, G. 1990. "The Core Competence of the Corporation." *Harvard Business Review*. 68 (3): 79–91.

Pucik, V., Hanada, M., & Fifield, G. 1989. *Management Culture and the Effectiveness of Local Executives in Japanese-owned U.S. Corporations*. New York: Egon Zehnder International.

Rosenberg, N., & Steinmueller, W. E. 1988. "Why Are Americans Such Poor Imitators?" *American Economic Review*. 78 (2): 229–234.

Stopford, J. M., & Wells, L. T., Jr. 1972. *Managing the Multinational Enterprise: Organization of the Firm and Ownership of the Subsidiaries*. New York: Basic Books.

Trevor, M. 1983. *Japan's Reluctant Multinationals*. London: Pinter.

Tsurumi, Y. 1968. *Technology Transfer and Foreign Trade: The Case of Japan 1950–1966*. Unpublished doctoral dissertation, Harvard Business School.

Tsurumi, Y. 1976. *The Japanese Are Coming: A Multinational Interaction of Firms and Politics*. Cambridge, MA: Ballinger Publishing Co.

Vernon, R. 1966. "International Investment and International Trade in the Product Life Cycle." *Quarterly Journal of Economics*. 80: 190–207.

Vernon, R. 1971. *Sovereignty at Bay: The Multinational Spread of U.S. Enterprises*. New York: Basic Books.

Vernon, R. 1979. "The Product Cycle Hypothesis in a New International Environment." *Oxford Bulletin of Economics and Statistics*. 41: 255–267.

Vernon, R. 1994. "Contributing to an International Business Curriculum: An Approach from the Flank." *Journal of International Business Studies*. 25 (2): 215–227.

Wilkins, M. 1970. *The Emergence of Multinational Enterprise: American Business Abroad from the Colonial Era to 1914*. Cambridge, MA: Harvard University Press.

Yoshihara, H. 1979. *Takokuseki Kigyo Ron*. Tokyo: Hakuto Shobo.

Yoshino, M. Y. 1968. *Japan's Managerial System: Tradition and Innovation*. Cambridge, MA: MIT Press.

Yoshino, M. Y. 1976. *Japan's Multinational Enterprises*. Cambridge, MA: Harvard University Press.

PART II

PUTTING JAPANESE AND LOCAL NATIONALS TOGETHER

Creating Third Cultures

3

MARY YOKO BRANNEN & JANE E. SALK

When Japanese and Other Nationals Create Something New

A Comparative Study of Negotiated Work Culture in Germany and the United States

The world as "global village" is a convocation used so often that the phrase itself has become a cliché. Most of us take for granted much of the outcomes of globalization. We navigate our lives daily through a panoply of cross-cultural choices such as which nation's food to eat, what foreign film to watch, or what country's fashions to wear. Most of us even quite comfortably intermix foreign words in our daily vocabulary, as when we say something analogous to "It's a *Zen* sort of thing," or "He's a real *macho* kind of guy." But one important arena where global navigation happens less smoothly is the multinational firm. In this setting, the culture, or the taken for granted rules and scripts that govern how people interact, is not so clear. And, as firms around the globe continue to internationalize, it is in this setting of the multinational firm that we are likely to experience the more poignant effects of the global village. Whether we venture into our cross-cultural experiences as expatriates, expatriate spouses, or as home-based employees of multinational firms, we find ourselves increasingly in complex cultural situations where rules of social interaction are often uncertain.

People turn to cross-cultural studies to help them navigate across cultural borders. Abundant in all the social sciences, these studies generally share the assumption that despite globalization of the world economy, differences in thinking and social action exist between people of different nations and that such differences matter, especially when it comes to executing transnational projects. Whether the transnational activity involves crossing borders to successfully manage overseas operations, effectively transferring technology, negotiating favorable trade policies, or providing cross-cultural guidance to expatriate individuals and families, people need cultural knowledge. With cultural knowledge, they can understand or predict, as the case may be, the consequences of the cross-cultural interactions.

The literature that takes up work culture formation in anthropology, communications, sociology, and management includes sophisticated single-culture studies that provide detailed descriptions of the practices, beliefs, and assumptions of disparate national cultures and comparative studies that elucidate potential areas of cross-cultural dissonance, but there have been relatively few studies of cross-cultural interaction. That is, hardly any studies explain how people with fundamentally different understandings and practices establish a means of cooperation toward shared goals. Moreover, most cross-cultural interactions are mediated through organizations, which, to complicate matters further, have their own cultures. Cultures have a variety of embedded layers. National culture represents only the outermost layer with organizational culture, work culture, regional culture, familial culture, and so on constituting the inner layers. Although few studies examine cross-cultural interaction where differences in "culture" are taken as national cultural differences, even fewer studies peel the outer layer of the culture concept down to the organizational and work culture level in order to gain understanding of how individuals from different cultural makeups are able to work together in multinational corporations.

In the field of management, a growing body of studies of multinational corporations examines of international joint ventures and foreign subsidiaries abroad. However, the lion's share of these studies has a macro-level focus on strategic and structural issues faced by top-tier executives. Very few studies have focused on micro-level process-oriented issues that affect cross-cultural interaction and work culture formation. In addition, such studies often invoke "cultural differences" (where "culture" is treated as a cognate for national culture) as an explanation for problems encountered in managing multinationals (Harrigan, 1988; Killing, 1983; Lane & Beamish, 1990). If we accept the notion that cultural differences inherently cause problems in the management of multinational organizations, many managers in this and subsequent decades can expect to continue tripping on cultural stumbling blocks without some basic understanding of the process by which differences can be overcome or at least arbitrated.

Given that multinational firms and cross-cultural contexts for doing business are only going to multiply, there is a pronounced need for cross-cultural scholars to conduct more micro-level research that documents what happens when managers from different cultures work together and how common working cultures evolve to facilitate the accomplishment of work goals in complex cultural organizations. This research focus has been endorsed by several international management scholars including Adler (1986), Boyacigiller and Adler (1991), and Parkhe (1993), who have articulated an increasingly urgent need for research focused on process and rich description that begins to advance the notion of a synergistic model of culture and cross-cultural interaction.

Through research on shared management international joint venture (IJV) teams (Salk, 1992; Salk, 1996; Salk & Shenkar, 1996) and comparative studies of Japanese management in multicultural work environments versus the monocultural context in Japan (Brannen, 1991, 1994a, 1994b, 1995; Peterson, Brannen, & Smith, 1994), we have been trying both on our own and now, together, to address the need for a better understanding of work culture formation in complex cultural organizations. Gradually we have converged on what we call a "negotiated culture perspective." Following Brannen's conceptual model of negotiated culture developed in her 4½-year ethnographic study of cultural change at a North American paper mill in the wake of a takeover by Japanese management (Brannen, 1994b) and Salk's observations of binational work teams in three disparate bicultural IJV settings (Salk, 1992), the negotiated culture perspective addresses the questions of how organizational actors use their various cultural identities and affiliations in influencing and participating in a new setting, how working cultures (team or organizational cultures) emerge in multinationals, and how both social and work contexts influence identity management and working culture creation.

In this chapter we compare two disparate cases of work culture formation experienced by a Japanese multinational paper company fictitiously referred to here as the Tomioka Paper Company (TPC), now Japan's largest paper manufacturer. The first case, Tomioka Specialty Papers, USA (a pseudonym abbreviated as TSP in the rest of the chapter) is a wholly owned unionized subsidiary in western Massachusetts that resulted from a takeover by TPC of an existing U.S. paper mill. The second case, Nutech IJV (again, a pseudonym), one hour's drive from Düsseldorf, is an equally shared joint venture between TPC and a large German paper manufacturer. The Nutech joint venture was an occasion for us to pool our learning and begin to deductively examine the assumptions about and conceptual understandings of the negotiated culture perspective induced in previous studies.

The chapter is organized in the following manner. We begin by briefly reviewing past research in order to situate and outline the negotiated culture perspective we use to analyze our cases. We then provide a brief overview of each case study and discussion of our research methodology. Our description of the processes by which work culture evolved in each case is then presented in a time-phased manner following the parallel developmental stages we witnessed in the U.S. subsidiary and German IJV. Here we examine the issues confronted by the American and Japanese employees in Massachusetts and the German-Japanese management team in Duerren, Germany. We examine first how the confrontation of these issues brought out certain problematic differences and then show how these differences became the vehicles for negotiated resolutions. We end by discussing the various methods of cultural negotiation available to multinationals and the conditions under which these methods might be more or less successful.

Theoretical Framework

Cultural Differences and Multinationals Abroad

Though the rising popular interest in Japanese management practices and in the management of multinationals abroad has resulted in growing bodies of research in both of these areas, significant gaps in empirical and conceptual understanding remain. With relatively few exceptions (cf. Brannen, 1994a, 1994b; Inkpen, 1997; Peterson, Brannen, & Smith, 1994; Salk, 1992; Yan & Grey, 1994) research on multinationals abroad has tended to use data at the organizational or interorganizational levels of analysis and has focused mainly on structural issues.

In IJV research, Ring and Van de Ven (1994) propose a process model emphasizing the roles of informal sense making, role and personal interactions among individuals, and a balance between formal and psychological contracts in the functioning of cooperative interorganizational relationships. However, their model does not fully address how and why cultural differences might affect IJVs and the model has yet to be put to an empirical test. Although a number of scholars have suggested that cultural differences among IJV participants increases the likelihood of failure or poor performance (Harrigan, 1988; Killing, 1983; Lane and Beamish, 1990; Parkhe, 1991), little research directly addresses and elucidates why this should be the case. Indeed, reviewing the state of knowledge in IJV research, Parkhe (1993) calls for concept development and generation of inductive theory through longitudinal, qualitative research, citing the limited amount of knowledge concerning processes within IJV organizations.

Likewise, although there is much scholarship on comparative Japanese/U.S. management and Japanese management practices abroad (Lincoln, Hanada, & Olson, 1981; Lincoln & Kalleberg, 1990; Lincoln, Olson, & Hanada, 1978; Peterson, Peng, & Smith, 1989; Peterson & Shimada, 1978; Yeh & Latib, 1990), there is little in-depth research that looks at dynamic processes in bicultural or multicultural organizations including multinationals that have Japanese participants. The few exceptions include Jill Kleinberg's (1989, 1994a, 1994b) ethnographic work on work group formation in a Japanese subsidiary in Los Angeles, Noriya Sumihara's (1992) in-depth field study of working culture formation in regard to performance appraisals at a sales-subsidiary of a large Japanese company in New York, and Brannen's own ethnographic study of organizational culture change in the wake of a takeover by Japanese management of a Western Massachusetts paper mill. In this volume, our chapter, together with the contributions of Kleinberg and Sumihara, begins to lay the groundwork for theory development around the issues of how "third cultures," as Sumihara refers to them, develop in the merger of people from distinct work and national cultures.

Research on Culture

The literatures on IJVs, multinational management, and Japanese management practices abroad have drawn on research and theory concerning culture. Research on national cultural differences is large and varied, and culture has been defined and studied in a variety of ways. For example, national and corporate cultures have been viewed as contextual or explanatory variables or as a dependent variable to be explained (Allaire & Firsirotu, 1984; Sackmann, 1991). Boyacigillar, Kleinberg, Phillips, and Sackmann (1994) have identified three types of international cross-cultural management research with a focus on (1) cross-national comparison, (2) intercultural interaction, and (3) a multiple cultures perspective. In IJV research, popular dependent variables include form of control, organizational learning, performance, longevity, and other organizational issues, and national culture typically is treated as an explanatory variable affecting dependent variables of interest (for examples, see Lane and Beamish, 1990; Parkhe, 1991, 1993).

Of those studies seeking to elucidate culture as a dependent variable, Hofstede (1984) has developed a typology that has been particularly influential in cross-cultural management research. He studied a large sample of IBM employees and used surveys to develop a way of viewing and describing culture in terms of similarities and differences of national groups on four dimensions: individualism-collectivism, power distance, uncertainty avoidance, and masculine-feminine. This approach documents substantial variation in national cutlures' mean scores on each of these dimensions. These differences are correlated with differences in management styles and the types of problems that a large number of intercultural collaborations between members of two cultures might encounter. However, this approach to culture has little to say about the dynamic aspects of intercultural encounters and how managers in a particular situation deal with difference.

In anthropology, and to some degree in sociology, some scholars are critical of approaches such as Hofstede's, because such approaches begin with a priori definitions of relevant groups and units of analysis and treat culture as a reified construct. A number of anthropologists (Abu-Lughod, 1986; Geertz, 1973; Ong, 1987; Roseberry, 1989), cultural historians (Anderson, 1991; Renan, 1990), scholars of cultural studies (Bhabha, 1990; Buel, 1994), and sociologists (Fine, 1979, 1984; Giddens, 1984; Strauss, 1978, 1982) view culture as sets of symbols, meanings, and practices created and reproduced through the interactions of a group's members. This approach to understanding culture is highly relevant to addressing the dynamics of interaction and culture creation. For example, Fine (1979) studied the creation of the idioculture of a Little League baseball team and found that broader social memberships of team members (e.g., religion), attributes of members (e.g., being fat or clumsy), and specific experiences of the team (e.g., winning or losing a game) contributed to the creation of the team's culture. In the same vein, Ong (1987) defines culture as follows:

> "Culture" is taken as historically situated and emergent, shifting and incomplete meanings and practices generated in webs of agency and power. Cultural change [and in our study working culture creation] is not understood as unfolding according to some predetermined logic (of development, modernization or capitalism) but as the disrupted, contradictory, and differential outcomes which involve changes in identity, relations of struggle and dependence, including the experience of reality itself . . . in situations wherein groups and classes struggle to produce and interpret culture within the industrializing milieu. (2–3)

Although Ong is writing about large-scale social systems, her approach to defining culture and cultural change is highly appropriate to multinational organizations.

In the two cases we analyze in this chapter, situational elements and change mattered greatly in highlighting particular kinds of differences and making some form of negotiated change desirable for team members. Another takeover by Japanese management, or IJV between Germans and Japanese that differed in the historical situations confronted, might have negotiated around different sets of issues sooner or later than did members of the cases we have studied, and, hence, these working culture outcomes might look very different.

Negotiated Social Orders and Key Assumptions
Regarding the Creation and Maintenance
of Working Culture

The negotiated culture approach views multinational organizations as settings in which members of different cultures encounter one another and in which the patterns of meaning and agency in the organization arise from the cultural negotiations of its members.[1] Our approach shares a view of organizations along the lines of

Anselm Strauss's notion of negotiated social order (1963, 1978). Although the concept of *negotiated order* antedates Strauss's earlier work comparing the negotiation at various levels of organization in two psychiatric hospitals (cf. Dalton, 1959; Goffman, 1961; Mead, 1934), he was the first to explicitly outline the approach. For Strauss the structure of the organization and the micropolitics of the negotiated order are closely linked:

> The negotiated order on any given day could be conceived of as the sum total of the organization's rules and policies, along with whatever agreements, understandings, pacts, contracts, and other working arrangement currently obtained. These include agreements at every level of organization, of every clique and coalition, and include covert as well as overt agreements. (1978: 5–6)

Strauss's approach was induced by research conducted in organizational arenas with members from a single national culture. Our work extends this approach to the multinational organizational arena. As stated previously, the goal of our present study was to combine our previous learning about negotiated culture induced through in-depth studies of bicultural organizations and then to move theory building forward by deductively examining our pooled assumptions. What follows is a discussion and listing of the assumptions of negotiated culture that guided our comparative study.

In our iteration of the negotiated order approach (fig. 3.1), what Brannen (1994a) terms the members' *cultures of origin* (the cultural orientation they bring with them into the work setting—a confluence of cultures such as national, regional, familial, etc.) are a point of departure and a set of meanings and behaviors that become the tacit basis from which the new MNC's organizational culture evolves. Salk (1992, 1996), and Salk and Shenkar (working paper) have found that in bicultural shared management IJVs, social identities based on the national cultures of origins of the team members tended

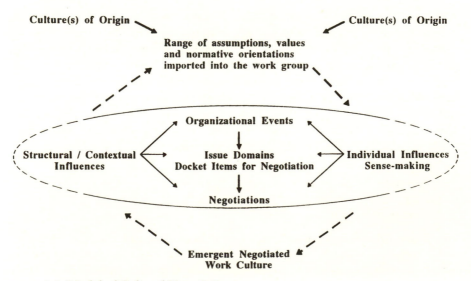

FIGURE 3.1 Model of Cultural Negotiation

to be enacted as the primary social identities early in the lives of such organizations and that one of the national cultural groups represented typically had a more dominant influence than the other in shaping the working cultures of IJV teams. Past research on national cultures (Hofstede, 1984; Ronen and Shenkar, 1985) can therefore provide important clues about the values, meanings, and behavioral norms that team members of a given culture might import into the new multinational organization. Hence, this is the first assumption of the negotiated culture approach:

Assumption 1: The national cultural origins of the multinational organizational members serve as initial anchors or points of departure for team members as a source of values, meanings, and norms they bring with them to the bicultural organizational context.

However, these sets of values, meanings, and norms anchored in national cultures are not impermeable cultural traits. In the cross-cultural management literature, more often than not such generalized cultural traits of two national cultural groups are used to construe what anthropologist Eric Wolf (1982: 34) has called a "two-billiard-ball" understanding of cultural interaction. Both national cultures are treated as monolithic entities (billiard balls) that either collide with each other, leading to unsuccessful ventures, or miss grazing each other, remaining intact in their original cultural forms. (We have generated a "billiard-ball" comparison for the three countries of interest in our study in the form of table 1 depicted and discussed later.) The negotiated culture perspective, on the other hand, sees national cultural traits that multinational organizational members bring to the venture as elements that over time can be recombined or modified through ongoing interactions among team members (Brannen, 1994b). The national cultural attributes are like items on a formal negotiation docket brought to the table for arbitration.

There are several critical determinants of the course of cultural negotiation, including both the structural as well as the negotiation contexts such as (a) the specific history of the multinational, (b) the number and training of the individuals involved in the interactions, (c) the relative balance of power and influence among the individuals, (d) the balance of power and influence of the national cultural groups, (e) the nature and complexity of the issues that come up in the course of the venture, (f) the extent of a priori knowledge of the other's culture, and (g) the degree of the internationalization of the individuals and their respective organizational cultures. Each of these factors is a key determinant regarding which of the many values, meanings, and norms of either culture will persist, which will collide and produce conflict, and which will be altered or modified to create a situationally specific organizational value, norm, or practice. Thus, while past research developing typologies of differences can point to areas where tensions and conflicts may be most likely to occur, which of these, and when (if ever) they will become problematic for the multinational management, depends on what kinds of work and other pressures confront the team. Hence, here is the second assumption of the negotiated culture perspective:

Assumption 2: The structure of the multinational, relations of power and interdependence among team members, and the specific issues and threats confronted by the team will shape which of these many cultural traits will become salient in the social negotiation of the multinational working culture.

For example, in multinational organizations confronting an external crisis spurred by competition, those cultural domains that pertain to decision making, working hours and the pace of work, and how to deal with customers are likely candidates for social negotiation, whereas those that pertain to other cultural domains (e.g., familial relations or the degree to which work is central to self-definition) might remain by and large untouched.

Cross-cultural experiences in multinational organizations challenge members to see themselves, situations, and others in new ways. The multinational organization provides experiences that also serve as selective mirrors for viewing one's self and one's own culture. As a mirror trained on the self, the other, and the situation, these experiences do not reflect all differences and similarities with equal clarity. Rather, experience in multicultural organizations selectively reflects and magnifies those aspects of one's own culture, one's self-identity, and one's beliefs that previously had been taken for granted. The "other" and what makes them such, therefore, is a product of how we understand ourselves and the situation and is subject to learning and modification over time. Differences and similarities that do not find expression in the work setting, or that might exist but that are not seen to impinge upon critical activities or goals, might continue to coexist without any substantial change or convergence.

Even though culture is generally spoken of as a group-level phenomenon, it is dynamically negotiated by individual members. And the "culture of origin" of an individual does not necessarily reflect neatly the general attributes of the individual's representative cultural group. Therefore, some members exhibit national cultural attributes ranging from those that might be considered "marginal" within a given national culture to those that would be considered "hyper-normal," embodying mainstream national cultural attributes to a very strong degree (Brannen, 1994b). Thus, an individual navigates and situates the self in organizational settings through taking the stance of a hyper-normal, normal, or marginal-normal member of his or her cultural group in terms of a given cultural dimension (Brannen, 1994b). Individuals exhibit a range of personal fit with their cultures of origin, reflecting their ongoing particular cultural histories in various cultural contexts (Brannen, 1994b). Hence, organizational cultures might not be representative of national cultures, and the orientations of particular representatives of a given national or organizational culture will mirror imperfectly either of those other two cultures. Hence, this is the third assumption:

> Assumption 3: When members from two distinct national and organizational cultures come together, a "negotiated culture" emerges.

The emerging negotiated culture will not be a blended or hybrid culture, nor will it reflect one or the other culture in its entirety. In other words, given culture A and B, the negotiated cultural outcome will be neither A or B or AB, but some other outcome more like a mutation containing parts of both parents as well as some aspects of its own making, idiosyncratic to its own context. The issues that become salient in the course of the multinational operation allow for expression of marginal-normal and hyper-normal tendencies of individuals vis-à-vis their cultures of origins as well as expressions mirroring the cultural norms. Hence, those domains brought to the surface as issues can be negotiated among the individual participants in a number of ways, and the resulting working culture will emerge from the influences of cultures of origins, individual stance taking, and the operating context. The multinational operation might be viewed as a contested terrain in which groups compete to assert their norms and practices in the context. For example, in an Italian-British IJV, Salk and Shenkar (working paper) found that critical domains of communication and decision making became dominated by an Anglo-Saxon style (much to the dismay of many Italian members who lacked the power to change it).

Alternatively, the homogeneity of members' stances might be low, and a more fluid process of cultural negotiation and innovation of norms and practices might be observed. Individuals who might be categorized as cultural-normals in terms of the parent organization might assume a marginal-normal cultural orientation in the emergent work culture while those who are marginal-normals vis-à-vis their parent organization or national cultures might be normals or hyper-normals in relation to the multinational organization's working culture (Brannen, 1994b). Hence, the last two assumptions of our negotiated culture perspective are the following:

Assumption 4: The specific attributes of a multinational operation's working culture will be emergent and cannot be predicted a priori.

Assumption 5: The cultural stances of organizational actors may map into "issue cultures" in unexpected ways.

These basic assumptions became the point of departure for the present study. We have pooled these assumptions from concepts that each of us induced from previous in-depth studies of bicultural work organizations. We approached our comparison of these two multinational sites with a research intent quite different from that either of us used before. Rather than conceptualizing the current study as exploratory, we took the above assumptions as given tenets of the negotiated culture perspective, choosing to learn more about them by comparing how negotiated culture evolved at the U.S. subsidiary to the one that emerged at the German-Japanese site. Before moving into a discussion of the research methodology and results, provide a brief history of the two sites.

The Two Multinational Sites

The History of the U.S. Subsidiary—TSP

In December 1986, a 44-year-old American paper-converting plant located in a small western Massachusetts mill town was taken over by a Japanese company—the TPC. The town and the plant had seen much better days. The town had been a productive mill town from the latter part of the 1950s until the late 1970s and was the home of four successful organizational facilities: a textile mill, a shoe manufacturer, a regional hospital, and the paper plant. But, in the late 1970s the town's industries began to decline, losing business volume to international competitors and personnel to the more lucrative computer industry cropping up in the eastern part of the state. Ironically, the town marker (an important ethnographic data source) reads, "The town that can't be licked. Population: 10,300."

The original U.S. plant was founded in 1916. The plant was run like a family business—the founders were "good with people" and ran an organization characterized by benevolent yet authoritative leaders. Under this management, employees enjoyed company parties three times a year, at Christmas, in the spring, and for a summer barbecue. In 1954 the company merged with another company and in 1957 became a wholly owned subsidiary of a manufacturing and sales company. As a result of the consolidation, the new corporation became an organization with a total of six manufacturing plants. Between 1954 and the midseventies, the plant experienced much growth but then began to decline in productivity. It was the town's second largest employer and in 1979 grossed $20 million in sales. Corporate headquarters operated the facility on an extremely tight budget "only spending money on equipment if it was broken."

From 1981 on there were no social gatherings, hourly workers were regularly laid off, and many of the office staff members were terminated. The management was characterized by a hierarchical structure with senior and middle managers supervising a unionized work force made up of 120 second- and third-generation workers of mostly Polish or French-Canadian ancestry. The most common metaphor used by the hourly workers to describe the American management style was "hammer and sickle." The management/union relationship had deteriorated to an all-time low by 1981—grievances were up to an average of 12 per month and ultimately a strike vote closed the plant for six weeks.

In 1983, the plant was sold to a holding company. From 1983 until TPC's acquisition of the plant in 1986, the predominant concern of the employees was the security of their jobs. During these three years the plant was operated on a sluggish three days a week schedule; hourly workers were laid off on an average of 12 weeks per year; over 30 out of the 116 office workers were given termination of employment notices during the three years; and management had a notoriously bad relationship with the United Paper Maker's International Union, indicated by a reported average of three formal grievances a month.

When the sale was final, the new Japanese management replaced top management and promoted the previous plant manager and marketing manager to senior positions while retaining the American middle management and hourly workers. The new management rehired approximately 170 of the 216 blue- and white-collar workers from the previous company (the remaining 36 employees were transferred as an entire division to another plant of the former owner). There are presently 271 U.S. employees at the plant: 122 office workers and 149 hourly workers. There are nine Japanese employees, three of whom are in top management positions.

According to the new management, the determining factors in deciding to purchase the U.S. plant were the equipment and the already trained workforce. In addition, a greenfield venture would have cost much more than the acquisition price, and it would have taken up to two years longer to get a new plant operating smoothly.

TPC took special care to gain the goodwill and support of both the community (a large part of whom are World War II veterans) and the U.S. employees during this changeover time. The summer before the takeover, TPC hosted a "Get Acquainted" picnic in the parking lot of the factory for the community. For the employees, the new president introduced himself to each person with a handshake and a word of goodwill. The only setback during the takeover was the collective bargaining agreement outcome with the union. Hourly workers were embittered by the fact that each lost an average of two weeks of paid vacation leave as well as the portability of their pension plan.

Before the acquisition, the plant was characterized by what might be called a conventional U.S. manufacturing culture. The new Japanese management replaced the top management while retaining the American middle management and hourly workers. One organizational structure of domination has therefore been replaced by another—resulting in a bicultural restructuring of power at the plant.

Three years after the takeover, the plant was operating seven days a week, there had been no layoffs or terminations of employees, and grievances were down to an unprecedented two in all of 1989. In addition, the plant underwent a $40 million expansion of its facilities to house a state-of-the-art thermal coating machine, which increased total plant capacity by over 200% and provided approximately 100 new jobs for the community.

The History of the German Joint Venture—Nutech IJV

The original plant was founded in 1710 as a paper mill in a small German town approximately one hour's drive from Düsseldorf. As one of the town's chief employers, the factory and the community had a close tie that persisted over the decades even while the factory had successive owners. Until just before the joint venture commenced, the plant was operated by a small family-owned company (in German, a mittelstandische firm). Townspeople we randomly encountered during our visits knew the plant and readily offered us its history. Many had either worked there at some point themselves or had friends or relatives who had. In fact, on our first visit to the plant our taxi driver said he needed no directions to the plant, he knew it and, in fact, identified it as "where the Japanese now are."

The paper industry had long been important to this rather small and conservative town. Thus, the factory and industry had deep roots in the community. However, this long history cut two ways, with the most recent owner of the facility feeling compelled to look for a way to keep the plant open and to keep the jobs there, even as competitive conditions in the European specialty paper industry were changing. This patriarchal management approach also echoed the general welfare corporatist nature of the German industrial structure that has many legal incentives making it quite expensive to shed workers.

At the time of this study, the IJV had been in production for approximately three years. Nutech is located at a single site in Germany; its ownership and governance is shared by the Japanese partner and the German partner. Equity is split evenly between these two partners, each having 47.5%. A Japanese trading company, which was to be the major distributor of Nutech's products, took a 5% ownership share. Production commenced under the IJV management in October 1991. As of the middle of 1994, the Nutech IJV employed 216 individuals, including 145 wage earners and 71 salaried managers. There were six Japanese managers at that time occupying the following positions: the managing codirector, director of technology, director of sales and marketing, director of business planning, quality manager, and manager of sales.

Of all the positions at the uppermost two levels (nine), the Japanese had four, and of the top three levels (18), the Japanese occupied a third of the positions. Looked at another way, by functional area, the Japanese dominated the top management of the sales / marketing and technology areas (two thirds of the top positions in these two functions were held by Japanese managers), while the Germans dominated production and administrative functions. The preponderance of Germans in the latter two functions was necessitated by the need to operate effectively with a German workforce and in a German legal / business context.

The relationship between the two major partners began in the early 1970s when the Japanese company licensed technology for the production of carbonless copying paper to the German company. This agreement resulted in ongoing, but arm's length contact between the two companies for the next 18 or so years, and this relationship was described by several veteran managers from both companies as a good one. In the mid-1980s, several factors prompted the companies to consider establishing a closer relationship. First, although the market for thermal papers in Europe was poised for rapid expansion, there was also the threat of rising protectionism against foreign competitors, especially the Japanese. Japanese producers such as the Japanese partner in the Nutech IJV wanted to establish a production base for thermal paper in Europe well in advance of 1992. Meanwhile, the plant was suffering from chronic low productivity, but the German partner had been reluctant to simply close it down for legal and social reasons. Therefore, there were discussions between the Japanese and German partners in the mid-1980s to explore the possibility of a joint venture that would take advantage of the excess capacity of the German partner and allow the Japanese partner to gain a production platform in Europe. These initial discussions, however, broke down sometime around 1986.

The reasons that led to the initial exploration of a joint venture did not go away during the next years, and in 1988 the companies were back at the table and engaged in serious negotiations. During these negotiations, International Paper, one of the U.S.'s largest paper companies, purchased the German company, which led to a slowdown of the negotiations. Nevertheless, an agreement for the IJV was reached and signed by the parties in September 1990. The Japanese were to provide the technology, while the Germans would provide the plant and manage the workforce. The top managers were appointed in late 1990. The Japanese did not begin moving to Germany until spring 1991. The final agreement was implemented in the fall of that year.

Approach to Data Collection and Analysis

Among our reasons for being interested in this comparative study was that the first author was familiar with the Japanese partner through her research on its U.S. subsidiary, therefore providing easy entry and a readily available binational case for comparison. Furthermore, the IJV was similar in structure and in governance to those studied previously by the second author in that neither the Japanese nor German partners had a controlling equity share and because the IJV used both German and Japanese managers to staff the top management team and to participate in the day-to-day governance of the organization. Our goal in this study was to compare the evolution of work culture in the two case settings to generate a list of methods of negotiating outcomes available to multinational managers.

Data collection on the U.S. subsidiary was accomplished by means of an in-depth ethnographic study, which followed the evolution of work culture at the subsidiary from immediately after the U.S. plant's takeover by TCP to four years thereafter. Ethnography, comprising of two essential elements—fieldwork and cultural study— is, as many have argued, perhaps the most effective method for gaining insights into micro-level cultural phenomena (Van Maanen, 1988: 2). Lincoln and Guba (1985) suggest that the more traditional positivist approaches to understanding organiza- tional culture fall short in adequately capturing the complexity of cultural phenom- ena in organizations. The difficulty of understanding micro-level cultural phenom- ena becomes even more accentuated when the research setting is rife with multilevel cultural interactions based on divergent organizational and national cultural assump- tions and beliefs brought together by the merging of two distinct national cultural groups into one newly formed organizational whole.

A second, equally important, determinant for choosing ethnographic method- ology is the relative newness of the organizational phenomenon under study. In an otherwise heated debate on the strengths and weaknesses of single-case versus multiple-case study methodology taken up by Dyer and Wilkins at Brigham Young University and Kathleen Eisenhardt at Stanford University in the *Academy of Man- agement Review* (1991: 613–27), scholars agree that the in-depth, single-case studies are particularly useful for inductive theory building in the early stages of a field of research. Eisenhardt argues further that the strength of such classic in-depth, single- site studies as Whyte's (1943), Gouldner's (1954), and Dalton's (1959) is in their gen- eration of strong constructs, which can then be used to advance theory and serve as the basis for deductive theory testing.

The primary data collection methods for the ethnography included participant observation and in-depth interviews. The researcher's formal role as participant observer was as an in-house intercultural consultant. The researcher's duties included giving workshops to the American employees on Japanese business culture, prede- parture briefings in language and culture for employees sent to Japan for training, workshops to the Japanese employees on U.S. business language and culture, and intercultural communication workshops for both Japanese and American employees. TPC provided the researcher with office space, open access to plant personnel and records in order to conduct the secondary data collection process, and a research grant that funded transcriptions of interviews and travel and research costs in Japan. The researcher spent an average of 10 hours a week at the research site for the duration of the 4½-year study. During this time she observed formal meetings, quality con- trol groups discussions, and two collective bargaining sessions.

In addition to the researcher's formal role at the plant, she was also a partici- pant observer in an informal sense. The informal portion of the role included joining employees for lunch in the break areas at the plant or at the cafeteria in the hospital next door to the plant and attending company functions such as picnics, yearly Christ- mas parties, and softball games. She also participated in the formation of two com- pany-related interest groups. One was a Japan-America club funded by six Japanese-owned companies in western Massachusetts. The other was a Japanese Saturday school, which met at a church on a local college campus and was founded to provide supplemental Japanese educational training for the children of the Japanese expatriates at the Japanese-owned firms in the area. Over the course of the 4½ years, the researcher formed friendships with many of the wives and families of the Japanese expatriates. In addition to the reciprocal intrinsic benefits resulting from these friendships, this union provided the researcher with another perspective on the life of expatriate managers and their families in their foreign home environment.

In Japan, the researcher conducted interviews and observed plant operations at the Japanese home office and two plant locations over the course of two summers. The informal aspects of the research process in Japan included after hours socializing with executives, which included joining them for dinner and after-dinner corporate bonding sing-ins at local *karaoke* bars. The participant observer process both in the United States and Japan generated 1,635 pages of field notes, which were accompanied by ongoing informal journal entries into an ethnographer's diary kept throughout the study.

The in-depth interviewing process was conducted in three steps: preliminary focus group interviews, follow-up structured interviews, and ongoing informal, unstructured dialogue. The data from these interviews took the form of 2,896 pages of interview transcripts. The field notes and interview transcripts were entered into Macintosh-compatible software called Hypercard, a semantic network analysis system, in order to facilitate the identification of themes within the field data. A content analysis facilitated by this software then helped to identify key constructs that emerged over the course of the ethnography in regard to intraorganizational dynamics in a binational setting. The content analysis generated five themes: (1) the effects of national culture on the labor relations structure and collective bargaining process, (2) national cultural differences in the ideology of innovation, (3) the alienation of the American middlemanager, (4) varied expatriate responses to the new organizational setting, and (5) national cultural differences in the understanding of organizational growth and decline processes. These themes led to the generation of a conceptual model of negotiated culture discussed earlier in the chapter.

Interviews were also an important source of data for the second comparative case at Nutech IJV. In this case study, since our primary aim was to compare findings on negotiated cultural outcomes with the first study—a deductive method of theory building as opposed to the inductive nature of the first study—we approached data gathering in a slightly different fashion. Rather than conducting long-term exploratory ethnographic inquiry, in this second case, we used the theoretical findings of our previous work to inform our data gathering. Hence, in the second case we were able to be more parsimonious with our method, limiting the parameters of our inquiry to semistructured interview questions that sought to confirm, disconfirm, or elaborate our previous findings.

We visited the Nutech IJV two times and have collected various types of data from several sources. Prior to the first visit, we collected organization charts and press clippings and gathered other information about the size, structure, and strategic rationales of the IJV. We interviewed all members of the top management team at least once. Semistructured interviews with team members lasted from one to over three hours each. All interviews except one were tape-recorded and typewritten transcripts of all interviews were prepared for subsequent analysis. One was not recorded at the subject's request. However, both researchers were present and took careful notes.

Among the topics covered were the past experiences of managers in working with or in other cultures in general and prior experience with the other parent organization in particular, descriptions of meetings and how decisions are made in the IJV, and types of contact among team members. We also asked individuals what their expectations had been about working in the IJV prior to its start and how their experiences so far in the IJV were consistent with, or different from, these expectations. Because the issues and critical incidents confronted by the team are posited to be of great importance in the development of cooperative relationships (Brannen, 1994b; Ring & Van de Ven, 1994; Salk & Shenkar, 1997), prior to the first visit we talked to several key informants who were familiar with the IJV to ascertain what might have been critical issues to date. These informants suggested that the installation of the new machinery, ongoing information demands by the Japanese parent, and product quality were issues that had been or that continued to be important to the IJV thus far.

For the Nutech case, we analyzed the data using NUDIST (Non-numerical Unstructured Data Indexing, Searching, and Theorizing), Version 3.0 (QSR Ltd., 1994). NUDIST is a textual analysis software program that allows researchers to code interview transcripts and analyze the frequency and degree of agreement in the themes and topics discussed by informants. NUDIST also allows for the building of hierarchical trees of themes and concepts, which greatly assists in analyzing and reducing themes into general categories. For this study, after having transcribed and cleaned our data, we input all of the interview transcripts into the NUDIST software program, developed a hierarchical coding tree based on the negotiated culture perspective, coded each of the transcripts using the categorical nodes we created for our coding tree, performed coder reliability checks, and finally analyzed the data across categories at each node location. As our main research goal in this study was to compare the process of cultural negotiation at the Nutech IJV and TSP in the United States, to understand what issues became salient, and how negotiated order evolved in each case, we concentrated our investigation around the categorical node we termed issues. We have reproduced the portion of the hierarchical tree used in NUDIST branching into the "Issues" node in figure 3.2. This node has seven subcategories of issue domains, each salient in both multinational settings—Nutech IJV and TSP: decision making, concept of work, job role perception, production and sales conflict, language, quality, and a final category labeled "other" for issues that did not fit neatly under a discrete title.

In the first round of interviews, we also asked informants to describe cultural differences between Germans and Japanese that were salient in the course of the history of the IJV. A similar method of inquiry was used in the case of TSP. We were therefore able to compile a list of comparative cultural differences that were salient in the course of the two multinational sites (table 3.1).

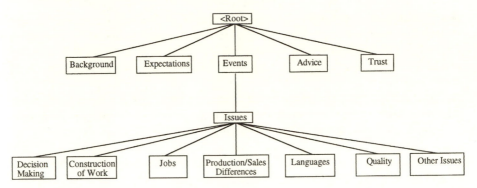

FIGURE 3.2 Coding Issues and Cultural Negotiations

Research Findings

In keeping with the notion that cultural negotiation cannot be separated from its historical context, we have organized our research findings by developmental phases in the multinational case histories as the contextual backdrop from which issue domains emerged. We present the findings in regard to the salient issue domains referred to before in the order in which they emerged within the context of three phases of production development described next.

Three Developmental Phases of Production

A time line of developmental phases experienced in both cases can be categorized as follows: Negotiation → 1) Phase 1: *Startup Period:* a period of foreign (both national

TABLE 3.1 German / Japanese / U.S. Billiard-Ball Comparison of Salient Cultural Attributes

German	Japanese	U.S.
Importance of individual	Importance of group	Importance of individual
Well-defined job roles	Job-role flexibility	Well-defined job roles
Leader as absolute authority	Leader as mediator	Leader as absolute authority
Rules more important than situation	Situation more important than rules	Rules and situation important
Importance of job security	Importance of lifetime employment	Job security with regular layoffs
Rigid work–personal life boundary	Fluid work–personal life boundary	Flexible work–personal life boundary
Fast & efficient decision making	Consensus decision making	Fast & efficient decision making
Limited consultative decisions	Participative decisions	Top-down decisions
Importance of expertise	Importance of age seniority	Importance of expertise and seniority
Importance of hierarchy	Importance of hierarchy	Importance of hierarchy
Uncertainty avoidance	Uncertainty avoidance	Risk taking

and corporate) occupation that coincided with installation and testing of the new technology → 2) Phase 2: *Adjustment Period:* characterized by problems and setbacks concerning consistency of product, output, quality, and wastage → 3) Phase 3: *Stable Growth Period:* most recent period of marked homeostasis during which members of the multinationals finally felt they were getting some control over production and quality and that they could begin to show better results.

The history of the cases from founding on is therefore divided into three distinct developmental phases that follow specific progressions in the plants' production capabilities. The first phase directly after the signing of the venture agreement was a time of much turbulence in both cases. The central event during this period both at TSP and Nutech was the installation and start-up of two pieces of state-of-the-art equipment including statistical process control monitors: (1) a paper machine that takes pulp (in the Nutech case—raw paper in TSP's case), converts it to raw paper, and then coats the paper with a thermal coating, and (2) a computerized "color kitchen" (or mixing room). The installation and start-up in each case were handled by teams of engineers and other specialists representing the various vendors of the equipment, most of whom were Japanese. The second phase was a period in which management and production workers were attempting to gain an understanding and mastery of the equipment and processes (a learning and ramping up phase). The third phase was a period in which the plant scaled up to full operation and commercial production and had reached a level of quality that was well regarded by customers. Each phase brought with it particular challenges that, in terms of dealing with other team members, brought particular issue domains related to cultural similarities and differences to the fore.

Phase 1: Start-up period, emergent issue domains, and some negotiated outcomes. Although in the case of both TSP and Nutech, TPC (the Japanese multinational parent) utilized a preexisting facility and employed many who had worked at the site previously, the technology was quite new, with production centering around two new pieces of equipment: the coating machine and color kitchen. Managers at both sites concur that the period during which the machinery was first installed represented a unique and distinct era in the history of both the U.S. subsidiary and the German IJV.

In both cases during the first year after inception, the Japanese vendors supplying the equipment sent technical and support personnel to the United States and Germany, meaning that rather than a handful of Japanese (seven in the TSP case and six in the Nutech case) concentrated at the top managerial levels, there were more than 20 Japanese on site. This situation was complicated even further by two other factors. One involved the multiple allegiances of these additional Japanese, who came from three other Japanese companies besides TPC: the vendor for the machine, a water machine manufacturer (in the Nutech case), and an electrical contractor supporting the vendor. Hence, individuals from five firms were working on site and were only loosely coordinated with one another. Another complication during this period, as one manager at Nutech put it, was that "there was very high pressure through the whole staff, because actually we were a little too late [behind plan] in the start up phase." Thus, not only were the top team members new to each other, they were encountering technological novelty and newness, they were highly dependent on the support people sent by the various vendors, and at the same time they were dependent on indigenous management and support people.

In both cases, under conditions of tremendous time pressure and the sense that not enough progress was being made to respond either to market needs or parental expectations, it is hardly surprising that the cultural issue domains that affected the speed and effectiveness of managerial action by the team were those that managers noticed most and were the most problematic. During this period, differences in decision-making styles, conceptualization of work, understanding of job roles, and tensions in regard to language use emerged as salient issues stemming predominantly from national cultural differences. The emergence of these critical issue domains led to divergent behaviors that created tensions and forced explicit recognition and negotiation on the part of individual managers. We treat each emergent issue in this first phase of production in the following discussion, making distinctions between the two cases as they were experienced.

Decision making.   All managers interviewed, at both TSP and Nutech, talked about decision making as a key issue in the first phase of production. There was consensus among the respondents that issues regarding decision making emerged due to national cultural differences in decision-making styles. At TSP, U.S. managers felt that decision making took an inordinate amount of time and that it was not clear if their participation was indeed valued. In fact, there were early indications in this phase of production of what Brannen (1994b) began to call "bicultural alienation"—a sense of malaise resulting from not feeling a part of the dominant culture of the organization. This alienation resulted when managers thought that their input was not valued in meetings. This type of malaise was encountered predominantly by middle managers in production, where the highest level of bicultural activity was taking place—around the new equipment in coating and in the mixing room. These managers felt that their inclusion in meetings was just proforma and that the Japanese managers had already reached their decisions prior to the meeting.

At TSP Japanese managers often in meetings would lapse into their native tongues for prolonged periods of discussion, which added to this feeling of malaise. The language factor is discussed in detail later. The managers who felt this type of alienation were clearly in the minority at TSP. In fact, U.S. managers in high-ranking positions or functional areas not directly affected by the changes in production were unlikely to experience this type of malaise. Brannen (1994b) attributed this to a sense of security that these managers had about their position in the company.

At TSP, much of the difficulties in decision making could be attributed to differences in decision-making styles and risk avoidance behavior of U.S. and Japanese members of the organization. The Japanese, who favored a consensus-gathering decision-making style, liked to include all members who would either have something to add to a decision or be affected by the decision in the meeting. In addition, because the Japanese managers did not like to take the risk of lack of consensus at the meetings, they tended to meet with each person involved in the decision making in a one-on-one dialogue before the actual meeting to hear his position and incorporate his position into the decision. Thus, often a decision would have been talked about and conclusions reached even before the actual meeting. However, this did not mean that the opinions of members at the meeting were not valued. Rather, it meant simply that the individuals whose input was required or who would be affected by the decision were consulted ahead of time. The managers who felt their opinions were not valued often felt this way because they were not asked to speak up in the meetings, even though in many cases the Japanese had consulted with them before holding the meeting.

The difficulties in regard to differences in decision-making styles continued through all phases of production at TSP. However, presumably because of the power imbalance resulting from a wholly owned subsidiary, no newly negotiated outcome around this issue evolved. Rather, the U.S. managers and employees began to resign themselves to respecting and even enacting the Japanese decision-making norms and style.

At Nutech, issues also emerged around decision making. However, rather than feeling excluded, German managers felt that they had little power to make decisions in a timely fashion. One German manager had this to say, "If you are responsible [for a certain outcome], you actually should have the power to make some decisions . . . particularly if you are responsible for waste and those sorts of things. [Here] you feel like you have little power. So [we—the Germans] have some trouble, I expect, (but not of a personal sort) with Japanese."

While some Japanese managers at Nutech felt they would rather speed up the decision-making process, all concurred that they were constrained by the expectations of the parent company that they achieve consensus among themselves and, most important, that they get approval from the Japanese home office. One Japanese manager said, "Here [in Germany] the responsibility [of the individual] is more than in Japan, because in Japan, for example, the production manager should consult the mill manager or department head of R & D or quality control. But, in Germany, they can do it by themselves. That means that action is [at a] rather high speed here."

Both the German and Japanese managers felt the disparity in reporting procedures to the home offices. One German manager said that the Japanese managers "had to report every hour what was going on, what happened, how to solve problems and so on. I felt at this time a very strong pressure." This issue, sometimes referred to as a feeling of having a Japanese "shadow management" also was experienced by U.S. managers at TSP. These discrepancies in decision-making style continued to plagued both the U.S. and Japanese managers at TSP and the German and Japanese managers at Nutech throughout this phase of organizational development without any significant movement toward a negotiated outcome.

Concept of work. At TSP the biggest issue in regard to differences in concept of work revolved around notions of job role definitions and responsibility. Whereas these differences might have been pronounced in any U.S./Japanese organization, they were quite polarized at TSP because of its brownfield, unionized status. The U.S. Paper Makers Union historically had experienced an adversarial relationship with management at the paper mill, and there were many remaining negative associations between management and labor at TSP. So there were many residual assumptions about job role categorizations, such as "that's not my job," and distinctions between management and others' hourly work, such as "a foreman cannot get his hands dirty," that inhibited the smooth implementation of technology at TSP. No significant negotiated outcomes were reached during this phase of development; however, Japanese management began to plant seeds of more flexible job role definitions, including concepts of teamwork in manning the new equipment.

There was also consensus about differences in job role definition issues at Nutech, where the Japanese felt that the Germans had a narrowly defined job scope, while the Germans felt the Japanese had an unrealistic expectation of broad role responsibility. One Japanese remarked, "In Japan, our feeling or some of our thinking is that we want to cover as much as possible. For example, I worked in quality control but I would like to know the production condition and the marketing condition. . . . But, my feeling is that German people at first concentrate on their own job." A German manager in production observed about a Japanese manager:

> [H]e is responsible for technology. And he feels a very strong responsibility for quality. Not only for manufacturing and coating machines, but [all the way] up to the customer, the end user. And if something is wrong, he always cares that he is responsible for that because it touches the quality. And for instance, in the German parent company, [the] quality control guy is of course responsible for quality as far as paper making is concerned, including the finishing department, [but] sending it out afterwards [the other department is responsible]. There is no responsibility after that because quality stops after coating. So this is a different way of thinking.

In regard to this particular issue of job-role perception, no significant negotiated outcome was reached. Individual managers have not been pressured to change their ways. However, in the cases where new employees have been hired, the codirectors have looked for German individuals who were more flexible in their perception of job roles.

At Nutech, all managers felt that there was a very large difference between Japanese and German notions of the boundary between work and private life. A Japanese manager described it this way, "A big difference between German and Japanese people is the workers. Workers in Germany care very much about their private hours. . . . [Even though] they may have some big order from the boss, if they have a prior personal commitment they will stick to their private life." The Japanese codirector said, "[Unlike the German employees] Japanese will give up their personal time."

This conflict came to a head when one Japanese manager (who was subsequently sent back to Japan earlier than intended) refused to allow a German manager to take his planned summer vacation leave. The Japanese manager insisted that the German change his plans, and the employee complained to the German copresident, who in turn informed the Japanese copresident that the employee had a legal right to take his vacation as planned. The Japanese copresident then overruled the Japanese manager's decision.

Language.   Language is an issue in any multicultural setting. Sometimes the venture language is familiar to one cultural group but not the other, as in the cases of Japanese-owned companies in the United States or the United Kingdom. In TSP's case the predominant venture language was English because the venture was located in the

United States and because the Japanese typically had some English instruction in high school and in college. Generally, language was not a major issue at TSP, with the exception of cases of a few U.S. middle managers who already felt excluded from the decision-making process and therefore felt most sensitive to those situations in which Japanese employees would spontaneously begin discussions among themselves in Japanese.

However, in the case of Nutech, English as the official venture language was of course not the mother tongue of the Japanese or the Germans. The Germans' English was generally more fluent than their Japanese counterparts', but, nonetheless, much difficulty arose from the lack of a shared language. For example, one German manager described the communication process at the plant in this manner, "We had to try to read [the Japanese] hearts and faces. But it is difficult when [they] can't speak English or German well. But you have to first be careful that you don't make your Japanese colleagues lose face." By one Japanese manager's account, "[In Japan] if [someone] says something, basically 100% of the [people] can understand, but here in Germany, Nutech, if I would [talk] in English maybe . . . 80 or 85% can understand, but 15% can't. In addition we can't express very detailed [thoughts]."

The negotiated outcome for language use was really the only one available. Namely, when a Japanese or a German was confused or needed help to be brought up to speed, he or she would confer with others of their same cultural group in their mother tongue. This was done solely to expedite matters and clarify issues rather than as a means of excluding one or the other cultural group from decision making. One German manager speaks about the negotiated outcome, "The work language is English. But during discussions they would sometimes speak Japanese and I thought this was a good thing because you know your own language better and can understand better and can discuss things more precisely. One has to be tolerant." However, this solution is seen as a temporary solution to a difficult situation, and most respondents tended to agree that it would be best if the level of English fluency were higher among both the Germans and Japanese.

Phase 2: Adjustment period, negotiated outcomes and more emergent issue domains.   At TSP the ground-breaking ceremony in fall 1989 (2½ years after inception) for the completion of the $43 million expansion housing the new equipment marked the success of the management team in realizing its goal to turn the plant into a state-of-the-art specialty paper manufacturing concern. The successful operations of the newly transformed plant rested not only on the transfer of technology from Japan, which was housed in the expansion in the form of leading-edge mixing and coating machinery, but also, most important, on the successful transfer or adaptation of organizational processes necessary to support the technology. The cross-cultural transfer of technology and organizational processes, again, were not done unilaterally but involved much adjustment of the original forms to fit within the new organizational context.

Many negotiated outcomes were reached at TSP during this period in regard to creating a work culture consistent with the requirements of quality control of the Japanese parent. Most of these negotiated outcomes were reached formally through two progressive collective bargaining agreements. Over the course of the two formal negotiations, the Japanese management and union officials were able to agree on several items including (1) new flexibility in language that allowed for more fluid job categorizations so that operators could assist each other as equal team members, (2) the concept of the working foreman, and (3) quality control as a line versus staff function. Some of the negotiated outcomes were also reached informally by on-the-job training both on the site as well as in Japan.

At the Nutech IJV, once the Japanese subcontractor support personnel had left (in summer 1991), the joint venture went into a period of adjustment when sales personnel were eager to make customer contact while production personnel were concerned with experimenting with the new equipment and ramping up to attain acceptable levels of quality. At this point, three new issues emerged as salient: (1) a conflict between production and sales departments about what output levels could be attained and when; (2) a conflict about production quality expectations (Germans accepting more frequent paper breaks than the Japanese; and (3) some issues about individuality and collectivism. While some of the cultural issues such as decision-making styles and differing conceptualizations of "work" that emerged in phase 1 continued to be important at this time, some understanding and successful negotiation around these issues began.

Conflict between sales and production.   This issue emerged both at TSP and Nutech. At TSP the most prominent difficulty stemmed from a divergence in understanding of sales roles between the U.S. and Japanese managers. The U.S. managers understood a strong demarcation between skills needed for those employees who were trained in sales versus those for employees skilled in production. On the other hand, it was common practice for Japanese managers to assign engineers previously assigned to production areas to the sales function so they could act as technical advisors to the sales force and TSP's clients. One particularly damaging outcome of this conflict at TSP resulted in U.S. engineers assigned to sales feeling ostracized and devalued by the Japanese management. They replied in interviews that this made them feel that they were being "put out to pasture," or made one of the so-called madogiwazoku (a Japanese term literally meaning one of the "by the window tribes"—an informal demotion reserved for underachieving managers). Only two middle managers felt so alienated by this practice that they eventually quit the company for jobs at a U.S.-owned paper plant in eastern Massachusetts.

At Nutech only a couple of managers in the production area mentioned that there was a conflict between what the sales staff would say they would deliver and what production thought they were capable of producing. Although this disparity is a common complaint in monocultural work settings as well, because each manager mentioned this as a national cultural discrepancy, we bring this up as an issue for cultural negotiation. One manager reported that

> the Japanese guys are following the market amount independent of the square meters they could sell—if there is one square meter they would like to have, they would develop it independent of costs and such things. And this is another way of doing, I think that we [Germans] have to learn that it is very good. In part, it is of course very expensive to develop such a grade. On the other hand, there is one way to enter a market. . . . [T]he Germans

would say 'Can we sell 20 million square meters? Then we should start to develop [it].'

Thus, the cultural difference may be in customer orientation. The Japanese tend to meet even small customer demand, whereas their German counterparts need a much larger order to justify product development and production.

Production quality expectations.   During phase 1 the key concern was to get the plant and machinery up and running. Now in the second phase of production development at TSP and Nutech, the quality of the product became a big issue of concern. Differences in regards to what level of quality would be the target for production emerged. Although the mills were doing well in terms of output, there was a lot of waste, mostly due to what the Japanese thought were excessive paper breaks.

The Japanese codirector of the Nutech IJV was articulate in describing the conflict:

> So, [in terms of operation] how many paper breaks should be okay? In TCP [the Japanese home company] and also in TSP after two years from starting, one paper break occurring in two or three days, means no paper breaks is the main condition. But this mill [Nutech] is 1.7 to 2 times per day on the average. . . . Japanese and [German expectations] are different regarding this case. . . . [T]hey [the German home company] did not find any difficulty allowing for this rate, but my thoughts are different.

While the quality of the products and the rate of paper breaks have gradually improved, at the time we wrote this chapter the discrepancy over product quality expectations has not been mediated at the Nutech IJV. TSP has had better success in meeting the zero defect standard over time. Managers at TSP attributed their success to the successful on-the-job training as well as positive collective bargaining agreements in regards to job-role definitions regarding quality control as an ongoing line function versus a periodical check staff function.

Individualism versus collectivism.   The differences between individualism and collectivism at the TSP plant curiously did not surface as a critical issue to be resolved during any of the three phases of production. We attribute this to a variety of reasons, not the least being the Japanese management's effort to run TSP as well as possible as a U.S. operation. Therefore, Japanese management did not enforce strict dress norms at the plant (although they did make available uniforms and laundry for those workers who wished to take advantage of the service) or regular group exercises. In addition, the Japanese management worked with the union in a win/win approach to collective bargaining and were able to negotiate the more critical aspects of work culture necessary to ensure a smooth-running paper facility.

At Nutech, the differences between individualism and collectivism played out a bit differently. A Japanese manager there spoke of this difference as follows, "The European style is independent behavior. How to protect their family and get higher status in the society or company. But the Japanese mind belongs to the organization or company—he must cooperate. This is a very different mind." Although individualism versus collectivism was not a difference explicitly taken up to any great extent, this basic difference between German and Japanese cultural stances seems to be at the root of many of the other issues confronted, such as decision-making styles and boundaries between work and personal life.

Over time a type of synchronization has begun to occur in regard to decision making at Nutech wherein the German component is beginning to tolerate a slower and more participative decision-making process while their Japanese colleagues are allowing for the meeting to be shortened and more pared down in terms of attendance. In addition, the codirectors have worked out a proactive system of reporting to the Japanese home office to receive approval before decisions are made to facilitate a faster feedback loop.

In addition, at Nutech a negotiated outcome to the divergence in concept of work and work boundaries emerged as a compromise by one or the other group. For example, Japanese managers tend not to expect that their German colleagues will join them in their late night socializing. Some German managers chose on their own to either forego vacations or take shorter ones during this first phase of production development. And Japanese managers have tended to realize that they cannot change this facet of German work life.

Phase 3: Stable growth period and more negotiated outcomes.   At this time no new critical issues became evident at either plant, but the issues around differing styles of decision making and expectations regarding quality, especially at Nutech, continued to be salient. A new iteration of negotiated outcomes emerged around the decision-making issue. Whereas in phase 2 there was a negotiated outcome around decision-making styles that was a compromise between the two national cultural tendencies, in phase 3 an even more expeditious outcome emerged. In this phase the codirectors began to handle local decisions between themselves as much as possible without the hitherto customary lengthy group discussions and checking with the parents.

In regards to quality norms, a negotiated outcome is still not forthcoming at Nutech. The Germans are generally content with an average 1.7 paper breaks a day, thinking that the Japanese expectation of zero paper breaks per day as the norm to be an unrealistic "pie-in-the-sky" figure.

TSP enjoyed more forward movement in the quality issue. However, the main issue still not resolved at the plant was that of certain employees feeling biculturally alienated. In some cases managers even perceived what they termed a "bamboo ceiling" for promotion due to lack of inclusion into the daily decision-making network at the plant. This finding is notably close to what Rochelle Kopp in chapter 5 refers to as the "rice-paper ceiling." Even though there were encouraging cases of promotion for non-Japanese managers, such as the vice-president of operations being promoted to president when the Japanese president was sent home to Japan, two middle managers continuing to feel discriminated against quit the company to join U.S. competitors, as previously mentioned.

Discussion

Disparate negotiated cultures were emergent in these two cases in that some individual and group differences persisted while members negotiated compromises or

innovations around those differences in behaviors or expectations that became problematic due to the pressures and challenges faced by the multinational organizations
over time. At TSP, whereas the issue of bicultural alienation remained unresolved
for some, many negotiated outcomes were reached surrounding conflicting issues
of decision making, concept of work roles, teamwork, and quality issues.

At Nutech, Japanese managers had to learn to respect the boundaries drawn
between work and private lives by many German colleagues and could not look to
them to spend evenings and weekends socializing. German managers set aside or
shortened planned vacations in the first two years of the venture when the IJV encountered technological and production problems, moving back toward their old
habits as the venture got onto a solid footing. Some of the Japanese managers adapted
to the German host country and IJV setting by working fewer hours than they would
have in Japan, and some were gradually coming to take longer vacations, though by
no means vacations as long as those taken by their German colleagues. The Japanese
had to learn to settle for more rapid decision making and less discussion than many
were used to while Germans had to settle for somewhat more lengthy discussions
and decision-making processes than many of them reported being accustomed to.
Conflicts that arose surrounding these and other organizational issues sometimes
had to be referred up to the level of the copresidents for resolution and a division of
labor emerged. For example, when issues arose concerning personal matters, Japanese managers would go to the Japanese copresident while German managers referred their problems and concerns to the German copresident. These negotiated
outcomes we have documented and discussed fall under four broad categories, as
summarized with examples in table 3.2.

The negotiated outcomes documented herein illustrate that the evolution of a
negotiated culture can both encompass and leave relatively undisturbed many aspects of the culture of origins of the members of a multinational organization, whereas
on some dimensions there can be convergence on a common approach to doing things.
Predicting the course of organizational culture evolution in complex cultural arenas
such as the two cases described in this chapter is not an easy task. Even if we can
accurately assess the two-billiard-ball cultural attributes of the separate cultural
groups, we have shown that these categories can at best serve merely as theoretical
and perceptual anchors for organizational culture determination.

Organizational culture as a negotiated entity evolves as a dynamic, ongoing, and
changing subtotal of interpersonal negotiations around organizational issues as they
come up in real time over the course of the organization's history. In the post–cold
war era, interactions between cultures are less hegemonic, exiting arrangements are
frequently changing, conditions are less certain, and actors have more influence over
multinational organizational outcomes. As a result, as we have shown in our comparative study, cooperative arrangements do not evolve along predetermined for-
mulae. Emergent working cultures do not simply reflect one or the other culture.
Neither are they a blend or hybrid of the constituents' best practices, nor are they
representative of some global universal work culture. Rather, cross-cultural actors
frequently face situations where no repertoires exist, so they create something new
for both parties—working cultures particular to and evolving with the multinational
context at hand.

TABLE 3.2 Methods of Negotiating Outcomes

	TSP	NU
Compromise by one group	Japanese management not enforcing Japanese dress norms or rituals such as group exercises Japanese management reinstating traditional company parties at Christmas, New Year's, and a summer barbecue U.S. management agreeing to not shutting down operations during the Christmas holidays U.S. management (with exception of a few middle managers) accepting and enacting Japanese consensus decision-making style	German managers foregoing vacations during the first two years of operations Japanese managers not expecting to socialize after work with their German counterparts
Meeting in the middle	Blending of both content and process of collective bargaining agreements between management and United Paper Maker's Union Process—change to more of a win/win strategy both sides coming to the table with leaner dockets. Content—acceptance of a middle of the road approach to job role flexibility U.S. workers and management accepting and adopting Japanese work concepts of multifunctional teams, quality control, and maintenance	Meetings shorter and less frequent than Japanese norm, longer and more frequent than the German norm Participation pared down for the Japanese
Innovating something new for both groups	Creation of the concept of the working foreman Evolution of a dual-hierarchy—a direct line to Japanese president for Japanese employees versus standard chain of command for U.S. employees	English language norm with an allowance for breakouts into mother tongues when necessary to expedite understanding Emergence of a proactive reporting structure with Japanese parent to facilitate faster decision-making loop
Division of labor to minimize need for further negotiation		Japanese managers go to Japanese codirector for "personal concerns" while Germans go to German codirector for same German managers in charge of production and administrative functions while Japanese managers dominate in the areas of sales/marketing, technology, and quality management

Notes

1. It is important to note here that "multinational" does not always indicate that the foreign operations are necessarily made up of members from disparate cultures. In fact, the term is generally used simply to indicate that a firm is doing business in different national cultures (see chapter 2 for a detailed definition). The two multinational case studies here, however, are in fact multicultural—both are run by bicultural (Japanese and American in one case and Japanese and German in the second case) management teams and have included some Japanese production operators working on the line at different times.

References

Abu-Lughod, L. 1986. *Veiled Sentiments: Honor and Poetry in Bedouin Society.* New York: Oxford University Press.
Adler, N. J. 1986. *Cross-Cultural Research: The Ostrich and the Trend.*
Allaire, Y., & M. E. Firsirotu. 1984. "Theories of Organizational Culture." *Organization Studies.* 5: 193–226.
Anderson, B. 1991. *Imagined Communities.* London: Verso.
Bhabha, Homi K. 1990. *Nation and Narration.* New York: Routledge Press.
Boyacigiller, N. A., & Adler, N. J. 1991. "The Parochial Dinosaur: Organizational Science in a Global Context." *Academy of Management Review.* 16 (2): 262–290.
Boyacigiller, N. A., Kleinberg, J., Phillips, M. E., and Sackmann, S. A. 1995. "Conceptualizing Culture in International Management Research." In Punnett B. J., & Shenkar, O. (eds.), *Handbook of International Management Research.* Cambridge, MA: Blackwell Publishers, Inc.
Brannen, M. Y. 1991. "Culture as the Critical Factor in Implementing Innovation." *Business Horizons.* 34 (6): 59–67.
Brannen, M. Y. 1994a. "Embedded Cultures: The Negotiation of Societal and Organizational Culture in Japanese Buyout of a U.S. Manufacturing Plant." In Murtha T. & Prahalad, C. K. (eds.), *Michigan International Organizational Studies Conference Proceedings.* Ann Arbor, February, 1994.
Brannen, M. Y. 1994b. *Your Next Boss is Japanese: Negotiating Cultural Change at a Western Massachusetts Paper Plant.* Doctoral dissertation, University of Massachusetts, Amherst.
Brannen, M. Y. 1995. "Does Culture Matter? Negotiating a Complementary Culture to Successfully Support Technological Innovation." In Liker, J., Ettlie J., & Campbell, J. (eds.), *Technology and Management: America and Japan.* Oxford: Oxford University Press.
Buell, F. 1994. *National Culture and the New Global System.* Baltimore: Johns Hopkins Press.
Dalton, M. 1959. *Men Who Manage.* New York: Wiley.
Fine, G. A. 1979. "Small Groups and Culture Creation: The Idioculture of Little League Baseball Teams." *American Sociological Review.* 44: 733–745.
Fine, G. A. 1984. "Negotiated orders and organizational cultures." *Annual Review of Sociology.* 10: 239–262.
Geertz, C. 1973. *The Interpretation of Cultures.* New York: Basic Books.
Giddens, A. 1984. *The Constitution of Society.* Berkeley: University of California Press.
Goffman, E. 1961. *Asylums.* Garden City, N.Y.: Doubleday.
Gouldner, A. W. 1954. *Patterns of Industrial Bureaucracy.* Glencoe, IL: Free Press.

Harrigan, K. R. 1988. "Strategic Alliances and Partner Asymmetries." In Contractor, F.J., & Lorange, P. (eds.), *Cooperative Strategies in International Business*. Lexington, MA: Lexington Books. 205–226.

Hofstede, G. 1984. *Culture's Consequences*. Beverly Hills: Sage.

Inkpen, A. 1992. *Learning and Collaboration: An Examination of North American—Japanese Joint Ventures*. Doctoral Dissertation, University of Western Ontario. London, Ontario, Canada.

Killing, J. P. 1983. *Strategies for Joint Venture Success*. London: Helm.

Kleinberg, J. 1989. "Cultural Clash Between Managers: America's Japanese Firms." In Benjamin Prasad, S. (ed.), *Advances in International Comparative Management*. Vol. 4. Greenwich, CT: JAI Press. 221–244.

Kleinberg, J. 1994a. "The Crazy Group: Emergent culture in a Japanese-American Binational Work Group." In Beechler, S., & Bird, A. (eds.), *Research in International Business and International Relations*. Vol. 6: Special issue on Japanese management. Greenwich, CT: JAI Press.

Kleinberg, J. 1994b. "Practical Implications of Organizational Culture Where Americans and Japanese Work Together." *National Association for the Practice of Anthropology Bulletin*. Vol. 14. Washington, DC: American Anthropology Association. 48–65.

Lane, H. W., & Beamish, P. W. 1990. "Cross-Cultural Cooperative Behavior in Joint Ventures in LCDs." *Management International Review*. 30: 87–102.

Lincoln, J. R., Hanada, M., & Olson, J. 1981. "Cultural Orientations and Individual Reactions to Organizations: A Study of Employees of Japanese-Owned Firms." *Administrative Science Quarterly*. 26: 93–114.

Lincoln, J. R., & Kalleberg, A. L. 1990. *Culture, Control, and Commitment*. Cambridge: Cambridge University Press.

Lincoln, J. R., Olson, J., & Hanada, M. 1978. "Cultural Effects on Organizational Structure: The Case of Japanese Firms in the United States." *American Sociological Review*. 43: 829–847.

Lincoln, Y. S., & Guba, E. G. 1985. *Naturalistic Inquiry*. Beverly Hills: Sage.

Mead, G. H. 1934. *Mind, Self and Society*. Chicago: University of Chicago Press.

Ong, A. 1987. *Spirits of Resistance and Capitalist Discipline: Factory Women in Malaysia*. Albany: State University of New York Press.

Parkhe, A. 1991. "Interfirm Diversity, Organizational Learning, and Longevity in Global Strategic Alliances." *Journal of International Business Studies*. 22: 579–601.

Parkhe, A. 1993. "'Messy' Research, Methodological Predispositions, and Theory Development in International Joint Ventures." *Academy of Management Review*. 18: 227–268.

Peterson, M. F., Brannen, M. Y., & Smith, P. 1994. "Japanese Leadership: Issues in Current Research." In Prasad, S. B. (ed.), *Advances in International and Comparative Management*. Vol. 9. Greenwich, CT: JAI Press.

Peterson, M., Peng, T. K., & Smith, P. B. 1989. "Japanese and American Supervisors of a U.S. Workforce: An Intercultural Analysis of Behavior Meanings and Leadership Style Correlates." Paper presented at the Annual Meeting of the Academy of Management, Washington, DC, August.

Peterson, R. L., & Shimada, J. Y. 1978. "Source of Management of Problems in Japanese-American Joint Ventures." *Academy of Management Review*. 3: 796–804.

Qualitative Solutions and Research Pty Ltd. 1994. Q.S.R. NUDIST, version 3.0.

Renan, E. 1990. "What is a Nation." In Bhabha, H. K. (ed.), *Nation and Narration*. New York: Routledge. 8–22.

Ring, P. S. & Van de Ven, A. H. 1994. "Developmental Processes of Cooperative Interorganizational Relationships." *Academy of Management Review*. 19: 90–118.

Ronen, S., & Shenkar, O. 1985. "Clustering Countries on Attitudinal Dimensions: A Review and Synthesis." *Academy of Management Review.* 10 (3): 435–454.

Roseberry, W. 1989. *Anthropologies and Histories.* New Brunswick, NJ: Rutgers University Press.

Sackmann, S. A. 1991. *Cultural Knowledge in Organizations: Exploring the Collective Mind.* Newbury Park, CA: Sage.

Salk, J. E. 1992. "International Shared Managment Joint Venture Teams: Their Developmental Patterns, Challenges and Possibilities." Doctoral dissertation, Sloan School of Management, MIT. Cambridge, MA.

Salk, J. E. 1996. "Partners and Other Strangers: Cultural Boundaries and Cross-Cultural Encounters in International Joint Venture Teams." *International Studies of Management and Organization.* 26 (4): 48–72.

Salk, J. E., & Shenkar, O. (1997 working paper). "Social Identities and Cooperation in an International Joint Venture: An Exploratory Study."

Strauss, A. 1963. "The Hospital and its Negotiated Order." In Freidson, E. (ed.), *The Hospital in Modern Society.* New York: Free Press.

Strauss, A. L. 1978. *Social Negotiations: Varieties, Contexts, Processes and Social Order.* San Francisco: Jossey-Bass.

Strauss, Anselm L. 1982. "Interorganizational Negotiation." *Urban Life.* 11: 350–367.

Sumihara, N. 1992. *A Case Study of Structuration in a Bicultural Work Organization: A Study of a Japanese-Owned and -Managed Corporation in the U.S.A.* Doctoral dissertation, New York University.

Van Maanen, J. 1988. *Tales of the Field: On Writing Ethnography.* Chicago: University of Chicago Press.

Whyte, W. F. 1943. *Street Corner Society.* Chicago: University of Chicago Press.

Yan, A. & Gray, B. 1994. "Bargaining Power, Management Control, and Performance in United States-China Joint Ventures: A Comparative Case Study. *Academy of Management Journal.* 37 (6): 1478–1517.

Yeh, R., & Latib, M. 1990. "Japanese Trust in Local Subordinates in Overseas Investments." Paper presented at the Annual Meeting of the Academy of International Business, Toronto.

4

JILL KLEINBERG

Negotiated Understandings

The Organizational Implications
of a Cross-National Business Negotiation

> Bargaining or negotiating is the generic term used to describe the cultural performance wherein different parties come together in an effort to reach what are interpreted as inconsistent goals (M. E. Pacanowsky and N. O'Donnell-Trujillo).

We commonly think of business negotiation as an activity physically and cognitively demarcated by the conference room, the table around which negotiators sit, and the time it takes to conclude the negotiation. The actors are there for the express purpose of reaching agreement on previously identified issues. Each "side" hopes to secure an outcome consistent with its own goals. Success or failure, either to agree or to win favorable conditions, hinges on a variety of factors, but foremost among them is the negotiators' behavior—how thoroughly they prepare, the effectiveness of their overall strategy, and their powers of persuasion, including the verbal and nonverbal tactics they utilize. When negotiation activity crosses nations, as in this case of the Japanese buyout of an American firm, the conventional model incorporates cognizance of cultural differences in negotiation behavior, differences that complicate the prospects for reaching agreement (Adler, 1991).

Here, I offer a different perspective on negotiation, which grows out of inductive ethnographic research focused on a Japanese-owned and -managed subsidiary in Los Angeles. The ethnographic lens sees the negotiation process as culturally embedded in a way far more pervasive than conventional conceptualizations of cross-national, cross-cultural negotiation. The present analysis, in fact, offers a multiple cultures framework. The "text" constructed through the interaction of the negotiators reflects Japanese and American cultural assumptions about how to conduct business negotiation. At the same time, however, it reflects cultural assumptions revolving around other foci. Negotiated outcomes, furthermore, transcend agreement on specific terms of the buyout. While informed by cultural assumptions, the interactions simultaneously create organizational culture(s). Existing shared understandings may be reinforced and new understandings constructed.

The sections that follow place this ethnographic study in the context of current research about cross-national, cross-cultural negotiation, set the stage for the buyout negotiation observed by the ethnographer, and analyze the negotiation text in order to clarify the proposed perspective on negotiated understandings.

Negotiating Cross-Culturally

As business has become increasingly global, scholars and practitioners have given growing attention to the negotiating styles and practices of persons from particular countries. Weiss (1993, 1996) labels the resulting "paradigm" of international negotiation "comparative, microbehavioral":

> The focus of this research paradigm has been face-to-face interaction between individual negotiators, which adherents view as *the* point of contact in negotiation. . . . From their perspective, the "mutual movement" that characterizes negotiation can occur only through interaction. . . . Thus what negotiators do (e.g., making offers, disclosures, threats) defines the process and determines the negotiation outcome. (1996: 214)

Thus, the comparative, microbehavioral stream of negotiation research encompasses not only cross-national comparison but consideration of intercultural communication processes as well (e.g., Adler, 1991; Adler, Brahm, & Graham, 1992; Fisher, 1980; Shenkar & Ronen, 1987). Researchers generally assume that societal culture affects negotiation. In the words of Shenkar and Ronen, "Conduct during negotiations is influenced by attitudes and customs, which to a great extent are embedded in a negotiating team's cultural and social traits" (1987: 263). Researchers also assume that cultural differences in negotiation conduct can lead to misinterpretation and misunderstanding. Therefore, cross-cultural understanding and accommodation are necessary if cross-national negotiation is to be completed successfully (Adler, 1991).

Despite conceptual emphasis on the consequences of cultural differences for cross-national (i.e., intercultural) communication, most negotiation research to date is single-country or comparative in focus. And most is based either on anecdotal description or analysis of simulated negotiations rather than observation of actual negotiations. (See Weiss, 1996, for a detailed overview of research methods.) Various types of behaviors receive attention for comparison across national groupings. Some researchers, for example, distinguish styles of negotiation, such as factual, affective, or axiomatic (Glenn, Witmeyer, & Stevenson, 1984), or dimensions, such as the value placed on emotional sensitivity or the degree of argumentativeness (Casse, 1982). Others look at verbal tactics—promises, threats, or normative appeals—and nonverbal behaviors—silence, facial gazing, or touching (Graham, 1985).

For the most part, the kind of research just described tells us little about the linkage between negotiation behavior and the societal culture. Nor does it capture the drama of interaction in the negotiation setting. Several studies of discourse style or discourse strategy place behavior surrounding negotiation more firmly in the larger cultural context. This work examines the culturally influenced cognitive maps (Spradley, 1979, 1980) that inform the way people put words together in order to persuade (Anderson, 1991; Friday, 1991; Young, 1992; Yum, 1991). In addition, these studies begin to explore the process of communicating across cultures, showing how and why people react to the negotiating approach of the cultural "other." Scholars argue for the urgency of more research on the intercultural aspect of negotiation (Adler & Graham, 1989).

Japanese and American Negotiation in the Literature

Since the 1970s, when the American business community first focused on Japan, initially as model and lately as nemesis (Boyacigiller, Kleinberg, Sackmann, & Phillips, 1996), the related negotiation literature has accumulated accordingly. This writing primarily targets the business practitioner and, interestingly, it generally emphasizes the embeddedness of negotiating behavior in the societal culture (e.g., Black & Mendenhall, 1993; Graham & Sano, 1984; March, 1988; Tung, 1984; Van Zandt, 1970).

Graham and Sano (1984), for instance, delineate successive stages of negotiation and contrast the way Japanese and Americans conceptualize the various stages. Whereas the heart of the drama for Americans revolves around the stages of persuasion, concessions, and agreement, Japanese negotiators emphasize two earlier stages: preliminary nontask sounding, particularly building relationships of trust through seemingly social activities, and the exchange of task-related information. Exchanging task-related information, in fact, constitutes an integral part of persuasion for the Japanese. Through this process, the character of individual negotiators, and of their organization, continues to be revealed. In addition, the process facilitates mutual understanding of each side's needs. Graham and Sano emphasize that the Japanese reach agreement only if they feel comfortable with the individuals and the organization with which they are negotiating. And, ideally, agreement implies a long-term relationship characterized by a spirit of flexibility and reciprocal cooperation. Americans, instead, concentrate on aggressively hammering out the most advantageous short-term agreement.

The negotiating style of Japanese and American actors also differs in significant ways. Graham and Sano (1984) describe the stereotypical John Wayne style of American negotiating. It emanates from a societal culture that centers the locus of action and decision making in the individual and extols a notion of fair play (Stewart & Bennett, 1991). A common script calls for an informal ("Just call me John"), "go it alone" hero who is eager to "get to the point" and force his counterpart to "lay your cards on the table." He lives (or dies) by the principles of "don't take no for an answer" and "a deal is a deal."

Contrast this to the stereotypical Japanese negotiating style built on a very different societal culture (see Lebra, 1976). Graham and Sano, for example, discuss a number of underlying principles. They include *tateshakai*, a Confucian-influenced notion of a vertically graded social order that requires clear status markers; *amae*, referring to emotion-laden reciprocal dependency; *wa*, or maintaining social harmony; and *ishin-denshin*, intuitive communication that expresses human empathy and helps preserve harmony by discouraging confrontation. Such principles are played out in an organizational context where convention dictates a broad pattern of information flow and buying into decisions ("consensus").

Although the culture-embedded argument for differences in negotiating behavior is compelling, an actor whose performance precisely reflects one or another of the contrasting styles would be portraying a clearly exaggerated cultural type. We must expect a range of behavior among same-country participants in actual negotiation settings, reflecting individual background and personality. Prior cross-national negotiating experience, for instance, may influence individual behavior. Furthermore, cultural assumptions about how to negotiate may be only one subset of societal culture that affects the negotiation process.

In addition, we must take into account the exigencies of the specific negotiating setting. Questions such as the following may be critical. What is the relationship between the companies involved in the negotiation? What are the relationships among the individuals conducting the negotiation—both across business entities and within a company? What is the nature of the focal organizations' cultures? Finally, we must consider, apart from the formal contract (ideally) concluded between negotiating parties, how negotiation activity has affected the organizations involved. A framework for conceptualizing cross-national, cross-cultural negotiation that encompasses the prior points extends the notion of cultural embeddedness. It also shows that negotiation is socially embedded.

An Evolving Conceptual Framework

Analysis of specific ethnographic data has resulted in the conceptual framework represented in figure 4.1. It reflects cultural influences on negotiated outcomes. Because culture constitutes a critical construct, it needs to be clearly defined. Culture here is considered "the acquired knowledge that people use to interpret experience and generate social behavior" (Spradley, 1979: 5). Cultural knowledge is widely shared by a group of people; its configuration is distinctive to the group, and it is constructed, passed on, and reinforced (or modified) through social interaction. Acquired cultural knowledge may be explicit, as in norms that people can consciously articulate, or it may be tacit, the unconscious assumptions that many scholars consider the innermost core of culture.

Japanese and Americans draw on three primary sets of cultural knowledge to conduct the buyout negotiation. In addition to cultural "rules" for negotiating, the actors' words and behaviors are influenced by a generalized nation-specific work culture and the culture(s) of the company they represent. Work culture refers to a loose set of assumptions about such concepts as responsibility, authority, trust, and decision making. These loosely shared assumptions develop out of individuals' experience as members of a society and members of work organizations in that society (Kleinberg, 1989, 1994a, 1994b, forthcoming). Organizational culture refers to cultural knowledge that emerges within a specific organization; it may comprise assumptions shared by all or most of an organization's members, or assumptions shared by an organizational subgroup. As figure 4.1 shows, intercultural interaction is mediated by particular relationships—relationships between the companies involved in the negotiation and among the individual negotiators.

Negotiation outcomes are visualized broadly. Most narrowly, they reflect the success or failure of negotiating parties to reach formal agreement on official issues. In the process of resolving these issues, however, the actors unconsciously "negotiate" culture. At the organizational level, existing organizational culture(s) may be

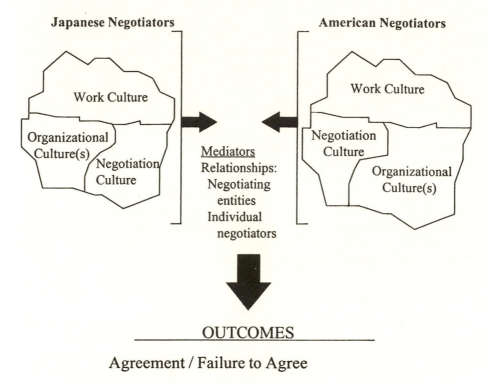

Japanese Negotiators   **American Negotiators**

Work Culture

Organizational Culture(s)

Negotiation Culture

Mediators
Relationships:
Negotiating
entities
Individual
negotiators

Work Culture

Negotiation Culture

Organizational Culture(s)

OUTCOMES

Agreement / Failure to Agree

"Negotiated" culture(s):

Reinforcement/reshaping of work and negotiating cultures

Reinforcement/reshaping of existing organizational culture(s)

"New" organizational culture(s)

FIGURE 4.1. Cultural Influences on Cross-National Negotiation

either reinforced or reshaped. Moreover, new organizational cultures may be created, in terms of an emergent subgroup or, as in the case discussed here, a new organizational entity that comes into being as a consequence of formal negotiations. At the societal level, the process may reinforce or reshape individual negotiators' interpretation of work or negotiating cultures.

Research Methodology

Negotiation data analyzed here were gathered through participant observation and intensive ethnographic interviews. I spent more than a year going almost daily to the focal company, identified by the pseudonym LASCO (Los Angeles Subsidiary Company). Over a 2½-month period, I observed four separate negotiating sessions and an agreement-signing meeting. In addition to the transcripts of over 20 hours of tape-recorded negotiation, the data set includes extensive field notes of observations along with related documentary materials. It includes as well transcripts of interviews with key participants in which their perceptions and feelings during the course of the negotiation were explored.

A mode of content analysis that Spradley (1979, 1980) calls domain analysis provides the main framework for discovering cultural (i.e., shared) assumptions. According to this framework, the largely tacit cognitive maps people use to navigate their world are organized into domains or categories of cultural knowledge. A domain is any symbolic category that includes subcategories (i.e., subdomains) of cultural knowledge. Certain cultural domains may be tied together by a "conceptual theme," a broad cognitive principle expressed in each domain.

Cultural knowledge relevant to the negotiation actors—influencing the way they negotiate a business deal, conduct daily work activity, or navigate their specific organization—became evident through repeated analysis of the data. Ideas, feelings, events, or behaviors that people recurringly talked about or enacted were identified and coded in field notes and transcripts. Themes and categories of underlying cultural knowledge were inferred from similar utterances and actions. (See Kleinberg, forthcoming, for a more detailed treatment of research methodology.)

The Context of Negotiations

About seven months after I began ethnographic fieldwork in LASCO, a subsidiary of a large Japanese trading company, the Japanese president invited me to sit in on negotiations about to take place. At this point in my fieldwork LASCO employed around 120 persons, including 11 *chuzaiin*, Japanese sent by the Tokyo headquarters to hold key management positions in the subsidiary. The Los Angeles operation formed the hub of the trading company's multinational "computer peripherals group." The bulk of the group's sales, as well as product research and development, emanated from LASCO. The trading company itself had no manufacturing capability. It subcontracted production to various Japanese manufacturers, but sold the products under the trading company brand name. The president, Matt (his adopted "American" name), had been with LASCO for 10 years. He was one of the founders of the subsidiary and the main architect of LASCO's business strategy.

Negotiations mainly involved the owner-managers of an American company, called here ROCA. This company had served almost two years of a five-year contract as exclusive sales representative for LASCO's video terminals product line. ROCA, in fact, had been formed expressly for the purpose of selling LASCO video terminals. Its owners, Tom and Jerry, had become acquainted with each other while working for different companies in the computer electronics industry. Together they approached Matt with the idea of a sales company to handle LASCO products, and LASCO loaned them start-up money. ROCA employed 15 persons in Los Angeles and regularly supplied 35 distributors in the United States. A subsidiary company,

ROCA Europe, handled European sales of trading company brand-name terminals from a base in Denmark.

Issues

At issue was a proposed buyout of ROCA by LASCO, thereby bringing responsibility for video terminals sales directly under LASCO management. Sales had grown tremendously since the LASCO-ROCA business relationship began. Matt now sought greater control of the burgeoning business. On the other side, Tom and Jerry, who were, respectively, president and vice president of ROCA, found themselves spending most of their time managing an expanding company instead of in the actual sales activities they both enjoyed. LASCO, therefore, planned to create a new sales subsidiary, LASCO Terminals, to handle the video terminals business.

The first formal negotiation session took place in early February. Three subsequent sessions occurred in March. In November of the previous year, however, there had been an initial meeting on the buyout at which Tom and Jerry presented their "requirements" to Matt. LASCO and ROCA failed to agree on a number of issues at that time, so negotiation continued on an informal basis. By February, the parties had reached certain understandings. Nevertheless, both sides acknowledged that, despite their mutual desire to reach accord, successful negotiations hinged on acceptance of particular conditions still in question.

Informal agreement already had been reached on the following:

LASCO will pay $500,000 in "front-end" money to Tom and Jerry for liquidation of ROCA.

Tom and Jerry will complete the three years remaining on the original sales representative contract as management-level employees of LASCO Terminals—Tom as vice president for marketing and Jerry as vice president for sales. Officially, however, for tax reasons, Tom and Jerry will form a "management services" firm, ROCA Consulting, and LASCO will employ their services through that firm.

LASCO will pay ROCA Consulting a commission of 1.5% of annual gross sales of video terminals in North America for a three-year period.

The new business arrangement will begin officially on April 1.

ROCA Consulting, with money loaned by LASCO, will buy 10% ownership of LASCO Terminals.

Tom and Jerry will be members of LASCO Terminals' board of directors, although they will not be "officers" of the company. (The meaning of "officer" is clarified later.)

Three points still needed to be negotiated. One concerned the date until which LASCO would pay ROCA the 10% sales commission guaranteed by the original sales representative contract. Jerry, in particular, considered this a key issue. ROCA payed its distributors a commission on orders placed by customers at the time the Japanese manufacturer shipped the order out of the factory. Orders went directly to LASCO for delivery to the customers. Customers payed LASCO for the product only after they received it, and LASCO paid ROCA's commission only after LASCO received payment. Therefore, Tom and Jerry contemplated the possibility of significant financial loss should a large number of video terminals ordered prior to the new agreement be delivered after the formation of LASCO Terminals.

A second point was the future business relationship between ROCA Europe and LASCO's sister subsidiary in England. The trading company had recently established ESCO (European Subsidiary Company), in London to promote computer peripherals sales in Europe. Up to this point, ESCO had not entered the video terminals market, concentrating instead on selling printers. Now ESCO planned to bring video terminals into its orbit. ROCA Europe, however, would remain a business entity owned by Tom, Jerry, and its Danish manager, Kristian, even after ROCA ceased to exist. So the question, a critical one to Tom and Jerry, became: would ROCA Europe continue to have responsibility for sales of trading company brand-name terminals and, if so, on what basis?

Finally, the negotiators needed to decide details of the service agreement. One point, settled without argument during informal discussions, concerned the amount of money that Tom and Jerry, through ROCA Consulting, would be paid annually. (The decision was $350,000, $400,000, and $450,000 over three consecutive years). Two other points were more problematic. One concerned the circumstances under which the three-year agreement between LASCO Terminals and ROCA Consulting could be canceled. The other concerned the work role of Tom and Jerry, specifically, whether they would be expected to act like normal LASCO Terminals employees.

The Actors

There are two central Japanese negotiators from the LASCO side. One, of course, is Matt. Matt's U.S. assignment has been unusually long—nearly 12 years. Most of this time he has been president of LASCO, which he helped establish. At age 47, he has a reputation among trading company colleagues for being a risk taker as well as a quick and autocratic decision maker. Many Japanese consider him too "American" to readjust to the Tokyo headquarters when he is rotated back to Japan. Matt has a distinctive gravelly voice and a slow, precise, economical manner of speaking English. In addition to Matt is Terry, LASCO's 41-year-old vice president of administration and Matt's long-time protégé. Terry, too, speaks English slowly, choosing his words carefully.

The key negotiators from ROCA are Tom and Jerry, ROCA's president and vice president. At ages 45 and 43, respectively, both men have an extensive background in computer electronics sales. Only Tom has management experience prior to the formation of ROCA, however. Tom is physically fit, a conventionally good dresser and, in the eyes of some LASCO female employees, attractive. Jerry is a much larger man than Tom, burly in both appearance and manner.

Besides these four men, the lawyers for each side, both Americans, also play important supporting roles in the negotiation drama. They are Roger, who has represented LASCO for many years, and Daryl, who has been ROCA's lawyer since the company's inception.

Characterization begins before the first negotiation session formally gets underway. At 1:30 PM, Matt and Terry wait for Tom and Jerry, typically late, to appear in the small conference room adjacent to Matt's office. Matt has seated himself at the head of the long oval conference table. Terry sits to Matt's left along one side of the table.

Around 1:45 PM, Tom and Jerry arrive. They chat with Matt and Terry. I tell Jerry I will be taping the negotiation. Jerry responds that he doesn't think it's a good idea, that the discussion could be "sensitive" and there could be "arguments." He says, "This could get rough, a lot of four-letter words." Matt jokes: "We need this on record." Jerry seats himself catty-corner from Matt, opposite Terry, while Tom places himself on Jerry's right. Later in the afternoon, the lawyers for the two sides arrive and sit beside their clients.

Matt gets the negotiation started. He exercises methodical control throughout, while Terry is LASCO's detail person. Terry passes out copies of a document that lists the issues which must be formally resolved in order for contracts to be drawn up. From this point, Terry joins Matt in moving the negotiation along. Matt frequently identifies possible problems that might occur with regard to the agreement. He plays, in his opinion, a hard-nosed negotiator, telling me after one session, "I'm acting very very tough guy, intentionally." Terry more often offers conciliatory remarks.

Jerry's presentation of self differs markedly from that of the Japanese. He speaks spontaneously, excitedly, and more frequently than anyone else, using repetition for emphasis. He jumps into discussions with an extreme or exaggerated stance, sometimes paying little attention to accuracy of fact. Jerry hones his characterization as a hard-hitting negotiator and, at the same time, as jokester and deep-down good guy. Tom maintains a calm, relaxed posture in comparison. He is the person from ROCA who tries to keep things moving smoothly. He typically softens Jerry's negotiating stance and corrects his factual lapses. Tom too jokes, but much less often than Jerry (or Matt).

The Negotiated Text

The analysis that follows centers on negotiation of the three main issues which LASCO and ROCA still need to resolve. By incorporating long excerpts from the negotiators' dialogue, it shows how the text created during the unfolding negotiations reflects both cultural inputs and negotiated cultures. Analysis gives primary attention to the impact of national differences in a generalized work culture and of LASCO's Japanese subgroup culture on negotiated outcomes. It emphasizes outcomes that represent the reinforcement of existing organizational cultures in LASCO and the creation of a new LASCO Terminals culture.

Negotiation text reproduced below is interspersed with the ethnographer's commentary. The bulk of the text draws from the first observed session, although some excerpts from subsequent sessions also are included. Analysis of each specific issue explicates the cultural "inputs" to the negotiation text—that is, the subtextual cultural themes or domains of cultural knowledge that thread through the utterances of Japanese and American actors as they strive for agreement. (The symbol . . . * . . .

means that a portion of the text that includes dialogue between two or more players has been deleted.)

Cultural assumptions about work recurringly expressed through dialogue organize around several overarching themes. For the Americans, critical themes concern money, trust, manageable risk, and autonomous action (personal and organizational). The themes of trust and the personal qualities deemed managerial are especially important to the Japanese. In addition, a primary theme of their organizational subgroup culture, the understanding that LASCO is inseparable from the larger trading company, helps shape Japanese input into the negotiation. (See Kleinberg, 1994, forthcoming, for a detailed treatment of LASCO's organizational cultures.) The existence of an area of thematic overlap, the notion of trust in a work setting, does not mean consonance in the assumptions Japanese and Americans respectively make about trust.

Outcomes, in terms of negotiated cultures, are discussed after the relevant cultural themes have been examined for all three critical issues.

Negotiating the "Old" Sales Commission

Differing Japanese and American conceptualizations of trust largely guide negotiation over how long to continue the 10% sales commission. Matt repeats the refrain, "You should believe." That is, Tom and Jerry should believe in LASCO's good intentions to play fairly. Jerry and Tom, however, enumerate the things that could go wrong. Jerry even brings up the possibility of willful manipulation of delivery schedules by LASCO. These Americans want avowed good intentions to be formally ensured in the agreement. The text excerpted here additionally illustrates the prominance of the theme of money in Jerry and Tom's discourse, as well as their preoccupation with reducing risk to manageable proportions.

> MATT: Okay, [item] number three. Anyway, as part of our present commission, our obligation to pay to ROCA up to March 31st is only towards, uh, invoice [of product received by customer] by that date.
>
> STEVE: Right.
>
> MATT: And the, after April 1st, if we cannot collect the money from the customer for that particular invoice, we have the right to ask ROCA for the invoice.
>
> JERRY: What? (laughter) What is this? Wait a minute, no, what did you just say, please?
>
> TOM: . . . What he's saying, that you're gonna go out there and unload the barrel and gonna ship five million dollars worth of product in March. If they can't collect, then they get that money back.
>
> JERRY: *Well, the only other problem is what . . . what keeps them from delivering April 1st, instead of March 30th?*
>
> MATT: *It's, uh, hundred percent in the control of LASCO.* (Laughter)
>
> JERRY: *That's the problem.*
>
> MATT: *You should believe us.*

JERRY: We had almost a million dollars not make it one month, that got slipped into the next month. Why?

MATT: Because our accounting, way of the, uh, accounting procedure in my country, every sales will close on 26 of every month. After that, we cannot, uh, enter to the computer.

JERRY: Why don't we just go one extra month [under the old commission agreement]? That way, we'll miss all the ones that. . . .

. . . * . . . The problem we're having, Matt, is, I mean, and honestly it's a problem . . . we're shipping anywhere from 300 to 500 thousand dollars worth of equipment between the 26th and 30th of every month. . . . Sometimes up to a million dollars. . . . * . . . And we had 400 thousand dollars of stuff this last month that went out on the first, on the second, because they [LASCO] couldn't get it out. . . .

TOM: . . . * . . . What Jerry's talking about is that we've been paying, we pay our guy's commissions based on, uh, when the product is shipped [to LASCO from the Japanese factory]. . . . And even though you miss a month, you know, [and] we don't get it [ROCA's commission] until the next month, we're still payin' our guys when they [the manufacturer] make the shipment.

MATT: Uh huh.

TOM: We just want to make sure we don't have a half million dollar differential that you say you're paying after the 31st, that could balance our books out. . . . * . . . Okay, just so . . . you know, right around that date we have a clear understanding, you know, with a little flexibility in there somewhere.

Matt adjusts LASCO's stance, indicating that Tom and Jerry will receive the 10% commission on any product paid for [by the customer] by April 15. They accept this, but Jerry pursues a related issue: *unusual* slippage in delivery.

JERRY: . . . * . . . Now, how 'bout the other half of the formula? . . . * . . . all of a sudden we see, in some significant manner—15%, 20%—some amounts falling into April. . . . I think *something should be triggered* then, because that means: either the factory is delaying it or, you know, *somebody is delaying the shipments into April and taking them out of March.*

MATT: Yeah, it need to something happen then. But, uh, it is kind of out of our control. Factory delay, delivery out of [our] control.

JERRY: Well, but you just told me earlier that LASCO had total control, so, uh. . . . (Laughter)

MATT: No, uh, if the product is at our hand here. But, unless, otherwise, it's out of control . . . if, uh, shipment boat sank, what happen then?

The debate continues. Matt suggests that the potential problem be handled by carefully checking March purchasing orders (POs) with Sam, a Japanese colleague who heads LASCO's present video terminals group. Sam has been identified as the future chief operating officer (COO) of the new subsidiary, LASCO Terminals.

MATT: . . . * . . . So, the only solution is, when, uh, briefing, uh, PO, you should discuss with Sam. PO by PO basis, this is including in the March shipment or not.

Jerry is not satisfied. He still worrys about the possibility of significant slippage into April of product that was supposed to be shipped in March.

JERRY: . . . * . . . So what is the recourse is all I'm asking, you know.

TERRY: *Are you worrying about the, uh, happenings beyond our control, or intentionally, you know. . . .*

JERRY: I would say, I would say to get April off to a nice start [for LASCO Terminals], *intentionally you might ship, you know, a portion of that business from late March to early April.* It doesn't hurt to come out flying you know. . . . Matt, I can't, I can't call up [the Japanese manufacturer] and say, "Well, why did you ship this on the 1st or the 3rd," [and learn that] because verbally somebody called and said, "Let's ship everything from the 1st to the 5th instead of from the 26th or the 20th. . . . Let's move half of it over, because, you know, we help you out sometimes, you help us out sometimes." *Do you understand the position?*

MATT: *No.*

JERRY: *You don't understand the position?*

MATT: *You should believe.*

JERRY: *Oh, I do believe, but see, in believing I can . . . by instituting something that makes it even easier to believe, right?*

TERRY: The person [at the Japanese manufacturing company] who is handling the accounting and, you know, daily inventory control of shipment, doesn't know our [LASCO-ROCA] deal.

MATT: Yeah.

TERRY: So they will do as usual.

JERRY: But Sam could sit and call [manufacturer's name].

TERRY: *So it depends on whether you can believe Sam or Matt or myself . . .*

Jerry continues to press for a clause protecting ROCA's interests, given a specified amount, that is, a "trigger point" of slippage. The debate over the issue of slippage ends inconclusively at this time. It is briefly resumed later in the first session when the lawyers are present.

JERRY: . . . * . . . All right, I've just seen this [slippage] happening a couple of times. That's what's bothering me.

TERRY: *I think uh we could always work out, regardless of the agreement, if anything happens.*

Jerry also brings up later the question of what happens if, "six or eight months after the subsidiary is operating, someone sues for money back." Does ROCA Consulting have the obligation to pay LASCO for returned product? The consensus is "no," but Jerry wants formal protection. He wants to ensure that ROCA Consulting's risk is minimized.

> JERRY: No. *Then we'd better put something in to at least limit liability.* I mean, who's to say that somebody might not come back and sue us and collect all the, the terminals they ever bought and resold, and send them all back here and say . . . there has to be a limit to our liability because we have no more, uh, no more source of funding. We've passed on, basically, all of it to you. . . . * . . . We're taking a gigantic reduction in the amount of monies we're taking in on a monthly basis, because we're pushing everything over to your side—to this new company, if you will. *Now, individually, we can't sit and take a risk that might have happened a year and a half ago without having some way to recoup it, which we don't have any longer.*
>
> DARYL: Well, there's got to be a cut-off date.
>
> JERRY: That's what I'm saying.

The potential problems of late product delivery and the return of payment to dissatisfied customers do not actually arise in subsequent negotiation sessions. The matter is handled through informal negotiation. By the time a LASCO-ROCA agreement is signed, LASCO has extended the cut-off date for the 10% commission to April 30, one month beyond the originally proposed date. Furthermore, the two companies have agreed to a date after which Tom and Jerry will not be liable for returned product shipped while ROCA was LASCO's sales representative.

Negotiating the Relationship Between ROCA Europe and ESCO

Discussion of the future relationship between ROCA Europe and ESCO gives insight into the complexity of relations between subunits of the trading company. Decision making clearly occurs within a multiunit framework, and Matt is well aware that proper protocol must be followed. The text particularly reflects one domain of cultural knowledge within the Japanese subgroup theme, "LASCO is inspeparable from the trading company." This is the understanding that "LASCO's strategy is part of the computer peripherals group strategy."

We see as well that this part of the negotiation is critical to Tom and Jerry's financial calculations. They emphasize, again, the theme of money. Trust also recurs as an important theme. The ESCO executives must believe that Tom, Jerry, and Kristian are trustworthy before they agree to a business relationship. Tom and Jerry place their trust in Matt to see that ROCA Europe's interests are protected.

> MATT: I think, uh, as I told you from the beginning of our negotiations, the Europe is out of my control, out of my responsibility. So, I will try to convince the President for ESCO to take the, uh, minimum three years, [that] ROCA Europe should be the exclusive rep for ESCO as far as this video terminal business is concerned. That I will try to let them accept, but I cannot guarantee.
>
> TOM: When will we know . . .

MATT: Uh, the President of ESCO and, uh, Tsutsui [executive responsible for day-to-day operations of ESCO] will be here by the 20th of this month for transaction of this, uh, deal. . . . So, I'd like to delete entire paragraph on Europe from the present agreement. But I understand your concern, so I will try the best and, uh, when UK [United Kingdom] president and, uh, Tsutsui come over here, we will arrange a meeting with you.

TOM: Okay, all right. So we make a deal directly with them?

MATT: Yes.

TOM: Okay.

MATT: But right now we are 90% no problem.

TOM: Okay.

JERRY: What's the 10%?

MATT: Ten percent is, uh, *they like to actually interview your guy* [*i.e., Kristian, who runs ROCA Europe*] *over this. Because without, uh, knowing him, he* [*ESCO's president*] *cannot commit to use as exclusive rep.* . . . .

TOM: Uh, Tsutsui knows Kristian.

MATT: Yes, Tsutsui knows, but, uh, new president.

Tom tells Matt that Kristian will be in Los Angeles the same week as the ESCO people, so Matt plans to arrange the meeting for a time when Kristian can attend.

MATT: . . . * . . . So, that's why I would like to propose that the entire article regarding Europe be deleted from the, uh, contract.

JERRY: I understand what you'd like to do, but you understand that we can't? Okay?

MATT: (Raises eyebrows) So, it means that you cannot accept?

JERRY: This is a very integral part of the whole, the whole deal. It always has been. . . . * . . . Do you understand that this is, you know, close to half the [buyout] deal.

MATT: (Raises head in questioning manner and makes a long "ummm" sound) . . . Because my impression was when, uh, I shared communication with you on this entire deal . . . I thought the European deal is not so significantly affect deal.

TERRY: We have seen that the, uh, European deal is, uh, out of [our control] . . . as Matt said, would try best to have the ROCA Europe to be the exclusive rep of ESCO, but as far as LASCO position is concerned, this deal, Europe deal, entirely separate. That's the basis we have been negotiating . . .

JERRY: We understand that it's a separate basis, but we also have been, you know, brought this far based on [the understanding that] C. K. [C. K. Tani, president of ESCO] has been, you know, informed of it; he approved of it; he liked it. And there would be two separate documents, but basically that it would happen. . . . *It's a very important part of the whole arrangement, and it's close to 50% of the deal.*

TOM: *It's not 50% but it's a building stone, a big block.*

JERRY: It changes everything else. It will change everything else if it doesn't go.

TOM: We can, you know, for purposes of right now, Matt, we can delete it from the package that we're talking about as a separate [deal]. . . . But realizing that, before we sign, we'll have that other thing. We'll have the European thing signed. . . .

MATT: But, uh, my understanding from the beginning after starting negotiation with you, the European deal, is, uh, . . . ESCO operation has, uh, choices. One is either they will use ROCA Europe as a sales rep, commission 5%, minimum three years, exclusively for European sales, or, ESCO can hire now the, uh, employee of ROCA Europe as the employee of ESCO. Right?

JERRY: No.

MATT: . . . * . . . Well, anyway, the Europe deal, we feel, as I said, uh, separate the deal. So, let's, uh, put aside.

JERRY: When you say put aside, there's nothing we can do about it until you sit down with C. K. Or, it sounds like, it sounds like we can't do anything until they interview, uh, Kristian and all, all they're looking at is possibly hiring him. . . . That's not our understanding.

MATT: Well, if so, then uh I have to change our proposal to, uh, ESCO.

TOM: *Do a sales, do a sales job on C. K. . . .*

Logo Negotiations

The theme of LASCO's inseparability from the trading company crops up again during a lull in the first negotiating session while the negotiators wait for the lawyers to arrive. The context is an animated discussion about logos. Utterances of the Japanese reflect their concern about the identity and future of the computer peripherals group (i.e., LASCO's strategy is part of the computer peripherals group strategy). Tom and Jerry have brought mock-ups of potential LASCO Terminals logos done by ROCA's ad agency. General interest in logos stems from the rapid expansion of the computer peripherals business worldwide. The need to coordinate LASCO's choice of logo with logo decisions made at the Tokyo headquarters complicates the issue. Indeed, a second set of Japanese subgroup understandings about LASCO's link to the trading company subtly colors the dialogue: the domain of cultural knowledge that "competition for control of the computer peripherals group" exists. Lack of agreement between LASCO and the headquarters about an appropriate logo can be viewed in the context of such competition.

In addition, this part of the text gives insight into Tom and Jerry's sense of autonomous action. In this instance, they feel that LASCO should be able to make decisions about the logo for LASCO and its subsidiaries, or even that the subsidiaries could independently make decisions. The Americans' concept of work clearly contrasts with Japanese assumptions about consultative decision making and interunit consensus.

JERRY: . . . * . . . Let's ask the question we've heard from two different sources—either the trading company [headquarters] or LASCO is looking to produce a new logo?

MATT: Yes.

JERRY: Yes, LASCO or, yes, Japan is looking for a new logo?

MATT: Japan. . . . All product [is] distributed worldwide, through distributors. It means, with the trading company's model number or name only. . . . All distribution product, standardized logo should be there. That is the [headquarters] focus, idea. We agreed, but the problem is they chose [already] a, uh, logo. We don't accept that logo.

JERRY: So, you can't use LASCO's [present] logo?

MATT: *No.*

JERRY: . . . * . . . *Well, okay. But can't we pick our own [logo]? LASCO Terminals?*

MATT: *That is . . . up in the air right now.*

Tom shows the logo mock-ups. He explains that the objective is to make LASCO a household name; the letters "LASCO" should be widely recognized in ads for any LASCO-affiliated company. He cautions Matt that speed is essential with regard to this decision.

TOM: . . . * . . . So, if you like basically that concept, we'd like to get going because LASCO Systems is waiting. They're trying to match [with us] their literature that's going to be printed, that's at the printers right now. So, if we can go with at least that "LASCO" [bold letters inside a rectangular block of contrasting color, to which the words Systems or Terminals can be attached], we can do the rest of it for the tie-in. . . . So, what do you think?

MATT: Well, uh, our problem is [we] always establish the new subsidiary, because of limitation of time, establish without thinking [about things like logos]. *But some kind of identity of group is needed. . . . That is true. . . . But if so, LASCO itself should change logo.*

TOM: *That's right. . . . Why don't you do that [at] this time?*

MATT: *Yeah, in that case, it takes a lot of time. We cannot, uh, decide this in a couple days. That is the problem.*

JERRY: Well, then how about if Terminals and Systems goes with that [proposed] "LASCO" block and then you can do what you want, and when you do, we'll change over, right?

MATT: It's very costly, no? Changing the logo?

JERRY: Well, we have to do something anyway.

MATT: . . . * . . . It's a big decision. . . .

JERRY: Well, obviously it is. And obviously we have no time. . . . So, the next year and a half, we'll probably all use this [the proposed logo]. Until we can get together and [the trading company headquarters] finally says this [a different logo] is what you'll use, right? I mean, that's how I feel. It's gonna happen, right? *Because you're gonna have to go back to Japan and ask them to come back with a new worldwide logo. But that'll take a year, right?* So which do you prefer. . . .

(Long pause. Matt nods. Matt, Terry, and another Japanese talk among themselves in Japanese.)

MATT: (To Jerry) So, you have to talk with everybody concerned.

JERRY: (At blackboard, gesturing and pacing) For what? . . . It's easy. We just checked almost everybody concerned. Sam says he likes that [logo]. Tom and I say we like that. So now it's up to you. You make the decision anyway. Doesn't matter what we say.

MATT: . . . * . . . *So, let's think it over a couple of days. . . . I have to talk to our marketing people and, uh, everybody concerned.*

JERRY: Okay, this *is* our marketing people. (Laughter)

MATT: No, LASCO.

JERRY: Well, this is LASCO Terminals.

MATT: Yeah, but, uh, in the future, we have to have a group image, one logo.

JERRY: Well, how 'bout if we bring the, uh, printer people in [right now], to see what they think of that [proposed logo], right? They'd like to see that.

MATT: Can you, uh, leave it, uh, couple of days?

TOM: Sure.

Negotiating the Management Services Agreement

The actors negotiate the management services agreement over all four of the formal sessions. This item encompasses an especially large number of cultural themes that have to do with concepts of work. Tom and Jerry express keen awareness of the autonomy they give up by becoming part of the LASCO Terminals organization; they are intent on preserving as much personal autonomy as possible under the new arrangement. Their preoccupation with the terms of the agreement, again, resonates with both their monetary concerns and their desire to manage risk. Japanese dialogue, more subtly, reflects notions about desirable personal qualities for a manager. In addition, trust resurfaces as a relevant theme. Once again, the Japanese negotiate with the understanding that LASCO operates within the web of the larger trading company.

Debate first centers on conditions under which the management services agreement can be canceled by LASCO Terminals.

MATT: . . . * . . . So, I. . . . uh, we have two problems or, I should say, two points we should discuss [about the management services agreement.] One is compensation, how much we should compensate. The other one, the number two point is: on what kind of occasion can we terminate this services agreement without any obligations within [i.e., before] three years. For example, if for some reason, we have to close LASCO Terminals, still have obligation to pay or not?

TERRY: I don't think so.

MATT: I don't know. We did not discuss in such a detail. . . .

JERRY: *Obviously, I think the draft we have is a "no cut deal" as they call it* [i.e., the contract cannot be canceled].

TOM: No . . . we didn't uh, we didn't address that in our deal.

Matt guides discussion toward possible reasons for ending the services agreement prematurely. He writes the following on the board:

Termination—automatic after three full years
Cancellation—without any obligation
  i. LASCO Terminals business stopped by any reason
  ii. Criminal [case against Tom or Jerry]
  iii. Disability [of Tom or Jerry]
  iv. Death [of Tom or Jerry]

MATT: (Still writing at blackboard) So in case of criminal cases, as I told you, we don't like to send large monthly checks to the jail. (General laughter)

JERRY: We told you we'd give you our P. O. box. (More laughter)

Attention focuses on point "i," the reasons LASCO Terminals might stop operating. Among the points mentioned are U.S. government intervention, or competition makes business unprofitable and the Tokyo headquarters shuts down the company. Jerry (forcefully) points out that if LASCO Terminals should cease operating, Tom and Jerry lose promised income from their commission on sales. They object to the risk.

JERRY: . . .* . . . The problem with doing any of this, and not making it, as I say, a no-cut deal on our account . . . *we tend to, uh, we tend to lose our ability to control item two* [on the agenda: the sales commission], *and item two is very important to us. So if we lose control of that, we've lost control of a lot of things.* . . .* . . . If you think you're going to shut the business down, that's not why we're here. . . .* . . . I don't wanna see number "i" happening. If there's a possibility of that, then we'd better start and renegotiate this whole deal.

TOM: You know we've gotta sit on, uh, we've gotta keep the services agreement going. 'Cause . . .

JERRY: Forget the services agreement. *Just look at what we're losing* [by giving up ROCA].

TOM: I know.

JERRY: We should invoke some rule, some penalty for that. That should be another item we should have: if for some reason [the Tokyo headquarters] can't maintain the company. . . . Cancellation clause, right? To us. To the benefit of the poor guys who gave up a running business. Does that make sense?

TERRY: To some extent.

JERRY: To some extent?

TERRY: To some extent.

JERRY: Say that a little bit louder. (Laughter) Mark the date, would you. (Laughter)

After the lawyers arrive, the negotiators return to the subject of cancellation. Jerry goes over earlier arguments, despite being told by everyone that it is unlikely LASCO Terminals would go out of business. His comments indicate his awareness that, in contrast to Tom and Jerry, the Japanese enjoy employment security within the trading company.

JERRY: . . . * . . . However, if they feel . . . that there might be some reason for canceling the agreement, then we're not dealing in good business practice. At least from our side, we're sitting here saying, "We're gonna be here for some time, other than death or disability," and they're saying, "Well, maybe the government looks like it's gonna shut this thing down. . . ." If that's the case, let's cancel all deals. I mean, everything falls apart then. Our management services contract falls apart, our 1½% for three years falls apart, and, uh, *theoretically, Tom and I are left holding the bag.*

MATT: Uh, we say, uh, the government—force majeure. Out of [our] control, although we desire to continue.

JERRY: Granted. . . . But, you all [the Japanese] go back. Either you sit here, or you all go back to Japan, *and you still have a position within the company. Where we sit [exposed], you know, for taking less money.* Well, you know we're selling certain rights now, based on this [deal] going on for a certain, you know, period. Where, theoretically, we might have been able to ensure some stability in our long-term lives, you know, financial stabilty. . . . And, if you're saying, based on any one of these [reasons], you can change your mind, then that. . . . You know, we have the most to lose, even though we're the smallest entity. *Personally, we have the most to lose.*

Barring an event on the scale of nuclear war, Matt verbally guarantees ROCA Consulting three years of monetary compensation, in the form of commissions and salary for management services. Nevertheless, he carefully explores the circumstances under which LASCO Terminals could substitute other persons for Tom or Jerry, or simply forgo any actual services by ROCA.

MATT: . . * . . . How about, uh, difference of opinion of the management?

ROGER: What flexibility do you want in that case?

MATT: Two flexibilities. One is we like to have the right to ask to this management (services) company to replace. . . .

JERRY: . . . * . . . Okay. To replace Tom and I. And what is the second one?

MATT: The second one is. . . . We don't terminate. We'll pay just three years, but, uh, I like to tell them [Tom and Jerry], no need to come over.

DARYL: ... * ... Well, members of the management team, under the managment contract, are subject to the direction of the board of directors ... They will do what you tell them to do.

ROGER: ... * ... So, you know, if you want a substitute, what you really do is, you say, "Jerry stay home," you pay Jerry, and then we go hire a substitute over here and just pay him ourselves. ... * ... The only time they have a duty to provide a substitute [at their own expense] is when there's a criminal [act] ... a death ... a disability.

DARYL: ... * ... With your reasonable discretion as to who.

MATT: So, as we said, as long as we are keeping the payments for the three years ...

ROGER: They have no right to do anything, if we tell them to do nothing.

MATT: Then, they cannot refuse.

ROGER: Correct.

In the third negotiating session, discussion gets down to the actual work role and work behavior of Tom and Jerry within LASCO Terminals. They are officially "consultants." Will they be bound by the policies and regulations that govern regular employees? Questions of vacation time, days off, work hours, overseas trips for ROCA Europe business, and so forth, arise.

ROGER: ... * ... Okay, shall we talk about this?

TERRY: I think so.

JERRY: Talk about what?

TERRY: Okay. Mostly, you guys are not employee, although you have to follow the, uh, company policies and regulations, ... right?

JERRY: Uh huh.

TERRY: For example, according to, uh, employee policy, vacations, uh, ... employees who worked for one year is entitled to take a vacation—10 days. The same rules apply.

JERRY: To us?

TERRY: Uh huh. Is that okay?

JERRY: No.

TERRY: ... * ... So where you have a problem? And, also, in case [of] employee ... if there is some person absent ... you know, [you can be absent] not more than 10 days [which would be covered by sick leave], okay? Then salary deducted automatically. [If you are] absent more than 10 days, then how the company will be compensated for that absence?

JERRY: It's a good point.

TERRY: We can deduct the pay ... the monthly payment, portion of it?

DARYL: Let me ask a question on concept. The concept of this agreement, which is what we discussed last time, is that, what in effect we're doing is, you [LASCO

Terminals] are contracting with a company. And that company, to perform under the terms of the agreement, must tender and provide the full-time productive efforts of Tom and Jerry, which is subject to your reasonable direction. And it provides that there must be a full-time, uh, rendering of services and all other productive effort during the terms of this agreement, unless you choose to say, "go away and stay home."

JERRY: Okay.

DARYL: . . . * . . . You know, I kind of would hope that the form of this agreement would provide that both of you are going to work together. If they start slacking off and taking trips around the world, then you have the abiltity to seek remedies under the agreement. Rather than saying, you know, "You took 11 days off this year, Jerry, and, therefore, we're going to dock you a day," or something like that. Roger, is that consistent with . . .

ROGER: I think what the problem is, very frankly, is not the concern that they will not devote their full-time best efforts. If there was any concern about that, there wouldn't be a deal.

JERRY: Right.

ROGER: *But the whole concept of their not being employees, which is what they have requested for their own tax reasons, is difficult for LASCO. And it's aggravated to the extent that they act less like employees even though they're not employees.* But to the extent that people in the company . . . say, "Well, we understand that Jerry and Tom do whatever they want. They don't want to come to work, they don't come to work."

JERRY: . . . * . . . Well, but that is a problem. Because, one thing . . . I mean, I can give you my own personal background. I get my children one month a year. In the summmer. Now that one month, if I want to take a week off, or two weeks off, or a month off, I will do it. Even though I keep working. He [Tom] does the same thing.

ROGER: Well, I don't think its just. . . . *No, I don't think we're trying to put the rules the same. . . .*

JERRY: . . . * . . . And, two, uh, Tom and I still have a responsibility in Europe, which we're going to have to go over there once in a while.

ROGER: I don't think that's a problem.

JERRY: Well, sure it is! Because unless it's deemed on this side to say that it is an official act, then you're taking time off to go across and do something else that there is some responsibility [to do]. . . . So there's going to be a certain amount of time there. That's one reason to have a management agreement.

TERRY: So your business in Europe is not relating to the LASCO Terminals?

JERRY: Why? . . . Well, it isn't and it is. Because sales of the product all over the world impact sales domestically. . . . [Strictly speaking], LASCO Terminals does not have any responsibility in Europe. Nor does ROCA Consulting. But Jerry and Tom have. So there will be times to be over there. Based on that, you gonna call it vacations? Time off? . . . * . . . So immediately, we can have a problem there. . . . Yet, we're still working. *We're not off playing all the time. We play very little. But to be regimented, versus, say, 10 days here. . . . Who is the one to say these 10 days are vacation and not work?*

TERRY: So . . . You have your own business as owner of ROCA Europe. You have to go to Europe. Who pays your travel expense?

JERRY: We have to . . .

TOM: It's our intent, certainly, to, uh, observe the . . . the, uh, rules and regulations of the company. Definitely. I mean, that's just. . . . Seriously, there's bound to be some exceptions. . . .

JERRY: In a large company, there is no exception. That's why we're on a management contract.

TOM: But . . . uh, certainly, the employee guidelines. . . . We assume the guidelines are for ourselves. . . . * . . . We have to act as employees or, otherwise, we have no respect from our [subordinate] employees. But I think that, uh, wording to the effect that, uh, we will observe the policies of the company. . . . Realizing, there's going to be a few basic exceptions which are reasonable. You know, . . . one of the toughest things is . . . is . . . as Matt pointed out several months ago, is that, you know, taking us from your [video terminals] group [as sales reps], and putting us into this . . . this . . .

JERRY: Structured . . .

TOM: Structure. *And, you know, it's a little tough squeezing back into that, that structure.* . . . * . . . So, it's a flexibility kind of thing, I guess.

As the preceding segment of text indicates, the Japanese notion of appropriate qualities and behavior for a manager conflicts with the Americans' notion of autonomous action. Additionally, trust is an issue. Matt and Terry do not trust Tom and Jerry to behave, in their view, properly. Can the Japanese, generally, place their trust in someone who does not conform? Authority relations with respect to Tom and Jerry and their Japanese bosses become a negotiated issue in the continuing exchange. We see possible divergence in the meaning attached to the words "working with" one's superior.

TERRY: . . . * . . . So the point is, uh, you guys are reporting to, uh, under [the new] organization, Sam [a Japanese], right? . . . * . . . So Sam is asked, you know, by Jerry. . . . Jerry takes one month off for some, you know reason. *In that case, Sam is asking, "How I have to deal with this, unless there is some rule?"* He can't say "yes" or "no." He does when he has such a rule.

JERRY: *Sam is asking?*

TERRY: *Uh huh.*

JERRY: *So this is a question from Sam, not . . .*

TERRY: *No, I have the same question too.* And even though you both taking off for one month, still we have to pay monthly [salary] charges. Is that right?

JERRY. Theoretically, yeah.

ROGER: . . . * . . . I think what Sam is concerned about—and he's not saying he has a concern because it's gonna happen and he's sure it's gonna happen. . . . *It's just [Sam wants] the understanding that there's a spirit of cooperation in that regard.* And, I don't think the agreement allows Jerry . . . to say to Sam, "I'm leaving. That's it. I'll see you next month. . . ." I don't think they could do that under the agreement, and Jerry's not going to do that, nor is Tom. It's the concept, I think, that Sam is concerned about. . . . Maybe the [observing] policies and regulations statement is enough.

JERRY: Yeah, but now that you bring it up, we will not . . . uh, or *I won't go under that policy if it's just, uh, if everything is so strict.*

ROGER: No, I think, uh, maybe we ought to say that, uh, they'll [Tom and Jerry] make every reasonable effort to comply with the policies and regulations, including matters relating to vacations, time off, and the like. And, to the extent that there's any dispute, the parties will attempt to work it out in good faith.

JERRY: . . . * . . . *We most certainly don't want someone telling us, though.* And if the purpose for Sam is to say . . . "I, Sam, can tell him, Jerry," then that's something else. *We plan to work with Sam, not for Sam, right?* Is that the spirit of the cooperation understanding?

ROGER: Well, I think the answer is they probably mean with, as opposed to for in the strictest sense.

(Roger, nevertheless, uses a personal anecdote to remind Jerry and Tom that "the whole is more important than you individually.")

ROGER: . . . * . . . And I think that's what they're saying. Sam would . . . it would be expected that you would just do what I did, sort of fight the best you can, then gracefully bow out and say, "Okay, Sam . . ."

TERRY: *My . . . my understanding, you know, the definition of with and for, okay. If they are employee, employee should work **with** his superior and **for** his superior. . . .*

The Signing

In early April, two weeks after the fourth session, negotiators from LASCO and ROCA meet to discuss several pending issues and to sign the buyout and management services agreements. The verbal banter threading through the text suggests Tom's and Jerry's trepidation, along with their sense of loss, in spite of their eagerness to embark on a new business venture.

JERRY: . . . * . . . You know, I'm signing more papers here than I did when I got unmarried. I thought that was the end of the world, but . . .

ROGER: Yeah, but that cost you money. This is making you money.

JERRY: *I don't know! I don't know what this is costing me to do this. . . .*

ROGER: . . . * . . . Tom, you want to leave us the keys [to the ROCA offices, so furniture can be moved]?

HARRY: On the way out, would you leave your keys? Your shirt and tie off, now, please.

After all the signing and initialing of pages is done, Matt and Terry smile at each other as they sit at the conference table, tired but relaxed. Matt remarks about Terry, "Ureshisoo wa ne," which can be translated, "He looks happy, doesn't he?"

Cultural Influences and Negotiated Outcomes

The text created as the actors negotiated agreement clearly reflects the cross-national, cross-cultural context. Separate sets of cultural assumptions unconsciously "motivate" the American and Japanese players.

Preliminary analysis of the text, for instance, indicates that a fair amount of individual communicative behavior is consonant with descriptions of American and Japanese negotiating "styles" found in the literature (e.g., Graham & Sano, 1984). Jerry, for example, comes near being the stereotypical John Wayne of American negotiating, characterized by a "shoot first, ask questions later" mentality. His discourse strategy and verbal tactics rest on direct confrontation and pressure for clear-cut answers. In contrast, as anticipated for the Japanese, Terry demonstrates greater concern for social harmony in the way he puts words together to persuade. Furthermore, the predicted Japanese emphasis on building relationships of trust is seen in the way ROCA-ESCO negotiations are handled. ESCO's president must get to know the ROCA principles before agreement can be reached. Another fundamental principle of Japanese societal culture infuses this segment of negotiation: the importance of enacting the vertically graded social order. Through his discourse and actions, Matt properly recognizes the status of the ESCO president.

Nonetheless, rigorous analysis of what is broadly termed negotiation style most likely would confound expectations based solely on the accepted wisdom. Personality and personal history mediate cultural rules guiding the conduct of negotiation. Matt, for example, had negotiated with Americans countless times and prided himself on being able to engage in "American style" negotiation. And, as noted earlier, Matt's personality evidenced an impatience and directness falling outside the Japanese cultural norm.

The long-standing working relationship between LASCO and ROCA also affected the communicative behavior of key Japanese and American negotiators. The principals now understood and had learned to adjust to each other's personality, capabilities, and culturally informed proclivities. Tom, for example, ruminated on what he had learned about negotiating trust from the initial encounters with LASCO, which led to the establishment of ROCA.

> An agreement of this nature is an agreement of working together. So many U.S. negotiators just assume you're going to work together and they get the legal stuff out of the way without paying a lot of attention, you know, to how we'll work together. . . . The negotiation, we really could have gotten it done in a couple of days, but apparently it was a way for us to get to know each other—a way for them to understand us. To get the trust built up.

Past experience thus conditioned the ROCA contingent to accept Matt's strategy for dealing with ESCO and the elongated time frame it imposed on negotiations. Similarly, knowledge of Jerry's personality conditioned the LASCO contingent to not take seriously his intimations that someone from a trading company subunit might fiddle product delivery schedules. The fund of mutual trust already accumulated allowed Jerry to play his role to the extreme.

This study particularly illustrates the impact of culturally specific concepts of work, as distinct from cultural rules for negotiating, for the negotiation process (see chapter 6). Concepts of work shape the text through a complex process. Players not only act according to their cultural motivation, they *react* as well.

For instance, one motivation for Matt's intentionally tough stance toward Tom and Jerry was "because of the difference of their characteristics." That is, their personal qualities differed from what the Japanese expect in an executive. Matt explained to me why, under the management services agreement, Tom and Jerry would hold the titles vice president of marketing and vice president of sales instead of being named executive vice president or general manager of LASCO Terminals. (The latter set of titles would make Tom and Jerry "officers" or key decision makers in the new subsidiary.) He said, "They could not pass my qualification." Their lack of qualification revolved around three areas: they put self-interest above the interests of the company; they were too concerned about money; and they did not think deeply enough before taking action. In Matt's culturally informed opinion, they were salesmen, not managers:

> He is [they are] selfish individual. Normally salesman is so. They don't like to be bound by the manager or the organization. . . . He is so much concerned about money for his pocket. This is also salesman type. For a young salesman, yes, understandable [but not for an older one]. . . . For business planning or product planning, three years relation with them. I could not satisfy [i.e., be satisfied with] their way of approach. No evidence. I just felt no deep studies.

To most U.S. business persons, Tom and Jerry's concern with the financial terms of the buyout (and the Americans' money-related joking) undoubtedly seems appropriate to the situation. Their desire to keep risk at a manageable level and their emphasis on autonomy of action also are familiar American cultural themes with regard to work (Kleinberg, 1989).

Tom and Jerry's contribution to the negotiation text, however, is understood in the context of their personal history as entrepreneurs in addition to their broadly American work culture. They were "giving up" a successful business; they felt the buyout terms should reflect ROCA's value. As Tom explained to me some months after LASCO Terminals had begun operating: "Because we were really the first and most successful worldwide sales agent in the country, we had a lot of opportunities in the final stages. That's why the negotiation was so centered on money—because we had to balance that money against what we could get on the outside."

But, just as important, the subtext was about giving up intangibles such as their entrepreneurial freedom, perhaps even their reputation in the industry. Contending that the business was being mismanaged under LASCO Terminals, Tom remarked:

My name is involved. . . . I started the thing [ROCA]. It was my deal. I brought Jerry and Hank [another original ROCA shareholder] in. I feel responsible for where it's gone and how it's gone. *I don't like being in the position of being in a secondary position.*

ROCA negotiators did not realize that each time they expressed these work-related themes through their utterances they merely reinforced existing cultural assumptions held by the Japanese. Japanese negotiators, for instance, came away with renewed belief that the interests of the "group" should outweigh self-interests, a commonly shared Japanese assumption about work (Kleinberg, 1989). Furthermore, negotiation strengthened certain understandings included in the subgroup culture of LASCO's Japanese managers. These include the domain of cultural knowledge that Americans are a problem to manage, because of their concern for power and money and because of their tendency to think mainly of what is best for them individually (Kleinberg, 1994a, 1994b, forthcoming).

Discomfited by Tom and Jerry's self-involvement and independent thinking, the Japanese reinforced a prominent cultural theme in LASCO's Japanese subgroup culture: LASCO is inseparable from the trading company (Kleinberg, 1994, forthcoming). One domain of cultural knowledge encompassed the understanding that LASCO's business strategy is part of the strategy for the whole computer peripherals group, another the understanding of competition among various individuals and subunits for control of the group. Thus, Matt gave Tom and Jerry lessons in interunit relations. Decisions about important matters such as logos or the video terminals business in Europe could not be made without the involvement of various subunits; autonomous action, personal and organizational, was exercised within narrow constraints. The future of the computer peripherals group took precedence over the interests of any one organizational subunit, despite competition for influence within the group.

Even the Japanese notion of trust in the workplace assumed an organizational emphasis in the negotiation text. Matt and Terry felt that Tom and Jerry should believe that LASCO or the trading company would not cheat them and that any problems which arose could be worked out in good faith. The long-standing business relationship, after all, gave ROCA quasi membership in the computer peripherals group. The text indicates that to some degree the Americans did believe in Matt's good intentions; dialogue concerning ROCA's European subsidiary certainly shows this. Nonetheless, within their work culture, trust required contractual safeguards.

Interaction between LASCO and ROCA negotiators laid the groundwork for emergent organizational culture in the new subsidiary. LASCO Terminals' place as one entity in the larger business group was negotiated clearly. At the same time, so was the dominance of LASCO's Japanese managers over LASCO Terminals business affairs. Tom and Jerry, along with other Americans (and Japanese) employed by LASCO Terminals, unquestionably would share an understanding of Japanese hegemony, paralleling assumptions embraced in organizationwide and Japanese and American subgroup cultures in LASCO (Kleinberg, 1994, forthcoming).

In addition, cross-cultural interaction during formal negotiations stimulated Japanese distrust of Tom and Jerry's ability to conform to organizational work norms once LASCO Terminals began operating. Matt and Terry, in response, attempted to construct social controls over their behavior through the negotiation process; this simultaneously stimulated the desire of Tom and Jerry to negotiate the absence of stringent controls. An organizationwide culture characterized by knowledge of tension between "the Japanese" and Tom and Jerry in fact did evolve in LASCO Terminals, as evidenced by later data gathering. Not surprisingly, tension revolved around issues relating to autonomy: how much autonomy could Tom and Jerry exercise, both in personal action and in deciding business strategy.

Discussion

Analysis of the LASCO-ROCA negotiation data results in a view of negotiation as being imbedded in wider organizational processes. Formal negotiation is not a discrete activity. The unfolding case study illustrates this point. The drama articulates with the politics of the larger computer peripherals group of the Japanese trading company, with headquarters-subsidiary relations, and with internal LASCO policy making, all of which are intertwined. It is shaped, in addition, by the cultures of the various organizational entities and subunits as well as by negotiation and work cultures that transcend organizational boundaries. The text constructed by the LASCO and ROCA negotiators not only reflects their past relationships, but, in constructing the text, they have begun to negotiate their future work roles, relationships, and organizational cultures. They have set the stage for the next act of the drama, much of which will revolve around LASCO Terminals.

The perspective on negotiation offered here grew out of an inductive analytic process typical of ethnographic research. Although this analysis evolved independently of negotiation research produced by Weiss (1993, 1996), the resulting conceptual and analytic framework exhibits considerable overlap and complementarity with the inclusive "Relationships, Conditions, and Behaviors" perspective on international, interorganizational negotiation Weiss proposes. According to Weiss:

> Real international business negotiations, especially between organizations, appear multifaceted, intrinsically complicated, and dynamic. To the extent that [existing] frameworks of analysis . . . produce pictures made up of fragmented and frozen elements, the frameworks need to be used with caution. (1996: 231)

Three key interconnected facets constitute the RCB framework, which "encourages assimilation" among and "provides a coherent structure" for a broad body of negotiation research that proceeds from different paradigms with different foci (Weiss, 1993: 295). These facets are relationships, behavior, and conditions. The relationships of the negotiating parties are seen as the central focus of a negotiation, directly accounting for negotiation outcomes. Describing and explaining various aspects of these relationships entails consideration of the negotiation actors and their behaviors, and of conditions that influence behaviors and relationships. Nonetheless, any facet of the model, as well as the connections among facets, may be the subject for "descriptive, explanatory, and prescriptive questions about complex, international negotiation" (Weiss, 1993: 291).

The conceptual framework which evolved out of the present case study concentrates on *cultures*, one of the "conditions" in the RCB model. Weiss (1993) anticipates that, in addition to societal culture, the common focus of the comparative, micro-behavioral research paradigm, ethnic and organizational cultures, and even a "negotiator subculture" might affect international negotiation. My prior ethnographic research on Japanese-owned firms has surfaced the culture construct of a nation-specific work culture or cognitive work maps (Kleinberg 1989, forthcoming). By incorporating this construct into its analytic framework, the present analysis extends our conceptualization of cultural influences on cross-national negotiation beyond that proposed by Weiss. Moreover, anchored in wide-ranging, intensive organizational ethnography, including observation of actual negotiations (and study of negotiation transcripts), the LASCO-ROCA analysis begins to comprehend the actual process by which various cultural foci affect negotiation. Empirical evidence illustrates how cultural assumptions unconsciously influence negotiators' communicative behavior, as well as their reactions to the cultural "other."

Finally, the LASCO-ROCA analysis helps fill another gap in international negotiation research. Weiss (1993: 277) notes that negotiation outcomes can have multiple attributes, some of which are neither explicit nor tangible and are, therefore, obscured by existing analytic frameworks. The present research findings add to a gradually accumulating body of data and analysis, based on ethnographic research, which gives insight into how cultures adapt and change (Weiss, 1993: 289) and how cultures are newly created through cross-national, cross-cultural interaction. It is precisely the phenomenon of negotiated culture that certain scholars studying Japanese and American or Japanese and German interaction within organizational settings currently seek to describe and explain (Brannen, 1992; Brannen & Salk, 1995, chapter 3; Kleinberg, forthcoming; Sumihara, 1992).

With regard to the Japan-U.S. interface, the broader perspective on negotiation and culture helps transcend the cultural stereotypes of Japanese and Americans that have gained a foothold in both scholarly and practitioner-oriented writing. The cultural influence is not monolithic, nor is it static. Nation-specific work and negotiation cultures do inform individual action, as do organizational cultures. But all of these cultural foci are mediated by personal experience and particular relationships among individuals and organizations. We need to be aware of those systems of meaning, those understandings that Japanese and Americans create together through their interaction.

References

Adler, N. J. 1991. *International Dimensions of Organizational Behavior*. 2nd ed. Boston: PWS-Kent.

Adler, N. J., Brahm, R. & Graham, J. L. 1992. "Strategy Implementation: A Comparison of Face-to-Face Negotiations in the People's Republic of China and the United States." *Strategic Management Journal*. 13: 449–466.

Adler, N. J., & Graham, J. L. 1989. "Cross-Cultural Interaction: The International Comparison Fallacy?" *Journal of International Business Studies*. Fall: 515–537.

Anderson, J. W. 1991. "A Comparison of Arab and American Conceptions of 'Effective' Persuasion." In Samovar, L. A., & Porter, R. E. (eds.), *Intercultural Communication: A reader*. 6th ed. Belmont, CA: Wadsworth. 96–106.

Black, J. S., & Mendenhall, M. 1993. "Resolving Conflicts with the Japanese: Mission Impossible?" *Sloan Management Review*. Spring: 49–59.

Boyacigiller, N., Kleinberg, J., Sackmann, S., & Phillips, M. 1996. "Conceptualizing Culture." In Punnett, B. J., & Shenkar, O., eds. *Handbook for International Management Research*. New York: Blackwell. 157–204.

Brannen, M. Y. 1992. *Your Next Boss is Japanese: Negotiating Cultural Change at a Western Massachusetts Paper Plant*. Doctoral dissertation, University of Massachusetts, Amherst.

Brannen, M. Y., & Salk, J. 1995. *A Model of Cultural Negotiation Between Japanese and Germans: A Joint Venture Case Study*. Unpublished manuscript presented at the Association for Japanese Business Studies Meeting, Ann Arbor, MI, June.

Casse, P. 1982. *Training for the Multicultural Manager: A Practical and Cross-Cultural Approach to the Management of People*. Washington, DC: SIETAR International.

Fisher, G. 1980. *International Negotiation: A Cross-Cultural Perspective*. Yarmouth, ME: Intercultural Press.

Friday, R. A. 1991. "Contrasts in Discussion Behaviors of German and American Managers." In Samovar, L. A., & Porter, R. E. (eds.), *Intercultural Communication: A Reader*. 6th ed. Belmont, CA: Wadsworth. 174–185.

Glenn, E. S., Witmeyer, D., & Stevenson, K. A. 1984. "Cultural Styles of Persuasion." *International Journal of Intercultural Relations*. 1, 3: 52–66.

Graham, J. L. 1985. "The Influence of Culture on the Process of Business Negotiations: An Exploratory Study." *Journal of International Business Studies*. Spring: 79–94.

Graham, J. L., & Sano, Y. 1984. *Smart Bargaining: Doing Business with the Japanese*. Cambridge, MA: Ballinger.

Kleinberg, J. 1989. "Cultural Clash Between Managers: America's Japanese Firms." In Prasad, B. S. (ed.), *Advances in International Comparative Management*. Vol. 4. Greenwich, CT: JAI Press. 221–243.

Kleinberg, J. 1994a. "Practical Implications of Organizational Culture Where Americans and Japanese Work Together." *NAPA Bulletin*. Vol. 14. Jordan, A. T. (ed.), *Practicing Anthropology in Corporate America: Consulting on Organizational Culture*. National Association for the Practice of Anthropology, American Anthropological Association. Washington, DC.

Kleinberg, J. 1994b. "'The Crazy Group': Emergent Culture in a Japanese-American Binational Work Group." In Bird, A., & Beechler, S. (eds.), *Research in International Business and International Relations*. Vol. 6. Greenwich, CT: JAI Press, 1994. 1–45.

Kleinberg, J. (forthcoming). "Making Sense of a Binational Organization: A Cultural Analysis of Japanese and Americans Working Together." *Academy of Management Journal*.

Lebra, T. S. 1976. *Japanese Patterns of Behavior*. Honolulu: University Press of Hawaii.

March, R. M. 1988. *The Japanese Negotiator: Subtlety and Strategy Beyond Western Logic*. Tokyo: Kodansha International.

Shenkar, O., & Ronen, S. 1987. "The Cultural Context of Negotiations: The Implications of Chinese Interpersonal Norms." *Journal of Applied Behavioral Science*. 23 (2): 263–275.

Spradley, J. P. 1979. *The Ethnographic Interview*. New York: Holt, Rinehart & Winston.

Spradley, J. P. 1980. *Participant Observation*. New York: Holt, Rinehart & Winston.

Stewart, E. C., & Bennett, M. J. 1991. *American Cultural Patterns: A Cross-Cultural Perspective* (rev. ed.) Yarmouth, ME: Intercultural Press.

Sumihara, N. 1992. *A Case Study of Structuration in a Bicultural Work Organization: A Study of a Japanese-Owned and Managed Corporation in the U.S.A.* Ann Arbor, MI: UMI Dissertation Services.

Tung, R. L. 1984. *Business Negotiations with the Japanese.* Lexington, MA: Lexington Books.

Van Zandt, H. E. 1970. "How to Negotiate with the Japanese." *Harvard Business Review.* November-December. 135–142.

Weiss, S. E. 1993. "Analysis of Complex Negotiations in International Business: The RBC Perspective." *Organization Science.* 4: 269–300.

Weiss, S. E. 1996. "International Negotiations: Bricks, Mortar, and Prospects." In Punnett, B. J., & Shenkar, O. (eds.), *Handbook for International Management Research.* New York: Blackwell Publishers. 209–265.

Young, L. W. L. 1982. "Inscrutability Revisited." In Gumperz, J. J. (ed.), *Language and Social Identity.* Cambridge, England: Cambridge University Press. 72–84.

Yum, J. O. 1991. "The Impact of Confucianism on Interpersonal Relationships and Communication Patterns in East Asia." In Samovar, L. A., & Porter, R. E. (eds.), *Intercultural Communication: A Reader.* 6th ed. Belmont, CA: Wadsworth. 66–78.

5

NORIYA SUMIHARA

Roles of Knowledge
and "Cross-Knowledge"
in Creating a Third Culture

*An Example of Performance Appraisal
in a Japanese Corporation in New York*

Introduction

This chapter focuses on how performance appraisals were handled at a Japanese company in the United States. It is based on ethnographic data involving intensive participant observation and interviews as part of a larger study of the New York headquarters of a sales subsidiary of a large-scale Japanese corporation (called TSDAL, a pseudonym that will be used hereafter) for 14 months from spring 1988 to summer 1989. The data presented here are concerned with face-to-face, cross-cultural negotiations about the performance appraisal of Japanese and American nonsales workers of this company. Thus, I am not dealing with generalized practices of performance appraisals at Japanese corporations in the United States, although I have drawn on what little literature exists concerning performance appraisal at other Japanese companies operating in the United States.

In 1989, I also paid three-day to one-week visits to the branches at Atlanta, Detroit, Chicago, and San Francisco. At all the branches in the United States at the end of the 1980s, the company was composed of a little over 700 regular employees, among whom 20% were Japanese expatriates. There were 38 Japanese and 80 Americans in the New York headquarters. At the New York headquarters, I assumed unpaid work, such as making an address database, doing translation, and making and distributing recreation announcements. Besides observation and informal conversation, I interviewed people at all levels in the office hierarchy, from vice presidents, junior and senior managers, and regular workers to the lowest-ranking secretaries, with the exception of the Japanese president, who refused to be interviewed even though he knew why I was there. After 1989, I returned to the company for one to three days each year from 1990 to early 1994, when I met with my informants to follow up on what changes, if any, had occurred.

In addition, in early 1995, I conducted half-hour to one-hour interviews (including telephone interviews) with five Japanese middle-level managers in other companies in Tokyo and Nagoya, Japan, in search of current patterns of performance appraisal. The companies were a large trading company, a large-scale Japanese bank, a large department store, and an energy corporation that is half government and half privately run. I chose them because they were all large-scale companies like the one I studied.

Theoretical Background

I had been dissatisfied with previous studies of Japanese corporations operating in the United States, because, until 1990, very few of them treated the dynamics of the face-to-face contact between American and Japanese workers, with the exception of Kleinberg (1989), who studied a Japanese trading company in Los Angeles based on a year's intensive field work, and Kidahashi (1987), who studied a Japanese security house operating in New York City for nine months. However, Kidahashi concluded that the Japanese security house was a "dual organization," where Japanese and American workers and their cultures conflict with each other, without either side yielding to the other. Brannen (1994) conducted a five-year ethonographic study of a Japanese paper company in the United States, focusing on interaction between Japanese and American workers. She critically noted a "two-billiard-ball model," by which she meant that a list of American versus Japanese cultural traits does not help explain the dynamics of cross-cultural interaction.

My fieldwork research enabled me to observe that face-to-face, cross-cultural contact did not necessarily end with conflict, although it did occur to some extent, nor did one side simply overwhelm and sweep away the other. The contact produced what can be called "a third culture," in which practices do not assume either a genuinely Japanese or American form. I found many such compromised practices in a variety of aspects of organizational institutions and individual worker's behavior, including the decision-making process (see Sumihara, 1993), the compensation system (see Sumihara, 1994), employment practices, and office space arrangements, among others (see, also, Sumihara, 1992).

The notion of a third culture was originally presented by Malinowski (1949), although he used "a cultural tertium quid" in his study of cross-cultural contact between Europeans and Africans in a colonial setting. Anthony King (1976) also drew on the idea to depict the British and Indian colonial relationship. Although I borrowed the term, I do not agree with Malinowski on the following two points:

1. Malinowski's unit of analysis was the institution, because conflict and interaction, he thought, took place on an institutional level. Malinowski assumed that in a "cultural tertium quid," "equilibrium" is reached through a "common measure" or a "common factor" on the level of the institution. Yet, little attention was paid to cross-cultural face-to-face interaction on the individual level.
2. He seems to view Europeans and Africans as two polarities having little knowledge about each other.

First, I cannot accept a static view of the notion of a third culture. In a cross-cultural encounter, at a glance both parties seem to find a "common factor," and thereby an equilibrium has been reached on an institutional level. Because Malinowski's analysis is confined to the institutional level, his view overlooks the dynamics of cross-cultural interaction on the level of day-to-day individual practice within the framework of the institution. Especially, as in my case, when Americans and Japanese workers who have significantly different sets of knowledge work together within the same workplace, the social effects of cross-cultural interaction on an individual level cannnot be disregarded.

By viewing Europeans and Africans as opposite cultural polarities who have no knowledge of each other's culture, Malinowski overlooks Europeans' knowledge about Africans and Africans' knowledge about Europeans. In the Japanese company I studied, Japanese and Americans shared each other's cultural knowledge to some extent while working together, and both acted taking into account the other's knowledge and sentiment, although this knowledge was limited. I think that this "cross-knowledge," as I call it, plays a significant role in shaping a third culture in practice.

As another facet of the notion of a third culture, Hayashi (1994: 216) says that a third culture refers to a culture born through cross-cultural contact and represents both cultures. According to his functional view, the third culture functions to bridge the two cultures (217–19). Thus, he limits the notion, suggesting that a third culture should contribute to bridging cultural gaps. My notion of a third culture is not based on a functional view and goes beyond his limits, encompassing both the intended and unintended consequences of face-to-face, cross-cultural interaction.

Because I aimed to follow the process by which the patterns of performance appraisal are produced and reproduced through cross-cultural social interaction between American and Japanese workers, Anthony Giddens's "structuration theory" was useful for my study.

According to Giddens (1979), individual social action that constitutes society cannot be explained only by the individual's intention or motivation, or simply by social and cultural factors. Giddens intends to deconstruct the binary oppositions such as individual/society, action/structure, and part/whole. To unite the oppositions, he never draws upon a functional or a structuralist view. Rather, he proposes a new approach, called structuration. According to Giddens's view, "[E]very social actor knows a great deal about the conditions of reproduction of the society of which he or she is a member" (1979: 5). However, this does not mean that the actor is always aware of this knowledge. Giddens says that there are two kinds of knowledge about a social system: "discursive knowledge," or knowledge actors are able to express on the level of discourse, and "practical knowledge," a tacit stock of knowledge that actors can draw on in social action, but which they cannot necessarily express on the level of discourse. Thus, the practical knowledge is not "unconscious," although Giddens does not rule out consideration of the unconscious in the production and reproduction of a social system through action. Not only Giddens, but many other theorists—including Geertz (1973) with his famous notion of "models of and for" a psychological reality, which teaches us a mechanism by which we of any culture learn to take for granted what we know, Bourdieu (1977: 164) and his notion of "doxa," Shein (1986: 6), and Adler (1991: 75)—pay attention to the importance of the taken-for-granted aspects of social action.

Individual action can be a source of social production and reproduction because drawing upon the two kinds of knowledge, individuals act *recursively* in a certain direction in time and space. In my study, Japanese and American workers have both discursive and practical knowledge about performance appraisal. Their stocks of knowledge are different, but they also share common knowledge to some extent. In action both of them try, consciously and subconsciously, to give form to their respective knowledge about performance appraisal. The actions are recursive, or self-reproduced, based on that knowledge. However, I believe that the knowledge is not static but is subject to change through experience and learning.

Along with the recursive nature of action, Giddens also claims, drawing on Wittgenstein's language game, that rules not only restrict action, but also enable it. When following the rules, one is free to act more than one way within their framework, but the action becomes meaningful only as social action because of the rules. This view suggests that, regardless of the formal, institutionalized performance appraisal system that TSDAL employed, in each appraisal situation there was more than one way to follow the rules of the system. It is too simplistic to think that the formal system definitively prescribes the action of individuals.

Japanese and American employees of the company I studied have significantly different views about performance appraisal; nonetheless, in each case they have to settle through negotiation at a certain point in the appraisal. In the cross-cultural negotiations in my study, Japanese and Americans influence or persuade each other through a variety of actions, including explaining one's own culture to the other, explaining how the other's action is interpreted in one's culture, and what the outcome of the other's action could be in one's social context. In general, negotiation is a communication whereby negotiators try to accomplish their aims. Through negotiation, both Americans and Japanese learn something of each other's knowledge. Consequently, they negotiate drawing on not only their own cultural knowledge, but the other's knowledge as well, which, as I show later, sometimes complicates the process by which a third culture is produced.

In relating to the previous discussion, I look at three interrelated areas of cross-cultural interaction I observed at the company:

1. Japanese stocks of knowledge and Americans' stocks of knowledge about performance appraisal;
2. "Cross-knowledge," that is, Japanese understanding of Americans' knowledge about appraisal and Americans' understanding of Japanese knowledge about appraisal; and
3. What the outcome of the cross-cultural negotiation is based on their respective stocks of knowledge.

Case Study

It is difficult to present a "typical" performance appraisal system and practice in Japan or in America because there are diverse types in both countries. Therefore, I prefer to focus on my own case study by showing what my informants in TSDAL said they thought Japanese or American performance appraisals were. My primary interest is learning what is brought about by Japanese-Americans' face-to-face, cross-cultural interaction in the workplace, rather than identifying typical Japanese or American performance appraisals.

There is very little literature on the performance appraisal practices conducted in Japanese corporations in the United States. Besides, among the few studies, both Abe et al. (1992: 117) and Tsuda (1993: 250) claim that performance appraisals of Japanese corporations in America have been largely "Americanized." This view parallels my interview research in Japan in early 1995. Two middle-level managers whose companies (a trading company and a bank) had overseas offices in America said in telephone interviews that they had heard in their companies that performance appraisals in their respective American offices have been Americanized, even though neither had experience in the American offices. My own experience indicates that it is misleading to determine that appraisals have been Americanized just because an "American" appraisal system has been employed in the Japanese corporation in America. If we look closely at the practices of each appraisal conducted by a Japanese appraiser, it proves to be hard to say that appraisals have been Americanized. By "Americanized," I mean that American employees perceive the system and the practices of the performance appraisal as American. As I have suggested before, the formal system is one thing, actual practices within that framework of the system are another, because there is more than one way to follow the rules of the system.

The Company's Formal System of Performance Appraisal

The formal appraisal procedure of TSDAL as I found it in 1988 was as follows. The immediate supervisor first fills in the official sheet of the performance evaluation for each of his subordinates. There are two kinds of forms; one is for nonexempt employees, low-ranked employees who are paid by the hour, and the other is for exempt employees, who are paid a salary. Then the supervisor sits with each subordinate and discusses the subordinate's performance based on the evaluation. This face-to-face meeting is held once a year for exempt employees and every six months for nonexempt. In the evaluation each element of the subordinate's performance and ability is rated by the supervisor from level 1 (poor) to level 5 (excellent). The supervisor explains why he gave his rating for each element. If the subordinate is discontent with the rating, he or she discusses the point. If the subordinate agrees with the supervisor's evaluation, he or she signs the sheet. The subordinate also has the right to write an excuse for or explanation of mistakes or poor performance as an appeal to the general manager of the division. The subordinate may do so at the evaluation meeting, and this document is taken as formal. After the evaluation meeting, the supervisor gives the evaluation sheets and the extra documents, if any, for approval to the general manager of the division. The general manager signs all the sheets and documents, indicating approval. The signed sheets and documents are finally forwarded to the personnel division, where they are preserved as records. Based upon the evaluation sheets and documents, and also on the division's budget, the general manager determines the percentage of each employee's salary raise and merit increase or promotion. Some general managers of small divisions determine these issues by themselves, whereas other general managers discuss them with each department manager. For their evaluation, each general manager is reviewed by the president of the company.

This formal procedure sharply contrasts with that of the parent company in Tokyo. In brief, the performance appraisal in the parent company is characterized by (1) no face-to-face meeting or discussion between the reviewer and the reviewed; (2) a once-a-year evaluation discussion about each worker is held by several superiors sitting together who know the worker, and (3) the result of the review is not reported in any way to the person reviewed. Thus, in the parent company in Tokyo, a subordinate does not know precisely how he is evaluated for the year. However, in the long run, he realizes whether he is advancing up the career ladder relatively quickly or slowly in his age group, because, given that seniority has a significant influence, at a certain age, someone else in the group may be promoted to a higher status before him, or he himself may be the first to advance.

Interviews with the TSDAL Japanese expatriates indicated that the one-way (from reviewer to reviewed) evaluation system of the parent company was also supported by the Japanese reviewees themselves. These workers did not find it particularly necessary to meet and discuss their performance review with their supervisors, because they trusted that the system guaranteed an "objective" review when one person was evaluated by many people from a variety of perspectives. They called the system *taju-kyakkan-houshiki* in Japanese, multiplex-objective-system. According to the system, the immediate supervisor prepares the original evaluation of each of his subordinates based upon his observation. The evaluation is then forwarded to his own superior and the same level managers of the department or the division for collective discussion at the meeting. The evaluators have varying degrees of knowledge of each worker evaluated, because, through work, they have some contact with him. More interesting, however, is that there seems to be a formula in the mind of the TSDAL Japanese workers that an individual judgement is "subjective," so not reliable, whereas a collective one is "objective," so it is a "right" decision. As one young Japanese worker at TSDAL said:

> I can't trust the individual evaluation of my supervisor, because misunderstandings are likely. Especially if he criticizes some of my performance clearly, I may take it personally, of course, depending upon the way he says it, because no single person can judge *objectively* correctly, so I think his personal evaluation is not free from bias. I always try to do the best I can, but my view is also *subjective*. I know I am myself far from perfect. Even I myself as an individual can't judge whether what I thought was the best I did is truly best or not. So it is possible that even when I think that what I did was probably not right, someone else may think that what I did was right. So, it is also likely that what my supervisor criticizes me about may be positively evaluated by someone else. That's why I believe that collective evaluation is better. (emphasis mine)

This appraisal procedure of TSDAL's parent company in Tokyo may not be a typical example in Japan. According to the interviews I conducted in early 1995, only the half-government-run energy corporation followed this procedure, while at the trading company, the Japanese bank, and the department store, a reviewer and reviewee meet at a table once a year for appraisal. My data are too limited to determine whether TSDAL's parent company's example is atypical or typical in Japan. However, as I have said, to show a typical Japanese example is not a purpose of this chapter; rather, I am concerned with how knowledge and what I call crossknowledge may shape a third culture.

Even though TSDAL is 100% owned by the parent company in Tokyo, the performance appraisal system has been Americanized, as both the TSDAL Japanese and American employees see it. However, within the framework of the system, TSDAL American employees find that at some important points, their Japanese supervisors evaluate them in "Japanese" terms or in ways that American counterparts are unlikely to do. Below are examples of how TSDAL Japanese supervisors evaluate their American subordinates and how the subordinates and personnel managers respond and negotiate to "correct" Japanese ways to American.

How Japanese Supervisors Treat American Subordinates in Evaluation

Egalitarianism.   As American personnel managers of TSDAL see it, the Japanese managers of TSDAL tend to be very reluctant to make a big difference between a high-performing subordinate and a low performer in salary raises. For example, TSDAL American managers take for granted that a high performer gets a 6% raise, while a low performer gets 1% or even nothing, depending upon the performance; by contrast, Japanese managers differentiate a high from a low performer with 4.5% and 2.5% raises at most.

Along the same line, among Japanese managers, there is what an American manager calls "inflation of grade points." As figure 5.1 shows, American managers tend to give low points on the grade sheet for performance appraisal, so that three points is an average, and four and five points are truly good. Japanese managers and supervisors tend to give high points, four points on average, to all of their subordinates. Consequently, there are only small individual differences among the subordinates. None of them can feel an absolute winner or loser.

Close examination revealed that the Japanese "egalitarian" review was associated with the Japanese managers' assumption that the company and the workers

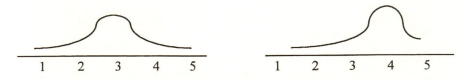

American Manager's Review   **Japanese Manager's Review**

FIGURE 5.1 American Versus Japanese Managers' Reviews

maintain long-term relationships. To indicate the importance of this point, one must take into account the Japanese principle of competition in the parent company in Tokyo. In the late 1980s when I conducted this research, most Japanese expatriates of TSDAL whom I contacted assumed that their relationship with the parent company had been and would be a long one. Even in 1994 when the parent company, like many other companies in Japan, was in the middle of restructuring due to severe recession, some Japanese expatriates whom I met in TSDAL believed that the workers' long-term relationship with the company was ideal, even though they no longer idealized lifetime employment.

Given the long-term relationship between workers and the company, in order to secure every member's job, cooperation among the members is very important. On the other hand, the Japanese management also wants to pick out able workers and place them in high-ranking posts. In order to solve the dilemma between cooperative work and competition for higher posts, the *nenko*, seniority, rule has played a significant role. With the *nenko* rule, there is no point in unnecessarily competing with people of a different age group. A senior person can, with security, guide and convey his skills and knowledge to his junior, because conveying skills across age differences retains hierarchical age relationships. However, *nenko* alone is not enough to create a cooperative work relationship, because the *nenko* rule wards off only unnecessary competition between different age groups. Able workers of the same age group have to be sorted out; at the same time, all workers have to be motivated to work together without dropouts. Egalitarian treatment of workers in terms of salary serves these contradictory purposes.

Because there is so little difference in terms of reward among same-age group members, even low performers have a second chance, "*haisha fukkatsu*," as a Japanese manager of TSDAL said in Japanese. High performers, even if not fully paid for achievements from a short-term perspective, can see that they have a higher possibility of getting promoted earlier than low performers when the age group reaches promotion age. In the parent company in Tokyo, besides a status title, such as *kacho*, manager, and *bucho*, general manager, each employee is endowed with *tokusho* or *shikaku* status associated with pay. Young workers of a same-age group tend to hold the same *shikaku*, because of the seniority rule. Given the *shikaku* system, each worker in the same age group is apt to be mindful of even a slight difference in salary among members of his group. A few hundred yen, a couple of dollars' difference may, by Japanese standards, make a good deal of difference in the long run, because a worker who receives the highest salary within the same *shikaku*-holder group is likely to get a higher *shikaku* first, when the age group reaches a *shikaku* eligibility age. The rest of the group has to wait for another six months or even a year to get the same *shikaku*.

A young Japanese worker at TSDAL said that in Japan, as a worker goes up from one *shikaku* status to another, he gets a significantly higher salary, by Japanese standards. Thus, egalitarianism is a relative term. If the system is seen as a whole, there is not much difference between high and low performers of the same age group, but each worker of the group feels that there is a significant difference. This may be a psychological trick. As Iwata says, "Japanese workers of the same age group in a company are placed in a race-like setting similar to that of professional baseball teams chasing a pennant. When many teams are close to one another, each game is more exciting to see and even a slight difference in runs feels like a great difference" (Iwata, 1985: 113). The trick may make great sense to the Japanese workers of a large-scale corporation, because they compete with one another over a long time span in the same company, but Americans who do not take for granted that the company is their long-term employer feel that it is not fair treatment.

In TSDAL, there is another immediate reason why the Japanese managers are reluctant to decide to give their low-performing subordinates no or little salary raise. The Japanese managers and supervisors are evaluated not only within TSDAL but also in the parent company in Tokyo. After all, all of them are supposed to return to Tokyo in a few years, so they are concerned about their evaluation in Tokyo. One of the most tangible, numerical elements by which they are evaluated is the turnover rate of the worker groups for which they are respectively responsible. In general, the lower the rate is, the better an evaluation in Tokyo. Therefore, the Japanese expatriates do not want to cause even low-performing subordinates to leave the company because of severe evaluation.

American TSDAL managers criticized their Japanese colleagues' appraisal practice: one of the American managers said that Japanese egalitarian treatment only helped low performers and dissatisfied high performers. A senior American personnel manager of a fast-growing sales division also critically said:

> I really spearheaded a project not to do that [to practice the principle of equality in salary raises]. . . . It should be the key contributors who receive the high merit increases, and other people should be left flat. I propose that people not receive any kind of merit increases at all, none, zero. It's our [personnel department's] responsibility to drive and push to discuss with Japanese managers not to propose those kinds of increases. American managers think of Japanese managers' egalitarian treatment as *unfair*. (emphasis mine)

Thus, American managers, especially those with personnel responsibilities, watch and advise Japanese managers, so that they differentiate high performers from low. An American personnel manager said that he made it a rule to advise newly arrived Japanese expatriates upon orientation about this matter. Despite the constant efforts of the American managers, however, Japanese reviewers are still reluctant to make a difference as big as a 6% salary raise for top performers and 0% for the lowest performer, as American managers and high performers would expect. For the Japanese reviewers who have had constant salary raises each year due to seniority, it is hard to imagine distributing 0% raises even to low performers, unless they are extremely lazy or have made serious mistakes. As a result of the constant negotiation between American and Japanese managers, the pay increase rate is settled somewhere between American and Japanese expectations, often 5% for top performers and 2% for the lowest performer.

Abstract elements in evaluation.   In Japanese performance appraisal practice, it is not just past performance, but abstract and subjective elements such as attitude toward work, cooperativeness, potential ability, and so on that are taken into consideration. According to my early 1995 interview research, all the companies, whether a trading company, a bank, a department store, or an energy firm, considered such abstract elements important in appraisal. Cooperativeness, *kyochosei* in Japanese, is an especially important element in the Japanese value system. Workers ready to undertake a job beyond office hours or a job that might have unexpectedly come into the department beyond anybody's responsibility are regarded as cooperative. Even in TSDAL, I observed that Japanese expatriates tended to evaluate American TSDAL workers based upon this value. As an extreme example, when I was on my way back from lunch along with two young Japanese managers, we saw a young, female American employee sitting in a very relaxed manner on the sofa of the entrance lobby of TSDAL listening to a Walkman with a headset. One of the Japanese managers said indignantly, "Look. I told her supervisor to advise her not to do that there even during lunch time." Then the other Japanese manager said, "She looks sloppy, but she actually is a cooperative person. When my department needed her help, she was quite helpful." Hearing that, the former manager, still looking angry, kept silent.

Attitude, *taido* in Japanese, is an abstract element by which to evaluate a worker, but the Japanese reviewers at TSDAL sometimes use the term even in appraisal meetings with their American subordinates, as American employees have observed in their own experience. A Japanese manager of TSDAL said that a worker's *taido* could be detected by "serious behavior" while working. Even though the American subordinates do not quite understand its meaning, insofar as their Japanese boss speaks highly of them on this point, they have no reason to complain.

Some American managers of TSDAL advise their Japanese colleagues not to take account of such abstract elements in appraisal. The American managers think that the efforts or good attitude will someday pay off in performance, so the worker should be rewarded only when his performance has been good. For the Japanese staff, in contrast, it is too simplistic and inconsiderate to evaluate a person based only upon his quantitative, tangible achievements, because, for one thing, not all kinds of work can be valued in numerical terms, and also even when one does not succeed, it may not be due to lack of effort, but more to circumstances such as an unpredictable business climate.

Because of the abstract nature of such elements of evaluation as attitude and cooperativeness, when the Japanese reviewer criticizes his subordinates in terms of those elements, Americans are straightforward and ask their boss to explain concretely. One young Japanese manager of TSDAL was discontent with his American subordinates' attitude toward work. He once told me that he was sometimes indignant because his American subordinates were often too relaxed or even humming when his department had a very important task to do. On the other hand, one of his American subordinates said that in American society, there was what he called "a culture of relaxation," by which he meant that even if one is serious, he pretends to take it easy. He also said that a too serious- or nervous-looking person would not be popular among friends. Thus, American TSDAL employees have to be mindful, if not seriously worried, that such cross-cultural misunderstandings may negatively affect the performance appraisal conducted by their Japanese boss.

As a consequence of cross-cultural interaction, one of the Japanese TSDAL managers confided to me that he made it a rule to take notes in his daily work life when he observed his American subordinates doing something he found wrong. He also said that he would not make notes for Japanese subordinates, because they usually did not challenge his criticism like Americans and also because the cross-cultural misunderstandings shown there are unlikely to happen between Japanese.

Deficiency of oral feedback.   One of the major complaints or disappointments of American TSDAL employees was that there was very little praise, or oral recognition from their Japanese supervisors. Not only nonmanagerial American workers, but senior American managers disappointedly complained that even when they had made remarkable achievements with hard, "uphill" efforts, their Japanese supervisors were usually calm: at best, they say, "You did well. I expected it of you."

This is not a matter of language, but a matter of the culture surrounding praise. Japanese also praise others, but in the eyes of the Japanese TSDAL staff, the way in which their American colleagues praise others looks overdone; for example, they say, "Terrific!" "Couldn't be any better!" "Genius!" The Japanese staff find it difficult to use such "big" words. By Japanese standards, those big expressions are saved for truly amazing occasions; otherwise, they are used for teasing, or for a sarcastic purpose, or they are delivered to children to please them. In a way, for Japanese supervisors not to praise or to praise in a conservative manner is to treat their American subordinates with respect as adults.

Some American TSDAL managers have learned what such oral praise means to the Japanese, but, even so, they are positive in making Japanese managers realize the importance of recognition in American culture. Even in informal talk, one senior American manager recursively stresses the point: for instance, referring to his school life, he explains how school teachers treated him in the class when he achieved remarkable results. As part of a recognition drive, the American manager also proposed an employee of the month program for nonmanagerial employees. A young American personnel manager also positively disseminated information about the importance of recognition to Japanese managers: he used examples of successful American companies like IBM to show how they improve workers' morale by way of spectacular recognition.

Because of the persistent efforts of American managers, Japanese managers came to realize the importance of what they said. I met many Japanese expatriates in TSDAL who said that they learned the importance of recognition in oral form in American society. However, even though they understood the importance, they were still reluctant to deliver oral recognition like Americans. One of them said that unless he was truly impressed, he was uncomfortable or had a sense of telling a lie if he praised his subordinates as Americans do.

On the other hand, some Japanese managers try to meet Americans' expectations in their own way, rather than by behaving like an American boss. For instance, a Japanese manager commented that he was impressed when he happened to witness his young, female subordinate neatly clean a booth after a public exhibition in California, a job that was not her responsibility. She said that he had said it in a conservative manner, but she was pleased.

However, Japanese managers cannot always respond properly to their American subordinates' expectations. The following are a few examples of misapplication of Japanese knowledge about Americans' expectations.

Example 1: In Japan, young workers of little experience are evaluated based on so-called *shitsumu-noryoku*, capability of handling routine work properly, training that is believed to be very important, and they are regarded as too young to worry about *kikaku-noryoku*, capability of planning. Therefore, when a Japanese manager evaluated his young American subordinate, because he thought he should praise American subordinates, he praised him by saying that he made relatively few mistakes in paper work, and so forth. However, the young American worker was not so happy, because he had expected that his Japanese boss would say something about the project he had planned. For the American subordinate, it was his planning ability that he thought would make him look capable.

Example 2: The grades that a boss puts in an evaluation form range from 1 (poor) to 5 (excellent). As shown before, Japanese managers tend to inflate the grade points to make their subordinates happy.

In an extreme case, a Japanese manager had continuously given good points to a low-performing American subordinate. When it turned out that he would not work harder to improve his performance, the Japanese manager wanted to fire him. This was also based on his understanding of American business culture in which a boss can easily fire his subordinate. His American colleague strongly advised him not to fire the American subordinate, because, in case the fired subordinate sued the company, the company would never win, because his grade record proved there was no reason to dismiss him.

These examples of misunderstanding show that having cultural knowledge is not good enough. It is not just knowledge of the rules of a game but knowledge of how to continue the game (how to apply the rules) that is more important. I will come back to this point in the concluding section.

Conclusion: Theoretical and Practical Implications

From my case study of a bicultural work organization, I want to clarify the theoretical implications for academic readers and offer practical suggestions for practitioners who have to deal with a bicultural workplace.

Summary and Theoretical Implications

First of all, although some researchers found a "dual organization" in Japanese corporations in the United States where the two cultures ended up in conflict with little room to yield, my study indicates that because common jobs have to get done, workers search for points of accommodation.

Second, it is not only on an institutional level that accommodation is reached; it is also on the level of individual practices within the framework of the institution. As we have seen, the formal procedure for performance appraisal in TSDAL had already been Americanized by 1988, as both Japanese and American employees of the company perceived it. However, on the level of each performance review practice, Japanese supervisors, basically following the formal procedure, tended to intentionally and unintentionally treat their American subordinates as though they were Japanese. For example, the pay increase rate tended to be egalitarian and the comments on performance tended to include abstract terms such as attitude and cooperation. It also seemed to American subordinates that the Japanese supervisors refrained from oral praise. Thus, TSDAL American employees tried to change Japanese practices with each individual performance review.

Here, I find that Malinowski's notion of a tertium quid has a limitation, because he assumed that the cross-cultural contact occurred only on the level of the institution. He, therefore, seemed to assume that by finding the common factors of two different institutions, cross-cultural conflict would be resolved. As my examples show, individuals have more than one way of following the rules that the institution prescribes. Especially in a face-to-face, cross-cultural setting, conflict and negotiation take place on the level of individual practices regardless of what kind of common factor has been found at the institutional level.

Third, through face-to-face, cross-cultural negotiation, new practices emerge. These constitute a third culture, which is neither genuinely Japanese nor genuinely American. As we have seen, more than once, a third culture emerged at the level of individual practices. Broadly speaking, a third culture emerged not only as an intended consequence but also as an unintended one. As examples of intended consequences, the pay increase rate was settled somewhere between Japanese and American expectations. In addition, Japanese supervisors started to make notes in daily work life when they found even small mistakes that their American subordinates made, because, unlike Japanese subordinates, the Americans would not easily accept criticism unless there was concrete proof.

A third culture as an unintended consequence is also very important in order to understand the face-to-face, bicultural process. As I have shown, both Japanese and Americans of TSDAL came to learn about each other through contact. They had a certain amount of cross-knowledge about each other. Based on this cross-knowledge, they communicated with each other, but sometimes, almost because of such cross-knowledge, miscommunication took place. For example, a Japanese supervisor praised his American subordinate, because he had learned that oral recognition was very important to Americans. However, the point for which he gave the praise was based on his own Japanese values. Such practices of misapplication of cross-knowledge constitute a third culture. Here, I think that Hayashi's (1994) analysis has a limitation, because he confined the notion of how a third culture emerges to a functionalistic view within a framework of its intended aspects. Thus, he disregards or overlooks the unintentional aspect of an emerging third culture. I will return to the importance of the misapplication of cross-knowledge in the following section.

Implications for Practitioners

First, all practitioners in bicultural settings should be aware that cross-cultural learning is a constant effort. One can never know enough about the other culture. Most people are curious about another culture when they meet it for the first time, but as time goes on, they feel that they have learned enough to conduct business and lose interest in learning further. However, as we have seen, it is always possible to apply cross-knowledge mistakenly. It is not just the amount of knowledge about another culture per se, but, more important, the knowledge as to how and when to apply it that counts. There is no instant solution to the problem of misapplying cross-knowledge, but constant effort is certainly one of the requisites. I suggest that practitioners exchange information and experiences as often as possible on concrete cases of miscommunication and misapplication of knowledge from both American and Japanese colleagues. Listening to the cases is not enough. Practitioners should also discuss them to analyze how and why such cross-knowledge was misapplied in each concrete case.

Second, all practitioners who handle cross-cultural processes should be aware that knowledge consists of both discursive and practical or tacit elements. We can know about another culture to some extent by listening to a person from that culture, but he or she cannot tell all he or she knows because much of cultural knowledge is tacit and too taken for granted to be expressed verbally. Although it is very important to discover the tacit knowledge of another culture, because it influences natives' behavior to a great degree, it is also more difficult to learn than discursive knowledge. Cultural anthropologists have sought to understand the natives' point of view through field work. They interview the natives and also observe their behavior and responses to social events. In other words, although some knowledge is tacit and not systematically expressed by the natives, it is symbolically expressed in behavior and in fragments of verbal expression. So practitioners, like field workers, should also be careful observers and interviewers, so that they can reach a deeper understanding of the other culture, that is, acquire tacit knowledge. While searching the tacit dimension of the other culture, practitioners should also become aware of their own tacit knowledge. They are in this sense researching not only other people, but their own taken-for-granted culture as well.

Third, practitioners, unlike anthropologists, have to make practical use of what they have learned. They have to determine in what way two conflicting cultures can compromise. As we have seen, a compromise on the institutional level is only a step toward a solution. There are vast areas of individual practices in which accommodation has to be sought. In the search for accommodation, mere cross-knowledge is not enough; practitioners have to identify the cross-knowledge, whether it is tacit or discursive, and whether and why it is or is not negotiable. In an example we have seen, Japanese managers were reluctant to clearly differentiate between high- and low-performing subordinates in the pay increase rate, partly because they were concerned that if the turnover rate of their department rose, they might be negatively evaluated by the parent company in Japan. Their concern, or knowledge, which is discursive in this case, may make negotiation difficult, unless there is some sort of guarantee or proof that the large gap in the pay increase rate would not affect the turnover rate. Thus, it is not good enough, in this case, for American negotiators to simply push Japanese managers to follow the American way merely by explaining American culture. If the relationship between the parent company and TSDAL Japanese expatriates in terms of evaluation cannot be changed, the Japanese managers are unlikely to change to an American system.

In TSDAL, Japanese expatriates know the significance of an English proverb, "When in Rome do as the Romans do," but, although they are physically in "Rome," they are socially still in close contact with their home. For practitioners, therefore, it is necessary to determine the best possible accommodation within the broader social circumstances. Acquiring tacit and discursive cross-knowledge in a wide social context helps to determine what the best possible accommodations are. Without these kinds of knowledge, practitioners and managers fall behind in helping to facilitate the third culture that makes the workplace operate smoothly.

References

Abe, E., et al. 1992. *Kaigai Nikkeikigyo to Jintekishigen (Overseas Japanese Companies and Human Resources)*. Tokyo: Dobunkan.

Adler, N. J. 1991. *International Dimensions of Organizational Behavior*. Boston: PWS-KENT.

Brannen, M. Y. 1994. *"Your Next Boss Is Japanese": Negotiating Cultural Change at a Western Massachusetts Paper Plant*. Doctoral dissertation, University of Massachusetts.

Bourdieu, P. 1977. *Outline of a Theory of Practice*. Trans. R. Nice. Cambridge: Cambridge University Press.

Geertz, C. 1973. *Interpretation of Cultures*. New York: Basic Books.

Giddens, A. 1979. *Central Problems in Social Theory: Action, Structure and Contradiction in Social Analysis*. Berkeley: University of California Press.

Hayashi, Y. 1994. *Ibunka intafeisu keiei (Cross cultural interface management)*. Tokyo: Nihon-keizaishinbunsha.

Iwata, R. 1985. *Nihon no Keiei Soshiki (The Structure of Japanese Management)*. Tokyo: Kodansha Gendai Shinsho.

Kidahashi, M. 1987. *Dual Organization: A Study of a Japanese-Owned Firm in the United States*. Doctoral dissertation, Columbia University.

King, A. 1976. *Colonial Urban Development: Culture, Social Power and Environment*. London: Routledge & Kegan Paul.

Kleinberg, J. 1989. "Cultural Clash between Managers: America's Japanese Firm." In Prasad, S. B. (ed.), *Advances in International Comparative Management*. Vol. 4. Greenwich, CT: JAI Press. 221–243.

Malinowski, B. 1949. *The Dynamics of Culture Change: An Inquiry into Race Relations in Africa*. P. M. Kaberry (ed.), 4th ed. New Haven, CT: Yale University Press.

Schein, E. H. 1986. "Atarashii Soshiki Bunkagainen eno Rikaiwo (Coming to a New Awareness of Organizational Culture)." In Senryaku Keiei Kyokai (eds.), *Koporet Karucha (Corporate Culture)*. Trans. by Urago and Ichikawa. Tokyo: Horuto Saundasu Japan.

Sumihara, N. 1992. *A Case Study of Structuration in a Bicultural Work Organization: A Study of a Japanese-Owned and Managed Corporation in the U.S.A.* Doctoral dissertation, New York University

Sumihara, N. 1993. "A Case Study of Cross-Cultural Interaction in a Japanese Multinational Corporation Operating in the United States: Decision-Making Processes and Practices." In Sims R., & Dennehy, R. (eds.), *Diversity and Differences in Organizations: An Agenda for Answers and Questions*. Westport, CT: Quorum. 135–148.

Sumihara, N. 1994. "Compensation System and Practice at at Japanese Owned and Managed Sales Subsidiary in the USA." In Campbell, N. & Burton, F. (eds.), *Japanese Multinationals; Strategies and Management in the Globa Kaisha*. London: Routledge. 240–250.

Tsuda, M. 1993. *Jinji Roumu Kanri (Human Resources Management)*. Kyoto: Mineruba Shobou.

6

ROCHELLE KOPP

The Rice-Paper Ceiling
in Japanese Companies

Why It Exists and Persists

Introduction

In chapter 3 Brannen and Salk make the point that defining the contrasts between Japanese and local cultures and management styles in terms of reified billiard balls is not a sufficient way to describe the dynamics that arise in the context of Japanese overseas subsidiaries and that it is necessary to examine the negotiated culture which emerges from interactions. This chapter represents an attempt to quantify and dissect what appears to be a common feature of the negotiated cultures that emerge in the overseas operations of Japanese firms: a heavy use of expatriates and a related barrier to the advancement of locally hired employees within the overseas operation.

Numerous observers of Japanese multinationals have (JMNCs) remarked on their tendency to dispatch large numbers of expatriates to overseas operations. That these expatriates dominate management posts to the exclusion of locally hired personnel is so often repeated that it has become virtually axiomatic.

This chapter discusses this phenomenon in detail, referring to it as a "rice-paper ceiling" that exists in JMNCs.[1] First, the rice-paper ceiling will be defined, and prior empirical research on this topic will be reviewed. Second, the existence of a rice-paper ceiling will be further documented by reference to comparative data on staffing patterns at American, European, and Japanese multinationals. Third, the various factors that contribute to the existence and perpetuation of the rice-paper ceiling will be presented.

Given this volume's focus on organizational learning, a discussion of the rice-paper ceiling is relevant because, in many respects, its key features and issues appear unchanged during the recent multinational development of Japanese firms. Twenty years ago, Yoshino (1976) said that "[t]he most serious problem of the Japanese management system in the multinational setting is that it cannot effectively integrate local nationals into the mainstream of management in the foreign subsidiaries." This is the essence of the rice-paper ceiling, and understanding the reasons for its persistence today sheds light on the extent to which organizational learning processes in JMNCs effectively address international human resource management (HRM) issues.

Defining the Rice-Paper Ceiling

The term rice-paper ceiling is derived from glass ceiling, popularly used in the United States to refer to barriers to advancement for women in business. Prior to defining the rice-paper ceiling, I will to examine in closer detail the concept of the glass ceiling. Although American women are protected by equal employment opportunity laws and have made great strides in the workplace in the past few decades, there are few women represented in the upper management levels of American corporations. Currently, women typically hold less than 5% of senior management positions in American industry (DeWitt, 1995).

Glass ceiling stands for an amalgam of cultural and organizational issues that are not official but may prevent women from rising in a company. These range from the "old boy network" that excludes women, business deals done on the golf course, the difficulties of balancing child raising and a career, the tendency to keep women in staff rather than line positions, and subtle differences in communication style between men and women.

In replacing "glass" with "rice-paper" (traditional Japanese *washi* paper), the concept of Japan is combined with the concept of advancement difficulties. Thus, the rice-paper ceiling refers to the advancement barriers facing non-Japanese who work for Japanese firms.

Multinationals must draw their worldwide management staff from sources that will best serve their business goals. To some extent, most MNCs will use personnel from the home country to staff senior posts. Kobrin (1988) suggests several reasons why a MNC might use an expatriate in a given overseas position rather than a local national: his or her knowledge of the global organization, identification with firmwide rather than local objectives, and role as an instrument of headquarters control, as well as the company's desire to develop the international expertise of a national by providing him with an expatriate experience.

Scholars who study JMNCs almost invariably remark on the preponderance of Japanese expatriates filling top-level posts. A recent survey of several hundred JMNCs confirmed this, showing that 78% of the chief executives or presidents of the overseas operations were Japanese expatriates and that department head positions were also often held by Japanese nationals (Yoshihara, 1995).

In addition, several researchers have documented that Japanese firms are more likely than American and European ones to staff the upper-level positions in overseas operations primarily with home-country expatriates. A study by Negandhi in 1979 comparing European-, American-, and Japanese-owned MNCs indicated that JMNCs were far less likely to have localized top management positions. In 78.9% of the Japanese firms, there were no locals in top management, whereas this was true for only 2.3% of the American and 15.2% of the European MNCs (Negandhi, 1979). A comparative study by Tung (1982) showed that JMNCs were particularly more likely to place expatriates in middle- and lower-level management positions around the world than were American and European MNCs. The comparisons were less consistent for top management positions. Shiraki (1995) gives comparisons between European/U.S. and Japanese MNCs within a single country, Indonesia. While 63.6% of the European/U.S. MNCs had put local university graduates in top management positions, only 25.0% of the Japanese firms had done so.

Confirming the Existence of the Rice-Paper Ceiling

In order to confirm previous observations and determine whether the rice-paper ceiling might have faded since the Negandhi and Tung studies, a comparative survey study of international HRM policies and practices in Japanese, American, and European MNCs was carried out (Kopp, 1994a).

Survey methodology

A database of major MNCs from the United States, Japan, and Europe was compiled by merging three listings: *Business Week* Global 1000, *Fortune* domestic, and *Fortune* international 500.[2] In order to bypass the companies that were unlikely to have multinational operations, all companies described as "utilities" were eliminated from the database. All American companies that were not also listed in the Directory of American Firms Operating in Foreign Countries[3] were also removed from the database. As a result, 918 firms remained: 272 headquartered in the United States, 309 headquartered in Japan, and 337 headquartered in Europe.

To facilitate a greater response rate, translations of the survey into Japanese, German, and French were prepared by native speakers familiar with business vocabulary.[4] The Japanese version was sent to the firms headquartered in Japan, the German version to firms headquartered in Germany, Switzerland, and Austria, and the French version to firms headquartered in France and Belgium. The remaining firms, all headquartered in other countries, received English versions of the questionnaire.

The survey was designed to be completed by one individual at each firm. I decided that the most logical choice to receive the questionnaires would be the individual responsible for the international HRM function, who would be most familiar with the statistics, policies, and problem areas the survey asked about. The choice of this type of subject, responding in an official capacity, also meant that the answers were likely to reflect the corporate employer's perspective. One response per firm was deemed adequate, as the majority of the questions in the survey were objective and were not expected to vary widely among respondents. The first mailing yielded an inadequate response. A second mailing was mailed approximately three months later to the non-responding firms.[5]

Eighty-one responses were received: 23 from Europe (France: 3, Germany: 3, Italy: 1, Switzerland: 1, United Kingdom: 13, and Netherlands: 2), 34 from Japan, and 24 from the United States. The majority of the individuals completing the survey were managers in the human resources or international departments of their firms.[6] The majority of the respondents to the survey were in the manufacturing/industrial sector: 79.2% of the

American firms, 60.9% of the European firms, and 73.5% of the Japanese firms.[7] The relatively low response rate (8.8%) reflected the underlying difficulty in obtaining corporate cooperation for survey projects that relate to potentially sensitive issues. However, the data obtained are sufficient to illuminate general trends and relationships.

Companies headquartered in different countries had different percentages of total sales derived from international operations. The average answer of the Japanese respondents to this question ($n = 28$) was 23.1%, 33.0% for the American respondents ($n = 20$), and 63.1% for the European respondents ($n = 14$). To correct for possible distortions resulting from this factor, a subsample of 15 Japanese companies was prepared with international sales averaging 34.8%.[8] In the results reported here, the data for this subsample are shown in parentheses following the results for the full Japanese sample. In most cases the data from the subsample do not contradict the conclusions derived from the full Japanese sample.

Survey Results

The results of the survey show a clear rice-paper ceiling effect, wherein Japanese firms fill more of their overseas management posts with home country expatriates than do American and European MNCs.

For example, comparing the staffing for the top manager positions at overseas operations, such as the so-called country manager or head of the local subsidiary, I found that American MNCs put home country expatriates in 31% of these positions, European MNCs put them in 48% of these positions. In Japanese JMNCs, 74% (75%) of these positions went to home country expatriates (see table 6.1)—very close to the 78% figure for Japanese expatriates in top overseas positions observed by Yoshihara (1995).

Significant differences appear in the broader group of all managerial positions at overseas subsidiaries. American firms fill 88% of these positions with local nationals, European firms, 82%, but Japanese firms fill only 48% (57%) of these positions with local nationals (see table 6.2).

The survey results also demonstrate that JMNCs are more likely to report complaints by local employees concerning lack of advancement opportunities. Of the Japanese respondents, 21% (20%) reported such complaints versus 4% of the European respondents and 8% of the American respondents. This demonstrates that the rice-paper ceiling not only exists but that it is noticed by locally hired employees.

TABLE 6.1 Top Management Positions (Country Manager or President of the Overseas Operation)

Headquarters country	% Home country nationals	% Local nationals	% 3rd country nationals
Japan ($n = 26$)	74% (75%)[a]	26% (24%)	0.2% (0.6%)
Europe ($n = 21$)	48%	44%	8%
United States ($n = 20$)	31%	49%	18%

[a]Percentages in parentheses are for the subsample of 15 Japanese companies.

TABLE 6.2 Managerial Positions (Defined as Supervisory, White-Collar)

Headquarters country	% Local nationals in managerial positions
Japan ($n = 27$)	48% (57%)[a]
Europe ($n = 17$)	82%
United States ($n = 22$)	88%

[a]Percentage in parentheses is for the subsample of 15 Japanese companies.

Why does this ceiling exist particularly in JMNCs? Just as the glass ceiling is not created by any written rules at American firms that say, "We won't put women in senior positions," Japanese firms do not have formal written policies that bar locally hired employees from managerial posts. In fact, JMNCs commonly endorse the goal of "localizing management," both to their employees and to outsiders. Yet they are frequently unable to make these statements a reality—just as many American firms fail to achieve their stated goals of eliminating the glass ceiling. The inability of JMNCs to achieve management localization in their overseas operations is due to a complex set of cultural and organizational factors that together work to inhibit non-Japanese from rising to senior positions in Japanese firms, analogous to the varied and complicated factors believed to contribute to the glass ceiling.

Causes of the Rice-Paper Ceiling

In examining the rice-paper ceiling, it is necessary to consider how Japanese firms determine that an individual is suitable for a management position. In Japan, the most important qualification for filling management positions is the employee's experience in the company. Japanese companies and individual managers are not used to giving important positions to individuals who have not been observed over a long period of time, who have not developed company-specific knowledge and relationship networks, and who have not earned trust and acceptance as long-standing members of the organization. Due to the lifetime employment tradition, there is no pattern of executive job mobility like that in countries such as the United States, which have more fluid labor markets. As a result, Japanese companies are not accustomed to incorporating externally hired unknown managers into their organizational power structures. Thus, even in their international operations, Japanese firms display a preference for putting known quantities in managerial positions, and most often these known quantities are Japanese expatriates.

In analyzing the causes of the rice-paper ceiling, the initial question is what is it that prevents locally hired employees from remaining in Japanese firms long enough for them to be considered known quantities? In other words, what factors contribute to turnover among high-potential locally hired employees of Japanese firms? In addition, what might hinder the development of trusting working relationships between Japanese and locally hired employees? And finally, what might prevent a locally hired employee from developing a network of contacts within the firm that would enhance his or her likelihood of success? These issues are at the core of the rice-paper ceiling phenomenon.

The following is an analysis of the key causes of the rice-paper ceiling, based on my survey research cited before, my interview research in the United States and Japan (Kopp, 1993; Kopp 1994b), and observations made in my work as management consultant to JMNCs operating in the United States. As many of these factors have been observed by others as well, related discussions in the existing literature will be cited. The intention is to fit the various factors into a useful framework.

The following discussion is intended to be general, pertaining to the typical JMNC. Nevertheless, it is important to keep in mind that there is wide variation among JMNCs in terms of the height and durability of their rice-paper ceilings, as well as the degree of their efforts to remove them. In other words, each contributing factor shown in table 6.3 may be present to a greater or lesser degree in any given firm. As Taylor pointed out in chapter 7, there are significant differences among JMNCs in the pace at which they are developing the organizational capabilities needed to be successful in the international environment.

Parent Company Issues

The rice-paper ceiling is determined in part by the corporate culture, management practices, and international HRM paradigm set in place by the parent company. The following paragraphs highlight the role of these factors in creating the rice-paper ceiling.

Control structure.   A major factor influencing the ability of Japanese companies to bring non-Japanese into the management ranks is the type of control structure they tend to favor. Two major ways in which companies institute internal control have been identified: *output-oriented* control systems and *culture-oriented* control systems (Dowling & Schuler, 1990: 30; Ouchi, 1979). An output-oriented control system focuses on objective, measurable data such as financial results and profitability indices. The manag-

TABLE 6.3 Summary of Contributing Factors to the Rice-Paper Ceiling

Parent co. issues	Local operation issues
Control structure	Day-to-day frictions and irritations
Parent co. human resource development goals for Japanese *seishain*	Language barrier
	Communication style
Lack of language skills or desire to communicate directly with local personnel	Leadership style
	Decision making
Lack of expatriate preparation prior to overseas posting	Human resource management
	Higher status of Japanese expatriates
Lack of autonomy of overseas operations	Difficulty attracting and retaining high-caliber local management candidates
Lack of international human resource policies that facilitate advancement of locally hired employees	Concern about locally hired employees' job mobility and company loyalty
Lack of parent co. involvement with, and awareness of, local employees (*genchi makase*)	Truncation of organizational learning
Different employee classifications (core versus peripheral employees)	

ers' actions are controlled by the fact that their output must match the performance goal expected of them. In contrast, a culture-oriented control system is less clear-cut, based on socialization of employees so that they understand the company's culture and goals. Thus, the managers' actions are controlled by training that leads them to act in accordance with accepted standards of behavior within that company.

All firms have control systems that combine both output-oriented and culture-oriented elements, but Western (and especially American) firms tend to rely more heavily on output-oriented control systems, whereas Japanese firms tend to use extremely culture-oriented control systems (Ouchi, 1981). This difference has a relationship with labor market structures. Output-oriented control systems are well-suited to an environment in which managers move from firm to firm, because the financial and other performance measures are explicit and thus easily grasped by new employees (Ouchi, 1979). On the other hand, the lifetime employment system of Japanese companies is the perfect environment for carefully inculcating culture-oriented controls.

The type of control system affects a company's ability to delegate authority to local nationals. The output-oriented controls that American and European MNCs rely on tend to be well-defined and easy to communicate to employees from other cultures. When such measures are used, locally hired employees can be given more autonomy and authority to meet the output goals as they see fit.

In contrast, the culture-oriented controls favored by Japanese companies are a barrier to decentralization because they are difficult to transmit to local employees. Since Japanese companies indoctrinate new Japanese employees into their cultures informally over a period of years, they are often at a loss as to how to train local employees in the culture quickly. Also, the training of an employee in a firm's culture traditionally takes place in Japan. Anyone who has not worked for a period of years in the head office will probably not be recognized as having adequately absorbed the culture (Bird & Mukuda, 1989). Finally, because Japanese companies' corporate cultures are firmly embedded in the Japanese language, culture, and labor practices, it is difficult to transmit them to local employees, who do not have significant prior knowledge of Japan. Given the difficulties of training local managers in their culture, many Japanese companies believe that only the thoroughly integrated Japanese employees can be entrusted with important managerial posts.

Parent company human resource development goals for Japanese *seishain*.   One common aspect of Japanese HRM practices applying to *seishain* (Japanese core employees under lifetime employment) is a series of rotations among posts used as a means to develop the individual's experience. This is particularly true for those on the "fast track." Recently, a foreign tour of duty has become a required rite of passage for up-and-coming executives in many Japanese firms. Thus, there is an additional rationale for Japanese firms to send expatriates overseas that is separate from the immediate business needs of the overseas operation. As Kobrin (1988) suggests, the foreign rotation becomes part of the home country's HRM development plan, with the overseas operation as the training ground.[9] This use of the overseas rotation as development opportunity tends to sustain the number of expatriates assigned to overseas operations.

Parent company employees' lack of language skills or desire to communicate directly with locally hired personnel.   The need to station Japanese expatriates at overseas operations is driven in part by the fact that they are used to facilitate communications with the parent company. These communications often take place in Japanese, necessitating that a Japanese individual be present in the overseas operation (Yoshihara, 1995). But if parent company personnel had greater ability or motivation to use English and communicate directly with locally hired personnel, the need for Japanese expatriates would be reduced. This issue might be referred to as lack of *kokusaika* (internationalization) of the parent company. Furthermore, most locally hired employees have the handicap of being only names on paper in the minds of parent company employees. In other words, locally hired employees generally do not have the opportunity to build the close network of mutual obligation and give-and-take relationships throughout the organization, which, it has been argued, is the key to power and advancement in Japanese firms (Lifson, 1992).

Lack of expatriate preparation prior to overseas posting.   Many Japanese firms provide their expatriates with little or no pre-departure training or orientation. Those that do tend to concentrate on English language skills and offer little or no cultural training (Nihon Zaigai Kigyo Kyokai, 1989: 37–40; Nishida, 1992: 10–13; Sugawara, 1993). The lack of preparation afforded Japanese expatriates tends to exacerbate culture shock and impairs their ability to build effective working relationships with locally hired colleagues.

Lack of autonomy of overseas operations.   A further issue is the lack of autonomy of the overseas operations of many Japanese firms. Japanese multinationals tend to have highly centralized control structures (Bartlett & Ghoshal, 1989; Bartlett & Yoshihara, 1988), which means that a great deal of decision making takes place in Japan or in consultation with Japan. This can make it difficult for locally hired employees to gain authority and power, especially when parent company employees prefer to communicate exclusively with Japanese expatriates.

Lack of international human resource policies that facilitate advancement of locally hired employees.   Japanese companies are less likely than Western multinationals to use personnel policies that would facilitate the evaluation and promotion of locally hired employees. The comparative survey discussed before (Kopp, 1994a) inquired as to whether four specific international personnel policies were in use:[10] respondents were asked to mark only those statements that accurately represented their company's international HRM policies.[11]

1. *Performance evaluation measures are the same in every one of our international operations.* Implementation of a standardized performance evaluation measure suggests that the parent company is concerned with consistent HRM policies across its overseas operations and that it is interested in the ability to compare managerial performance across countries. Such an orientation would facilitate use of human resources on an international basis.[12]

2. *A training program has been put in place to groom local nationals for advancement in our company's managerial ranks.* A company that implements such a training program explicitly views local nationals as candidates for management.

3. *Local nationals are often transferred to headquarters or to other international operations so that they can gain experience and learn more about the company as a whole.* Implementation of this policy suggests an even greater commitment to use of local nationals in management than does the implementation of a training program. This is because transferring local nationals requires greater planning and allocation of resources. Implementation of this policy also suggests a broad view of the capabilities and role of foreign nationals, going beyond their usefulness in their country of origin.[13] Furthermore, such international transfer opportunities give locally hired employees greater knowledge of and identification with the global firm, thus reducing the importance of one of Kobrin's (1988) rationales for the use of expatriates.

4. *At headquarters we maintain a centralized roster of all our managerial employees (both home country nationals and foreign nationals) throughout the world in order to facilitate worldwide managerial development.* Implementation of such a policy indicates that the parent company is actively keeping track of local employees and is better able to consider them when planning for international management needs, as well as activities such as training programs.[14]

Japanese firms are far less likely than U.S. or European firms to have adopted any of these policies (see table 6.4). The lack of such policies results in the perpetuation of the rice-paper ceiling.

Lack of parent company involvement with, and awareness of, local employees (*genchi makase*).   The lack of certain international HRM policies is a reflection of the fact that many JMNCs do not consider locally hired employees to be within the purview of the head office. Rather, locally hired employees and all human resource matters pertaining to them are considered the responsibility of the overseas operation that hired them. This is often referred to by the phrase *genchi makase* (entrusting it to the overseas operation). While local autonomy with respect to HRM is certainly necessary to some extent, due to differing labor laws and the impracticality of making all human resource decisions at a head office, the fact that local employees are not closely tracked, much less nurtured, by a head office limits their ability to get ahead in the head office–determined personnel hierarchy.

A related issue is that although Japanese firms can be thought of as resource accumulators with respect to human resources (Bird & Mukuda, 1989), key organizational knowledge belongs primarily to core Japanese employees, and in many cases the knowledge of locally hired employees is not granted the same importance or even recognition. For example, many Japanese firms spend large sums of money sending Japanese employees to prestigious graduate business schools, yet do not make similar investments in the training of locally hired employees.

TABLE 6.4 Implementation of International Personnel Policies

Description of policy	Japanese firms, % implemented (n = 34)	European firms, % implemented (n = 23)	U.S. firms, % implemented (n = 24)
Performance evaluation measures are the same in every one of our international operations	24% (0%)	48%	58%
A training program has been put in place to groom local nationals for advancement in our company's managerial ranks	24% (27%)	43%	33%
Local nationals are often transferred to headquarters or other international operations so that they can gain experience and learn more about the company as a whole	15% (27%)	65%	54%
At headquarters we maintain a centralized roster of all our managerial employees (both home country nationals and foreign nationals) throughout the world in order to facilitate worldwide managerial development	18% (13%)	61%	54%

Percentages in parentheses are for the subset of 15 Japanese companies.

Different employee classifications (core versus peripheral employees).   In JMNCs there is a contrast between the periodic and automatic rotation of Japanese employees and the lack of rotation of locally hired employees. (This is underscored by the previous data showing that Japanese multinationals are less likely to transfer locally hired employees for developmental purposes.) This is a result of the difference in status of employees from Japan and employees hired locally. While Japanese employees hired in Japan are *seishain* (core, permanent employees) of the parent company, locally hired employees are considered employees of the local operation that hired them and thus lack a direct employment relationship connection with the parent company.[15] *Seishain* form a pool of core employees who are rotated from post to post, from country to country. Locally hired employees are generally not rotated in this manner. They tend to stay within the operation where they were hired, and they often work on only that specialty for which they were hired.[16] The locally hired employees are analogous to non-*seishain* employee categories in Japan such as *shokutaku* (contract employee), *paato* (full-time "part-timer"), *kogaisha no shain* (employee of a subsidiary), and *haken jugyoin* (employee sent from a temporary agency), which are all nonmanagement classifications that have no upward advancement potential.

Because non-Japanese employees are not in the rotation pool, they are not likely eligible for positions reserved for those in the pool. The following is a typical example. An American is hired to work for a Japanese bank in the project finance area. He has an MBA from a top business school and had previously worked in the project finance area for several years at an American bank. He is assigned to work under a Japanese manager who has recently come from Japan. He is surprised to find that his superior has no prior project finance experience. In fact, the superior's job assignment prior to coming to the United States had been in foreign exchange.

The American sets about patiently teaching his new superior the ins and outs of project finance. After they have worked together for three years, the superior has learned a lot about project finance. But then the superior is called back to Japan, and another Japanese employee is sent from Japan to take his place. The new superior has no knowledge of project finance.

Why was the new superior assigned to the position? Because this assignment was part of the standard employee rotation system, determined by the personnel department at the head office. The philosophy of this firm's personnel department is to build a cadre of generalists by rotating them through different locations and positions. The parent company's belief is that a capable person can learn what is necessary to do a job.

The American employee is extremely frustrated. He wonders why the company did not promote him to the manager's position rather than bringing in an expatriate who does not have specific knowledge of the work at hand. In this case, the parent company never considered the possibility of putting a local hire in the post. It just automatically did what it had always done, send an expatriate. Also, as mentioned before, the personnel managers at the parent company are disconnected from human resource matters concerning the overseas operations. They had never met the American employee. They do not know what he is like, nor do they know anything about his background, qualification, or skills. They were not aware that he would have liked to fill the manager's position.

The American employee, facing the prospect of training another superior all over again, says to himself, "What's the point? In a few years they'll just send another green manager who I'll need to train, and who I'll need to prove myself to." Soon after, he takes a job with another company, and the bank loses one of its better employees.

This anecdote shows the difference in how the organization views the roles of Japanese core *seishain* and peripheral locally hired employees. This example also illustrates the potential clashes between the generalist-oriented career paths prevalent in Japan and the specialist-oriented career paths common in the United States. It also demonstrates how the parent company–oriented personnel rotation system can overlook the potential of local employees.

Local Operation Issues

Day-to-day frictions and irritations.   Also playing a major role in the creation and perpetuation of the rice-paper ceiling are the everyday issues that involve the day-to-day interactions between locally hired employees and Japanese expatriates in the context of the local subsidiary. As discussed by Brannen and Salk in chapter 3, the specific tasks and pressures faced by the overseas operation will cause the different values, meanings, and norms of the Japanese and locally hired employees to surface and potentially collide and produce conflict. If not adequately resolved, these day-to-day frictions can prevent locally hired employees and Japanese expatriates from developing effective working relationships. They can cause Japanese to view the abilities of their locally hired counterparts negatively and to want to retreat from interaction with local employees and work only among themselves. These frictions can also cause locally hired employees to feel frustrated and potentially result in low job satisfaction and high turnover. The ultimate outcome is a failure to develop the trust relationships that would make the Japanese firm comfortable putting locally hired employees in key positions.

The following examples and explanations are based on my research and observation concerning interaction between Japanese expatriates and American employees. However, analogous culture clashes have been reported by those studying Japanese investment in other countries as well.

Language barrier.   First and foremost among everyday issues is the language barrier. Few business people outside of Japan are able to speak Japanese, and even fewer can read and write it. By the same token, many Japanese lack confidence in their English and are unfamiliar with the colloquial speech used in the workplace. (The effect of this factor seems largely unchanged in the 20 years since it was noted by Yoshino, 1976.)

Many everyday misunderstandings can be traced to linguistic crossed signals. For example, an American employee of a Japanese company was working very hard on a project with a tight deadline and was putting in long hours every night. One evening at about 7:00, his Japanese superior walked by and said to him, "You must work harder." The American employee was extremely upset. He wondered why his superior did not realize that he was already working hard and why his efforts were not appreciated.

In fact, what his superior was trying to say was the Japanese phrase *ganbatte kudasai.* When translated literally, it's a command to work harder. But it really means something more like "keep up the good work." When misunderstandings of this type occur on a daily basis and remain unaddressed, they can sour the office atmosphere and prevent the development of effective working relationships.

Communication style.   A further, deeper level of issues goes beyond pure language into the realm of communication style. Many scholars in the intercultural communication field have studied these differences, which include issues such as directness (Gudykunst and Nishida, 1994: 40–44); tendency to discuss or debate (Becker, 1986); use of high context versus low context communication (Hall, 1976); and use of specific communication strategies in various instances, such as apologies (Barnlund and Yoshioka, 1990), persuasion (Neuliep and Hazleton, 1985), or embarrassment remediation (Sueda and Wiseman, 1992).

As an example, consider an American employee working on a new project that she initiated. Her Japanese supervisor tells her that further progress for the project will be "a bit difficult." She interprets this phrase in an American manner, as a sign that the project is possible but that more effort is needed, thus perceiving it as a challenge. She spends more time and energy on the project but gets nowhere. Eventually, she gets frustrated and wonders why she is beating her head against the wall, while her boss wonders why she did not take the hint to give up and try something else. In Japan, the subtle comment that something is "difficult" reveals that it is basically impossible.

This example illustrates one of the differences in communication style that can contribute to the rice-paper ceiling—Japanese tend to be less direct and are reluctant to present negative information (Gudykunst and Nishida, 1994: 40–44). This can be extremely confusing to Americans and other Westerners, who are used to a more straightforward style of communication. Meanwhile, Americans can be oblivious to the signals that Japanese try to send them.

In this situation, if you asked the employee, she would say, "Why didn't he just tell me?" And if you asked the supervisor, he would say, "I tried to!" Misunderstandings caused by differences in communication style are seldom recognized as such by managers and employees. Instead, the tendency is to ascribe the misunderstanding to negative aspects of the individual involved, which further undermines working relationships and acts to decrease trust.

Leadership style.   Leadership style is also quite different in the United States and Japan, and this difference can also be a barrier to effective interaction. (This is likely to hold true in other Western countries that have leadership models similar to those of the United States.) An analogy is perhaps the easiest way to capture this difference. The American model of a good manager can be characterized as being like a football coach, whereas the Japanese model of a good manager is more like a karate teacher,[17] along the lines of the Pat Morita character in the movie *The Karate Kid*.

The football coach maps out the game plan and gives detailed assignments, while the karate teacher gives little formal instruction. Instead, the karate teacher demonstrates and expects the students to learn through imitation and practice.

The football coach gives a pregame pep talk and cheers when the team does well. The karate teacher seldom praises his students and does not subscribe to the American concept of positive reinforcement. Rather than celebrating past victories, the karate teacher focuses on future improvements.

The football coach may use charisma and emotion as a way to bond with the players. On the other hand, the karate teacher is circumspect and unemotional. He believes that "silence is golden," "talk is cheap," and "it's better to be strong and silent."

The following is an example of how these differences can come into play in the workplace. An American joined a Japanese firm. In his previous jobs he had always worked for American-style strong leaders. The way to get along and get ahead in these past positions was to do exactly what was asked and not step on anyone's toes by going off into different areas. So when he joined the Japanese firm, he waited for his new Japanese boss to give him direction, to tell him what to do. However, the Japanese boss was accustomed to the Japanese leadership model, in which superiors expect their subordinates to take initiative. He had hired a talented person and was looking forward to seeing what he would do. So he waited for his new employee to take action. Meanwhile, the new employee waited for direction, which he did not receive. The situation amounted to paralysis. After about a year the American quit in frustration, and his manager was quite disappointed. This example demonstrates a conflict in role expectations and is typical of the complex cultural interactions where, as Kleinberg notes in chapter 4, "players not only *act* according to their cultural motivation, they *react* as well."

Decision making.   Another recurring issue in JMNCs is the decision-making process (Kopp, 1994b; Pucik, Hanada, and Fifield, 1989; Trevor, 1983; Yoshino, 1976). There are two issues involved when discussing decision-making in Japanese firms. The first is the process by which decisions are made. Non-Japanese are usually not familiar with typical Japanese decision-making processes such as *nemawashi* (behind the scenes consensus building) or *ringisho* (circulating proposal documents). This lack of familiarity with decision-making practices and related cultural norms can prevent non-Japanese employees from effectively influencing the decision-making process. However, JMNCs seldom provide cross-cultural training to their locally hired employees that would improve their skills in this area.

The second issue is to what extent locally hired employees can even participate in the decision-making process. In some Japanese companies, locally hired employees are wholly or partially excluded, because the decision-making process occurs in Japanese, in a meeting to which non-Japanese staff are not invited, or even takes place in Japan. A recent study of Japanese affiliates in the United States and Europe (Beechler et al., 1995a) showed that local managers are not involved in nearly half of the decisions involving the local operation.

In addition to being excluded from much decision making, the locally hired staff may not have the opportunity to find out how the decision was made. For example, in one Japanese bank's U.S. branch, the American loan officers refer to their approach as "throwing spaghetti on the wall to see if it sticks." This is because they never get any explanation from the bank's credit department in Tokyo as to why certain loans are accepted or rejected. For example, if they submit four loans to hospitals and all of them were rejected, they assume that the credit department does not want to make loans to hospitals.

When one asks Japanese managers why they feel reluctant to include locally hired employees in the decision-making process, they usually give two reasons. The first one traces back to the language barrier—"It's just so much more convenient and comfortable to use Japanese." The second reason traces back to Japanese discomfort with the job mobility of locally hired employees, discuss next.

Human resource management.   Japanese HRM practices are vastly different from those practiced in other countries, a difference driven by both the fundamental difference between human resources as practiced in the Japanese low labor mobility environment and practices that pertain to high labor mobility environments, as well as the different laws and customs of various countries. As a result, virtually every aspect of HRM—hiring, firing, compensation, benefits, performance evaluation, career paths—may be handled differently in the host country than it is in Japan. The differing values and expectations held by Japanese and local employees concerning these issues necessitate negotiation and can lead to misunderstandings. In chapter 5, Sumihara presents an example of this process in the context of performance evaluation.

Because Japanese companies and Japanese managers likely lack an in-depth understanding of human resource management as it is practiced in the host country, and in many cases choose to apply the parent company template in terms of policies and practices (as discussed by Bird, Taylor, and Beechler in chapter 12), the resulting compensation, benefits, or other personnel practices at many Japanese firms may be out of place in the local context or are merely adequate rather than truly competitive. In some cases the practices of JMNCs may be actively irritating to locally hired employees or even contradict local laws and customs.

Higher status of Japanese expatriates. The higher status of Japanese expatriates is a perennial complaint of locally hired employees. Japanese companies, reflecting their society, are quite hierarchical and pay very close attention to the allocation of symbols of rank. Any benefits and privileges actively withheld from locally hired employees can become tangible reminders of the other frustrations they feel. Examples include a firm where only Japanese expatriates were given the security code to enter the office after hours, a firm where Japanese expatriates were allowed to entertain clients by playing golf but locally hired employees were not, a firm where only Japanese expatriates were invited to wear company lapel pins, and a firm in which only Japanese expatriates were allowed to meet and socialize with top company executives visiting from Japan.

Difficulty attracting and retaining high-caliber local management candidates. The "everyday friction" factors described before, combined with the perception of a rice-paper ceiling blocking advancement opportunities, make it difficult to attract the best employees and to retain them over the long term.

In the comparative study mentioned previously (Kopp, 1994a), difficulty recruiting high-caliber local employees was a problem reported more often by Japanese firms than by European and American companies. In fact, 44% (53%) of the Japanese firms reported this problem, while 26% of the the European firms and 21% of the American firms did. Statistical evidence on HRM issues at Japanese companies operating in the United States also points to recruiting difficulties. When asked to describe problems encountered in establishing their U.S. affiliates, 39.5% of the respondents to a Japan Society survey cited "finding qualified American managers to work in the affiliate" and 30.8% cited "hiring a qualified work-force" (Bob & SRI, 1990). Similarly, a survey of Japanese companies operating in the United States conducted by a human resource consulting firm found that 35% felt recruiting personnel to be very or extremely difficult, and 56% thought it to be difficult (The Wyatt Company, 1990).

The issue of retention can be measured directly in the form of turnover. Many Japanese firms suffer from chronic high turnover in their American affiliates, particularly among white-collar and managerial employees. The comparative study above also showed more Japanese firms reporting high turnover of locally hired employees—32% (20%) versus 9% of the European firms and 4% of the American firms (Kopp, 1994a).

Due to the difficulty of attracting and retaining high-caliber local personnel, many Japanese firms find themselves with employees of lesser quality, whom they are then reluctant to place in key positions. Also, those high-caliber management candidates who do join may not stay long enough to satisfy the frequent Japanese requirement of long length of service in the firm before appointment to a management post. Furthermore, it can be argued that in some cases, employees who were comparatively high-caliber when they entered a Japanese firm may, after a long length of service, fall behind their peers in other firms. This reflects the comparative lack of developmental opportunities in many Japanese firms, such as lack of job rotation for locally hired employees, lack of investment in internal or external training programs for locally hired employees, lack of autonomy and decision-making opportunities for local employees that would hone their managerial abilities, and Japanese expatriates' lack of skill and effort in coaching and mentoring locally hired employees.

In conversations with Japanese expatriate managers, they often cite "lack of readiness" or "lack of suitable managerial qualities" as reasons for not promoting locally hired employees. In addition to the issues mentioned before that might influence the *actual* management abilities of locally hired staff, it is important to keep in mind that different concepts of appropriate role behavior for managers can negatively affect the *perceived* managerial qualities of locally hired staff. In chapter 4, Kleinberg's study presents an example of how such negative perceptions can be formed.

Concern about locally hired employees' job mobility and company loyalty.   The mobility of locally hired employees, which may be exacerbated by the high turnover situation common to JMNCs, is of great concern to Japanese firms. The fact of local employees' mobility is frequently used as justification for withholding sensitive information from them, excluding them from decision making, and not placing them in upper-level posts.

In the United States and other countries where there is a fluid labor market, it is not considered unusual for managers to change jobs and join a competitor. Accustomed to the low labor mobility environment in Japan, Japanese companies tend to view the possibility of defection with extreme discomfort and are reluctant to share confidential information shared with locally hired employees, who could potentially leave the firm.

As a result, the following scenario can take place. The Japanese expatriate managers think, "We don't want to give too much information and responsibility to locally hired employees right away, because they might job-hop to another company." The locally hired employees sense that they are not being included in the company's decision-making process and conclude that their future prospects are limited.

They decide to leave to join other firms. The Japanese expatriate managers say to themselves, "Ah, it's just as we thought, non-Japanese aren't loyal to their companies. They didn't stick around long enough for us to get to trust them!" Their negative stereotypes are confirmed, and the cycle begins again. This "vicious circle of lack of trust" is a recurrent theme in Japanese companies' interactions with locally hired employees (Kopp, 1995).

Truncation of organizational learning.   A final factor contributing to the rice-paper ceiling is truncation of organizational learning. It is necessary for Japanese organizations to learn how to more effectively recruit, motivate, and retain locally hired employees at the overseas operation level. Also, individual Japanese expatriates need to form trusting relationships with locally hired employees. At the parent company level, human resource managers need to gain an understanding of international HRM issues, as well as the specific issues related to locally hired employees. Also, the staff of departments having contact with overseas offices need to develop greater comfort in communicating with locally hired employees, as well as in establishing the beginnings of trusting relationships on a person-to-person level.

These learning processes are truncated by three factors: turnover among locally hired employees, periodic rotation of expatriates in and out of the local operation, and rotation of Japanese employees within the parent company. These three factors lead to a lack of continuity and a loss of institutional memory, inhibiting organizational learning. Further, due to rotations and turnover, Japanese employees at either the local operation or the parent company seldom work with any given local employee long enough to develop the kind of strong relationship, or to afford the local employee the same "reputation" among Japanese employees, that is necessary to encourage ascendancy of local employees into key positions. Because the assumption of competence is not as strong for local employees as it is for Japanese employees, local employees often find themselves in the position of having to prove themselves over and over again to each new Japanese employee they begin to work with.

Conclusions

Persistence of the Rice-Paper Ceiling

As noted by Beechler, et al. (1995b), and also Westney in chapter 2, the argument has been made that Japanese companies have expatriate-intensive personnel practices because their international expansion has been relatively recent, and that as time passes they will follow the same path that Western MNCs have taken, reducing the number of expatriates and localizing the management of their overseas operations (Tung, 1988; author's interviews). Westney terms this the life cycle effect explanation. Although this may be true for those relatively few JMNCs who have made significant investments of money and effort in adapting their policies to the international environment, the mere passage of time does not guarantee that a company's practices will change, and it may even serve to solidify current practices. As chapter 12 demonstrates, not all JMNCs follow the same learning path, and some view their experiences as validating their original approach.

Recent findings on expatriate-intensive international personnel practices in JMNCs (Kopp, 1994a, Yoshihara, 1995) are consistent with research performed significantly earlier (Negandhi, 1979; Tung, 1982; Yoshino, 1976). Furthermore, in a study of staffing practices in Japanese firms' U.S. affiliates in 1978 and 1988, Boyacigiller (1990) found that they did not tend to localize their affiliates by hiring more local nationals over time. These findings are consistent with the prediction made by Trevor (1983) that a "universally applicable 'logic of multinationalization' is incompatible with the evidence from the [Japanese] subsidiaries" he studied.

Japanese multinationals have not taken the path of Western MNCs in becoming less ethnocentric in their staffing policies because of the various cultural and organizational factors discussed at length earlier in this chapter. This combination of factors is particular to Japanese firms and accounts for the persistence of the rice-paper ceiling in their overseas operations.

Over the years, many scholars have pointed out that ethnocentric practices handicap Japanese multinationals (Bartlett and Yoshihara, 1988; Kopp, 1993, 1994a, 1994b; Pucik, Hanada, and Fifield, 1989; Trevor, 1983; Yoshino, 1976). This negative impact occurs through operational difficulties in the local operations (Negandhi, 1979), friction between expatriates and locally hired employees (Bob & SRI, 1990), high cost of using expatriates as compared to locally hired employees (Yoshino, 1976), strain on the limited pool of Japanese staff qualified to take overseas positions (Kopp, 1994a; Yoshino, 1976), HRM problems such as high turnover and low morale among local employees (Kopp, 1994b), litigation by local employees (Jacobs, 1990; Kilborn, 1991; Thompson, 1989), stress and career disruption experienced by Japanese expatriates (White, 1988), and lack of local responsiveness (DeNero, 1990).

However, the explanation for the persistence of the rice-paper ceiling may be one or more of the following:

1. The problems discussed here are not perceived by Japanese expatriates. Indeed, the very factors that cause these problems may prevent Japanese expatriates from perceiving them.
2. Even if Japanese expatriates are aware of the problems, they may not notify the parent company of them, because either they do not perceive them to be important or they wish to avoid transmitting negative information that may reflect badly on them.
3. Even when the problems become known to Japanese expatriates as well as the parent company, they may not link them intellectually to corporate human resource policies and practices that can be changed, linking them instead to external factors out of the company's control, such as market conditions, "cultural differences," or "poor moral quality of local nationals."
4. Even if the problems are perceived by Japanese expatriates and the parent company to be linked to corporate HRM policies and practices, they may feel that the potential negative consequences of changing these policies outweighs the expected benefits. This is demonstrated vividly by Yoshihara (1995), whose survey study shows that Japanese firms are concerned about potential problems associated with placing local nationals in management posts. Japanese parent companies were concerned that naming local nationals as presidents of the overseas operation would have a detrimental effect on the relationship with the parent company (28%), and the relationship with Japanese expatriates (35%), and would lead to violations of company policies (48%). Japanese respondents to his survey cited a variety of problems associated with undertaking discussions with local managers (the types of discussions necessary if local managers are to take on key posts and participate in decision-making processes): time-consuming nature of these discussions (55%), difficulty in having frank discussions (41%), psychological tension (23%), decline in the quality of discussion (20%), and hesitation of Japanese managers to speak (19%). Significantly, only 5% of Japanese parent companies felt that placing a local national in the top position at a local operation would improve its performance.

Even if the problems are perceived by Japanese expatriates and the parent company to be linked to corporate human resource policies and practices, and the potential benefits of changing those policies are perceived to counterbalance or even outweigh the potential negative effects of doing so, changes may not be made due to the aversion to risk often seen in Japanese firms (Kopp, 1994b). Actions of the type necessary to bring true change to the structure of international HRM in Japanese firms are particularly risky to would-be internal proponents, because they involve those elements at the core of traditional practices, such as the rigid distinction between *seishain* and non-*seishain*.

Two-tier system as true export of "Japanese-style human resource management." There has been much discussion in the literature about whether Japanese-style HRM is transferable to other countries, and to what extent JMNCs are indeed applying Japanese management methods in their overseas subsidiaries (see, for example, Beechler & Yang, 1994; Dicle, Dicle, & Alie, 1988; Ishida, 1986). However, those discussions have focused on the aspects of Japanese management associated with one category of employees, the *seishain*, namely long-term employment, internal labor markets, seniority-based compensation, high investment in human resource development, etc.

Yet the policies used to manage *seishain* are only one aspect of Japanese-style HRM. The core group of *seishain* employees may make up as little as 20% of a company's workforce, depending on the particular industry and the state of the overall economy (Klee, 1986: 366).[18] The other workers needed by a Japanese company are utilized on a non-*seishain* basis, forming a two-tier employment system that is a hallmark of Japanese HRM.

The criticisms of how JMNCs tend to treat locally hired employees (lack of job security when compared with lifetime employment status of *seishain*, lack of access to decision making and upper-level posts when compared to *seishain*, and lack of training and development opportunities when compared to *seishain*) are all true of non-*seishain* in Japan as well. In fact, it could be that the rice-paper ceiling observed in Japanese firms is an artifact of their export of two-tiered personnel structures to their overseas operations.

Thus, the rice-paper ceiling can be seen as evidence that Japanese multinationals are indeed applying Japanese-style HRM overseas. It just happens to be the aspect of Japanese-style HRM that involves having rigid categories of core and peripheral employees who have highly contrasting levels of job security and prospects for advancement.

Notes

1. This phenomenon was termed the bamboo ceiling by scholar Nakiye Boyacigiller (1990).

2. The *Business Week* list was from July 15, 1991. The Fortune lists were the *Fortune* 500, April 29, 1991 and the *Fortune* 500 Largest Foreign Companies, July 22, 1991. The *Business Week* list ranked companies on the basis of stock market value, while the *Fortune* lists ranked companies on the basis of sales volume.

3. 11th ed. New York: World Trade Academy Press, 1987.

4 Resource constraints did not permit back-translation of the French and German questionnaires. My ability to read Japanese obviated the need for back-translation of the Japanese questionnaire.

5. The second mailing was directed toward the "Chief Personnel Officer—Int'l Div.," and "direct to the person responsible for international human resources" was handwritten in Japanese on the envelopes directed to Japan.

6. In addition, nearly 50 companies, primarily American and European, responded by indicating that they would not be able to complete the questionnaire. Approximately a third cited reasons of confidentiality, another third cited a lack of personnel to complete the quantity of questionnaires they received, and the remainder indicated that the management of their international human resources was so decentralized that it would not be possible to gather the information requested. The respondents in the last category may in fact be highly polycentric firms, using the definition given in Perlmutter and Heenan (1979), Heenan (1975), and Perlmutter and Heenan (1974).

7. The firms were categorized into industry sectors using Morgan Stanley Capital International's definitions. This categorization has six industry sectors: energy, materials, capital equipment, consumer goods, services, and finance. Due to data constraints, for the purposes of this analysis companies in the first four sectors were grouped together as "manufacturing/industrial," and companies in the last two sectors were grouped together as "service." Two American firms were of unknown category.

8. The subsample was created by removing the 6 Japanese respondents who did not give an answer to this question and also removing the 13 Japanese firms with the smallest responses to this question.

9. Kopp (1994b: 117, 174) discusses the issue of trainees at further length.

10. These four policies were suggested by the ethnocentric/polycentric/regiocentric/geocentric classification of firms described in the following: Perlmutter and Heenan, 1979; Heenan, 1975; Perlmutter and Heenan 1974.

11. In the questionnaire, the policies were phrased exactly as they are italicized in the text.

12. Perlmutter and Heenan (1974) discuss the adoption of worldwide performance appraisal systems as an alternative to ethnocentric appraisal systems.

13. Perlmutter and Heenan (1974) and Ondrack (1985) discuss the nonethnocentric policy of transferring local nationals for career development purposes.

14. Perlmutter and Heenan (1974) refer to such rosters as "managerial inventories."

15. This subject is treated at greater length in Kopp (1994b: ch. 10).

16. It is important to note that the term locally hired employees includes Japanese nationals who are hired directly by the local operation rather than having been sent from the parent company. These locally hired Japanese face many of the same structural obstacles as local national employees.

17. This analogy is developed at greater length in Kopp (1994b: ch. 6).

18. Haruo Shimada of Keio University estimated that in the mid-1970s approximately half of Japanese workers were covered by lifetime employment and that the figure today would be closer to 25% (Schlesinger & Kanabayashi, 1992).

References

Barnlund, D., & Yoshioka, M. 1990. "Apologies: Japanese and American Styles." *International Journal of Intercultural Relations.* 14: 193–205.

Bartlett, C., & Ghoshal, S. 1989. *Managing Across Borders: The Transnational Solution.* Boston: Harvard Business School Press.

Bartlett, C., and Yoshihara, H. 1988. "New Challenges for Japanese Multinationals: Is Organization Adaptation Their Achilles Heel?" *Human Resource Management.* 27 (1): 19–43.

Becker, C. 1986. "Reasons for the Lack of Argumentation and Debate in the Far East." *International Journal of Intercultural Relations.* 10: 75–91.

Beechler, S., & Yang, J. 1994. "The Transfer of Japanese-Style Management to American Subsidiaries: Contingencies, Constraints, and Competencies." *Journal of International Business Studies.* Third quarter: 1–25.

Beechler, S., Stephan, J., Pucik, V., & Campbell, N. 1995a. "Decision-making Localization and Decentralization in Japanese MNCs: Are There Costs of Leaving Local Managers Out of the Loop?" Paper submitted to the Academy of International Business, November.

Beechler, S., Stephan, J., Pucik, V., & Campbell, N. 1995b. "The Transnational Challenge: Performance and Expatriate Presence in the Overseas Affiliates of Japanese MNCs." Paper presented at the Academy of Management, August.

Bird, A., & Mukuda, M. 1989. "Expatriates in their Own Home: A New Twist in the Human Resource Management Strategies of Japanese MNCs." *Human Resource Management.* 28 (4): 437–453.

Bob, D., & SRI International. 1990. *Japanese Companies in American Communities.* New York: Japan Society.

Boyacigiller, N. 1990. "Staffing in a Foreign Land: A Multi-level Study of Japanese Multinationals with Operations in the United States." Paper presented at the Annual Academy of Management Conference, August.

DeNero, H. 1990. "Creating the 'Hyphenated' Corporation." *McKinsey Quarterly.* 4: 153–174.

De Witt, K. 1995. "Panel's Study Cites Job Bias for Minorities and Women." *The New York Times.* November 23, p. A16.

Dicle, U., Dicle, I. A., & Alie, R. 1988. "Human Resource Management Practices in Japanese Organizations in the United States." *Public Personnel Management.* 17 (3): 331–339.

Dowling, P., & Schuler, R. 1990. *International Dimensions of Human Resource Management.* Boston: PWS-Kent.

Gudykunst, W. B., & Nishida, T. 1994. *Bridging Japanese/North American Differences.* Thousand Oaks, CA: Sage.

Hall, E. 1976. *Beyond Culture.* New York: Doubleday.

Heenan, D. 1975. *Multinational Management of Human Resources: A Systems Approach.* Austin: University of Texas at Austin Bureau of Business Research.

Ishida, H. 1986. "Transferability of Japanese Human Resource Management Abroad." *Human Resource Management.* 25 (1): 103–120.

Jacobs, D. 1990. "Differences between U.S. Workers and Japanese Managers Wind Up in Court." *The New York Times.* September 9, sect. 3, p. 25.

Kilborn, P. 1991. "U.S. Managers Claim Job Bias by the Japanese." *The New York Times.* June 3, p. A1.

Klee, A. R. 1986. "Worker Participation in Japan: The Temporary Employee and Enterprise Unionism." *Comparative Labor Law.* 7: 365–380.

Kobrin, S. J. 1988. "Expatriate Reduction and Strategic Control in American Multinational Corporations." *Human Resource Management.* 27 (1): 63–75.

Kopp, R. 1993. *Koyo Masatsu (Employment Friction).* Tokyo: Sanno Institute of Management Press.

Kopp, R. 1994a. "International Human Resource Policies and Practices in Japanese, European, and U.S. Multinationals." *Human Resource Management Journal.* Winter: 581–599.

Kopp, R. 1994b. *The Rice-Paper Ceiling.* Berkeley: Stone Bridge Press.

Kopp, R. 1995. "Careers and Ambition." *Japan Related*. March/April: 8–15.

Lifson, T. 1992. "The Managerial Integration of Japanese Business in America." In Kumon, S., and Rosovsky, H. (eds.), *The Political Economy of Japan*. Vol. 3. Palo Alto: Stanford University Press. 231–266.

Negandhi, A. 1979. *Quest for Survival and Growth: A Comparative Study of American, European, and Japanese Multinationals*. New York: Praeger.

Neuliep, J., and Hazleton, V., Jr. 1985. "A Cross-Cultural Comparison of Japanese and American Persuasive Strategy Selection." *International Journal of Intercultural Relations*. 9: 389–403.

Nihon Zaigai Kigyo Kyokai (Japanese Overseas Enterprises Organization). 1989. *Kokusaika Yoin Ikusei Kenkyu Iinkai Hokokusho (Report of the Committee on Development of Human Resources for Internationalization)*. Tokyo: Nihon Zaigai Kigyo Kyokai.

Nishida, H. 1992. "Beikoku Funin Shain ni Hitsuyo na Kyoiku to wa, Kami (Necessary education for employees sent to the U.S., part 1)." *Jinzai Kyoiku*. August: 10–13.

Ondrack, D. 1985. "International Transfers of Managers in North American and European MNEs." *Journal of International Business Studies*. 16 (3): 1–19.

Ouchi, W. G. 1979. "A Conceptual Framework for the Design of Organizational Control Mechanisms." *Management Science*. 25 (9): 833–848.

Ouchi, W. G. 1981. *Theory Z*. Reading, MA: Addison-Wesley.

Perlmutter, H., & Heenan, D. 1974. "How Multinational Should Your Top Managers Be?" *Harvard Business Review*. November–December: 121–132.

Perlmutter, H., & Heenan, D. 1979. *Multinational Organization Development*. Reading, MA: Addison-Wesley.

Pucik, V., Hanada, M., & Fifield, G. 1989. *Management Culture and the Effectiveness of Local Executives in Japanese-Owned U.S. Corporations*. Ann Arbor: University of Michigan and Egon Zehnder.

Schlesinger, J. & Kanabayashi, M. 1992. "Many Japanese Find Their 'Lifetime' Jobs Can Be Short-Lived." *Wall Street Journal*. 8 October, p. A1.

Shiraki, M. 1995. *A Comparative Analysis of the Human Resource Development and Management of Multinational Corporations in Indonesia with Reference to Industrialization*. Kokushikan University (mimeograph).

Sueda, K., & Wiseman, R. 1992. "Embarrassment Remediation in Japan and the United States." *International Journal of Intercultural Relations*. 16: 159–173.

Sugawara, Y. 1993. *Silence and Avoidance: Japanese Expatriate Adjustment — Summary of the Results of a Thesis Project*. California State University, San Bernadino (mimeograph).

Thompson, M. 1989. "Japan Inc. on Trial." *California Lawyer*. May: 43–46.

Trevor, M. 1983. *Japan's Reluctant Multinationals: Japanese Management at Home and Abroad*. New York: St. Martin's Press.

Tung, R. 1982. "Selection and Training Procedures of U.S., European, and Japanese Multinationals." *California Management Review*. 25 (1): 57–71.

Tung, R. 1988. *The New Expatriates: Managing Human Resources Abroad*. Cambridge, MA: Ballinger.

White, M. 1988. *The Japanese Overseas: Can They Go Home Again?* New York: Free Press.

Yoshihara, H. 1995. "Management Localization and Performance of Overseas Japanese Companies." *Association of Japanese Business Studies Best Papers Proceedings, Eighth Annual Meeting*. June 2–4. Ann Arbor, Michigan. 145–156.

Yoshino, M. Y. 1976. *Japan's Multinational Enterprises*. Cambridge, MA: Harvard University Press.

The Wyatt Company. 1990. *A Report on the Survey of Human Resource Management in Japanese-Owned Companies in the United States*. Washington, DC: The Wyatt Company.

PART III

TRANSPLANTING AND TRANSFORMING HUMAN RESOURCE MANAGEMENT

Philosophies, Policies, and Practices
at the Subsidiary Level

7

SULLY TAYLOR

National Origin and the Development of Organizational Capabilities

The Case of International Human Resource Management in Two Japanese MNCs

In the last few years, the competitive landscape for multinational firms (MNCs) has changed enormously. Due to changes in transportation systems, communication, and government policies, there is increasing equalization of access to input resources, whether material, financial, or technological (Bartlett & Ghoshal, 1989; Ohmae, 1995; Pfeffer, 1994). This equalization has led to a reassessment of the distinctive features that enable a particular firm to compete globally (Bartlett & Ghoshal, 1990; Ohmae, 1995; Pfeffer, 1994). At the same time, MNCs cannot retreat to home markets. They are increasingly forced to compete globally due to economies of scale, strategic moves of competitors, and actions of governments (Porter, 1986; Prahalad & Doz, 1987). There is as a result an interesting paradox: just as MNCs are being inexorably forced to increase their global activities in order to remain competitive, the ability of an individual firm to differentiate itself from another is being worn away through the equalization of access to the resources on which they rely. Inevitably, what distinguishes the competitiveness of one MNC from another is its internal resources to outmaneuver its competitors. Organizational resources are becoming the keystone of what makes a MNC competitive (Pfeffer, 1994).

One key resource receiving increasing attention is organizational capabilities. Briefly, an organizational capability is a firm's ability to use its resources to achieve its ends. In this chapter, I first define and differentiate organizational capabilities from the strategic resources that serve as inputs to the corporation and then consider the organizational capabilities needed for knowledge-intensive MNCs today. In order to study the development of these organizational capabilities within MNCs, and the influence of national origin, I examine the Spanish affiliates of two Japanese MNCs (JMNCs) from the same moderately high knowledge-intensive industry. I suggest that while firms from a particular country, in this case Japan, face similar institutional forces, they have developed different levels of the organizational capabilities required to effectively use their resources in international competition. After reviewing the methodology used to collect data on the organizational capabilities in each affiliate, I present the results of the study and offer implications of this research in the concluding section.

Firm Resources and Capabilities

The importance of firm resources has received increased attention with the advent of the resource-based theory of the firm (Barney, 1986, 1991; Rumelt, 1984; Wernerfelt, 1984), which emphasizes the management of the internal environment of the firm as a key to competitiveness, rather than focusing only on the external environment. The internal resources of the firm are crucial in this view and are defined as "the fixed, firm-specific input factors of production" (Nanda, 1992: 12). Firm resources that are capable of distinguishing one MNC (or any firm) from another and give it a competitive advantage over other firms in the global economy are termed strategic resources and have several features. They must be inimitable (Barney, 1986, 1991; Grant, 1991), rare (Barney, 1986, 1991; Hamel & Prahalad, 1990), immobile (Barney, 1986, 1991; Grant, 1991; Peteraf, 1993) and nonsubstitutable (Barney, 1986; Grant, 1991). The differences in firm strategic resources lead to differences in sustainable competitive advantage (Black & Boal, 1994).

Drawing on prior writing in this area, I group strategic resources into two categories: strategic input resources and organizational capabilities (Henderson & Cockburn, 1994). Strategic input resources are the knowledge and skills or technical systems (Leonard-Barton, 1992; Teece, Pisano & Shuen, 1992), resources (Amit & Schoemaker, 1993), and other assets that are the inputs that can lead to increased efficiency and hence competitive advantage for the firm. For example, the tacit knowledge developed by skilled engineers with a particular production process can be a strategic input resource (Leonard-Barton, 1992). The second category is organizational capability, which has recently been defined as "the socially complex routines that determine the efficiency with which firms physically transform inputs into outputs" (Collis, 1994). Some theorists have argued that organizational capabilities are the ultimate source of competitive advantage (e.g., Hamel & Prahalad, 1990; Ulrich & Lake, 1990). Essentially, organizational capability is the ability of a firm to utilize its strategic input resources, often drawing on several simultaneously, in order to achieve a desired outcome. It is an implementation resource, which includes the ability to "deploy the firm's resources and to develop new ones (Henderson & Cockburn, 1994: 65). In short, organizational capabilities are essentially enabling mechanisms or characteristics that can help give a firm a competitive advantage but that have value only if the firm possesses strategic input resources. As with any resource, firm history may lead to heterogeneity in the development of these organizational capabilities (Bartlett & Ghoshal, 1989; Nelson & Winter, 1982).

This discussion points to a crucial question: what are the *organizational capabilities* required for knowledge-intensive MNCs to be effective in the global economy today? In order to answer this question, I first look at the overall organizational task that faces these MNCs. I turn in the following section to a consideration of these questions.

Organizational Tasks and Capabilities Required for International Competition in Knowledge-Intensive MNCs

The key organizational task required of all knowledge-intensive MNCs today is to use its internal resources to generate and utilize knowledge that can provide them a competitive advantage over competitors (Hamel & Prahalad, 1994). While knowledge creation by itself does not lead to a competitive advantage—after all, it could be the wrong knowledge, or the firm may not possess the complementary assets to utilize the knowledge well (Teece, 1986)—an MNC that lacks knowledge that distinguishes it from its competitors is not likely to survive. I define knowledge here as an intangible good such as process technology, research results, or knowledge of customers that can enhance a firm's ability to compete. Of course, knowledge is itself a strategic input resource.

Because knowledge is created by people, two keys to knowledge creation and utilization in the MNC are its managerial systems and its expertise in managing the firm's human resources (Pfeffer, 1994). The tasks of generating and using knowledge have predictable implications for the organizational capabilities that must exist in the MNC. As Henderson and Cockburn's (1994) study of the knowledge-intensive pharmaceutical industry shows, a firm must have the ability to "access new knowledge from outside the boundaries of the organization and the ability to integrate knowledge flexibly across . . . and within the organization" (Henderson & Cockburn, 1994: 66). Thus, *knowledge access* and *integration* are key, overarching organizational capabilities required of the human resource management (HRM) system of the knowledge-intensive MNC.

This overarching organizational capability can be used in conjunction with prior research in international management to elaborate a set of four organizational capabilities and to logically derive ways they can be manifested. Each of these four organizational capabilities fits under the umbrella of knowledge access and integration and appears in turn in the following discussion.

To access knowledge, the MNC, through its international HRM system, must be able to tap into human resources who have the ability to create this knowledge, regardless of nationality or location. I call this first organizational capability *dispersion of creativity*. In other words, foreign subsidiaries must have human capital slack in order to produce high levels of knowledge or innovation (Bartlett & Ghoshal, 1988). Without the dispersion of creativity within the organization, learning becomes centralized (Bartlett & Ghoshal, 1990). However, any MNC that relies only on the talent at headquarters or on its expatriates to create knowledge is denying itself access to the increasingly capable human resources that exist throughout many countries (Bartlett & Yoshihara, 1992) and access to "pockets of innovation" throughout the world (Hakanson, 1990: 261). For example, as chapter 10 notes, there is a shortage of researchers in life sciences in Japan, particularly in biotechnology, while the United States and other Western countries have strength in this labor market, leading Japanese firms in that industry to invest in the West. Additionally, because the overwhelming majority of MNCs are headquartered in developed and thus expensive countries, the cost of relying only on home country talent results in higher than necessary expenses. For example, Western software firms are increasingly taking advantage of the large pool of software engineers in India, which the local market cannot absorb, by setting up software development centers there. Thus, a critical component of this organizational capability is the ability to hire well-qualified people, throughout the units of the MNC, who are capable of producing valuable knowledge for the firm.

A second organizational capability required in order to access and integrate knowledge is the creation of *knowledge transfer mechanisms among the network*. The creation of knowledge in multinational firms necessitates use of the output of as many of the knowledge creators within the firm as possible, regardless of their geographical location or level in the organization (Bartlett & Ghoshal, 1990; Hamel & Prahalad, 1994; Hedlund & Rolander, 1990; White & Poynter, 1990). An American MNC, for example, that ignores the contributions of the research personnel in its European subsidiaries will lose the opportunity to garner the fruits of their research projects, even if these apparently have only local applications (cf. Bartlett & Ghoshal, 1990: 221–22). In order to take full advantage of all the knowledge created within the MNC's system, transfer mechanisms must exist that permit the diffusion of knowledge to occur, which in turn lead to efficiencies for the MNC. With this creation of a high density of linkages between units, it is "no longer necessary to establish a comprehensive range of resources in each market because exchange linkages can now be established across borders, without the need for complementary facilities on a location-by-location basis" (Ghoshal & Bartlett, 1990: 613–14). For example, "Dow's information system facilitates the sourcing process . . . by making relevant information widely available. Managers everywhere within Dow can access detailed cost, revenue, and profit data for any product category in any geographic area" (White & Poynter, 1990: 103–4).

Yet even if transfer mechanisms are put in place, they will not function well unless there is *dispersed authority to utilize the transfer mechanisms*. As Bartlett and Ghoshal found, "[S]ubsidiaries with low levels of local autonomy neither created nor diffused innovations" (1988: 370). This dispersal of authority to utilize the transfer mechanisms is the autonomy of knowledge creators to communicate with those members of the MNC's units that can best utilize their locally created expertise. This third organizational capability of dispersed authority enables the knowledge creators to spread their knowledge to the unit(s) within the MNC that will most readily benefit from it (Hamel & Prahalad, 1994; Kogut, 1990; White & Poynter, 1990), often leading to "complex interlinkages" between affiliates (Bartlett & Ghoshal, 1990: 223). While certainly headquarters' personnel usually have a wider perspective on the MNC and understanding of what individual units and unit members are doing, to rely solely on centralized authority for the use of the transfer mechanisms will of necessity underutilize the firm's internal resources. White and Poynter (1990) call this organizational capability of dispersed authority "horizontal organization," and underscore the need for managers to be able to access information anywhere it exists within the firm as one way of overcoming the cognitive limitations of organizational members.

A final organizational capability necessary to ensure utilization of knowledge within MNCs is *top management recognition of and respect for expertise* created in units outside the home country (Bartlett & Yoshihara, 1992; Hakanson, 1990). This enables the MNC to be flexible in the assignment of strategic missions to affiliates (Doz, Prahalad, & Hamel,

1990). From a knowledge access and transfer perspective, there are two reasons why this flexibility is necessary. First, as the MNC hires increasingly talented individuals to staff overseas affiliates, the capability of the affiliate to carry out organizational tasks changes. The ability to recognize and change the strategic mission of the affiliate thus becomes an important competitive ability. For example, Intel recognized that a procurement system development project team in Israel had a high concentration of the knowledge and skills Intel needed. The local educational environment had endowed those team members with those crucial capabilities. As a consequence, a greater role for the Israeli affiliate in the project was developed, even though this necessitated greater travel for both the team coordinator and several team members.

Second, as the affiliate's local environment changes, the role of the affiliate must adapt. For example, the maquiladora plants of MNCs in Mexico, placed there before the advent of the North American Free Trade Agreement (NAFTA), could acquire a larger strategic role to serve the Mexican market as the local economy develops. MNCs that ignore the potential new roles their overseas affiliates acquire run the risk of ignoring a possible venue for utilization of the MNC's knowledge. In the case of Hewlett-Packard (H-P), for example, the ability of the Singapore affiliate to design products for the Japanese and other Asian markets was recognized and developed as the growth potential of those markets increased (Harvard Business School, 1993). Based on this recognition, H-P changed the mandate of the Singapore affiliate and initiated the required transfer of knowledge from U.S. design centers to Singapore.

Based on this analysis of the main organizational capabilities required in knowledge access and integration in knowledge-intensive MNCs, it is possible to examine the degree to which an individual firm has developed them. As resource-based theory suggests, not all MNCs have developed equal levels of these organizational capabilities. While multiple factors lead to differences in levels of organizational capabilities, one major influence that has been suggested is the administrative heritage of the MNC (Bartlett & Ghoshal, 1989), which is defined as an organization's "configuration of assets and capabilities, built up over the decades; its distribution of managerial responsibilities and influence, which cannot be shifted quickly; and an ongoing set of relationships that endure long after any structural change" (Bartlett & Ghoshal, 1989: 33). One key aspect of administrative heritage is the national origin of the firm. Bartlett and Yoshihara (1992) in fact suggest that Japanese firms in particular may have limited ability to develop the organizational capabilities required for competing internationally today. To examine the degree to which national origin of the MNC in fact affects the ability of the MNC to develop the needed organizational capabilities, this chapter studies the Spanish affiliates of two JMNCs. I examined the international HRM (or IHRM) system itself.

The next section provides a brief description of the methodology used in this study and an overview of the two affiliates used as the basis of this study.

Methodology

The information in this section is based on a study of the affiliates of two moderately knowledge-intensive JMNCs in Spain conducted during summer 1992. These two affiliates were chosen from a larger study of five Japanese affiliates due to their striking similarities along crucial dimensions. In each affiliate, semistructured interviews were conducted with members of top management. In affiliate 1, the HRM director of the production plant, the director of training and development in the sales division, and the affiliate's public relations director—all Spanish—were interviewed. In affiliate 2, the HRM director of the production plant, who was Spanish, and the managing director of the plant, who was Japanese, were interviewed together. Later, a separate, informal interview was conducted with this same production plant HRM director. All interviews were conducted in Spanish by the interviewer, who is fluent in the language, and recorded for later transcription. In addition, the interviewer took extensive notes during the interviews.

Each interview lasted between 45 minutes and 2 hours. In addition to gathering information about the start-up of the affiliate and data about its present operations, the questions focused on the HRM system of the affiliate and on the IHRM system of the firm, as well as some questions on performance indicators. All except the performance indicators are described in detail in the results section.

Table 7.1 provides basic data concerning the operations of the two affiliates. Both affiliates began operation in 1973 in Spain, neither as a greenfield. Due to legal restrictions at the time, both firms were compelled to set up operations by going into partnership with local Spanish firms or by acquiring an existing firm. Due to the increasing economic integration of the European countries, the operations of both affiliates were changing from supplying the Spanish market with a full range of products to specializing in a few products for the European market, leaving the other products they sell to be supplied by other affiliates within the European network of affiliates.

TABLE 7.1 Descriptive Statistics of the Two Affiliates

	Affiliate 1	Affiliate 2
Year of founding in Spain	1973	1973
Manner of founding	Licensing agreement	Acquired existing firm
Present ownership structure	Bought out licensee; now 100% owned	Acquired; 100% owned
Products	Consumer electronics	Consumer electronics and consumer durables
Functions	Assembly, manufacturing, distribution, development, sales, applied research	Assembly, manufacturing, sales, applied research, service, development
Number of employees	1,400	620
Gender of employees	50% women; 50% men	35% women; 65% men
Average age of employees	28	29
Number of expatriates	15	13
Strategic role	Moving from serving the Spanish market to specialized producer within company's European system of affiliates	Moving from serving the Spanish market to specialized producer within company's European system of affiliates

The similarities between the two affiliates on a number of other dimensions are striking. Both operate in the consumer electronics field, although affiliate 2 also produces consumer durable goods. Indeed, in conversations with managers at both affiliates it became clear that they consider each other to be their principal rival within Spain. Both have operations in the industrialized Cataluna area of northeast Spain, although both have placed their manufacturing plants outside of the provincial capital of Barcelona. While affiliate 1 is considerably larger than affiliate 2, both have similar ratios of males to females in their workforces and almost identical average employee ages.

The Organizational Capability of Dispersion of Creativity

The organizational capability of dispersion of creativity relies first and foremost on the ability of the MNC to hire well-qualified people to staff overseas affiliates, for reasons already described. Thus, one predictor of this organizational capability would be the hiring of local staff with highly developed job skills. There are two additional elements of dispersion of creativity that could logically be expected. One is the ability of the MNC to use expatriates sparingly. This, in a way the opposite of hiring well-qualified people to staff the overseas affiliates, does not always occur. In some MNCs expatriates continue to dominate the management and technical levels of the affiliates even after highly qualified people have been hired, due to either their utilization as control mechanisms or because the entire MNC staffing system has not been reexamined. A final element of dispersion of creativity is the independent action in job tasks of the skilled personnel hired in the overseas affiliates. They are more likely to produce knowledge valuable to the firm if they are allowed to put their skills to use solving firm problems, rather than being tightly controlled by headquarters. I examine each of these elements of dispersion of creativity.

Staffing quality.   For HRM knowledge to be created throughout the units of a MNC, well-qualified people must be hired and placed in positions of authority. In the study, staffing quality differences were examined for HRM director position. In affiliate 1, the HRM director had an extensive and impressive background in HRM in a variety of large, successful Spanish firms. Two years previously, in his early forties, he had come to the Japanese firm after serving as the director of personnel in a Spanish firm. In addition, he had an advanced degree in labor relations from a Spanish university. As a side note, the director of training and development at affiliate 1 was also highly educated and had extensive experience in other firms. In contrast, the HRM director of affiliate 2 had little experience in other firms, having joined the company before he was thirty, and had received almost all his training in HRM within the Japanese company itself, after being hired. He had no advanced degree in industrial relations. In short, the staffing quality for HRM seems lower in affiliate 2 than in affiliate 1, which, it should be noted, confirms my findings at overseas affiliates of the same companies in other parts of the world. The greater education and diverse experience of the HRM personnel in affiliate 1 give it an edge over affiliate 2.

It should be noted that the role of the affiliate (Gupta & Govindajaran, 1991) may be an influence on the type of personnel needed for a particular site, and thus the lower skill levels of the HRM director in affiliate 2 may suggest that the affiliate itself is fulfilling a different role within its MNC's network than affiliate 1 is fulfilling within its network. However, given the similarity of strategic tasks that the two affiliates seemed to have (see table 7.1), this does not seem to be a likely rationale for the lower skill quality of the HRM director of affiliate 2.

Use of expatriates.   In the use of expatriates, affiliate 2, with less than half the number of employees, had almost the same number (13) of expatriate managers as affiliate 1 (15). Moreover, affiliate 1 had expatriate managers in only two of its top management positions (head of the affiliate and head of sales) while affiliate 2 had seven. Interestingly, affiliate 1 had a third country manager who, after working at the head office in Japan for several years, had been posted to the Spanish affiliate. In affiliate 1, the plant HRM director stated that the expatriate managers, most of whom were in technical areas, were the affiliate's "windows on Japan" with regard to technology, and he did not foresee the total number declining appreciably in the future because of this technology transfer function. In contrast, the HRM director at affiliate 2 reported that the company was in fact making a push to reduce the number of expatriates overseas, which according to him was due to the expense and the reluctance of young Japanese to serve abroad. He felt the reduction process would take a great deal of time, however. In both affiliates, the reported average time for an expatriate to stay in Spain was five years.

In short, as would be expected, affiliate 2 has not emphasized the hiring of highly skilled local people (at least in the HRM area) and consequently has not reduced the number of expatriates. Given the high cost of retaining expatriates overseas (Black, Gregersen, & Mendenhall, 1994), likely over time the MNC to which affiliate 2 belongs will experience greater costs than the parent company of affiliate 1.

Independence of action.   The ability of an affiliate to create knowledge is influenced by the degree to which knowledge creators within the affiliate have the ability to act on their own insights and utilize their skills (Bartlett & Ghoshal, 1988). Obviously, the MNC would wish to allow for this independence only if it had in place highly skilled and capable people in its affiliates. Yet this independence of action gives the affiliate the ability of "not only implementing the company's strategy, but also of making important contributions to it" (Bartlett & Yoshihara, 1992: 291). One indicator of the degree to which the affiliate has developed independence of action is the way in which the HRM approach in the affiliate was created. A second indicator is the job autonomy of the HRM director, the key knowledge creator in this area. This study asked questions about the degree of similarity of the HRM system to that of the parent company and the Spanish competitors and about the origin of the HRM system. The results appear in the following sections.

Similarity of HRM system to parent company's.   A key issue was to determine the degree to which the affiliate's HRM policies are similar to those in use at the parent company, given as item 1 in the appendix. As can be seen, affiliate 1 saw absolutely no similarity between the HRM policies and practices it used and those utilized by the company in Japan, for either blue- or white-collar employees. Affiliate 2, on the other hand, perceived that the HRM policies it used bore moderate to significant similarity to those used by the parent company. The least similarity was found for blue-collar employees, notably in the areas of compensation, training, job rotation, and career development, although even in these areas the respondents thought there was some similarity.

Similarity to Spanish competitors.   The perceptions of the respondents regarding the similarity to Spanish competitors can be seen in their answers to a question regarding the similarity of specific HRM practices to those in use in Spanish firms. Their answers are given in item 2 of the appendix. For both affiliates, the hiring of new employees seems to be closest to the practice of Spanish firms. For almost all the practices, however, affiliate 1 sees itself as quite distinct from Spanish companies, while affiliate 2 sees itself as differing from Spanish companies but not greatly so. It should be noted that the plant HRM director at affiliate 2 said that any deviation from Spanish companies was in a "positive" direction, that is, was an improvement over local practice, except in the area of compensation. He indicated that, relative to that of local companies, the bonus and benefit system left something to be desired. In affiliate 1, the plant HRM director mentioned that he felt that the affiliate differed completely from Spanish companies in several areas in particular: work autonomy, horizontal job rotation, and social activities.

Origin of HRM approach.   In order to determine how the HRM approach of the affiliate was actually created, the HRM directors were asked to indicate the source and degree of influence on their HRM systems of the following: parent company's HRM policies, Spanish competitors' HRM policies, Japanese competitors' HRM policies, and local Spanish labor law. Degree of influence was measured on a 5-point scale, with 5 the strongest influence. A comparison of the answers of the two affiliates reveals some strong differences in source and degree of influence, as item 3 in the appendix shows.

While both affiliates see the influence of local Spanish law as approximately the same, the influence of parent company HRM policies is very different. Affiliate 1 perceives a moderate influence on its policies from the parent company, while affiliate 2 sees very strong influence of the parent company policies on its own. Affiliate 1 also appears to have learned from Spanish competitors, while affiliate 2 perceives no influence from this source. Neither affiliate indicated any significant influence from other Japanese affiliates operating in Spain and equal amounts of influence from local labor laws.

Thus, while the actual resulting HRM approaches may not differ a great deal, as indicated by the responses to item 4, the source of the HRM policies is in fact very different between the affiliates. Evidently, affiliate 1 borrowed moderately from both the parent company and from other Spanish firms, while affiliate 2 borrowed only, and heavily, from the parent company. The differences regarding the source of their HRM "template" (see chapter 12) does not in itself have performance implications for the MNC. The differences do indicate, however, the degree to which knowledge creators within each affiliate have independence of action, and thus indicates possible differences between the MNCs in access to knowledge.

Other data gathered during the interviews provide further insight into the origins of HRM systems at the affiliates. In affiliate 1, the two respondents from the HRM department were asked how they had learned about the parent company's overall approach to HRM. In neither case had they received any training at the company's headquarters in HRM, nor at the affiliate itself. Asked whether there was an overall philosophical approach to HRM within the company, both the plant HRM manager and the head of training and development answered an unequivocal "yes." Yet, asked how he had learned the philosophy, the head of training and development stated that it was simply "in the air," a pervasive knowledge of the corporate values and norms that infused the HRM system and that should be used to inform HRM design decisions. Even when pressed, however, he could not say how he had learned the underlying philosophy.

In affiliate 2, on the other hand, the transfer of HRM competence from the parent company to the affiliate was overt and systematic. The HRM director had been sent to Japan twice. The first time was for a three-week orientation given to all new affiliate HRM directors. The second time, seven years later, was for a month-long study of the HRM policies and practices and see "how they could be applied to Spain." While studying HRM at the plant in Japan, he was asked several times if he intended to stay with the company for a long time. If not, according to his report, the Japanese managers told him that the conversation would end right there, and no further information about HRM would be shared. The clear intention of the parent company to transfer the HRM philosophy to the affiliate was further illustrated in later written communications with the HRM director, who wrote:

> In principle, the same [HRM] strategy is applied here as in Japan, but always taking into account the different characteristics and laws between Japan and Spain. So, basing it [our approach to HRM] on the policies of Japan, it is adapted to the culture, situation, customs, etc., of Spain, but always following the designated objectives and trying to maximize the similarity to the original. (my translation)

Job autonomy.   Some indirect indicators of the job autonomy of the managers at these two affiliates were gathered. In affiliate 2, I interviewed the head of the plant and the plant HRM director together. The interview lasted over two hours, but in spite of many other pressing matters the managing director must have had, he remained throughout the interview. In contrast, I never met any of the Japanese managers at affiliate 1. After the initial brief correspondence with the Japanese managing director to set up the visit to the plant, all contact concerning the visit was made through a Spanish manager. A brief meeting for me and the managing director had been set up, but an emergency trip to the regional headquarters took him out of the office the day of the visit. Thus, the entire visit was planned and conducted by Spanish HRM managers within the affiliate.

In short, affiliate 1 demonstrates more characteristics of independence of action, an element of dispersion of creativity, than does affiliate 2. The high quality of its HRM staff, less reliance on expensive expatriates and thus the inclusion of greater diversity of views through use of locals, less centralized control of the HRM system itself, and the greater autonomy of the HRM director all indicate that affiliate 1 has substantially greater capability to create knowledge than does affiliate 2. This in turn increases the knowledge "pool" available for access by the MNC. Organizational capability may not create a competitive advantage for the MNC in and of itself, but in combination with other resources it may.

The Organizational Capability
of KnowledgeTransfer Mechanisms

A resource such as knowledge is useful to a knowledge-intensive MNC only to the degree that those who can best utilize the knowledge within the firm are privy to it. Consequently, a key organizational capability that MNCs must have in place to compete effectively is an established network of knowledge transfer mechanisms (Bartlett & Ghoshal, 1988). Through such mechanisms knowledge created in one unit can be dispersed to those parts of the system that can capitalize on its creation.

A question concerning transfer mechanisms was asked of the interviewees. Specifically, they were asked to describe the ways and the degree to which the HRM policies and practices developed at the affiliate were shared with either the parent company or with other overseas affiliates of the firm.

In affiliate 1, the plant HRM director said that no sharing of HRM policies and practices developed in Spain were shared with the head office, although he thought that they should be. The difficulty, according to this interviewee, is that Japanese workers are significantly different from Spanish workers. The Japanese were characterized as like "soldiers." Spanish workers, on the other hand, have to be persuaded. As a result, HRM policies effective for Spain may not apply easily in Japan, although some might particularly apply given changes in the work attitudes of younger Japanese. In affiliate 2, the plant HRM director simply gave an emphatic "no" to the question of whether HRM policies and practices developed in Spain were shared with headquarters.

The most striking difference between the two affiliates was in the area of sharing HRM expertise with other affiliates. Both affiliates send their directors to biannual meetings of the HRM directors of the European affiliates. Moreover, both HRM directors work on subcommittees looking at specific HRM issues, such as developing a recruiting pamphlet. The difference, however, was in the way in which these meetings are organized. The company to which affiliate 1 belongs does not organize the meetings. Rather, they are instigated by the HRM directors themselves. Occasionally someone from the Tokyo personnel department attends the meetings, mostly to observe. In fact, as a consequence of these meetings, the HRM directors of the European affiliates had recently developed a plan for job rotation of a select group of managers between the affiliates within Europe, in the hope of increasing the promotion possibilities of all their managerial talent, and had begun talking to the U.S. affiliate with the idea of eventually including rotations to the United States. Queried as to whether the head office was involved in developing this plan, the plant HRM director said "no," although they now knew about it. The European affiliates had not informed them yet of the idea of including the United States, however.

The regional meetings of the HRM directors attended by the HRM director of affiliate 2, on the other hand, are always organized from Tokyo by the vice president of HRM of the entire company. Workshops in different areas of HRM are provided, and the HRM directors are free to chose among them. One of the purposes of the meetings is to exchange ideas with the HRM directors of the other European affiliates on how they have adapted the parent company's HRM philosophy and practices to their local environments. The HRM director of affiliate 2 also participates in subcommittees on particular areas of HRM. The participation of different affiliates in these subcommittees is coordinated by the head office HRM department.

In short, while both affiliates reported that transfer mechanisms such as regional meetings exist in order to transfer HRM expertise throughout the system, both the amount and the direction of knowledge flow differed significantly between the two, with affiliate 2 experiencing less lateral use of transfer mechanisms, as well as fewer transfer mechanisms in general. Again, while the existence of transfer mechanisms is not in and of itself a competitive advantage, it can be a key organizational capability in knowledge-intensive MNCs, where integration of knowledge across and within the organization is of paramount importance.

The Organizational Capability of Dispersing the Authority to Transfer Knowledge

In the previous section we saw some evidence that the ability of knowledge creators within the affiliates to utilize the transfer mechanisms differs considerably between the two affiliates. While the HRM managers in affiliate 1 are initiating unilateral contact with other affiliates concerning HRM issues and policies, the transfer mechanisms are highly controlled either by headquarters or an expatriate in affiliate 2. To test more concretely the degree to which knowledge creators have access to use transfer mechanisms based on their own judgment, the study examined the number of independent contacts the non-Japanese managers at the affiliates have with counterparts in headquarters. To the degree that managers have direct access to knowledge users and creators in Tokyo, they will increase the dispersion of the knowledge created within the firm.

As can be seen in item 5 of the appendix, the two affiliates have similar frequencies of communication between the affiliate and the head office in Japan. What is distinctly different, however, is that at affiliate 1 both the Japanese top management and the Spanish HRM director have almost equal frequency of communication with Japan, using the same means of communication, whereas in affiliate 2 there is a clear distinction between the Japanese and Spanish managers with regard to communication with Japan. Clearly, affiliate 1 has established a norm in which affiliate managers can independently utilize the avenues to transfer knowledge within the firm, without having to go through an expatriate posted to the affiliate. This is an indication, although limited, that there is greater dispersal of authority to utilize transfer mechanisms in affiliate 1 than in affiliate 2.

The Organizational Capability of Top Management Respect for Expertise

As mentioned previously, the ability to change the role of an affiliate is important to the successful utilization of the knowledge created within the MNC, and this is based on respect of managers in the parent firm for expertise in its foreign affiliates. Those firms that cannot change the tasks of their foreign units will not be able to respond to changes in strategic capabilities and strategic requirements of the local environment.

In order for the affiliate's role to be flexible, top management in the MNC must be able to respect the expertise developed in units not located in the parent country (Bartlett & Yoshihara, 1992). To explore this issue, I asked interviewees at both affiliates to describe the degree to which top management, both Japanese and Spanish, saw the HRM expertise of the parent company as central to competitiveness (see item 6 in the appendix). While interviewees at both affiliates reported that the firm saw HRM policies and practices as sources of competitive advantage, the average of the six questions for affiliate 2 (4.5) was higher than at affiliate 1 (3.5), although the small numbers of respondents makes meaningful statistical comparison of this difference impossible. In short, affiliate 1 appears to have greater openness to sources of competitive advantage not originating with the parent company. This openness would allow top management of the MNC of affiliate 1 to make changes in the strategic roles of affiliates with greater ease than could the top management of the MNC of affiliate 2.

A caution should be inserted here, however. It may simply be that HRM is not seen as a source of competitive advantage at all by local Spanish managers, indicated by their responses to the fourth question in item 6. Moreover, it must be pointed out that both of these affiliates had changed strategic roles rather recently, as described in the first part of the results section, which indicates that there may be somewhat less difference between the two affiliates in this organizational capability than in the other three organizational capabilities.

Discussion

The purpose of this chapter was to explore whether the development of four organizational capabilities that are important for knowledge-intensive MNCs is primarily determined by the national origin of the firm. Examining in depth the existence of these organizational capabilities at the Spanish affiliates of two JMNCs in the same industry has provided a tentative answer to this question—and the answer is no.

The results of this study indicate that Japanese firms are developing the organizational capabilities needed by knowledge-intensive MNCs at differing rates. In affiliate 1, there is a great degree of decentralization in the design of its HRM system, indicating that the affiliate has become a center of knowledge creation. The resultant HRM policies are seen as distinctly those of the affiliate, although not in conflict with those of the parent firm or other affiliates because of the subtle infusion of parent company HRM philosophy. The affiliate has developed a cadre of highly skilled HRM managerial personnel with extensive experience in other companies and given them the autonomy to act on their own, including developing contacts with counterparts at the parent company headquarters. And finally, the top management of the firm is perceived as less ethnocentric in its belief in the superiority of the parent company's expertise, a key ingredient to building the requisite respect for the knowledge in the affiliate organizations.

The parent company of affiliate 2 does not seem to have made as many of the assumed needed changes. The affiliate's HRM system is highly controlled from the center, and deviations from parent company HRM philosophy and policies are grudging concessions to local imperatives. Given this control, it is not surprising that the plant HRM director had little HRM expertise developed independently of the firm and is in fact more an "implementor." The mechanisms for sharing HRM developments among the European affiliates are also highly controlled from the center, and the purpose is clearly to ensure as much consistency as possible with parent company practices. Given this, it is not surprising that the parent company top management's belief in the superiority of the HRM system is quite high.

An important question that arises is whether the differences in organizational capabilities between the two affiliates makes any difference with regard to affiliate or MNC performance. Although the study did in fact gather some data on the affiliates' performance, the differences were small, indicating that affiliate 2 was having trouble meeting performance goals. Both affiliates, however, were facing the beginning of the economic recession that began in 1992 in Spain. Given this larger environmental factor in performance, as well as the fact that only one organizational type of knowledge—HRM expertise—was examined, it is probably not surprising that larger differences in performance were not discovered.

However, if the development of the organizational capabilities studied in this research are indeed key skills for knowledge-intensive MNCS competing in the global environment of the late twentieth century, as research and theory suggest, then the accumulated impact of the differences in organizational capabilities found in only two affiliates could be substantial at a wider network level (Ghoshal & Bartlett, 1990). That is, whereas the performance of an individual affiliate may not differ substantially from that of the affiliate of another MNC operating in the same country, the small differences summed across the entire MNC's operations may have significant impacts on the MNC's overall competitiveness, particularly over time. Future research must address this issue by examining organizational capabilities across the entire network of a MNC and study longitudinal influences.

Several other findings from this study should be highlighted. One is the apparent lack of differences between the two affiliates with regard to strategic role flexibility. Even though affiliate 1 appears to receive greater respect for its HRM competence than does affiliate 2, as noted, both affiliates had undergone a substantial change in strategic roles fairly recently. An interesting question that emerges from this is whether the process of strategic role change was similar between the two firms. That is, did affiliate 1's role flexibility emerge from a consensus between top management and affiliate management based on respect for the latter's evolving capabilities, while affiliate 2's change was a unilateral decision imposed from central headquarters? If so, what difference does it make? These are purely speculative questions, but ones that should be added to future research on the organization capability of flexible affiliate roles.

A surprising finding is that while the HRM director at affiliate 1 saw no similarity between the HRM policies at the affiliate and those at the parent company, he also did not see any real similarity with Spanish companies. In most discussions of integration and localization, the trade-off is usually seen as between adapting the practices at the center or those locally (Bartlett & Ghoshal, 1989; Rosenzweig & Nohria, 1994; Rosenzweig & Singh, 1991). In fact the choice could be not between integration and localization, but rather between integration and nonintegration. National organizations may in fact develop organizational processes that, while borrowing from or using information from both the parent company and local firms, are distinctly their own. This is parallel to the open hybrid model of organizational learning discussed in chapter 12.

As mentioned before, the limitation of this research is that it is based on a detailed examination of only two affiliates of JMNCs. Obviously, no firm conclusions concerning the differing abilities of JMNCs to develop organizational capabilities can be drawn from such a small sample. At the same time, the consistency of the pictures of each of the affiliates that emerges from the results across all the measures is impressive and leads to the implication that there are indeed significant differences in the pace at which JMNCs are developing the organizational capabilities they will need in the future. Because of the possible enormity of these implications for the future viability of both the firms involved in this study, as well as for other MNCs, this area deserves a great deal more research attention to substantiate the tentative conclusions of this study and to probe further into the causes of the differences in the speed with which these companies are changing.

Appendix

Item 1

Please use the scale below to indicate how similar the following human resource management functions are between your affiliate and the Japanese parent company. Please write in the answer that best fits your answer for each function. If you don't know, please leave a blank.

0	1	2	3	4	5
Not applicable/ function doesn't exist at the affiliate	Not at all	Somewhat similar	Fairly similar	Mostly the same	Exactly the same

_1,3__Blue Collar employee selection   _1,3__Managerial employee selection
_1,2__Blue Collar employee training   _1,3__Managerial employee training
_1,2__Blue Collar employee compens.   _1,2__Managerial employee compens.
_1,3__Blue Collar employee promotion   _1,3__Managerial employee promotion
_1,2__Blue Collar employee career dev.   _1,3__Managerial employee career dev.
_1,2__Blue Collar employee appraisal   _1,3__Managerial employee appraisal
_1,2__Blue Collar employee job rotation   _1,1__Managerial employee job rotation

Note: the first number in each space is the response given by affiliate 1, while the second number is that given by affiliate 2.

Item 2

Please indicate how similar your company is to Spanish-owned companies on the following items.

0	1	2	3	4	5
Don't Know	Exactly the Same				Completely Different

Work environment   (3,2)

Way employees are hired   (1,2)

The type of compensation system   (3,1)

Amount of training   (4,2)

Type of training   (2,2)

Type of work   (4,1)

The way supervisors manage   (3,2)

Promotion opportunities   (3,3)

The pay level   (3,2)

The way job performance is evaluated   (3,2)

Work organization   (3,1)

Way of getting along with the other employees   (4,2)

The social activities   (2,2)

In both cases the answers were with references to white-collar employees.

Item 3

Factors influencing business unit's HRM policies and practices: Below are a list of factors we believe might influence a business unit's HRM policies and practices. On a scale from 1 to 5 using the scale below, indicate how much impact each factor has.

1	2	3	4	5
Very little influence		Some influence		Very great influence

Factors:

Parent company's HRM policies	_____2,5_____
Spanish competitors' HRM policies	_____3,1_____
Japanese competitors' HRM policies	_____0,1_____
Spanish government regulations	_____3,3_____

Item 4

HRM practices: Companies can adopt different HRM strategies. For each item below, please circle the number which most closely corresponds to the philosophy at your company.

a. The staffing processes of this company focus on:

Filling vacancies by promotion from within the firm.	A combination of filling vacancies through internal and external.	Filling vacancies by hiring from the external labor labor market.
1 2 3	4 5	6 7

(4,1)

b. Hiring decisions in this company are based primarily on:

Personality fit between the company culture and the hiree.	A combination of personality fit and job-relevant skills, knowledge, and abilities.	Job-relevant skills, knowledge, and abilities.
1 2 3	4 5	6 7

(4,4)

c. In terms of training at this company:

Employees are not expected to enter the firm with the skills necessary to perform their job, but are trained after they are hired.	Employees are expected to have some of the skills necessary to perform their job and are encouraged to get the skills they need.	Employees are expected to enter the firm with all of the skills necessary to perform their job.
1 2 3	4 5	6 7

(4,3)

d. Skill and knowledge development of employees at this company is:

Valued, and support and guidance are provided by the company.	Valued, but not provided by the company.	Not valued, and not provided by the company.
1 2 3	4 5	6 7

(2,3)

e. The appraisal system at this company focuses primarily on:

Job performance.	A combination of job performance and other factors which contribute to the employee's total contribution to the company.	Factors which contribute to the employee's total contribution to the company.
1 2 3	4 5	6 7

(4,5)

f. The compensation system at this company focuses primarily on:

Short-term job performance.	A combination of short-term job performance and the employee's long-term contribution to the company.	The employee's long-term contribution.
1 2 3	4 5	6 7

(3,5)

Item 5

For each of the four modes of communication listed below, please indicate the frequency of communication between yourself and executives from the headquarters of the parent corporation using the scale below. Do the same for communication between Japanese managers in the affiliate and executives from the headquarters of the parent corporation.

	Daily	3–4 times a week	1–2 times a week	3–4 times a month	1–2 times a month	once every 2 months	once every 6 months	once a year	less than once a year
Face to face communication							O	X	x
Over the telephone communication	O,o		X		x				
Routine and periodic formal reports					X,O,o				x
Electronic or paper-based letters or memos	X,O,o	x							

O = top Japanese executives at affiliate 1; o = plant HRM director at affiliate 1
X = top Japanese executives at affiliate 2; x = plant HRM director at affiliate 2

Item 6

Please use the scale below to indicate how much you agree or disagree with the following statements about human resource management practices and policies in your company. Human resource management (HRM) policies and practices refer to the ways in which your company recruits, hires, promotes, pays, trains, and develops its employees. Please circle the number of the appropriate response for each question. If you don't know, please leave a blank.

1	2	3	4	5
Strongly Disagree				Strongly Agree

The Japanese managers in this company believe that the HRM policies and practices of the parent company are better than those used by other firms.   (3,5)

The Japanese managers in this company believe that the HRM policies and practices of the parent company give it a competitive advantage over other competitors.   (4,4)

Japanese managers at this affiliate believe that the HRM policies and practices of this company are a key to its success.   (4,5)

Spanish managers at this affiliate believe that the HRM policies and practices of this company are a key to its success.   (3,4)

Japanese managers at this affiliate believe that Japanese-style HRM policies and practices are better than those used by local firms.   (3,5)

Spanish managers at this affiliate believe that Japanese-style HRM policies and practices are better than those used by local firms.   (4,5)

References

Amit, R., & Schoemaker, P. 1993. "Strategic Assets and Organizational Rent." *Strategic Management Journal.* 14 (1): 33–46.

Barney, J. B. 1986. "Types of Competition and the Theory of Strategy: Toward an Integrative Framework." *Academy of Management Review.* 11: 791–800.

Barney, J. B. 1991. "Firm Resources and Sustained Competitive Advantage." *Journal of Management.* 17 (1): 99–120.

Bartlett, C., & Ghoshal, S. 1988. "Creation, Adoption, and Diffusion of Innovations by Subsidiaries of Multinational Corporations." *Journal of International Business Studies.* 19 (3): 365–388.

Bartlett, C., & Ghoshal, S. 1989. *Managing Across Borders.* Boston: Harvard Business School Press.

Bartlett, C., & Ghoshal, S. 1990. "Managing Innovation in the Transnational Corporation." In Bartlett, C., Doz, Y., & Hedlund, G. (eds.), *Managing the Global Firm.* London: Routledge. 215–255.

Bartlett, C., & Yoshihara, H. 1992. "New Challenges for Japanese Multinationals: Is Organization Adaptation their Achilles Heel?" In Pucik, V., Tichy, N., & Barnett, C. (eds.), *Globalizing Management: Creating and Leading the Competitive Organization.* New York: John Wiley & Sons. 276–299.

Black, J., & Boal, K. 1994. "Strategic Resources: Traits, Configurations and Paths to Sustainable Competitive Advantage." *Strategic Management Journal.* 15: 131–148.

Black, S., Gregersen, H., & Mendenhall, M. 1992. *Global Assignments.* San Francisco: Jossey-Bass.

Collis, D. 1994. "How Valuable are Organizational Capabilities?" *Strategic Management Journal.* 15: 143–152.

Doz, Y., Prahalad, C.K., & Hamel, G. 1990. "Control, Change, and Flexibility: the Dilemma of Transnational Collaboration." In Bartlett, C., Doz, Y., & Hedlund, G. (eds.), *Managing the Global Firm.* London: Routledge. 117–143.

Ghoshal, S., & Bartlett, C. 1990. "The Multinational Corporation as an Interorganizational Network." *Academy of Management Review.* 15 (4): 603–625.

Grant, R. M. 1991. "The Resource-Based Theory of Competitive Advantage: Implications for Strategy Formulation." *California Management Review.* 1991 (Spring): 114–135.

Gupta, A., & Govindajaran, V. 1991. "Knowledge Flows and the Structure of Control Within Multinational Corporations." *Academy of Management Review.* 13: 287–301.

Hakanson, L. 1990. "International Decentralization of R&D—the Organizational Challenges." In Bartlett, C., Doz, Y., & Hedlund, G. (eds.), *Managing the Global Firm.* London: Routledge. 256–278.

Hamel, G., & Prahalad, C. 1990. "The Core Competence of the Corporation." *Harvard Business Review.* May-June: 79–91.

Hamel, G., & Prahalad, C. 1994. *Competing for the Future.* Boston: Harvard Business School Press.

Harvard Business School. 1993. "Hewlett-Packard: Singapore (A)." Case # 9-694-035.

Hedlund, G., & Rolander, D. 1990. "Action in Heterarchies: New Approaches to Managing the MNC." In Bartlett, C., Doz, Y., & Hedlund, G. (eds.), *Managing the Global Firm.* London: Routledge. 15–46.

Henderson, R., & Cockburn, I. 1994. "Measuring Competence? Exploring Firm Effects in Pharmaceutical Research." *Strategic Management Journal.* 15: 63–84.

Kogut, B. 1990. "International Sequential Advantages and Network Flexibility." In Bartlett, C., Doz, Y., and Hedlund, G. (eds.), *Managing the Global Firm.* 47–68.

Leonard-Barton, D. 1992. "Core Capabilities and Core Rigidities: A Paradox in Managing New Product Development." *Strategic Management Journal.* 13 (Summer Special Issue): 111–126.

Nanda, A. 1992. "Resources, Capabilities and Competencies." Boston: Harvard Business School, working paper.

Nelson, R., & Winter, S. 1982. *An Evolutionary Theory of Economic Change*. Cambridge, MA: Harvard University Press.

Ohmae, K. 1995. *The End of the Nation State: The Rise of Regional Economics*. New York: Free Press.

Peteraf, M. A. 1993. "The Cornerstone of Competitive Advantage: A Resource-Based View." *Strategic Management Journal*. 14: 179–191.

Pfeffer, J. 1994. *Competitive Advantage Through People*. Boston: Harvard Business School Press.

Porter, M. E. 1986. "Competition in Global Industries: A Conceptual Framework." In Porter, M. E. (ed.), *Competition in Global Industries*. Boston: Harvard Business School Press. 15–60.

Prahalad, C., & Doz, Y. 1987. *The Multinational Mission: Balancing Local Demands and Global Vision*. New York: Free Press.

Rosenzweig, P. M. & Nohria, N. 1994. "Influences on Human Resource Management Practices in Multinational Corporations." *Journal of International Business Studies*. 25 (2): 229–251.

Rosenzweig, P. M., & Singh, J. V. 1991. "Organizational Environments and the Multinational Enterprise." *Academy of Management Review*. 16 (2): 340–361.

Rumelt, R. P. 1984. "Towards a Strategic Theory of the Firm." In Lamb, R. B. (ed.), *Competitive Strategic Management*. Englewood Cliffs, NJ: Prentice-Hall.

Teece, D. 1986. "Profiting from Technological Innovation." *Research Policy*. 15: 285–305.

Teece, D., Pisano, G., & Shuen, A. 1992. "Dynamic Capabilities and Strategic Management." Haas School of Business, University of California, Berkeley.

Ulrich, D., & Lake, D. 1990. *Organizational Capability: Competing from the Inside Out*. New York: John Wiley & Sons.

Wernerfelt, B. 1984. "A Resource-Based View of the Firm." *Strategic Management Journal*. 5: 171–180.

White, R. E., & Poynter, T. A. 1990. "Organizing for World-Wide Advantage." In Bartlett, C., Doz, Y., & Hedlund, G. (eds.), *Managing the Global Firm*. London: Routledge. 95–116.

8

MARTIN KENNEY, JAIRO ROMERO,
OSCAR CONTRERAS, & MAURICIO BUSTOS

Labor-Management Relations in the Japanese Consumer Electronics Maquiladoras

Introduction

In the last 15 years Japanese manufacturers have expanded their global manufacturing operations, establishing production facilities in both developed and developing countries. In the last decade Japanese manufacturing management techniques have been hailed as global best practice by firms in Europe and North America (Womack, Jones, & Roos, 1990). In the developing countries Japanese manufacturing investments have been eagerly sought not only for their employment impacts, but also in hope that the host country could improve its capabilities by learning advanced production organization and industrial relations techniques. The largest developing-country recipients of Japanese investment have been in East Asia. Since 1982 Mexico has been the largest non-Asian developing-country recipient of Japanese investment (Kenney & Florida, 1994). The spearhead for this investment has been the electronics industry and related parts makers (Szekely, 1991). In the last 15 years nearly all of the major Japanese consumer electronics firms have opened production facilities known as maquiladoras, which are factories licensed to produce duty-free if all products are exported (Kenney & Florida, 1994; Sklair, 1989; Szekely, 1991).

Some developing countries have seen foreign investment as a vehicle for the transfer of global best practice manufacturing techniques. They assume that by working in foreign manufacturing facilities indigenous workers and managers are experiencing and learning advanced production technology. The premise is that the tax income and workers' wages should not be the sole benefit of foreign manufacturing investment. The potential for personnel from the developing country to learn is seen as crucial benefit.[1] If one accepts this perspective, then the entire investment process can be interpreted in a new light. For the host country, foreign investment is not a mere mechanism to garner foreign currency. Rather, the foreign manufacturing facilities are reconceptualized as resource institutions that allow the host country to exchange inexpensive labor for an opportunity to learn and to upgrade national capabilities. From this perspective, successful learning can transform the host country's entrance in the global economy.

This chapter combines the results of two separate studies of the transfer of the Japanese management and production system to the Mexican maquiladoras. The first study, reported on in Kenney and Florida (1994), gathered information from Japanese managers on the transfer of Japanese practices to their Mexican maquiladoras. The second study used personal interviews with workers to obtain data on the industrial relations in the Japanese consumer electronics maquiladoras. The purpose of both studies was to understand the extent of the transference of Japanese labor-management relations to the maquiladoras. The data reported here are unique in that one study was conducted with Japanese managers (with the exception of one American manager) and the other study was confined to the Mexican production workers.

The chapter begins with a stylized outline of the Japanese management system.[2] The second section describes the maquiladoras and outlines the dimensions of Japanese investment in them. The third section summarizes the previous research on the transfer of Japanese management techniques to the maquiladoras. The fourth section describes the two studies reported on in this chapter, and the fifth section examines the general characteristics of the worker's study. Then the sixth section presents the results of the studies and discusses the transfer of the Japanese industrial relations system to the maquiladoras on dimensions such as suggestions, teamwork, work evaluation, work satisfaction, training, quality control, and management's treatment of nonmanagerial employees. Finally, the conclusion summarizes the results, remarks on the degree of transfer, and affirms that the transfer process remains limited.

The Japanese Management and Production System

In the postwar period, Japanese industry developed a management and production system that was significantly different from that of the United States (Aoki, 1988; Dore, 1986; Fruin, 1992; Kenney and Florida, 1988, 1993). The most salient characteristic is that the Japanese factory is not merely a site for the production of physical products. More significant, the factory also generates knowledge about producing; that is, it is reflexive and reflective on its own praxis. It is thereby able to evolve to ever higher levels of productivity as it produces. In the process, the individual in the factory and the factory as a social system learn skills and add capabilities (Fruin, 1997).

The fundamental tenets of the Japanese industrial system are the enterprise unions, long-term employment, and seniority-based wages. These basic features mean that the role of workers in production developed quite differently than in the other countries of the Organization for Economic Cooperation and Development. Whereas Western firms have treated the individual as the fundamental organizing unit, Japanese firms emphasized the team as the organizing unit for production (Fruin, 1992). In this way Japanese firms deliberately and consciously harnessed the social to managerial goals.

The Western distinction between blue-collar and white-collar employees is blurred in Japanese firms. Though clearly there are white-collar and blue-collar tracks, there are no immutable barriers against internal promotion between these two classes of employees. The more prominent distinction is between the long-term regular employees and the other employees such as temporaries or subcontractors who work on the factory premises. Because workers are employed by the firm for their entire career and cannot be easily terminated, they resemble what economists call a fixed cost. This different context and organization meant that the logic of investment in workers was strikingly different. In Japanese firms this changed the economic calculus for managers, and training became an investment to be amortized over the employee's career (Koike, 1988).

Within the Japanese firm training occurs on a number of different dimensions. One of the most distinctive methods of training is job rotation, a system by which team members are trained in all or most of the jobs undertaken by the team (Cole, 1989, 1979). Off-the-job training includes teaching workers to do the routine cleaning and preventive machine maintenance. There are also significant off-the-job training programs aimed at upgrading workers by providing new skills. This constant learning provides the context for the emphasis on the workers' role in spearheading the continuous improvement and quality control activities (Cole, 1989).

The Japanese production system also has a number of other distinguishing features. For example, in Japan workers wear uniforms, sing company songs, work in open offices, do prework exercises, and participate in various company functions. In this chapter we are mainly interested in the factory floor level of management because this is the locus of activity in the Japanese maquiladoras.

Research on the Transferability of the Japanese Production Management System

The history of research regarding the transferability of the Japanese system production system to foreign countries is now well into its second decade (see chapter 2). Until recently, most research examined the transfer of Japanese management to developed economies. The literature indicates that transference varies by firm and industry. With reference to the United States, the general conclusion is that the most thorough transfer has occurred in the traditional heavy industries such as autos, auto parts, steel, and tire industries (Florida & Kenney, 1991, 1992; Shimada and MacDuffie, 1987), whereas in electronics assembly the transfer has been less complete (Abo et al., 1994; Kenney & Florida, 1993). While some research on Japanese management systems in Europe has been less industry-specific than in the United States, the most important exceptions here are the studies on the Nissan plant in the United Kingdom (Garrahan and Stewart, 1992; Wickens, 1987). Also, Oliver and Wilkinson (1988), based for the most part on studies of Japanese consumer electronics factories in Wales, found significant evidence of successful transfer.

The transfer process has not been complete and, in most cases, enterprise unionism, long-term employment, and seniority wages have not been transferred. However, in the automotive industry some functional analogues of these features can be found in the U.S. transplants (Kenney & Florida, 1993). Moreover, it is often, as chapter 3 shows, a negotiated process. Team-oriented production, emphasis on quality production, and the other "functional" features of the Japanese production system have experienced far more widespread transfer in the U.S. context. Finally, the more culturally laden aspects of the Japanese system, such as singing the company songs or mandatory exercises, have not been transferred. The single exception is that most Japanese companies retained the requirement that all plant employees wear a uniform. To explain the transfer process, Beechler and Yang (1994) developed a set of factors hypothesized to affect the transfer of Japanese-style human resource management (HRM) practices to overseas subsidiaries. Their particular formulation framed in the HRM perspective did not consider industry-specific factors as significant.

Until recently, there have been fewer studies of the transfer of the Japanese system to developing countries. The largest body of work relates to the adoption of the Japanese production system in subsidiaries in Southeast Asia. In the only global study using quantitative measures, Abo et al. (1994) found that the transfer to Southeast Asia was approximately equivalent to the transfer to the United States. Koike and Inoki (1990) studied the skill formation systems of Japanese subsidiaries in Southeast Asia and found little evidence that the Japanese skill formation practices had been transferred. This was somewhat contradicted by Kawabe (1991) and Beechler (1990), who found that in Malaysia a hybrid of local and Japanese management styles was developing.

The evidence for the transfer of the Japanese system to motor vehicle production in the United States is substantial. In the electronics sector the evidence is less convincing, however. Recently there may be more effort to transfer the Japanese system to countries such as Malaysia, because the subsidiaries are exporting consumer electronics products to Japan (Hiramoto, 1995). The Mexican case study is interesting because Mexico's insertion in the international division of labor of Japanese electronics firms is quite similar to that of Malaysia. Many of the firms and products are identical. Thus, comparing the results in this chapter with those of studies of other developing countries should be quite productive as firm and industrial process effects are controlled. This provides an almost laboratory-like setting for comparing the impacts of environment on industrial relations systems.

The Japanese Consumer Electronics Industry and the Maquiladora Program

Mexico established the maquiladora program in 1965 to provide employment for a rapidly growing population and to improve Mexico's foreign exchange balance (Sklair, 1989). By the 1980s the maquiladoras had become the most dynamic sector of the Mexican economy and provided more foreign exchange than any Mexican industry except petroleum (Alonzo, Carrillo, & Contreras, 1995). From the Mexican perspective the maquiladora program can be said to have accomplished its initial goals.

The total number of maquiladoras is now in excess of 2,000, with a total employment of more than 500,000 (Alonzo et al., 1995). Japanese investment is still relatively small. In 1991 there were only 107 Japanese maquiladoras employing approximately 25,000 Mexicans (Kenney & Florida, 1994). Though Japanese plants constitute only 5% of all maquiladoras, many are large and are operated by global-class companies such as Hitachi, JVC, Matsushita, Sanyo, Canon, Pioneer, Casio, and Sony. Moreover, the number of Japanese firms operating maquiladoras has been increasing rapidly. In 1991 there were 20 Japanese electronics component suppliers in Baja, California. By 1995 the total had risen to approximately 40 consumer electronics assemblers and parts suppliers. Moreover, most of these companies are expanding and having affiliated firms relocate to Mexico. So, for example, Matsushita Electric has been joined by Kyushu Matsushita and Matsushita Industrial Components.

In 1995 the pace of investment accelerated. For example, Matsushita announced the termination of television assembly in Chicago and the transfer of all production to Tijuana. Matsushita also decided to move its North American television headquarters and television R & D to neighboring San Diego, California. In 1995, JVC opened a television assembly facility in Tijuana. This leads most observers to believe that Japanese investment in Mexico will continue to grow (see, for example, Piturro, 1995).

The Japanese firms were initially attracted to North America because of increasing competition in the U.S. market and the rising value of the yen. Investment in maquiladoras has occurred in a number of industrial segments, but Japanese investments are concentrated in consumer electronics and electronics parts sectors. More recently, the passage of the North American Free Trade Agreement, with its North American content requirements for televisions, and further increases in the value of the yen convinced many more Japanese firms and, especially, parts suppliers to relocate production to North America. The low labor costs Mexico provides are crucial for ensuring that Japanese producers can remain competitive against increasingly severe competition from Korean and Taiwanese firms.

Mexico's most significant advantage is inexpensive labor. In 1994 (before the most recent 50% devaluation) the average wage a production worker received was approximately $1.60 per hour (including benefits). A worker discharging similar tasks in the United States or Canada would receive in excess of $6.00 per hour. The $1.60 per hour wage contrasts with Shaiken's (1990: 92) estimate that in 1987 entry-level wages were $.87 per hour. Most observers believe that wages in Tijuana will increase at 10% per annum. Of course, the recent devaluation of the peso decreased wages in dollar terms by 50%, making Mexican labor costs even more attractive.

Nearly all Mexican plants along the border are nonunionized. The lack of unionization means that Tijuana is an excellent case study for transfer because union resistance does not affect the transfer process. The lack of unions is appreciated by Japanese managers. For example, the Japanese manager of an electronics supplier suggested that Mexico was a good alternative to U.S. unions and problems of U.S. labor-management relations. The president of a Japanese electronics component supplier described it: "In the United States, there are union problems, and some other kinds of problems. I have no experience with these but according to some data and some people with experience they are always fighting against unions and lawyers. Small enterprises cannot cope with it."

Given the current situation, even more Japanese electronics firms likely will continue to invest in Tijuana and Baja, California. If this growth continues, there is a possibility for Mexico to share in the rapid growth that has characterized Southeast Asia. Tijuana is an interesting case study of a non-Asian developing country site with an Asian firm–dominated electronics manufacturing center.

Previous Research on Industrial Relations in the Maquiladoras

Much has been written regarding industrial relations and manufacturing techniques in the maquiladoras (see Alonzo et al., 1995, for a review). The initial studies undertaken in the early 1980s described the maquiladoras as dimly lit sweatshops (Carrillo & Hernandez, 1985; Fernandez-Kelly, 1983). Recent studies have found that the electronics maquiladoras have a quite different work environment than that described in earlier studies (Gonzalez-Arechiga & Ramirez, 1992; Pelayo-Martinez, 1992; Wilson, 1992). In an overview article Gereffi (1994) held that the older "sweatshop" view of the maquiladoras was not applicable to the new modern plants operated by the multinational corporations and using sophisticated new production techniques and labor-management relations.

The "new" maquiladora position is reinforced by the work of Shaiken (1990; Shaiken & Browne, 1991), who concluded on the basis of interviews at three Japanese-operated electronics maquiladoras that advanced manufacturing techniques such as just-in-time (JIT), *kaizen*, and job rotation characterize production in the Japanese electronics maquiladoras. This conclusion is confirmed by other scholars studying the Japanese maquiladoras (Echeverri-Carroll, 1988). In this view Japanese firms are actively implementing their production system in the maquiladoras, and by implication the management system is being transferred to Mexico.

The optimistic reports of the transfer of Japanese management techniques and organization to Mexico have been challenged. For example, research conducted by Kenney and Florida (1994) found less evidence of the transfer of Japanese management techniques. Using the quantitative framework developed by Abo et al. (1994), Kamiyama (1994) concluded that the "transfer of the Japanese production system to maquiladoras has had some success." This evaluation is less positive, if the actual categories used for reaching such a conclusion are examined. The maquiladoras resemble the management system in Japan in wage-setting and promotion, where management is powerful in both Japan and Mexico. In the important areas of worker responsibility for maintenance and quality, Kamiyama's scores are quite low. In critical activities such as quality control and the worker's role in machine maintenance and routine repair, practices in Mexico differ substantially from those in Japan. Also, small-group activities are nearly nonexistent and training is limited. The greatest "transfer" was in the areas where management could unilaterally impose its will because of the lack of unions on in the use of imported Japanese production equipment. The results reported by both Kamiyama (1994) and Kenney & Florida (1994) indicate only a quite limited transfer of the Japanese industrial system.

There are also a few studies of Japanese maquiladoras by HRM scholars. Comparing the management styles of U.S., Japanese, and Korean maquiladoras, Paik and Teagarden (1994) found that Japanese maquiladoras used a "control"-oriented HRM system. Beechler and Taylor (1995), in a comparison of Japanese and U.S. electronics maquiladoras in Tijuana, concluded that the HRM techniques practiced by the Japanese firms had hybridized with Mexican management, though the dimensions of this hybridization were not described. This literature concludes that Japanese HRM practices have been only partially transferred to Mexico.

From the perspective of the production system, the extant literature mirrors conclusions in the HRM literature in that are quite contradictory. An aspect of this disagreement is probably due to the different perspectives of these researchers. The more optimistic scholars compare the relations in the Japanese maquiladoras with those of Mexican firms, whereas the more pessimistic use relations in Japan as the referent. The results reported in this chapter provide significant new evidence for the debate about the transference of the Japanese system to Mexico.

The Characteristics of the Study

This chapter integrates the results of two separate studies of industrial relations in the maquiladoras. The first study was conducted in 1991 and extensively reported on in Kenney & Florida (1994). In this study Japanese managers from 11 maquiladoras were interviewed. The respondents were acquired through a letter sent to all the Japanese maquiladoras and then followed by a phone call seeking to schedule an interview. Also, in the case of three companies, personal connections with managers at the Japanese headquarters were used to secure the interviews. All the interviews were conducted in English and 10 of the 11 included a plant tour. A prepared interview schedule was used. However, open-ended responses were encouraged, and 10 of the 11 interviews were taped. Both personal and corporate anonymity was guaranteed to all respondents.

The second study was conducted from October through November 1993. In this study interviews were conducted in Spanish with 75 employees from eight Japanese consumer electronics and electronics component maquiladoras in Tijuana. In contrast to nearly all other studies of workers in Japanese transplants, this study did not depend on management to provide access to interview subjects. The respondents were acquired by members of our interview team, who were stationed outside the plant gate at the end of the day shift. Each subject was approached and asked to participate.[3] For those who agreed, an appointment was made for an interviewer to visit their home to conduct the interview. All interviews were conducted employing a prepared questionnaire with the opportunity for open-ended comments. The typical interview took one hour and nearly half the interviews were tape-recorded. Anonymity was given to all respondents.

The initial goal was to complete 10 interviews at 8 Japanese maquiladoras for a total of 80 interviews. Ultimately, only 75 interviews were conducted. The reason for the discrepancy was that the interview team usually arranged 13 to 15 appointments at each firm; however, for a variety of reasons not all interviews could be undertaken. The reasons for not undertaking the interviews included wrong addresses, the inability to find the domiciles of subjects because of a lack of street signs, lack of building addresses, nightfall, or the general difficulties of remaining on schedule. The houses of many respondents were on unpaved roads in the shanty towns of Tijuana. Therefore, because of the limited budget and interviewers' time, we decided that it was more important to acquire respondents from a wider sample of firms than to try to increase the respondents to 10 at each firm.

This chapter reports the results of both studies, thereby providing both a managerial and a worker perspective on industrial relations in the maquiladoras. One caveat is necessary. As table 8.1 indicates, the firms included in the manager's study were not in every case the same as those in the workers' study. Therefore, the comparability is not perfect because the studies had different research teams and funding agencies.

General Characteristics of the Mexican Respondents

The workers' sample has roughly the same socioeconomic and gender characteristics as those reported in general studies of the maquiladoras such as Carrillo et al. (1991). Among our respondents 91% worked the day shift (this is not surprising as we contacted our respondents at the end of the day shift). The gender ratio in the sample was 56% female and 44% male. This is roughly in keeping with the gender ratios reported in other studies and the overall gender ratio in the maquiladoras as calculated by the Mexican government (57.2% female and 42.8% male). The majority of the respondents (63%) were 21 years of age or younger. The average age was 21.2 years and the modal ages were 18 and 19 (16% each). The majority were single (77%) and 25.3% had children. Finally, 75% of the respondents were born in states other than Baja, California and 25% were born in Baja, California. This is an immigrant workforce.

The average weekly wage was 205.8 new pesos (NP; at the time, $59). However, one respondent who was a trainee received only 30 NP per week, which is 20 NP lower than the next lowest wage of 50 NP (when the 30 NP response is eliminated, the average is 208.1 NP). The survey indicated a significant disparity between wages for men and women. Women received an average of 175.64 NP per week and men received 245.64 NP. The nonwage benefits for regular production workers were rela-

TABLE 8.1 Japanese Maquiladoras Included in Samples

Company name	Study[a]	Number of employees	Product	Date of establishment
Matsushita	M, W	2,100	Televisions	1982
Sony	M, W	3,000	Televisions	1980
Mutsutech	M, W	100	Plastic parts	1980
Hitachi	M	1,050	Televisions	1986
Sanyo TV	W	2,000	Televisions	1982
Casio	M	300	Musical instruments	1988
Sanmex	W	270	Electric fans	1982
Canon	M	800	Typewriters	1988
SMK	W	500	Remote controls	1988
Pioneer	M	500	Speakers	1989
Arcosa	W	300	Wire harnesses	1986
Nishiba	M	170	Plastic parts	1987
KSC	W	360	Remote controls	1987
Kyowa Electric	M	110	Plastic parts	1990
Sanoh	M	65	Wire harnesses	1987
Kyocera	M	120	Ceramic parts	1987

[a]M = manager's study, W = workers' study

tively minor and varied by firm. They included combinations of the following: food coupons, on-site dispensary medical treatment, a small transportation subsidy, company-sponsored parties for Christmas and other holidays, a subsidized cafeteria, medical insurance, and paid vacations (some of these are required by Mexican law). One smaller supplier provided shower rooms, as the homes of many employees did not have running water. It also provided sports facilities and outdoor picnic tables. A number of managers cited employee parties as a significant benefit. One firm offered two weeks' paid vacation at Christmas and one week paid vacation in August, a transportation bonus, and a small weekly food bonus. Even with these benefits, this firm had the highest turnover rate of any firm interviewed. The average work week was between 45 and 48 hours. The length varied by whether the company's employees worked six 8-hour days a week or five 9-hour days a week. One firm gave its workers every other Saturday off and had an 8-hour day.

The managers reported turnover rates of between 4% and 15% per month. The average turnover rate calculated from the manager's survey was 10% per month on an annualized basis. Turnover was high at all firms, but was highest for the suppliers and newly established plants. The turnover rate fluctuates seasonally. From April to August, when students are on vacation, turnover is low (at one company, 5%). During September and October, it increases to 8% as students return to school. Then during the Christmas season, turnover increases dramatically as workers return home to central Mexico for the holidays. Often they do not return to the same factory. This problem became so severe that Sony sent buses to collect its workers in central Mexico after the New Year's holiday.

Turnover rates also vary by the number of other maquiladoras in the vicinity. The area with the largest number of plants has the greatest competition for workers. Poor public transportation and low wages effectively limit the labor market to areas close to the plant. As the labor pool in the vicinity of a particular industrial park is depleted, newer maquiladoras must locate in new industrial parks, which are in close proximity to untapped residential areas. One manager said that his plant, located outside the major concentration of maquiladoras, had lower turnover due to reduced opportunities for mobility.

The managerial explanations for the turnover rate varied greatly. One manager believed turnover rates were so high because his employees "are not used to acquiring sums of money and when they do, they leave." The president of yet another maquiladora attributed the higher turnover rates among women to the fact that the women often left to get married.

Another factor cited by one manager was that Mexican workers would switch employers for as little as 100 old pesos (three cents) an hour. Most thought benefits mattered only slightly. And yet one maquiladora cited its air-conditioned facility as a reason for relatively low turnover rates. Finally, it should be understood that not all the maquiladoras considered the turnover rate a serious problem. For example, the president of another Japanese maquiladora suggested that a viable situation was if 10% to 15% of employees stayed permanently as a stable core—the other workers were expendable.

When workers were asked their reasons for quitting, 31% answered "to look for other jobs," 19% answered "they did not like the work or the salary was too low,"

16% answered to "return to their home or leave Tijuana," and 12% answered they would "return to school." Interestingly, the belief of some managers and U.S. researchers that the high turnover rates are due to a desire to return home or to emigrate to the United States is not strongly supported. It seems that labor market turbulence is more important.

Unexcused absenteeism was also high by Japanese or U.S. standards. In most Japanese maquiladoras absenteeism was between 3%–5% per day. But this varied considerably by company. One manager said that absenteeism on Monday was 5%, while on Friday (pay day) it was essentially 0%. The companies were strict on attendance. As a general rule, either three or four days of unexcused absences were grounds for dismissal. To encourage attendance, some firms offered small bonuses for perfect attendance.

This high rate of worker turnover was reflected in the fact that the majority of our respondents had been working in their factories for less than one year (62%) and 44% had been working for less than six months. This is true in the case of both men and women, as 64% of the women and 59% of the men had been working in the plant less than one year. However, there was a difference in seniority. On average women had worked at the factory for 15 months and the men for 23 months. Curiously, even though workforce tenure was short and turnover rates were high, 75% considered their job permanent. This highly fluid labor force creates an interesting situation because the Japanese system is premised upon low turnover and absenteeism.

The high turnover was seen as a problem by most, but not all, managers because it interrupted the accumulation of knowledge and expertise in the plant. And yet this has not discouraged Japanese firms from increasing their investments in Mexico. The low wages apparently are more significant than the possibility of creating a skilled, capable labor force.

The Transfer of Industrial Relations Techniques to the Maquiladoras

The first act for any firm establishing a plant is hiring employees. In the Japanese consumer electronics transplants in the United States there is extensive screening of employment applicants (see, for example, Beechler & Yang, 1994). Actually, in Japan screening is often less rigorous because graduates are a known quantity so there is less uncertainty. One would think that screening in Mexico would be rigorous. However, only 49% of our respondents received written examination before employment. Only 36% received oral interviews. The most prevalent test was a preemployment medical examination, which was taken by 72%.

According to most workers, their previous training and skills were not important. This is in keeping with Japanese practice both in Japan and in the United States of employing recent graduates so as to be able to better socialize them into firm-specific work patterns (see, for example, Cole, 1979). Only 15% had previous work experience necessary for their current job. The young age of the average worker means that many came to the maquiladoras with little industrial experience. For 19% it was their first job and for another 30% it was only their second job.

Training and Quality Control

Because only a few workers had relevant skills upon employment, any skills involved in the work process must be acquired by training. The amount and dimensions of training provide an important insight into the degree of transfer to Mexico. Most managers said quite frankly that their firms offered only rudimentary training. For most workers training is almost exclusively accomplished on the job. The reasons for this include the unskilled nature of the work and the high turnover rate. In 1991 the president of one supplier said, "Even if we have high turnover as far as this production is concerned, it does not matter so much because the jobs do not require technical skills. It is easy to hire people and put them on the line. So, we do not have so many problems." From this manager's perspective there is little economic incentive to invest in his workers.

The workers' responses were quite similar to those of the managers. The amount of initial off-the-job training varied, but two thirds received minimal training. Upon hiring 33% received no training at all and another 33% received one day or less training. The next largest category (24%) was five days training (one work week). The actual source of training varied: 24% were trained by fellow workers and 31% by supervisors. However, the largest category (35%) was trained by others, usually the lowest supervisory person, the line assistant. Most training was received on the assembly line (53%), another 29% were trained in a special work area, and the remainder received training in both places.

For those who did receive initial training, the topics varied by firm and individual. The most frequent type of training was in task-related skills (93%). The second most frequent area of training concerned safety and cleanliness (59%), followed by quality control (57%). Much less important was plant policy (42%) and teaching workers to work in groups (22.6%). Of least importance was statistical process control (17%). Given the length of the training, it can only be cursory introductions. To create a global-class factory, continuing training is a central activity. One method of upgrading workers is to dispatch them to conferences, seminars, or classes. Some workers have been dispatched from the factory to special training programs. Though few of those interviewed went to classes, 28% said that they knew of fellow workers who had been dispatched for further training. One supervisor said, "The managers send workers out for training to Japan too, but in my case since I am third in line, the Japanese managers asked the first and the second in the hierarchy to go to training. If my supervisor is too busy to go, then he offers the opportunity to me and I go." Curiously, another respondent who had been working in the same maquiladora for 10 years said that only managers are sent to Japan for further training. It was difficult to draw any specific conclusion, but formal extrafacility training of operator-level workers and lower-rank supervisors seems quite limited.

The Japanese system emphasizes improving quality. However, understanding the necessity of producing quality products is not natural; rather it is learned. This is especially true for Mexican workers who, for the most part, have not had experience owning or producing high-quality manufactured goods. Seemingly, this should make it of even greater importance to provide quality control training to workers. However, only a few workers (13%) received quality training away from their normal work position.

The use of rotation and job changes also has an important training function. Respondents were asked how often they changed their tasks. Among our respondents, 46% never changed tasks, 10% changed tasks several times during the week, 10% changed tasks as frequently as every three weeks, 7% changed tasks every week, and 4% changed tasks every day. Cross-training and providing a broader range of experience did not appear to be a significant managerial goal. Most managers also said that they did not use rotation, although one assistant manager said that at his plant the women rotate jobs during the day. The president of another company did not practice rotation to cross-train workers but thought that they should consider it.

Rotation or job change is clearly an important training and motivational device, but it should be noted that in Japan it is only used in certain production processes. In some positions, such as a machine technician, supervisor, etc., rotation is not used as these individuals develop important job-specific skills. Similarly, in some operations such as the production of plastic injection-molded parts there are only a few tasks, so there is little opportunity for job rotation. Therefore, in both Japan and Mexico rotation is not practiced for certain jobs.

Teamwork

The organization of workers into teams is a fundamental feature of the Japanese production system. Sixty-seven percent of the respondents worked as members of groups. Though the workers are organized into groups, great care must be taken in assuming that these are the highly interactive teams similar to those described in studies of Toyota. These groups do meet regularly to discuss production issues, though the communication is almost entirely one-way. The most frequently discussed topics in group meetings are the following: quality problems (46%) and working together (22%). These work groups do not include active rotation for skill upgrading, ongoing measures to improve production, or other features that make the team such a powerful force for competitiveness. Thus, the term team means something different from its meaning in Japan. Frequently for the workers the team leader was simply the *jefe de linea* (hereafter, line chief) or the supervisor. This leads us to conclude that these work groups are quite different from the teams normally encountered in Japan.

Suggestions and Continuous Improvement

An important aspect of the Japanese system is worker involvement in providing suggestions for production improvement. Therefore, it is interesting to know whether workers were asked for suggestions for improving the work process and organization. Three categories were used: frequently, sometimes, and never. Thirty-five percent of the workers said they were asked frequently, 31% sometimes, and the remainder (34%) answered never. The fact that nearly one third was not asked at all may in part be explained by our managerial interviews. Two different managers said that workers in the "turnover zone" were not asked for suggestions because they knew little and would just confuse the operation. The workers said the majority of the suggestions they submitted related to improving product quality and improving the production process (39% and 35%, respectively). Only 7% provided suggestions on how to solve production problems and 13% provided suggestions on improving group performance.

Generally speaking, there was little evidence of the transfer of the Japanese emphasis on worker involvement in continuous improvements. One company said its Mexican employees do engage in a limited form of *kaizen,* or continuous improvement activities. One manager described his continuous improvement activities: "Each department's Mexican manager sometimes holds a meeting for *kaizen* for improvement. So, let's say the QA Department, they have a regular meeting once a week or once a month. Sometimes they set up a project for improvement. This is *kaizen.* So, yes, we are implementing *kaizen.*"

There was limited evidence of organized continuous improvement or quality control circle (QC) activities that included operators. The company mentioned before did not use QCs and believed implementation in the Mexican environment would be too difficult. Another factory had some small-group quality control activities, but these were not comparable to those in Japan. However, even these limited activities were exceptions to the rule.

There appear to be three reasons inhibiting the implementation of Japanese style continuous improvement and QC activity. First and most fundamental, the production processes used in the plants are highly routinized, thereby limiting the need for continuous improvement or QC activity. Second, the average education level (8.5 years) of the workforce is not high by Japanese standards, and most workers lack the mathematical skills to engage in activities such as statistical process control (SPC). Third, high turnover disrupts activities such as continuous improvement that depend upon workers' knowledge of a plant's operations.

An important aspect of the Japanese model is decentralizing routine quality control activities to workers. For example, 87% of the workers were responsible for checking their own work. Among the 68% of the sample working on the assembly line, 79% said that they were responsible for rejecting defective parts or parts not assembled correctly at the previous work station. This is an important finding because worker responsibility for routine quality is a fundamental component of the Japanese production system. Eighty-two percent of the workers said that they were responsible for keeping their work stations clean.

A more important gauge of the training and involvement of workers is whether they perform routine machine maintenance. Machine maintenance is an important indicator of worker training and the responsibility and the trust management has in worker competency. Here, there was less transfer. Only 33% of the respondents did any maintenance on their machines, and, of those, only 32% (11% of the entire sample) received any maintenance training.

Worker-Management Relations

The blurring of the boundary between labor and management is well documented in Japan. In the United States, especially in auto manufacturing, Japanese firms have also deemphasized the differences between blue- and white-collar workers. This Japanese practice diverges sharply from traditional Mexican management in which relations between managers and workers are extremely hierarchical. In the typical Mexican firm, the manager operates more like a patriarch. White-collar workers as a class are considered to be the significant members in the Mexican firm, while blue-collar workers are treated as distinctively inferior. To gauge these distinctions, we asked whether better treatment was given to white-collar or blue-collar workers. Fifty-six percent of the blue-collar workers believed there was a difference with white collar office workers receiving preferential treatment (but this percentage is likely far lower than it would be in a comparable Mexican-operated factory). In addition, communication between blue-collar workers and white-collar workers is limited. Generally, the workers had little interaction with the managers and 53% had no relations at all with the managers.

From the literature on maquiladoras and the general literature on Japanese labor-management relations, we expected the treatment of males and females to differ significantly. However, differential treatment on the basis of gender did not seem serious, as 72% found no differences in treatment by gender. Interestingly, this seems to contradict the president of one Japanese maquiladora, who suggested that the gender division of labor was easier to handle than in the United States because of the greater acceptance of "traditional" gender roles in Mexico. In this case the gender division of labor meant women did circuit board insertion and some of the other more repetitive jobs. Men, on the other hand, assembled cabinets, drove forklifts, and did work requiring more physical exertion. Here, the gender division of labor may have appeared as "natural."

Relations with supervisors were surprisingly positive, as 61% thought they had good relations, 28% had mediocre relations, and 11% had no relations. None of the workers said that they had bad relations with their supervisors. Worker-manager relations also were good; though 53% said they had no relations at all with the managers, another 32% said they had good relations with their managers. From the workers' responses there was no indication that the workers were being treated badly or openly oppressed. There is some evidence of promotion from the shop floor. However, the internal promotions were limited compared with both Japan and Japanese transplants in the United States. Nearly all of the supervisory (i.e., nonmanagerial) employees (78%) were recruited from the operators. The barrier between blue- and white-collar workers is not so strong at the supervisor level. However, in the Mexican environment, class is very difficult to overcome and no workers have yet become managers. One company president said the following:

> There is a line between labor and management. But, we have only two years' experience here in Tijuana. In 10 or 20 years time actually I do not know if we will still keep a line. In case of a worker who has improved so much and knows operations perfectly, and speaks perfect English and Spanish. Maybe he can be promoted to manager like in Japan.

There is a distinct hierarchy in the factories. Invariably, the president is Japanese and often alternates between the Mexican plant and an office in California. In most cases, the plant manager is also Japanese. College-educated Mexican nationals occupy the middle levels of management and are typically responsible for personnel administration and liaison with the government authorities, though a number of Mexican engineers hold operations management positions.

Some more superficial aspects of the Japanese production management system, such as the companywide use of uniforms, have been implemented in most plants. All plants required uniforms for shop floor workers. However, at two plants new recruits did not receive a uniform until after their first and third months, respectively. This served two purposes: to assist in identifying new employees and as a cost-saving measure given high labor turnover. At one plant neither the Japanese nor Mexican managers wore uniforms. At another office clerks did not wear uniforms in the office but wore a uniform plus tennis shoes for safety and cleanliness (to protect the product from dust) when they entered the factory. Interestingly, in some cases white-collar workers were not required to wear uniforms, whereas factory workers were. This status indicator is not prevalent in Japan.

All plants used open offices with the exception of private offices for the president, plant managers, and the highest-ranking Mexican staff members. At factories all personnel use the same cafeterias. In Mexico only managers can afford to drive cars to work, so there were few reserved parking spots, except for the president and visitors. It should also be noted that most of the Japanese managers commuted from San Diego to the Tijuana plant.

Work Satisfaction

The oppressiveness of work in the maquiladoras, especially those operated by Japanese firms, has been often noted (see, for example, Paik & Teagarden, 1994). To measure this, we asked about work satisfaction. Forty-seven percent felt that their job was "interesting and pleasant," 39% said that the job was "all right, but not too interesting," and 9% thought that the work was "boring and monotonous." From these results it is reasonable to conclude that workers are relatively satisfied with their work. This result stands in sharp contrast to the common perception of the maquiladoras as sweatshops populated by unhappy workers. However, it is also true that turnover and absenteeism are quite high, which could indicate that unhappy workers simply leave the firm. Therefore, those remaining might be expected to be satisfied by the fact that they are still with the company.

Conclusion

The transfer of industrial relations systems to new environments is difficult in any case. Mexico offers unique challenges for Japanese firms. From the perspective of Japanese managers, the high turnover and absenteeism rates mean only that the plant is accumulating expertise at a slow pace. Introductory training must constantly be repeated and these training investments are difficult to recoup due to rapid turnover. A minimal investment in initial training makes sense in economic terms. However, due to a lack of training, these plants are having difficulties maturing and increasing their capabilities. Here, further research should be done to examine whether Japanese firms might be concentrating their training investments on longer-term employees, whom they will promote to supervisory positions. In other words, training investments might be concentrated on the more stable employees. These experienced employees then guide the untrained new recruits. Thus, there may be a core group of workers who more resemble the regular employees in the Japanese home factories.

The results of both the worker and manager research gave little indication that the majority of the workers were expected to actively participate in upgrading production. For the most part the maquiladoras did not appear to be "knowledge works" or "learning" institutions (Fruin, 1992, 1997). Rather, a better term might be to call them "reproduction" factories; that is, the role of these factories is to accurately reproduce production processes that have been moved down the learning curve and stabilized in the Japanese knowledge works. One major piece of evidence for this is that most plants use far more quality control inspectors than in Japan.

Though we have only circumstantial evidence, there is reason to believe that Japanese firms have accepted the Mexican dichotomy between white- and blue-collar employees. Currently, the internal promotion opportunities for operators were limited to promotions to line chief or first-level supervisor. These limited upward mobility opportunities may also reinforce the pattern of high turnover.

From these two separate studies, we believe that there is a very partial transfer of the Japanese management model. These practices include uniforms, open offices for managers, and group meetings. However, the fundamentals of teamwork, high levels of training, and worker-based quality control were not prevalent. At the same time, there may be a more determined effort to implement the Japanese management system in the future as the production process becomes more complicated and competition increases.

Notes

1. There is a large literature on technology transfer to developing countries. Chapter 12 here conceptualizes the establishment of Japanese HRM systems in overseas subsidiaries as a type of learning process. More recently, learning has become a central issue in the new institutional economics (for an overview see Teece, Pisano & Shuen, 1994).

2. There is a significant debate regarding the changes the Japanese industrial relations system is undergoing due to the recent economic crisis. I continue to believe that it is too early to draw any firm conclusions regarding fundamental changes in the Japanese system.

3. One problem with acquiring respondents in this way is that often "malcontented" workers are more willing to respond. We could not control for this possibility. However, our question regarding job satisfaction indicated that dissatisfied workers were a distinct minority.

References

Abo, T. et al. 1994. *Hybrid Factories.* New York: Oxford University Press.

Alonzo, J., Carrillo, J., & Contreras, O. 1995. "Working in the Mexican Maquiladoras: Challenges of the Contemporary Industrial Transition and Its Interpretation." Unpublished mimeo, El Colegio de la Sonora.

Aoki, M. 1988. *Information, Incentives and Bargaining in the Japanese Economy.* Cambridge: Cambridge University Press.

Beechler, S. 1990. *International Management Control in Multinational Corporations: The Case of Japanese Consumer Electronics Subsidiaries in Southeast Asia.* Unpublished doctoral Dissertation, University of Michigan Business School.

Beechler, S., & Taylor, S. 1995. "The Transfer of Human Resource Management Systems Overseas." In Campbell, N., & Burton, F. (eds.), *Japanese Multinationals: Strategies and Management in the Global Kaisha.* London: Routledge. 157–185.

Beechler, S., & Zhuang Yang, J. 1994. "The Transfer of Japanese-Style Management to American Subsidiaries: Contingencies, Constraints and Competencies." *Journal of International Business Studies.* 25 (3): 467–491.

Carrillo, J., & Hernandez, A. 1985. *Mujeres Fronterizas en la Industria Maquiladora.* Mexico, SEP-CEFNOMEX.

Carrillo, J. V., et al. 1991. *Mercados de Trabajo en la Industria Maquiladora de Exportacion.* Tijuana: COLEF.

Cole, R. 1979. *Work, Mobility and Participation.* Berkeley: University of California Press.

Cole, R. 1989. *Strategies for Learning.* Berkeley: University of California Press.

Dore, R. 1986. *Flexible Rigidities.* Stanford: Stanford University Press.

Echeverri-Carroll, E. 1988. "Maquiladoras: Economic Impacts and Foreign Investment Opportunities: Japanese Maquiladoras—A Special Case." Austin: University of Texas, Bureau of Business Research, Graduate School of Business.

Fernandez-Kelly, M. P. 1983. *For We Are Sold: I and My People: Women and Industry in Mexico's Frontier.* Albany: State University Press of New York.

Florida, R., & Kenney, M. 1991. "Organizational Transplants: The Transfer of Japanese Industrial Organization to the U.S." *American Sociological Review.* 56 (3): 381–398.

Florida, R., & Kenney, M. 1992. "Restructuring in Place: Japanese Investment, Production Organization and the Restructuring of Steel." *Economic Geography.* April: 146–173.

Fruin, M. 1992. *The Japanese Enterprise System.* Oxford: Clarendon Press.

Fruin, M. 1997. *Knowledge Works.* New York: Oxford University Press.

Garrahan, P., & Stewart, P. 1992. *The Nissan Enigma.* London: Mansell Press.

Gereffi, G. 1994. "Mexico's Maquiladoras in the Context of Economic Globalization." Paper presented at the workshop on "The Maquiladoras in Mexico: Present and Future Prospects of Industrial Development," El Colegio de la Frontera Norte, Tijuana, B.C., Mexico, May 23–25.

Gonzalez-Arechiga, B., & Ramirez, J. 1992. "La Silenciosa Integracion de la Industria Baja California a la Cuenca de Pacifico." In Palacios Lara, J. J. (ed.), *La Apertura Economica de Mexico y la Cuenca del Pacifico: Perspectivas de Intercambio y Cooperacion.* Guadalajara: Universidad de Guadalajara. 169–191.

Hiramoto, A. 1995. "Overseas Japanese Plants under Global Strategies: TV Transplants in Asia." In Frenkel, S., & Harrod, J. (eds.), *Industrialization and Labor Relations: Contemporary Research in Seven Countries.* Ithaca, NY: ILR Press.

Kamiyama, K. 1994. "Comparative Study of Japanese Maquiladoras with the Plants in the United States and Asian Countries." Paper presented at the workshop on "The Maquiladoras in Mexico: Present and Future Prospects of Industrial Development," El Colegio de la Frontera Norte, Tijuana, B.C., Mexico, May 23–25.

Kawabe, N. 1991. "Problems of /and Perspectives on Japanese Management in Malaysia." In Yamashita, S. (ed.), *Transfer of Japanese Technology and Management to the ASEAN Countries.* Tokyo: University of Tokyo Press. 239–268.

Kenney, M., & Florida, R. 1988. "Beyond Mass Production: The Social Organization of Production and Innovation in Japan." *Politics and Society.* 16 (1): 126–158.

Kenney, M., & Florida, R. 1993. *Beyond Mass Production: The Japanese System and Its Transfer to the United States.* New York: Oxford University Press.

Kenney, M., & Florida, R. 1994. "Japanese Maquiladoras: Production Organization and Global Commodity Chains." *World Development.* 22 (1): 27–44.

Koike, K. 1988. *Understanding Industrial Relations in Modern Japan.* New York: St. Martin's Press.

Koike, K., & Inoki, T. 1990. *Skill Formation in Japan and Southeast Asia.* Tokyo: University of Tokyo Press.

Oliver, N., & Wilkinson, B. 1988. *The Japanization of British Industry.* Oxford: Basil Blackwell.

Paik, Y., & Teagarden, M. 1994. "Strategic Human Resource Management Approaches in the Maquiladora Industry: A Comparison of Japanese, Korean and U.S. Firms." *International Journal of Human Resource Management* 6 (3): 568–587.

Pelayo-Martinez, A. 1992. "Nuevas Tecnologias en la Industria Maquiladora de Autopartes en Ciudad Juarez: Materiales y Observaciones de Campo." Quadernos de Trabajo no. 6, Unidad de Estudios Regionales, Universidad Autonoma de Ciudad Juarez.

Piturro, M. 1995. "Asian Invasion." *Mexican Business.* July / August. www.nafta.net/mexbiz/articles/turningj.htm.

Shaiken, Harley. 1990. *Mexico in the Global Economy: High Technology and Work Organization in Export Industries.* San Diego: Center for U.S. Mexican Studies, University of California, Davis.

Shaiken, H., & Browne, H. 1991. "Japanese Work Organization in Mexico." In Szekely, G. (ed.), *Manufacturing Across Border and Oceans.* 25–50.

Shimada, H., & MacDuffie, J. P. 1987. "Industrial Relations and 'Humanware': Japanese Investments in Automobile Manufacturing in the United States." Briefing paper for the First Policy Forum, International Motor Vehicle Program, MIT.

Sklair, L. 1989. *Assembling for Development.* Boston: Unwin Hyman Inc.

Szekely, G. (ed.). 1991. *Manufacturing Across Border and Oceans.* San Diego: Center for U.S. Mexican Studies, University of California, San Diego.

Teece, D., Pisano, G., & Shuen, A. 1994. "Dynamic Capabilities and Strategic Management." Consortium on Competitiveness and Cooperation, University of California at Berkeley CCC. Working paper no. 94–9.

Wickens, P. 1987. *The Road to Nissan: Flexibility, Quality, Teamwork.* Houndmills, England: Macmillan Press.

Wilson, P. 1992. *Exports and Local Development: Mexico's New Maquiladoras.* Austin: University of Texas Press.

Womack, J., Jones, D., & Roos, D. 1990. *The Machine that Changed the World.* London: Macmillan.

9

VLADIMIR PUCIK

When Performance Does Not Matter

Human Resource Management in Japanese-Owned U.S. Affiliates

One of the themes in this book is organizational learning of Japanese MNCs (JMNCs). Another theme running though many of the chapters is the critical role of human resource management (HRM) in the globalization of Japanese firms. In this chapter I look at both of these issues by drawing on qualitative and quantitative data on management practices in Japanese affiliates operating in the United States my colleagues and I have collected over the past 20 years (Brecher & Pucik, 1979; Hatvany & Pucik, 1981; Pucik, 1993; Pucik, Hanada, & Fiefield, 1989). In this context, the chapter specifically focuses on white-collar HRM. With the data collected in a major study of management practices in the Japanese-owned affiliates in the United States (Pucik, Hanada, & Fiefield, 1989) as a base and observations from follow-up field research, I use the findings to illustrate the "Japanese" approach to globalization, the reasons why so little has changed in Japanese management overseas over the past two decades, and why so little has been "learned."

During this period Japanese direct foreign investment expanded very rapidly. From the outset, a large portion of it has gone to Japan's principal market—the United States. By the end of 1995, the volume of net Japanese investment in the United States, excluding real estate, was estimated at close to $200 billion. More than 3,000 Japanese-owned firms employ about 500,000 Americans, and there is little doubt that the number will continue to grow (Toyo Keizai, 1996). Having a job with a Japanese-owned firm is becoming a common experience for many Americans.

The rapid growth of Japanese investment in the United States has attracted a great deal of attention from the academic community as well as from the popular media, in comparison to investment from the United Kingdom, or the Netherlands, for example, which, in absolute terms is larger than investment from Japan. Much of the public interest came out of curiosity about how "Japanese management"—which by now attracted an appeal of almost mythical proportions—would fare on American soil. The study of the "transplants" has become almost an academic discipline (e.g., Fucini & Fucini, 1990; Graham, 1993; Kenney & Florida, 1993; Womack, Jones, & Roos, 1990).

Predictably, due to differences in focus, methodology, and research ideology, researchers studying transplants have not arrived at a common set of conclusions. Even more, as pointed out in chapters 2 and 7, different conclusions arose because the heterogeneity among Japanese firms in the way they approach foreign operations may be even more prevalent than previously believed. However, while a debate continues about how unique are the Japanese management methods on the factory floor, or how "genuine," or how successful are the transplants, there is no dispute that the spread of Japanese investments abroad has contributed to a major reexamination of manufacturing organization among academics and, most important, among practitioners.

The majority of observers view the work culture and organization of Japanese manufacturing transplants not uncritically but generally in a favorable light, especially in comparison with traditional approaches of the U.S. automotive firms. At the same time, it has been asserted, in particular by the media, that while Japanese-owned firms may indeed be employers of choice for many rank-and-file Americans, their record with respect to the white-collar professional and managerial organization, employment, and effectiveness is not very good (DeNero, 1990). Much of the criticism focuses on the large number of expatriates used by Japanese firms in managing their U.S. operations, the lack of autonomy delegated to local affiliates, and the resulting subordinate roles of local managers and executives, in other words, the slow pace of globalization of the human organization (Kopp, 1994). Some observers even described the inability of Japanese companies to globalize as the "Achilles Heel of Japanese Management" (Bartlett & Yoshihara, 1992).

In order to understand the globalization process inside the Japanese MNCs, my colleagues and I have studied the scope and methods of Japanese direct investment in the United States over a sustained period of time. In particular, our focus was on the organizational implications of globalization and on HRM practices with respect to the professional and managerial workforce. Since the late 1970s we have conducted more than 500 interviews with American and Japanese executives and two comprehensive in-depths surveys of management practices in Japanese-owned U.S. affiliates (Brecher and Pucik, 1978; Pucik, Hanada, & Fiefield, 1989), and we have examined globalization practices and policies in the corporate offices in Japan. The objective of this chapter is to review and summarize the overall findings of this research stream in relation to the key themes of this book: the evolution of JMNCs, transferability of their HRM practices abroad, and organizational learning.

Why Focus on Human Resource Management?

In today's global competitive environment, when the handful of proven strategic recipes is well known, the key to success is the organizational ability to execute. Regardless of their national origin, companies worldwide that aspire to compete on a global scale are embracing global integration, but at the same time they must push for local flexibility and speed. Global companies have to nurture global organizational learning by stimulating creativity, innovation, and the free flow of ideas across boundaries, but also advocate a disciplined approach to global continuous improvement. To succeed in global competition requires an open and empowered organizational climate but also a tightly focused global competitive culture (Pucik, 1997).

When organizational capability becomes the key to sustainable competitive advantage, the globally aligned mindsets, attitudes, and behaviors of employees worldwide become one of the principal factors for the successful implementation of competitive strategies. Human resource management infrastructure, systems, and practices that directly influence such "soft" organizational elements then become the critical tools for effective corporate globalization. In a global competitive environment, we would therefore expect to see a direct link between the degree of globalization in the human resource area, especially the ability of the firm to access management talent worldwide, and the company's success in the global marketplace (Pucik, 1992).

This decision to focus on human resource practices in Japanese affiliates as the lens through which to analyze the globalization process was reinforced by feedback that my colleagues and I received throughout our research. Regardless of industry sector, initial investment mode, or length of Japanese presence in the United States, most American and expatriate Japanese executives whom we spoke to cited *the need to attract and motivate high-caliber local managers and executives as the key success factor* for future performance of Japanese firms overseas, and in particular in the United States. Many of them believed that even though the management teams in place in their firms were strong, the organization lacked depth and few could identify their successors in house. This lag in global leadership development in the most important market for JMNCs was seen as a major constraint on the future ability of Japanese firms to compete.

Why is this problem so prevalent among the JMNCs? What are the specific manifestations of this issue in Japanese affiliates in the United States? Does it affect their performance, and, if so, what measures are Japanese firms taking to learn from the past and to remedy this situation?

In order to provide a framework for a detailed inquiry into human resource practices in JMNCs operating in the United States, my colleagues and I first asked a sample of American managers employed in Japanese-owned firms a number of questions that focused on specific characteristics of HRM systems in their firms (figure 9.1). The responses highlighted several common trends that provided a context for our follow-up interviews with a larger group of American and Japanese executives.

Not surprisingly, given the Japanese origins, the employment security in the affiliates was considered higher than in comparable American firms and management turnover was seen as lower. Compensation was seen as essentially meritocratic, and only a small percentage of the respondents did not agree with the statement that performance affects salary increases. However, a significant proportion of American executives complained about the lack of clarity of performance objectives and, even more important, about the quality of performance feedback they received. The linkage between performance and promotion was perceived as substantially weaker, and most American managers and executives believed that promotion chances were smaller than in comparable U.S. firms. Opportunities for horizontal mobility were perceived as relatively high, again in line with what one expects in a Japanese organization. However, contrary to the image of Japanese companies as investing heavily

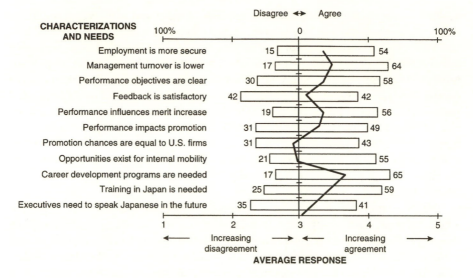

FIGURE 9.1 Human Resource Practices in Japanese MNCs

in training and development, nearly two thirds of executives were not satisfied with the amount of training provided. A large group of executives even advocated more training in Japan, including learning the Japanese language that many perceived as necessary for local executives in Japanese-owned firms to master in the future.

Building on these initial observations, we proceeded to explore a number of these issues from a more detailed perspective, using a variety of methodologies to collect data: a case study approach—a large number of interviews within a single organization—to understand intraorganizational differences, replication of cases across industries to observe interorganizational variations, and a broad cross-sectional sampling of interviews complementing our 1989 study to validate and anchor our findings. In addition, valuable insights were obtained during management training workshops conducted with JMNCs in the United States as well as in Japan.

For the purpose of this chapter, I have organized observations along a traditional human resource framework: focusing on specific human resource activities and functions—from recruitment and selection to rewards and careers. I then proceed to examine the question to what extent there is a relationship between human resource practices and corporate performance, as background to conclusions about the patterns of organizational learning as JMNCs attempt to globalize.

Recruiting Local Executives: "A Bricklayer for a Mason, a Mason for an Architect"

Recruiting high-caliber local executives is often seen as the first essential step for any MNC attempting to establish local presence in new markets. Japanese MNCs should not be an exception, and similar sentiments regarding the need to attract capable local managers are often voiced by at least some Japanese top executives. The view is, however, far from unanimous. Some Japanese executives told us, in essence, that such efforts may not be worth the trouble and that a having a localized top management group may not be a strategic imperative for success in the U.S. market, especially given the difficulties some Japanese firms experienced with their American executives—in and outside of Hollywood. They assume that, if need be, deficiencies in the quality of the local team can be remedied by a heavier reliance on Japanese expatriates. Observed a senior American executive, "To many of my Japanese colleagues, 'globalization' implies placing the best people in the best jobs in the world. And to them, Japanese are the best."

In fact, up to the early 1990s, most Japanese companies operating in the United States had faced few difficulties in recruiting competent American senior executives or middle managers. The ease of recruitment and retention was due to the strong competitive position of Japanese firms, the turmoil in the U.S. labor markets from the wave of acquisitions and restructuring by major U.S. firms, and the perceived long-term growth prospects for the Japanese affiliates. The employment security in Japanese-owned firms was considered high and management turnover was low. As their U.S. competitors have reduced their staffs, many of these managers joined Japanese companies and provided the backbone for growth and expansion. However, whether the American management talent will continue to be available now in the depth and breadth required, after the Japanese "miracle" has faded, is an untested question.

What kind of local executives would a typical Japanese firm hire?

In contrast with American MNCs in Japan who are willing to pay a premium for a Japanese executive with previous experience with a foreign company, most Japanese firms in the United States generally do not look for executives with a Japan-related background, although a number of firms are experimenting with recruitment strategies that emphasize a candidate's broad interest in Japan at the lower levels of the organization. Such programs generally involve posting to Japan for an extended period of time. In this respect, one seasoned American executive commented in our 1989 study: "Recruitment of people with little insight into Japan and Japanese companies poses no problem. However, if they have been in other Japanese firms before, they know that we are more of the same. They know that opportunities for professional development are limited." Often, the problem is developing executives and bringing people up through the subsidiary. In the words of an American Human Resource manager, "It is in the middle management that we had a lot of failures. They don't understand a Japanese company or culture and they get so frustrated that they leave before they learn. Unfortunately, we don't learn from that. We blame the person. We say that they don't fit, it's not the organization."

In the interviews with local as well as Japanese executives, three personality traits were consistently identified as essential for a local manager's success within a Japanese-owned firm: "aggressive patience," flexibility, and commitment to teamwork. Many newly hired U.S. managers often reported initial difficulties with the slow pace of decision making in many of the Japanese affiliates—without patience it may be difficult to survive. But just waiting is not enough; initiative is essential. Flexibility is also considered very important, in terms of working through unclear reporting and communication channels. The constant requests for data can be unnerving, and "a common reaction of many Americans to data request is resentment, especially if they don't know why the data are required," explained one local manager. The first six months on the job are critical. The newly hired executive either adjusts to the different pace of decision making and to the lack of clear job definitions, or he or she leaves the company.

In many Japanese affiliates, the selection process itself is often very intensive all the way up to the middle management ranks. While there is a growing tendency to rely on executive recruiting firms to ferret out potential candidates, the internal screening process is rigorous and consumes a great deal of top executive time. In a number of firms, the senior Japanese executives interview all management-level candidates. Professional qualifications are paramount, together with personal characteristics. But how well are Japanese firms able to make appropriate judgments about the candidates' qualifications, in particular on the softer criteria? Is the consensus-driven selection process weeding out future leaders? One former Japanese automotive executive commented: "If Mr. Honda applied for a job in our U.S. affiliate, most likely he would have been rejected. He was too different, too visionary to pass our screening."

However, many Japanese managers seem to have expectations regarding the necessary managerial qualifications that are different from what is customary in the United States. As explained by one local executive, "American employees expect managers to know and do more. An American manager gets the job only if he or she is qualified. On the other hand, Japanese managers get the job first and then learn the skills." A former personnel executive of a large Japanese manufacturer concurred: "We always hired a little below the necessary qualifications—a bricklayer for a mason, a mason for an architect, an architect for a city planner." In some cases, this approach may encourage new initiative, provide challenging opportunities, and contribute to the dynamism of the organizational culture. In other cases, the weak managerial infrastructure may have serious consequences for the effective management of the business. "We have lots of mediocre American managers around here," remarked an executive with an electronics firm. "As a result, once the Japanese expatriates get the experience, they want to run the business themselves and they don't hire the top quality people or the top quality people get frustrated and leave."

The lack of visible role models may further diminish the attractiveness of these firms as employers of choice for many career-minded young Americans. In marked contrast to the recruiting practices in Japan, only a few Japanese-owned companies recruit regularly on college campuses and maintain an active presence there. Very little recruiting is based on a candidate's long-term potential, often contrary to the Human Resource strategy espoused in the corporate literature. Most young professionals employed by Japanese subsidiaries are hired to meet current job requirements only, without any clear plans for their future career path and development. Not surprisingly, in 1997, only one Japanese firm was ranked among the top 50 firms to work for among graduates of MBA programs.

The pool of talented candidates is further restricted because of the perception by the American public that the treatment of women and minorities still poses a challenge to many of the Japanese affiliates. The "glass ceiling" and the "rice-paper ceiling" overlap. At issue is not only the attitude and behavior of Japanese executives, whose awareness of the problems has grown rapidly, but often the advice they receive from some of the senior Americans who themselves do not see this as a priority item (e.g., the recent Mitsubishi Motors sexual harassment case). Some Japanese executives complain that, because of their high visibility, they are being unfairly criticized by the media and that American social problems cannot be solved by the Japanese. However, much more can be done in this regard, including stronger guidance from the parent corporation.

Career Development: "I Have a Good Job. But Is It Really a Great Career?"

Few human resource topics in Japanese subsidiaries elicit such unanimity of opinion as the need for enhancement and improvement in management and executive development. This involves both an introduction of company-specific education programs and a creation of long-term career-development paths for middle- and upper-level executives. Most American as well as Japanese executives would probably concur with the opinion of a senior local banker in a Japanese-owned financial institution: "We are staffed with capable people, but we have no strength on our bench: our key successors are not in place." Such executive succession concerns are often the key driver of management development from the corporate side. From the perspective of a young-up-and-coming marketing manager, concerns are of a different nature: "To work in this company is a great opportunity. I have a great job. But is it really a great career?" The tendency is to hire a manager to fill a specific position and to perform specific responsibilities. With only limited activities in place to enhance the manager's skills and capabilities, individuals are given little encouragement beyond their current roles. This short-term emphasis is interpreted by many local managers as an indication that there are few career or promotion opportunities within the organization.

Although most agreed that management development is one of the critical issues to be addressed (we heard many comments such as "Everyone needs to be measured on their ability to develop people"), the quality of development programs is very uneven. Several companies reported multiple false starts, with global development programs in place that were based more on faith than on detailed analysis of developmental needs. Even in affiliates with a long history in the United States there seems to be little coordination with the headquarters concerning human resource development. The existence or absence of management development activities is mainly determined by the capabilities of the local HRM executives and the willingness and interest of senior Japanese officers to provide support and resources. A critical roadblock to effective development is seen as an unwillingness to free the time for managers to learn. However, this was not a Japanese issue; problems just as often originated from the American side. As pointed out by an American HRM executive, "We don't spend time on training anymore. We don't have time or we don't take the time. Our people change constantly, and we really need to do more."

In our survey, nearly two thirds of executives responded that more career development programs were necessary. While there were already significant opportunities for internal mobility within the affiliate, the new emphasis was on mobility that would take American managers to subsidiaries in other countries, and in particular to Japan (figure 9.1), with the objective to acquire a global perspective on the business and to enhance international management skills. More than half of the managers in the survey regarded training in Japan as essential for the development of future local executives. Such training and exposure is seen as critical in learning the core business as well as developing important contacts and relationships across the parent organization. However, under the present circumstances, and in the foreseeable future, the key constraint to such opportunities is language. Most local managers agreed that without at least some ability to speak Japanese, transfers to Japan would probably not be effective.

The local executives interviewed were split on the necessity to learn the Japanese language. More than a third of the managers surveyed believed that, in the future, it will still be possible to succeed in a Japanese-owned firm without Japanese language skills, but a slightly larger group was convinced that such knowledge will be essential for a Western executive to rise to the top. Still, no Japanese affiliates provide opportunities for Japanese language training that would be even close to what is offered to the Japanese staff to improve their ability to speak English (e.g., one year intensive classes at a local university). Somewhat paradoxically, however, the few American executives who are effective speakers of Japanese, and who use it frequently to communicate with their Japanese colleagues and directly with the head office, play down the role of language. Well aware of the political climate in their organization, they do not want to be seen as advancing in the organization only because of their language and cultural skills.

In the long run, Japanese companies recognize the challenge of opening management training programs in Japan for their high-potential local staff or incorporating on-the-job training in Japan into career development plans of non-Japanese executives. Already some Japanese companies have begun to address the social and cultural problems and cost (housing, schooling, spouse employment) associated with such programs. Global development activities at the executive level already take place in some of the firms, but even there, the effort is seen as insufficient. "We need more meaningful interchange, like sending Americans to Japan. We do it, but don't do it enough," was a typical comment. One experienced local executive in a Japanese consumer electronic firm added: "The company should hire young college graduates and send them to Tokyo for training as well as initiate international job rotations for Americans, Europeans, etc. We need to inculcate a broader, international horizon in all our people. To be global, the company must exchange personnel."

Setting realistic expectations on both sides of the Pacific about the development objectives of training in Japan was another issue of concern: "When young Japanese are sent to us from Japan, for the first year they aren't very effective. They really don't start to perform until the second or third or even the fourth year. But when we send Americans to Japan, the top Japanese complain that the Americans aren't useful right away." Americans sent to Japan are often seen as "token gaijins" with only a symbolic involvement in daily business activities of the head office. Such outcomes were disappointing to the individuals who were dispatched to Japan, as well as to the advocates of these programs who could not demonstrate any long-term benefits from such activities. Again, language is part of the problem, but even the overseas staff who have Japanese language skills complain of difficulties in getting included when it matters. Their problems are similar to the hurdles facing midcareer management recruits entering the home office in Japan. Within the highly rigid internal labor market, where one's career progresses in the context of a particular "year-of-entry class," the midcareer recruits are valued for their specialist skills, but they are not really considered insiders (Pucik, 1989); they lack contacts and influence that come from the affiliation with the respective "class." Although their formal employment status is the same as for those who entered immediately after graduation, their career progress is handicapped from the very beginning.

To get around this problem, some Japanese firms have begun to recruit foreign college graduates in Japan who have a significant headstart in language and cultural understanding and who can take advantage of the socialization opportunities available to their Japanese colleagues. However, the retention rate is very low (at least for Americans and Europeans), as vague promises of long-term opportunities cannot match the attractive job offers from Western firms that appreciate the immediate unique contributions that these individuals can make. MBA programs also pose a retention challenge. It is very rare for a Japanese firm to sponsor a non-Japanese high-potential employee to study full-time for a full MBA degree. Simply, they are not trusted enough, although the rapidly increasing turnover of Japanese MBA graduates indicates that the desire to pursue career opportunities over loyalty to the firm is not limited to individuals from any particular culture.

In theory, developmental moves into a third country may be seen as more promising, as the language is less of an issue, but so far only a handful of American managers have been assigned outside of their parent company in Japan, mostly to Europe and Southeast Asia. It is fair to say, however, that even when opportunities are presented, local high-potential managers are not always very interested. Maintaining high value as a specialist in the local labor market is seen as more valuable than building trust through contacts in Japan, or investing in relationships with the Japanese in general. According to a veteran American executive vice president, "In any international firm you must develop mutual trust and respect. Personal relationships and communication are the key. However, some American managers, especially the younger ones, don't think that this is important."

Performance Management: "Good People Should Know That They Are Good"

The key factor in implementing an effective management development and career planning system is the quality of the performance management process. However, the main conclusion concerning performance management in Japanese-owned U.S. affiliates that emerged from our interviews and was supported by findings from our earlier 1989 study was straightforward: a significant proportion of American executives indicated that they were not happy about the quality of feedback on their performance (fig. 9.1). No other questions in our study elicited as many negative responses. The quality of the performance feedback process came up in the numerous follow-up interviews as well. Most managers and executives reported only a limited knowledge of their performance objectives. In the absence of a performance dialog, most senior executives, outside of sales and manufacturing, had little idea of what was expected of them, other than do their best and perform well as a part of the management team.

As pointed out in chapter 5, performance feedback, in a traditional "American" sense that involves one-on-one discussions between a superior and subordinate, is largely nonexistent for the professional workforce in Japanese-owned overseas subsidiaries. This is not surprising, given that in Japan, at least in the past, there was very little formal feedback provided to employees on the managerial track. "Good people should know that they are good, and the others don't want to know," was the prevailing attitude. Therefore, most Japanese executives have little, if any, experience in conducting an American-style direct and open performance appraisal. As a result, few Japanese superiors provide any direct feedback to their American subordinates. Written performance evaluations are very rarely conducted, and those who do receive such an evaluation seldom sat down with their Japanese superiors to discuss the ratings.

Even when feedback occurs, cultural expectations concerning its scope and directness may differ. With less emphasis on informal communication than is customary in Japan, it is not surprising that many local managers have only a vague idea of where they stand. According to a veteran American executive, "I have been with this company for 15 years and I have had only one evaluation. I have been advised of my performance in informal ways. But I always must take the initiative. I get criticism from the Japanese, but I am never told you have done well." However, complaints of local managers regarding performance feedback need to be put in proper perspective: most American employees working in Japanese firms are actually evaluated by other Americans. At the same time, very few American executives evaluate the Japanese, even though they may formally be their direct superiors.

The American managers who reported to the Japanese generally assumed that they were doing well unless directly told otherwise. Many of them, however, found this unsatisfying and wanted more direct performance feedback. The following comment was quite typical in this respect: "My results were communicated to me by the Japanese president in a meeting which lasted about three minutes. I have never seen my appraisal, although we should be able to. When I asked human resources about it, the response was that the Japanese are not ready. They don't even want to rate the simple four criteria now on the appraisal sheet (attitude, ability, achievement, overall performance)." The assumption that all is well, unless one is specifically told otherwise, often created problems for the Japanese. They could not understand why their local subordinates were not responding to indirect suggestions that performance improvement was needed. As a result, the high performers were frustrated because of the perceived lack of recognition, but those with mediocre performance were convinced that they were doing fine.

However, would more feedback from the Japanese make a difference? The responses from the managers whom we interviewed indicate that the answer is, probably not. Many of the local executives are not at all keen on receiving their evaluations from the Japanese, as they do not trust their judgments. One such executive said, "The Japanese aren't great in assessing American top talent. For example, the Japanese are more comfortable with people who play the game better, but who are not necessarily sensitive to the company's long-term needs. People who disagree vigorously are shunted aside, although they may be acting in the best interest of the company." This opinion was seconded by a young executive in another firm: "American managers who go along politically sometimes seem to fare better than those who occasionally are willing to differ." It seems that having more feedback from Japanese superiors without improving their ability to evaluate the attitudes and behaviors of the local staff would not improve the situation very much.

The ambiguity of performance standards also puzzled many of the local executives. Some executives have pointed out that, as a consequence of the lack of clarity, "the overall standards are not as stringent as in a similar U.S. company," and the incidents of mediocre performance were seldom addressed. The ambiguity concerning performance standards often led to different conclusions about the performance management system by executives in the same company. One top executive commented, "In our bank, individual goals must be achieved. If there are two consecutive shortfalls, that individual is gone." His description of the uncompromising "tough" climate in the firm was, however, implicitly contradicted by his colleague across the hall, who said, "I always worry about keeping the organization from developing into a retirement home."

In one important dimension, Japanese-owned firms were rather different for their local counterparts: outright dismissals for poor performance were reportedly very rare. Even when they happened, the action was often initiated by Americans, notwithstanding the uneasiness of the Japanese. The reason for this is simple: "Firing an individual is a poor reflection on the organization and management. Consequently, the company tries to fit the individual elsewhere in the organization puzzle." While a majority of the Americans considered the relative job security a positive feature of Japanese organization, several, mainly younger executives complained that low turnover in spite of poor performance "led to complacency, too much fat, and a fossil culture."

In the case of dismissals due to a major error of judgment by managers or executives, several Americans pointed out the double standards: "If a U.S. executive breaks a company rule, he is fired, if a Japanese breaks a rule, he is transferred." Such policies, although perhaps understandable in the context of differences in the employment systems of the two countries, create resentment and suspicion. In addition, a number of U.S. executives were irritated by what they considered a Japanese tendency to cover for each other and blame the local staff for any mistakes. "One of my roles here is to be the fall guy for the Japanese. I understand this, but sometimes even I wonder why I put up with this stuff," said an American executive in charge of strategic planning. In several firms we observed a "creeping localization" in outplacement practices: growing reliance on and consultations with legal counsel before any dismissal in order to reduce the risks of lawsuits and unfavorable publicity.

Rewards and Career Opportunities: "You Can Go Only So Far. Above That, There Are Only Japanese"

As in the case of other human resource practices, there was a wide variety of opinions expressed in our survey and in the follow-up interviews with respect to the compensation and promotion systems implemented by Japanese companies in the United States. Most respondents agreed that existing compensation practices are not a major handicap in attracting capable Americans (figure 9.1), indicating that Japanese firms are quite willing to pay what it takes to attract the necessary local talent. This trend was accelerated after the yen strengthened in the late 1980s and the dollar-based cost of Japanese expatriate salaries increased considerably.

Most Japanese companies would typically put in place entry-stage compensation schemes at levels at or slightly below the market median, but the salary average is slowly moving upward. However, the entire package for a typical higher-level executive is still generally less than peer compensation in American companies. Nevertheless, in the words of a general manager in an automobile company, "The Japanese are very compassionate—they want people to do well. The company does not pay top salary, but does remember people at the end of the year."

This opinion was supported by others. Although most executives we spoke to were aware of some salary differentials with executives in comparable American firms, this did not have an impact on their overall satisfaction with their jobs. It can only be speculated that many of the executives were aware that it may be very difficult for them to change jobs relatively late in their careers or, as observed by one high-ranking American, "We are paid just right. It is only that American executives in general are too well taken care of as a class—they are overpaid." In addition, the disfunctionalities of the Japanese approach to managers' compensation—paying for seniority and title, rather than for performance—were embraced by quite a number of American executives. Or, as poignantly pointed out by one of them, "I have a great title, but no power and not much responsibility. I accept it, but they better pay me for it."

American executives in firms that were acquired by the Japanese were generally paid more than in firms that were started greenfield. In fact, in the case of an acquisition, the HRM systems were generally retained and little direction was provided from the new owners on HRM policies and procedures. The level and composition of compensation for the top-level American executives continue to be the subject of frequent discussions, particularly as the income of most American executives in acquired firms often exceeds the earnings of most senior Japanese at the parent company. However, in most cases there has been no apparent resolution of this disparity: the U.S. executives receive compensation comparable with or greater than they did prior to the acquisition.

In general, Japanese firms compensate managers based on changing market expectations. However, this flexibility does not transfer to pay structure, which has not yet changed away from the traditional annual merit increase focus. The current trend in the U.S. labor market toward pay-for-performance variable compensation, whether on an individual, group, or company level, does not seem very visible in Japanese-owned firms. Obviously, any shift to pay-for-performance compensation would require restructuring the performance management system, particularly the objective setting and the feedback process, areas where Japanese firms have the greatest difficulties. It would also put on the table profit allocation questions, which in many Japanese firms are basically off-limits to local executives.

Another potential problem area is the lack of long-term incentive pay. In fact, the only major complaints regarding compensation were expressed by local managers employed in sectors such as high-tech or investment banking where U.S. companies offer some sort of incentive pay (mainly bonuses and stock options) that plays an important role in the overall compensation package even at the lower level of the organizational hierarchy. The absence of incentive compensation in Japanese-owned firms was cited repeatedly as a major long-term retention issue. Some Japanese financial firms have now introduced more performance-related compensation, partly to satisfy the aspirations of their Japanese staff, who can clearly see the compensation disparity with their counterparts in American firms. However, we did not find any Japanese firms contemplating stock options or other forms of equity participation for their U.S.-based managers and executives.

While the level of compensation was, with a few exceptions noted above, only a marginal issue, the opportunities for long-term career progression in Japanese-owned firms were of more immediate concern. As pointed out earlier, promotion opportunities above a certain level are limited at best, and even at lower levels some patience is required, relative what may be customary in an American company in a similar industry. One executive declared, "If you want a promotion in six months, you will die here." However, the theme of discontent covers more than the speed of promotion. Ultimately, what are the career opportunities available? In the absence of a regular dialog about performance and career planning, the answers were full of skepticism: "Compensation and promotion are fair. But you can go only so far. Above that there are only Japanese."

The dissatisfaction with long-term promotion chances was strongest at the lower management levels. Dissatisfaction did not always imply an immediate desire to resign on the part of the Americans, but in the long term, the more talented, aggressive, and ambitious managers leave, whereas the others gradually adjust to a more limited future. In particular, American executives currently in relatively senior positions within their firm perceived little or no prospects of moving up. Most were recruited to those positions, although several had been promoted one or two levels since they joined the firm at the middle management ranks. All seemed reconciled to the fact that they would never get to the top of the company. As an American EVP observed, "This is a Japanese-owned company. Senior Japanese executives will always be required here." Paradoxically, in the same firm, because of the rapid growth, good opportunities exist for division heads, perhaps even better than with comparable U.S. firms. However, because there are no visible opportunities to advance further, another senior American asserted, "In our firm we have a hard time to keep our managers, because everyone above them is Japanese."

The limited career opportunities perceived by high-potential and ambitious American managers make it very difficult for Japanese companies to develop stable local leadership teams, especially in sectors wherein Japanese-trained executives are thought to possess unique know-how. For example, a number of high-level local executives, valued for their intimate knowledge of "lean manufacturing," already left Japanese automobile manufacturers to work for their U.S. or European competitors. As a result, even after more than 30 years of presence in the United States, with only a handful of exceptions, there are no local executives in top-level decision-making positions in most Japanese firms in the United States who would project a leadership image attractive enough to serve as a role model for young American managers to follow. If leadership development is what globalization is ultimately all about, the Japanese have so far failed, at least in their U.S. operations. More important, there seem to be little chance that an improvement is imminent.

Human Resource Practices and Corporate Performance: Is There a Need to Change?

In summary, a detailed examination of white-collar HRM practices in Japanese-owned firms operating in the United States does not reveal a very positive picture. While many of Japanese firms operating in the United States are reasonably successful, this may be in spite of, not because of, their local HRM policies. Certainly, many of their U.S. factories are world-class; studied, admired, and emulated because of their work flow design and shop floor management, but nothing even remotely comparable can be said about Japanese management in the office environment. The only publicity the Japanese firms get in this area is when another lawsuit is filed by disgruntled American employees.

However, why did Japanese firms not move aggressively to remedy the obvious shortcomings, just as they learned quickly from, and reacted to, problems and difficulties in managing the American blue-collar workforce? Also, as total returns on Japanese overseas investments in the United States are not very attractive (e.g., lower than comparable investments in Asia, or even negative, according to most recent figures [MITI, 1995]), pursuing opportunities to improve performance by focusing on human organization may seem to be a rather obvious strategy. Or is it?

Part of the failure of the Japanese firms to respond to their HRM challenges may be attributed to the fact that even the most visible shortcomings in HRM are *not perceived* to matter to a degree that would attract immediate attention of top-line executives. It is important to note that in our survey and in interviews, Japanese expatriates (with few exceptions) do not seem overly concerned with HRM constraints. Most of them came from manufacturing and marketing backgrounds, and their knowledge of HRM issues seemed to be rather limited. They accepted ineffectiveness of their U.S. white-collar operation as given and believe that because the measurement of progress is not very obvious, it is probably something that can be postponed until another occasion.

However, the opinions of the American executives are surprisingly similar to those of the Japanese. A majority of respondents in our survey felt that organizational and HRM constraints are still not very serious, in particular with respect to middle managers (figure 9.2.)

The limited career advancement and promotion opportunities were cited as the only serious obstacle to recruitment and retention of qualified American executives, and with respect to middle managers, the limited autonomy in decision making was

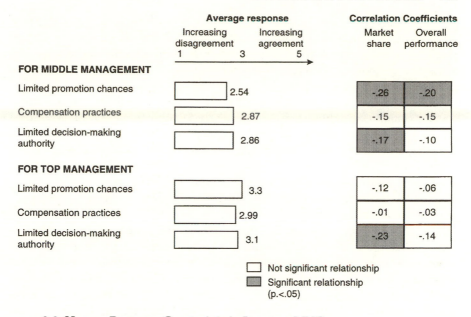

FIGURE 9.2 Human Resource Constraints in Japanese MNCs

also often cited. Most respondents agreed that existing compensation practices are not a major handicap in attracting capable Americans, confirming the observations made earlier that Japanese firms may be quite willing to pay what it takes to attract the top-level local talent (perhaps sometimes even too much, even by Hollywood standards).

Part of the reason why HRM issues do not seem to be perceived as requiring an urgent and specific action—as opposed to a general belief that these issues are of critical long-term importance—is that HRM constraints, at least in the minds of managers, lack direct impact on the immediate performance of the subsidiary. In our survey data (figure 9.2), this relationship is rather weak. It does not seem to matter very much, at least in the immediate future, if the existing HRM practices restrict the flow of capable local managers. The affiliate performance does not seem to be affected in any significant way, as the JMNCs are probably able to work around this constraint by continuing their reliance on expatriates.

The only HRM constraint that showed a consistent significant relationship with any of the indicators of affiliate performance is the "limited promotion chances for middle managers," which is negatively correlated with overall performance and market share achieved by the affiliate. Even in this case, however, the direction of the causal relationship is ambiguous. It may be that low-performing firms simply do not grow rapidly, thus limiting promotion opportunities for middle managers. The relationship of other HRM constraints with affiliate performance is even more limited. The decision-making autonomy for both top and middle groups of managers may have an impact on market share, but the relationship with overall performance is not significant. All of this may provide some explanation about why so few

U.S.-based JMNCs are willing to take a concerted action to modify their existing HRM practices. In the minds of Japanese executives, the HRM constraints are still "manageable," there does not seem to be a penalty for low affiliate performance, and, most important, the payouts from change are not clear (e.g., "Americans will eventually quit anyway, no matter what").

This raises an important question. Is there any evidence to suggest that HRM systems could make a difference? Is there a way to examine the contribution HRM practices can make to corporate performance independent of perceptions of individual managers? In other words, is the apparent neglect of white-collar HRM area a pragmatic decision reflecting a trade-off between risks and returns, or are we seeing here another example of Japanese of corporate myopia, where the pressures and details of everyday business, together with limited incentives to maximize performance, prevent executives from embracing new opportunities?

To what extent are the specific HRM practices of Japanese affiliates related to various dimensions of their business performance? Figure 9.3 explores this question, using information collected in our 1989 survey. It is important to note, however, that the relationships shown here imply association, not necessarily causality. In some cases, certain levels of performance may lead to certain HRM practices, not the other way around. For example, in healthy and profitable organizations, employment security may be relatively high. At the same time, many other observed relationships between HRM practices and business performance make intuitive sense and parallel other findings from the management literature.

Among the HRM practices examined, promotion chances equal to U.S. firms show by far the most consistent significant and positive relationship with the various dimensions of business performance. Japanese-owned affiliates that provide career opportunities for their local managers and executives that are perceived at least

HUMAN RESOURCE MANAGEMENT PRACTICES	Correlation Coefficients		
	Level of profits	Market share	Overall performance
Employment security	.28	.19	.30
Clear performance targets	.12	.21	.14
Sufficient feedback	.02	.26	.15
Appraisals impact promotions	.10	.17	.17
Appraisals influence salary	-.01	.14	.04
Promotion chances equal to U.S. firms	.31	.29	.23

☐ Not significant relationship
▨ Significant relationship (p<.05)
▰ Very significant relationship (p<.01)

FIGURE 9.3 Human Resource Management Practices and Corporate Performance

as good as those in comparable U.S. firms seem to outperform their competitors. Another HRM practice, employment security, has a similar positive association with the performance measures, but as pointed out, the direction of this relationship is not clear.

Among the performance measures, market share is the most strongly linked to HRM practices, probably because this is a more reliable indicator of local performance than financial data affected by funding method and transfer pricing. Performance feedback and clear setting of performance targets are also positively and significantly related to market share, suggesting the importance of addressing some of the issues raised earlier in the discussion of performance management. Finally, there is some evidence that affiliates that link appraisals to promotions perform better than those do not; however, no similar effect can be observed for the linkage of appraisals with salaries.

In summary, while Japanese and American executives in the U.S.-based Japanese affiliates do not consider existing HRM policies to be an immediate constraint influencing the performance of the affiliate, there seems at be at least some amount of empirical evidence suggesting that progressive HRM practices are indeed linked to successful organizational performance. Yet, if there may be opportunities to improve affiliate performance through better HRM, those opportunties are not pursued. The gap between the professed "human resource" orientation of Japanese MNCs and the willingness to ignore benefits from improving HRM practice is striking and does not show any sign of being closed in a relatively near future.

In Search of Globalization: "They Do the Thinking, and We Do the Acting"

At the level of corporate public relations. Japanese MNCs take no back seat in putting forward their goals of globalization of organization and human resources. However, in our interviews, one local executive provided this comment on the Japanese-style globalization: "You probably have heard the corporate slogan concerning globalization of our company: 'Think globally, act locally.' It sounds great. But in reality, not much has changed. *They* do the thinking, and *we* do the acting."

From this perspective, while generalizations may be misleading in some specific instances, probably the most striking observation one can make about HRM practices of white-collar local employees in Japanese-owned subsidiaries in the United States is that, at the core, *very little has changed in the last twenty years.*

Recent follow-up interviews with American and Japanese executives have highlighted the same problems with competent local managers, career development, and performance management practices that my colleagues and I observed in our in-depth survey conducted during the late 1980s, which in turn are comparable to findings from the early studies on Japanese investment in the United States dating from the late 1970s. The size of the operations, the length of experience, the complexity of the organization, and even the great degree of change in the competitive environment do not seem to have had much impact on Japanese HRM practices abroad, at least in the United States. From an institutional perspective, the JMNCs have not learned, or, at best, they have learned very little. Yet, without learning, the organizational performance of JMNC's operating in the United States will continue to be marginal. Why have JMNCs not learned, when organizational learning is supposed to be one of their "core competencies" (Nonaka & Takeuchi, 1995).

In chapter 6, Kopp suggests that the fact that Japanese firms do not act on their HRM problems is perhaps due either to the fear of change that could make matters even more difficult from the Japanese headquarters viewpoint, or because the HRM system in Japanese affiliates is in fact a mirror image of the core and the periphery differentiation embedded in the Japanese HRM system at home, and thus, from at least the Japanese point of view, there is no need to change. The system may not be optimal, but it does not *completely* prevent things from getting done, and it is what the companies know best how to manage. However, there may be at least another alternative explanation why so little change has occurred and why learning has not occurred.

The Japanese HRM system as we know it today evolved during the 1960s and 1970s in response to a highly competitive environment in Japan and in the world markets. It was based on two core assumptions about the challenges facing Japanese corporations: growth and competition. The assumption about continuous growth underlies the pattern of interactions with the labor markets, and the assumption of competition underlies the external orientation and the internal organization of the firm (Tezuka, 1997). However, for large JMNCs that form the bulk of Japanese investments in the United States, both of these assumptions have not been valid for at least from the mid-1980s. The companies stopped growing, but because of their past successes and abundant resources in the highly productive blue-collar sector, the white-collar employees were protected from any negative consequences of declining competitiveness (Hori, 1993). The system of Japanese corporate governance, wherein the upper strata of white-collar employees effectively run the firm without interference from equity markets, prevented, and still to a large degree prevents, any rapid meaningful change that would shift the balance of the corporate HRM system back to its past focus on competitiveness.

Without white-collar organizational competitiveness at home and few visible negative consequences, at least in the short run, it is not surprising that the productivity and effectiveness of white-collar employees abroad is not high on the Japanese corporate agenda. In fact, even companies altering their HRM practices in Japan, by learning and applying the Western HRM tools, such as 360-degree feedback, show no inclination of upgrading their HRM systems overseas. The fundamental obstacle to effective globalization is simple: the continuous expatriate orientation of JMNCs. The HRM practices will not likely become global as long as the top management infrastructure of Japanese firms worldwide is heavily Japanese.

The bias for expatriates is built into the core of JMNCs. Many previous studies of Japanese foreign investment, including several chapters here, point out the large number of Japanese expatriates dispatched to manage overseas affiliates, relative to American and European MNCs. However, even as Japanese affiliates matured, and contrary to the often-voiced expectations, the ratio of Japanese expatriates did not decline. Of course, the operational obstacles of language and culture could be one explanation for the lack of progress in the localization of management. But it has to be recognized that, in the present "no growth" environment, these expatriate positions are also very valuable, as they provide places for the surplus Japanese managerial workforce. If they are lost to the locals, the pressure to find more managerial jobs at home will increase.

This all implies that hesitation about, and resistance to, any meaningful localization will continue as long as the maximization of managerial employment in Japan at all cost remains the hidden but paramount corporate objective. Japanese affiliates cannot be localized overseas; this process can only follow a mindset change in the parent company. Not much will change there until Japanese firms become again focused on competitiveness and performance.

In summary, the lack of progress in globalization of human resources on the part of most JMNCs is not due to cultural bias against foreign employees, or because of poor international management skills, but because these firms don't see the linkage of globalization efforts to company performance. They see no linkage, not because of a lack of knowledge about the benefits of globalization, or poor knowledge of globalization tools, but because, in principle, they are not profit-motivated in the first place. They can afford not to be profit-oriented because they have huge reserves of assets, and a profit orientation would necessarily disrupt the status quo.

Effective globalization of JMNCs would first require radical changes and pain at home, but most Japanese companies today still do not have the leadership and accompanying vision and courage to take on entrenched internal interests. Naturally, change will eventually come, because JMNCs cannot escape forever the pressure of the global markets, but, for most of them, it will come very slowly.

References

Bartlett, C., & Yoshihara, H. 1992. "New Challenges for Japanese multinationals: Is Organization Adaptation Their Achilles Heel? In Pucik, V., Tichy, N., & Barnett, C. (eds.), *Globalizing Management: Creating and Leading the Competitive Organization*. New York: John Wiley & Sons.

Brecher, C., & Pucik, V. 1979. *The Economic Impact of Japanese Business Community in the United States*. New York: Japan Society.

DeNero, H. 1990. "Creating the Hyphenated Corporation." *The McKinsey Quarterly.* 4: 153–74.

Fucini, J., & Fucini, S. 1990. *Working for the Japanese: Inside Mazda's American Auto Plant.* New York: Free Press.

Graham, L. 1993. Inside a Japanese Transplant. *Work and Occupations.* 20 (2): 147–173.

Hatvany, N., & Pucik, V. 1981–1982. "Japanese Management in America: What Does and Doesn't Work." *National Productivity Review.* 1 (1): 61–74.

Hori, S. 1993. Fixing Japan's White-Collar Economy: A Personal View. *Harvard Business Review.* 71 (6): 157–172.

Kenney, M., & Florida, R. 1993. *Beyond Mass Production: The Japanese System and Its Transfer to the United States*. New York: Oxford University Press.

Kopp, R. 1994. "International Human Resource Policies and Practices in Japanese, European, and United States Multinationals." *Human Resource Management.* 33 (4): 581–599.

MITI (Ministry of International Trade and Industry). 1995. *Kaigai jigyo katsudo doko chosa no gaiyo.* Tokyo: Okura-sho.

Nonaka, I., & Takeuchi, H. 1995. *The Knowledge-Creating Company: How Japanese Companies Create the Dynamics of Innovation*. New York: Oxford University Press.

Pucik, V. 1989. "Managerial career progression in large Japanese manufacturing firms." In Rowland, K., & Ferris, G. (eds.), *Research in Personnel and Human Resources Management*. Greenwich, CT: JAI Press. 257–276.

Pucik, V. 1992. "Globalization and human resource management." In Pucik, V., Tichy, N., & Barnett, C. (eds.), *Globalizing Management: Creating and Leading the Competitive Organization*. New York: John Wiley & Sons.

Pucik, V. 1993. "The Strategic Role of Local Managers in Japanese-Owned U.S. Subsidiaries." In Campbell, N., & Burton, F. (ed.) *Japanese Multinationals: Strategies and Management in the Global Kaisha*. London: Routledge & Kegan Paul.

Pucik, V. 1997. Human Resources in the Future: An Obstacle or a Champion of Globalization? *Human Resource Management*. 36 (1): 163–167.

Pucik, V., Hanada, M., & Fiefield, G. 1989. *Management Culture and the Effectiveness of Local Executives in Japanese-Owned U.S. Corporations*. Ann Arbor: University of Michigan.

Tezuka, H. 1997. "Success as the Source of Failure? Competition and Cooperation in the Japanese Economy." *Sloan Management Review*. 38 (2): 83–93.

Toyo Keizai. 1996. *Kaigai Shinshutsu Kigyo Soran 1996*. Tokyo: Toyo Keizai Shimposha.

Womack, J., Jones, D., & Roos, D. 1990. *The Machine that Changed the World*. London: Macmillan.

PART IV

ORGANIZATIONAL LEARNING AND THE PARENT-AFFILIATE CONNECTION

10

DAVID T. METHÉ & JOAN D. PENNER-HAHN

Globalization of Pharmaceutical Research and Development in Japanese Companies

Organizational Learning and the Parent-Subsidiary Relationship

Introduction

With the quickening pace of change brought about by technological innovation and globalization, organizations have had to scramble to keep pace. The relentless drive for responsiveness has focused much attention on organizational learning (Senge, 1990), seen as crucial to a company's success (Garratt, 1987). It has been studied in a number of contexts (Brown & Duguid, 1991; Nevis, DiBella, & Gould, 1995), but one area that needs more systematic study is globalization, particularly because one of the key assets attributed to multinational corporations (MNCs) is their greater learning opportunities as a result of operating in diverse environments (Ghoshal, 1987). As more and more companies put facilities overseas, their executives confront the managerial challenge of transferring information and knowledge related to best practices from where they were generated to where they are needed.

One obvious, but no less crucial aspect is that in order for learning to occur, this transfer process must cover vast geographic distances often across organizational boundaries. The organizational boundaries exist between a parent company in the home country and a subsidiary organization in a host country. With the geographic distance also come barriers of organizational culture and country culture to contend with as management attempts to move knowledge between these business units. As more companies establish a global presence, it is essential that they understand what learning in the global parent-subsidiary relationship entails.

In this chapter, we study the phenomenon of organizational learning in a global context within Japanese companies. Two aspects of the Japanese business context make this study particularly relevant. First, Japanese firms are often held up as examples of companies proficient at organizational learning (Cole, 1989, 1995; Imai, Nonaka, & Takeuchi, 1985; Pucik, 1988). In addition, many Japanese companies have been extending operations overseas only in recent years. There have been few studies of organizational learning in this context. In particular, our study focuses on Japanese companies active in the pharmaceutical industry, which has only recently begun to globalize, giving us the opportunity to examine the entire history of these companies' globalization efforts.

We focus our study further by examining the learning relationship of parent to subsidiary in the context of the globalization of research and development (R & D) activities, seen as a primary source of value creation in all technology-intensive industries such as the pharmaceutical industry. The R & D process has been characterized as more than the movement of material from design to sales. It requires higher-order activities, which result in the creation of knowledge and the learning of that knowledge as ideas move from concept to market (Nonaka, 1991). Learning,[1] in particular organizational learning, is central to the R & D process. Our study, then, will focus on globalization of R & D activities by Japanese pharmaceutical companies.

Globalization in the Pharmaceutical Industry

The pharmaceutical industry is undergoing two fundamental changes. The first was triggered by the discovery of the DNA molecule by Watson and Crick, which lead to a fundamental change in the way R & D is done by researchers in new drug discovery. In addition, research knowledge began to become systematized, and innovation began to rest on this accumulated knowledge. Innovation, no longer a process of "hit or miss" as a group of pharmacologists screened a large number of compounds developed by organic chemists, became a process by which a wide variety of disciplines were needed to develop new drugs. As a result, the average firm in 1965 spent $21.9 million on discovery, but by 1990 this amount had increased to $68.2 million in constant dollars (Henderson and Cockburn, 1994). This movement toward the systematization of knowledge changed the innovation process from random to accumulated discovery in that a researcher's ability to discover new compounds was a function of the knowledge base and the researcher's experience in using it. This process accelerated during the late 1970s and 1980s with the development of recombinant DNA and monoclonal antibody techniques.

In addition, the downstream research activities leading to final approval of a pharmaceutical continue to be complex. The entire development process can take an extremely long time and is also expensive. The Pharmaceutical Manufacturers Association sponsored a study in 1991 that reported that it takes an average of 12 years and $231 million to get a drug from the laboratory to the pharmacy. Consequently, organizational changes in research strategy take a long time to manifest themselves.

These changes in the innovation process for pharmaceuticals triggered another fundamental change in the industry. Because the cost of development was increasing and because the knowledge bases for new drug discovery were centered in various parts of the world, pressures for globalization of markets began to overcome the inertial forces that kept country markets separate. Companies play a central role in attempting to globalize this industry as they search for researchers with the knowledge necessary to develop new drugs and for as large a market as possible to recover the development costs. Companies, in addition to government regulatory bodies and the local medical establishment, can also play a role in resisting globalization pressures because they wish to protect domestic markets.

These forces have slowed, but not stopped, the process of globalization in pharmaceutical markets. More countries are beginning to allow the use of preclinical work done by companies in other countries in their drug approval process. As a result, some harmonization of regulations and standards is occurring. However, the pharmaceutical industry is still a long way from being as globalized as the consumer electronics or aircraft industries. The speed at which the pharmaceutical industry reaches the state of globalization exhibited in these other industries will depend on a number of factors, some of which we examine in this chapter. These relate to the success or failure that companies experience in their own individual attempts to globalize. We examine the experience of several Japanese companies in globalizing their research and development activities.

The Japanese Pharmaceutical Industry

Japanese pharmaceutical companies enjoyed a relatively protected market until the late 1970s. Until that time Japanese patent protection was granted only to process, and not product, making it very easy to "reverse engineer" drugs developed in other countries. Further, regulations made it difficult for non-Japanese companies to enter except as joint ventures. Consequently, throughout most of the 1960s and 1970s, Japanese companies licensed-in drugs developed abroad. With the granting of full patent protection and the easing of entry regulations, along with the accelerated pace of change in the innovation process for new pharmaceuticals, Japanese companies confronted a future that would require new capabilities to ensure survival.

In this chapter we present the experience of five Japanese pharmaceutical companies' attempts to globalize their R & D. The information used in this study resulted from interviews with 15 Japanese companies involved in the pharmaceutical industry. The companies profiled were selected to provide a cross section of the variety of activities companies had undertaken. Some firms had established overseas activities, others had not. The five we profile are representative of those that had established overseas R & D activities. The semistructured interviews with the vice president of R & D (or the equivalent) lasted from one to two hours. The interviews were conducted as a preliminary part of the research reported in Penner-Hahn (1995), which examines the globalization process of 66 Japanese companies engaged in over 116 foreign pharmaceutical R & D activities between 1980 and 1992. The period 1980 to 1992 was chosen to capture the beginning of the internationalization of R & D in the Japanese pharmaceutical industry. The first instance of a Japanese firm initiating a foreign R & D activity was in 1980. While firms have continued to establish overseas R & D activities since 1992, the study period was chosen to capture the initial efforts at globalization.

For the purposes of this chapter, we examined the motivations for establishing foreign R & D activities as expressed during the interviews we described. We then classified these companies that undertook foreign R & D activities according to their strategic intent toward globalization of R & D. We focus on representative companies within each category to illustrate the issues germane to parent and subsidiary relationships and organizational learning. Our focus will be on how these companies have learned in setting up their overseas subsidiaries. Due to the complexity of the research process itself and the newness of the globalization activity, information on the outcomes of the R & D projects is unavailable.

Approaches to Globalization of R & D

In this chapter we define organizational learning as the process by which errors or weaknesses are corrected (Argyris & Schön, 1978). As such, we see this learning as the acquisition of knowledge new to the organization that can lead to the building of new capabilities that exhibit themselves in changes in the organization's operating routines to counter changes in an organization's environment. Consequently, organizational learning should enhance an organization's chances of survival. However, what is perceived as the "error" to be corrected may in itself be in error.[2] Also, the process of correcting the error, assuming the correct one is identified, may cost more than the benefits derived. We will return to these issues later in the chapter. For now, we note that the benefits and costs of engaging in various types of organizational learning need to be carefully weighed by management.

This brings us to our first of two distinctions concerning organizational learning in the context of the globalization of R & D. Globalization is any activity conducted away from the company's home country. Organizational learning in a global context means acquiring not only the information needed to compete but also the management process, systems, and structures by which an organization obtains knowledge. Organizational learning occurs at two levels, the management level and the functional knowledge level. Management must determine what functional knowledge along the value chain it should acquire and how best to acquire it. In general, management must decide which functional area to target, such as marketing, production, or R & D knowledge. Management must also determine how it will acquire the targeted knowledge. In our study we observed that firms structured their acquisition activities in a number of ways such as contracting in the market, engaging in alliances, acquiring another firm, or setting up their own greenfield subsidiary.

In our study we examine firms that target the acquisition of R & D knowledge, in particular knowledge related to the discovery of new pharmaceuticals. This leads to our second distinction, between research content knowledge, such as that related to understanding the metabolism of plasma lipoproteins, and research process knowledge, which is related to how to conduct the research (Corisini, 1987). Research knowledge, then, includes not only the specific knowledge of a particular scientific discipline such as molecular biology, but also the skills, methods, and mind set required to carry out discovery research in the discipline. What is important about this distinction is that process knowledge does reside at the individual level and requires individual learning, but for a company to take competitive advantage of it, this individual-embodied process knowledge must be translated into knowledge that is embodied in organizational routines and requires organizational learning.

Organizational routines are the procedures, both formal and informal, for carrying out tasks in a company (Nelson and Winter, 1982). These routines are independent of the individuals who carry them out, but individuals can contribute to their formation and continuance (Levitt and March, 1988). These organizational routines, along with the shared norms and values attendant with them, make up the cognitive systems and collective memories that help to translate individual learning into organizational learning (Hedberg, 1981). The socialization process that individuals undergo in becoming acquainted with an organization's culture (i.e., its collection of norms, value's, and routines) is the primary process by which individual learning becomes organizational learning (Schein, 1985). The distinctions between management and functional level knowledge and within the R & D function between content and process are critical to understanding the various challenges that the companies arrayed here confront with their various globalization strategies.

In particular, the distinction between content and process reveals itself strongly in R & D because content knowledge can often be acquired without acquiring the process knowledge, but the reverse is not a given. Learning the process of R & D more often requires learning the content of a scientific field. This relationship of process to content is closely tied to the notion of tacitness.[3] Tacitness relates to the inability to codify knowledge and therefore affects the ease and cost of transmitting it. This inability to codify knowledge means that learning often requires the actual participation and movement of people in a process in order for organizational learning to occur. The role that tacitness plays in learning new ways of conducting discovery in pharmaceutical research influences the management of global R & D. Tacitness relates more to the process of how to generate and use technological knowledge and less to the content of the technological knowledge itself, which can be codified and learned in a classroom. For example, a company can acquire a license covering technological knowledge about a breakthrough chemical entity without learning the process of how to generate a similar chemical entity of equal significance.

Even when a company sets up a subsidiary unit overseas, it may gain the capability to create new breakthroughs in the subsidiary unit, but never learn to internalize the process in the home company itself. To take full advantage of the capability, the company must establish absorptive capacity, that is, the capability to translate and use knowledge created elsewhere (Cohen and Levinthal, 1990). In the context of our study, we see absorptive capacity as composed of organizational structures that can act as memory devices for the firm and strategic awareness to learn at the organizational level. This absorptive capacity is necessary for the utilization of information flows across organizational boundaries. Having both memory and awareness are critical, for simple collection and storage of knowledge, without the awareness of using it to change organizational routines, will not lead to organizational learning. Further, having strategic awareness and mechanisms to carry out that intent will lead to trial and error without the appropriate functional knowledge stored in organizational memory mechanisms. Building this absorptive capacity is particularly tricky in the R & D context because the organizational routines for basic research, called discovery in the pharmaceutical industry, are different from the organizational routines utilized in development, called clinical research in the pharmaceutical industry. More often than not, proficiency in one does not automatically lead to proficiency in the other. Consequently, the issue of organizational learning becomes one of how to build the absorptive capacity without having the organizational routines of the one overwhelm the organizational routines of the other.

This issue is amplified in Japanese companies in that the dominant technical logic of the organization is weighted toward the development of products based on existing scientific knowledge as opposed to basic research needed to create new scientific knowledge (Methé, 1995). Some have argued that Japanese companies create knowledge through their product development process (Nonaka, 1991; Nonaka and Takeuchi, 1995), but this kind of knowledge creation is far different from that of discovery of new scientific and technological knowledge bases. These activities place an imperative on efficiency in resource and time utilization in bringing new products to market. Consequently, more emphasis is given to using already existing knowledge, concepts, and off-the-shelf components than on creating new ones, and organizational units designed to create new scientific knowledge are vulnerable to capture by existing units (Methé, 1997). The dominant technical logic of Japanese companies is seen as the efficient exploitation of existing knowledge bases with incremental additions through the product development process. From our research it was evident that one of the fundamental issues confronting Japanese organizations over the next decade will revolve around their ability to transition from adept exploiters of existing scientific and technological knowledge bases to creators of new ones. Developing the capabilities and routines needed to create and explore new knowledge bases will mean the introduction of a new technical logic, which is often incompatible with the current one. Consequently, any attempt to build up the new organizational routines needed for knowledge discovery must shelter or insulate them from the already entrenched dominant technical logic. The more the organizational distance (Methé, 1997) between the units, the greater the insulation. Setting up a subsidiary to do discovery research in a distant country will provide a great deal of organizational distance and, consequently, the needed insulation, but at the risk of losing control and slowing the organizational learning across the organizational boundaries between the home company and its overseas subsidiary.

Such a situation arose in the context of the entertainment industry when Sony bought Colombia Pictures and Matsushita bought MCA. Both Japanese companies took a "hands off" approach toward managing their acquisitions because each company was acutely aware that the organizational routines for new product development of electronic hardware are different from those exercised in the new product development of movies. This quarantine of the two organizational entities may have made sense, since the value chain connection between electronic hardware and movies is tenuous at best. The recent failure of Sony's and Matsushita's efforts raises even stronger concerns for the need for balance in organizational processes where the value chain linkage is strong, such as in R & D activities. Such isolating mechanisms would be disastrous in the case of the discovery of new drugs and their eventual development. In this case, information must flow between those charged with both aspects of the product development process. Some balance between absorptive capacity and insulation from the dominant technical logic must be established.

It is important to distinguish between various companies' strategic approaches to these issues when confronted with a change toward globalization in the environment. Not all companies view the same environment in the same way. In fact, some argue that this is the source of competitive advantage in industries because it allows firms to gain access to and utilize important resources (Dierckx & Cool, 1989; Peteraff, 1993; Wernerfelt, 1984). Although it is beyond the bounds of this chapter to review the literature on the resource-based theory of the firm, one of the key elements of this theory relates to a firm's capability to use its resources or to identify and acquire those available in the environment before its competitors do. As the environment changes, the capabilities required to identify and use the resources must adjust, and that adjustment implies organizational learning (Teece, Pisano, & Sheun, 1997). This is particularly true when new markets open through processes such as technological innovation or globalization (Methé, Mitchell, & Swaminathan, 1996). The opening of markets through globalization presents opportunities to identify and capture resources ahead of competitors.

In examining these pharmaceutical companies, we set forth their expectations about globalization before attempting to evaluate the process. Our approach to understanding and classifying the various paths that Japanese pharmaceutical companies have taken toward the parent-subsidiary relationships is exploratory and used Argyris and Schön's (1978) work in describing deutero, double loop, and single loop learning as a broad conceptual framework. In this study's context of the globalization of R & D we use this broad framework in a way similar to Dodgson's (1993). The Japanese pharmaceutical firms perceive that they are weak in using the organizational routines for pharmaceutical discovery research, especially in biotechnology. Thus, the error to be corrected is the lack of knowledge related to discovery of new chemical entities, especially through biotechnological research. We see single loop learning as acquiring that knowledge and double loop learning as correcting this weakness not only by acquiring the knowledge but also by acquiring the organizational routines needed to develop such knowledge independently in the future. Further, we believe that deutero learning may develop in firms that experience double loop learning if managerial structures provide the opportunity for learning at the managerial level.

In our study, we define a subsidiary in broader terms than those used in most of the globalization literature. Because we are concerned with learning, and especially learning in the context of research and development, the concepts of firm boundaries need to be extended beyond the traditional equity definition (Pisano, 1990). We include as subsidiaries not only wholly owned organizations, but also joint ventures and alliances for scientific research, as well as product development with companies and other institutions, such as universities. This is consistent with our definition of globalization and more accurately reflects the actual activities of companies in the study. Each of the globalizing activities is seen as a dyadic relationship between the parent and subsidiary. As a result, a company may have several sets of these relationships.

How a management structures its globalization process in order to facilitate the information flow in acquiring research knowledge and moving it between the parent and subsidiary is important. These structures can be an integrated two-way flow, a one-way flow either from the parent to the subsidiary or vice versa, or a disjointed two-way flow. The main difference between an integrated two-way flow and a disjointed two-way flow of information is that in the former, the information flow occurs within one set of parent-subsidiary relationships operating in a coordinated fashion, whereas in the latter the information flow is spread out among several sets of parent-subsidiary relationships operating relatively independently. Further, we divide the companies by how much they emphasize acquiring content-specific research knowledge versus both process and content knowledge. These companies are arrayed according to the degree of organizational learning built into the globalization of R & D that each has engaged in at the time data were collected, in 1993.

As can be seen in figure 10.1, the previous discussion is arrayed along two dimensions. The horizontal axis lists the strategic structure of the globalization activities and the vertical axis the R & D functional knowledge targets. Along the side and bottom of each axis are the potential organizational learning outcomes. For the R & D knowledge targets, those firms that engage in acquiring just content knowledge are more likely to experience single-loop learning at the functional level, whereas those that target both content and process knowledge will likely experience double-loop learning at the functional level.

Along the horizontal axis, the strategic structure of the globalization activities are arrayed, with the potential managerial learning outcomes along the bottom of

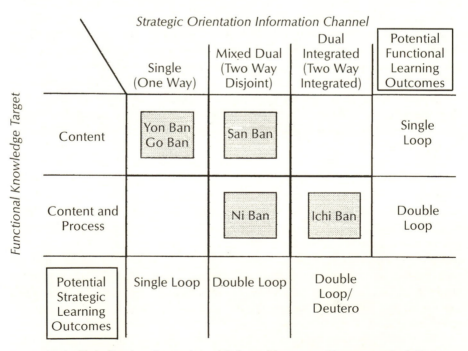

FIGURE 10.1 Globalization Strategies of Selected Japanese Pharmaceutical Companies and Potential Learning Outcomes

the table. A one-way channel refers to an activity in which the firm's search is dominated by the need to acquire the functional R & D knowledge and no attempt is made to engage in a dialogue with other organizations, whereas a two-way channel does establish a dialog between the firm and the other organization. The focal firm using a two-way channel is more likely to share information at a deeper level and consequently is more likely to need to develop structures that have absorptive capacity. Hence, it is more likely to engage in double-loop learning.

The resource-based theory of the firm would suggest that one of the key aspects to competing in an industry characterized by multiple knowledge bases located in multiple locations is that one must be able to tap into these when needed. To do so, a company must add to its repertoire of capabilities in understanding these various knowledge bases. As noted earlier, this can be accomplished through a number of different strategic alternatives such as contracting, alliances, merger / acquisition, or internal development. How would these activities map into the organizational learning matrix presented in figure 10.1?

Companies characterized as following a dual-channel integrated globalization strategy have likely established a research facility overseas.[4] This research facility is an integral part of the company's future research capability and requires that information and learning flow in both directions. The parent company's relationship with the overseas research facility acts as a coordinating mechanism for all the other globalization activities undertaken. As a result, the flow of information from all overseas activities is "housed" within one parent-subsidiary relationship forming an integrated two-way flow of information. Further, this information is concerned with both the content of the research and the process of how the research is accomplished. These companies tend to emphasize learning about the process of conducting research, especially discovery research, as well as the content knowledge derived from the research. There is a need to have two-way flows of information between the parent and subsidiary and to create governance mechanisms to manage that flow. Companies engaged in this intense set of activities are more likely to be strategically aware that they must learn from their globalization attempts and to establish knowledge storage or memory structures inside the parent. By structuring the parent-subsidiary relationship in this way, the company is more likely to engage in double-loop learning and will open the organization to the strong possibility of engaging in deutero learning.

Those companies in the single-channel globalization strategy have established some form of research activity overseas. This activity may be a joint venture, a wholly owned research facility set up to do clinical or discovery research, or a series of contract / licensing relationships between the company and individual researchers in other institutions in the host country. However, this activity has been structured in such a way that information flows primarily in one direction, either from the parent to the subsidiary or from the subsidiary to the parent, and is primarily concerned about the content of the research knowledge, not the process by which the research is carried out.[5] The earlier examples of Sony and Matsushita in their acquisitions of movie companies is an illustration of this type of relationship. Because this type of parent-subsidiary relationship does not build structures within the parent for knowledge storage or does not have a strong strategic awareness for organizational learning, this type of arrangement does not alter the organizational routines for conducting research inside the company and focuses primarily on correcting weaknesses in the company's technological knowledge base. This type of organizational learning is likely single-loop learning.

Companies following a mixed-mode globalization strategy have structured their R & D activities in such a way that some of the channels are concerned with learning content while others are concerned with learning process, and these can be either a one-way or two-way channel between the parent and the subsidiary. Again, these can be joint ventures, alliances, contract research, or individual research laboratories. There are usually several different types of parent-subsidiary relationships that make up multiple sets. Each of these sets, or dyads, of parent-subsidiary relationships was formed for a different purpose and lacks the integrative approach of the dual-channel strategy. In aggregate the information flows are two-way, but no single parent-subsidiary relationship acts as a focal point for integrating the information flows, and, consequently, these are disjointed two-way flows of information. Companies in the mixed-mode strategy thus have a sense of the need to build absorptive capacity and balance it with insulating mechanisms, but not the coordinated efforts exhibited by the dual-channel strategists. The type of organizational learning occurring in the mixed-mode globalization strategy depends on the degree of strategic awareness and the extent of knowledge storage structure development. Clearly the greater the development of absorptive capacity, the more likely double-loop learning will occur.

We have identified one company as following an integrated dual-channel globalization strategy. Another two companies are following a mixed-mode channel globalization strategy. And finally, two more are following a single-channel globalization strategy. All the companies have attempted some form of globalization of R & D; the distinction between them is the degree to which their globalization strategy requires a one-way or two-way flow of information and whether they emphasize content or process learning. We now turn our attention to examining several of the companies in more detail. Each of these companies is representative of the category of global strategy/organizational learning described earlier. The names of the companies have been disguised to preserve confidentiality.

Company Profiles

Dual-Channel Deutero Learning

Ichi Ban.   Ichi Ban company as of 1994 is the fourth largest Japanese pharmaceutical firm with sales of Y297 billion and net income of Y20 billion. The company spent 11.5% of sales, or Y34.2 billion, on R & D in 1994. Ichi Ban was founded in 1941 and has focused primarily on pharmaceuticals, which account for 90% of its sales.

Ichi Ban established its first overseas research facility in 1987, the Ichi Ban Research Institute of Boston. Ichi Ban also has a number of other types of relationships with overseas research institutes. Ichi Ban has funded three projects with a U.S. biotechnology company. This first laboratory was rented and a new facility was constructed in 1989 in Andover, Massachusetts. A close personal contact between the president of Ichi Ban and a professor at Harvard University played an important role in getting the laboratory established. Research in this laboratory is in organic synthesis, with about 10 researchers doing postdoctoral research. The purpose of this laboratory is the discovery of new chemical entities.

In 1990, Ichi Ban established its London Research Laboratory, affiliated with the University College of London. Research into molecular and cell biology was begun at the London laboratory in 1991. The university had contacted Ichi Ban to establish a partnership and currently holds three of the four positions on the scientific board that guides research at the laboratory. The other position is held by a professor from Cambridge. Currently the research staff is 16, one of whom is Japanese. Ichi Ban plans to eventually have 20% of the research staff as Japanese. Although the London laboratory is essentially a foreign operation run by a foreign staff, the Japanese researchers are intended to play a vital role as a link between basic research at London and in Japan. The intention is to help speed the movement of research from discovery to a final product.

The activities of the Boston and London laboratories are complemented by Ichi Ban's own laboratories at Tsukuba, Japan. Ichi Ban was the first private company to open a large-scale research complex at Tsukuba when it established its laboratory in 1982. The major activity is exploratory drug research, carried out via a project-oriented system that matches the chemistry group with the pharmacological group for each disease area. Another key activity is to act as a link between the Boston and London laboratories. The Tsukuba laboratory helps to advance projects initiated at the Boston laboratory, particularly because the Tsukuba laboratory is better equipped to carry out in vivo studies. Also, the Tsukuba laboratory is charged with implementing research related to new concepts discovered at the London laboratory.

Although strong personal relationships between the president of Ichi Ban and people initially responsible for setting up the Boston and London Laboratories still exist, the channels for learning have broadened and deepened in both instances. While individual learning occurred through the personal relationships, by establishing permanent structures and systems, individual learning can be more easily converted into organizational learning. For instance, in addition to the scientific boards, there is also a management board for each laboratory. While the scientific boards set the directions for each of the laboratories and help to coordinate between the three laboratories, the management boards also coordinate personnel movements, budgets, and other logistical issues. Further, the research directors of each of the three laboratories meet periodically to discuss how research is going in each laboratory and what can be done to enhance the transfer of knowledge. Once a project has been selected that requires the interaction of the Tsukuba laboratory and either the London or Boston laboratory, project-level research managers also coordinate at each of the sites. The work of transferring learning among the laboratories has been one area of top management attention, especially from the president. Areas that still need to be developed include how to evaluate the work at the various laboratories and how successful the transfer process has been. Ichi Ban management referred to researchers at Tsukuba as "catchers," who have the function of capturing ideas from the various overseas laboratories. These people and the systems and structures that support them play a crucial absorptive capacity role in that they act both as information collectors and as storage or memory mechanisms in the parent firm. These people are also seen as playing a critical role in any future evaluation system. As such, they must be cognizant of both process and content knowledge.

Ichi Ban has sought to alter its R & D routines by establishing facilities overseas that are specialized and closely linked in the value chain of new drug development. This has required their management to develop structures and systems that would enhance the absorptive capacity at Ichi Ban in Japan in dealing with its two overseas subsidiaries. It has established dual channels between the three laboratories both at the scientific and management levels and at the strategic and operational levels as well. Although there are two parent-subsidiary relationships, attempts are made through the various boards to integrate them. Further, concern is placed not only on transferring knowledge but also on understanding the research process that goes on at each of the laboratories, in order to better evaluate research progress. Because this is a very recent activity, Ichi Ban appears to be engaged in an experiment in deutero learning, in that it must reflect on how it learned in the past and what elements worked and did not work. Its senior management has established several high-profile parent-subsidiary relationships and is integrating these into the core R & D process. As a result, they must devote considerable time and other resources to overseeing the management and functions of these relationships. Consequently, Ichi Ban is experiencing organizational learning at the management level as well as at the research process and content levels. Its current coordinating mechanisms are a new strategy for organizational learning, and these in turn are undergoing continual scrutiny for which elements can be generalized to the organization and which elements can be discarded.

Mixed-Mode Double-Loop Learning

Ni Ban.   Ni Ban, established in 1943, is the eleventh largest Japanese pharmaceutical company, with about 2.6% of the Japanese market. Ni Ban's sales were Y171.6 billion in 1994. Its net income was Y8.2 billion in 1994, and Ni Ban spent Y5.4 billion on R & D in that year. Although 98% of sales are derived from pharmaceuticals, Ni Ban also makes diagnostic products, personal health care products, and agrochemicals.

Ni Ban began its overseas involvement in 1985 with a joint venture with Genetics Institute (GI) to help develop and market the drug EPO. Ni Ban received the rights to sell EPO in Asia. Because of a 1991 court ruling awarding patents to Kirin-Amgen for EPO, Ni Ban's joint venture with GI is in some doubt, although it can still market EPO in Asia. Ni Ban also became involved in another joint venture with Gen-Probe of San Diego, California, in 1987. Ni Ban provided funding into biotechnology related to diagnostics. In 1989, Ni Ban acquired Gen-Probe and moved its research efforts in this area to the San Diego laboratory. Ni Ban has also made a large investment in Vertex, a Cambridge, Massachusetts, company that focuses on drug design. The initial investments were made in 1990, and since then Ni Ban has sent three of its researchers to Vertex. Ni Ban in 1988 also made an investment in British Biotechnology (BT) to tap into the basic work in molecular biology conducted at that company.

In 1993, Ni Ban sent 15 researchers from Japan to work at Gen-Probe. This action merged the two research units, creating a greater critical mass for conducting research into biotechnology-related diagnostics. In essence, this action also corrected an error in the previous R & D structure since there had been difficulties in coordinating the research activities of the two separate facilities. The Gen-Probe facility is managed independently, for there is now no need for coordination. Although there is a top-management meeting between the parent and subsidiary to aid in information exchange, Ni Ban has not developed an in-depth management system to facilitate the development of an integrated dual-channel structure, such as scientific or management boards. As a result, the top management of Ni Ban must still confront the coordination issue in that they would like Gen-Probe to move more into the medical therapeutics area. As yet, Gen-Probe is still considering the idea.

In the case of Vertex, the type and degree of channel building is different. Ni Ban owns about 5% of Vertex's stock and has sent three researchers to work in areas such as immunosuppressant research, organic synthesis, and biotechnology. However, most of the information exchange is carried out through electronic mail between researchers at Ni Ban's laboratory and those at Vertex. It is difficult to determine what mechanisms are in place to convert this individual learning into organizational learning. The relationship with BT is even more loose. Ni Ban was made aware of BT through an investment banker in London and, currently, Ni Ban owns stock in BT but does not have any ongoing projects.

In each of the three sets of parent-subsidiary relationships between Ni Ban and its overseas affiliates, most of the knowledge transfer is concerned with content and it is one-way. There is two-way knowledge transfer between Ni Ban and Vertex, but this appears to be limited to content knowledge. No attempt has been made to learn research process knowledge. Ni Ban is engaging in double-loop learning at the management of globalization level in the sense that it is trying to correct errors in its current organizational routines for conducting global R & D. Its transfer of its diagnostic group to Gen-Probe is evidence of this. Further, it is currently evaluating what it will do with the BT relationship and is aware that it must modify its relationships somewhat in order to enhance its current organizational routine for conducting R & D.

San Ban.   San Ban had Y293 billion in total sales in 1994, with Y23.1 billion in net income. About 95% of its sales are in pharmaceuticals. This placed San Ban as tenth in the Japanese market among pharmaceutical companies. It spent about 11.8% of sales, or Y26.8 billion, on R & D in 1994.

San Ban began its overseas research activity by funding research work on Interferon at a major U.S. biotechnology firm in 1981. In return for its funding, San Ban received marketing rights to the drug but did not engage in any collaborative research. In 1982 it set up a subsidiary in the United States to do marketing and clinical work for pharmaceuticals developed in Japan. It subsequently set up similar relationships with a joint venture in France in 1990 and a wholly owned subsidiary in the United Kingdom in 1993. Both do clinical research for drugs developed in Japan.

San Ban began its first real foray into collaborative research when, in 1988, it established an alliance with a California biotechnology firm to do research into the central nervous system, particularly Alzheimer's disease. One researcher was sent from San Ban, and after two years some basic knowledge was developed, but the relationship was terminated because it was determined that it would take far longer than initially anticipated to develop a drug from the research. Again in 1988, San Ban established another alliance with a Norwegian firm to do basic research on contrast agents. San Ban does not have the capability to do such basic research work in its Tokyo laboratory, but it can do developmental work. It helps by funding the research in Norway and has established a board that meets twice a year to oversee the work. The relationship is still ongoing. This board represents a possible mechanism for converting individual into organizational learning, at least at the global management level. It may facilitate the conversion at the research level.

San Ban has also engaged in research with universities in the United States as a way to develop experience in areas that will be needed in the future. Utilizing some of the experience gained from the relationship with the California biotechnology company, San Ban set up two contract research relationships with universities in the United States. They have established a board to oversee the research and are planning to send some of their own researchers in the future. They also established an endowed chair at a third university. Although this chair was set up because of a close contact between San Ban and a particular professor, who has subsequently left for another university, the funding for the chair continues.

San Ban has established several other sets of parent-subsidiary relationships. The relationships related to overseas clinical research and marketing are primarily a one-way channel from the parent to the subsidiary. There are also relationships that are alliances with venture companies or universities that are primarily a one-way channel from the subsidiary to the parent. The focus in these relationships has been on content knowledge learning, but because of the "failures" experienced with the California biotechnology company, and to a lesser extent with its endowed chair at a U.S. university, San Ban has gained knowledge in the process of managing these relationships. It has engaged in double-loop learning in that it has modified some of the underlying organizational routines for managing these relationships, as seen in the subsequent development of the various boards.

Single-Channel Single-Loop Learning

Yon Ban.   Yon Ban had overall sales of Y341.8 billion in 1994. Approximately 51%, or Y174 billion, were from pharmaceuticals placing Yon Ban about fourteenth in terms of pharmaceutical sales in the Japanese market. Yon Ban spent Y17.5 billion, or 5% of total sales on R & D and about 50% of R & D expenditures were devoted directly to pharmaceutical research.

Yon Ban linked into overseas knowledge bases early. It first sent two of its researchers to the University of Wisconsin in the mid-1970s to learn about recombinant DNA technology, and it funded research on the blood clot breaking drug TPA at a U.S. biotech firm in 1982. The pattern established with these alliances has been repeated in several more cases during subsequent years. Yon Ban funded the TPA research in exchange for the marketing rights in Japan. It did not engage in collaborative research with the biotech firm, choosing instead to fund their research. Consequently, Yon Ban was interested only in absorbing the content knowledge regarding TPA. This is indicative of a single-channel structure in that the information flows in only one direction. It is also indicative of single-loop learning in that the relationship is aimed at learning about research content areas that currently do not exist within Yon Ban. Yon Ban currently has a similar relationship with two biotechnology companies in the United States, one knowledgeable about cardiovascular disorders and the other about neurodegenerative disorders. Again, both are funded, primarily on a milestone basis, with little collaborative work with Yon Ban. It has focused most of its R & D efforts at its primary laboratories in Mishima and Tokyo. Most of the discovery work is carried out at the Tokyo Laboratories.

Very selectively, Yon Ban has sent a small number of its researchers to work in foreign institutions. Based on the project and the needs for specific content knowledge to reinforce activities carried out in Japan, Yon Ban has sent a few of its researchers to work on projects at the National Cancer Institute and the National Institutes of Health. Likewise, similar relationships have been established with universities in the United States and Europe. In each of the cases the selection of institutes and projects is based on the need to acquire certain knowledge about a particular discipline or chemical compound. In addition, the research relationship is tied to particular researchers, not the institute. In other words, Yon Ban will fully fund its researchers or fund the project of a university's researcher but has not established a permanent relationship with the institution by endowing a chair or laboratory, as San Ban did.

Yon Ban has set up some overseas subsidiaries in the United States and Germany, but these are mainly for marketing drugs. Although the marketing of pharmaceuticals requires that clinical research be done, both in the United States and Europe, these are handled on a contract basis. As yet there is no plan to develop even this type of research capability overseas. Further, there is no relationship between these marketing offices and Yon Ban's researchers who are in the United States or Europe.

These patterns of parent-subsidiary relationship are likely to continue in the near future. Yon Ban may increase the number of researchers abroad and also the number of links with biotechnology firms, but has no plan to establish a major joint venture or permanent laboratory. It has established a one-way channel to collect content knowledge and engages in single-loop learning.

Go Ban Pharmaceutical.   Go Ban Pharmaceutical company is ranked about thirteenth in the market by pharmaceutical sales. Its overall sales in 1994 were Y384 billion, with about 40% from pharmaceuticals. It is estimated that about Y27 billion was spent on research in 1994.

Go Ban has a very decentralized R & D structure, with about 850 researchers spread out over 12 research "institutes." Go Ban began its overseas R & D activities in 1985 with the opening of a laboratory for clinical work in Maryland and another in Frankfurt. The Frankfurt laboratory currently does some preclinical work in eye and skin areas, but the main aim of the work at these two laboratories is to get drugs developed in Japan certified for the U.S. and European markets. Formal meetings are held once a year with these overseas research institutes to determine progress and to coordinate future action.

Go Ban did engage in funding some overseas research that was closer to discovery. Through a close personal contact at a western U.S. university, a research institute was established in 1986. Research in this institute focused on cell surface membranes and cancer. Although the research has been ongoing, Go Ban decided to terminate the relationship in 1994. Go Ban is classified as having a single-channel single-loop learning strategy, primarily because of the relationships between the Japanese parent and the Maryland and Frankfurt laboratories and because it funded research at the institute with no involvement on the part of its Japanese researchers. In essence, the relationships were initiated to correct specific weaknesses in content knowledge of the parent firm. This is achieved by one-way flows of information from the overseas subsidiary to the parent.

Conclusions and Implications

Our study addresses several issues at the interface of strategy and organizational learning and has implications for executives as they attempt to manage the parent-subsidiary relationship, especially as it relates to R & D. First, we agree with the research that suggests a relationship between individual learning and organizational learning. All learning in organizations begins as individual learning, and the process of spreading what an individual has learned throughout the rest of the company constitutes organizational learning. In the context of our study, Japanese organizations have certain advantages and disadvantages in this conversion process. The advantages spring from the HRM policies of Japanese companies (Pucik, 1988). In particular, the long-term employment and job rotation aspects allow Japanese individuals to be in an organization longer and to interact with a greater number of people throughout the organization. Both enhance the opportunity for converting individual learning into organizational learning. These same HRM policies are at work in each of the companies studied. Consequently, it is more likely that researchers sent overseas will return and act to spread their individual knowledge to others in the organization. Given that these individuals will likely stay with the company during their entire career, as a natural outgrowth of the normal rotation and promotion process, their individual learning can affect how research is done in the company. By altering the research routines over time, the individual learning is converted into organizational learning.

The conversion of this individual learning into organizational learning is affected first by the fact that researchers going overseas are subject to the same forces at work in negotiating a third culture as those noted in chapters 3 and 5. The question of what research routines will be developed in the subsidiary and transferred to the parent arises. The conversion of individual learning into organizational learning is further affected by the general orientation toward learning observed in Japanese organizations. However, this is a double-edged sword. As noted earlier, one of the most important factors affecting this conversion process is the socialization of the individual into the mainstream culture of the organization. Further, the mainstream culture of Japanese organizations is composed of a dominant technical logic that emphasizes efficient product development (Methé, 1997). The strength of the dominant technical logic can act as a filter that strips away research process learning that tends to contradict it. The power of this inertial tendency can be seen in that a number of Japanese researchers, beginning with Dr. Esaki, have left Japan for the United States and subsequently won Nobel prizes. They left because the organizational culture built up by the dominant technical logic of product development did not support changes to the organization that encouraged discovery. Consequently, it is important to recognize that companies that engage in activities that build absorptive capacity are more likely to experience, at the very least, double-loop learning.

These companies have a greater chance of overcoming the inertia of the dominant technical logic than companies that engage only in single-loop learning. Companies engaged in double-loop learning exhibit a strategic awareness of the need to learn and combine that awareness with structures for organizational memory that aid changes related to the management of the globalization process and the research process. These alterations can, over time, create a new technical logic that includes both the knowledge exploration and knowledge exploitation aspects of R & D. We found, in results similar to those described in chpater 7, that although Japanese firms use "Japanese" management systems, they adapt these in very different ways.

One explanation for these differences stems from interfirm differences in strategic resource endowments. This leads us to our second point that there are strategic implications of the various approaches to learning for the company from the standpoint of resources expended versus output gained. The kind of organizational learning that is most appropriate depends as much on the resource and capability endowment of the company and its overall strategic approach to globalization as it does on any abstract hierarchy of learning types. Although deutero learning is a more complex, involved type of learning that should yield more profound results concerning a company's strategy and changes in its dominant logic than either double-loop or single-loop learning, its very complexity and requirement for multilevel managerial involvement taxes the resource base of the company more both in terms of the learning process itself and in incorporating the lessons learned into the organization. This may be a very inefficient use of the resources, and although the company may learn and change its strategy and dominant logic, it may still fail in the marketplace.

Consequently, it may be just as strategically appropriate to structure the parent-subsidiary relationship for Yon Ban or Go Ban in single-channel single-loop learning as it is for Ichi Ban to structure theirs in a dual-channel deutero learning. What is most important from a strategic point of view is matching the type of learning needed with the current resource and capability level of the organization. Further, for Yon Ban or San Ban or Ni Ban to consider changing from single- to double-loop or double-loop to deutero learning would require not only the alteration of the parent-subsidiary structure from single-channel to dual-channel, but also the building of absorptive capacity inside the parent, in order to take full advantage of the strength of the subsidiary. This would require considerable expenditure of resources, especially managerial talent and time, and may not yield the benefits in new discoveries and product development that would enhance company survival. Parent-subsidiary relationships that overtax the organization are just as debilitating as those that cause the company to underperform in learning and will increase the probability of organizational failure and bankruptcy.

Third, the previous two points converge in this recognition: although all learning is individual, this individual learning is strongly influenced by the social context in which it takes place (Simon, 1991). An important part of that social context is the organization and its dominant logic. For a company to achieve the proper strategic match, it must be aware of the dominant logic in its strategic thinking and how much it needs to be changed to enhance its capabilities to respond to its environment. The structure of the parent-subsidiary relationship is a critical part of this process, but it is only the beginning.

Another important aspect of managing these relationships, no matter how they are structured, is that special attention must be paid to the personnel utilized in the relationship. Several issues must be addressed, and the type of approach will also influence the type and success of learning. For example, whether people are from the technical part of the organization or the managerial part will influence the type of content, as well as process knowledge imported. A worker's age or seniority in the organization will also influence the type of learning and the manner in which it is converted into organizational learning. More senior people will have more immediate impact and perhaps generate longer-term changes in capabilities. The number of people sent to subsidiaries is also important. A larger number of junior people sent may be able to insulate themselves long enough to have a dramatic impact on the parent organization after they return. Where and how these people are housed when they return is also critical to converting individual learning to organizational learning. The more central, as opposed to a peripheral, location will increase the likelihood of spreading the learning throughout the organization.

In addition, whether the people move from the parent to the subsidiary only or also move from the subsidiary to the parent as well will influence the type of learning. This final point has a direct impact on the building of absorptive capacity. If both sides of the organizational equation have knowledge of the other, it is easier to build receptor sites into the parent and the subsidiary. These receptor sites can more easily transfer knowledge, especially tacit knowledge, between the two organizations because they will share more of the language, values, and norms of their counterpart. In setting up these receptor sites, however, the balance between the dominant logic of the parent and that of the subsidiary must be considered. If the subsidiary is primarily charged with clinical research, then there is less of an issue. If the subsidiary has been established to do discovery work, then the parent must emphasize insulation. This can be accomplished positively through building its own basic research capabilities in the receptor site in its home laboratory. This would also create absorptive capacity inside the parent.

Finally, in a number of the cases discussed—Ichi Ban, San Ban, Go Ban—personal contacts and relationships played a significant role in helping to establish the parent-subsidiary relationship. These personal relationships were also noted as important in helping to facilitate the flow of information between the parent and subsidiary. However, the overreliance of personal contacts can fall prey to the vagaries of personal career moves and individual motives, as Kleinberg pointed out in chapter 4. This can hinder the continued development of the relationship or result in its termination. From our study we find that information flow is enhanced and organizational learning is increased where these personal contacts are supplemented by more formal mechanisms for governance, such as the scientific and managerial boards. These boards and other formal structures help to set up the "skeletal" framework that can allow for greater informal contact to develop. This tends to increase the spread of the *jinmyaku*, or personal network, more rapidly and deeply between the parent and subsidiary and not only facilitates the governance of these relationships but also increases the absorptive capacity in the organization.

Our study has revealed that learning in the context of globalization of R & D activities can take many forms in structuring the parent-subsidiary relationship. The ultimate value of these forms is a complex and dynamic mix of the company's initial endowment of resources and capabilities, and its strategic intent. The managing of these relationships places a strong emphasis on HRM development and strategy. Although the various strategic approaches may differ, one common trait of all these companies is their recognition that they must engage in this globalization process and that they must enhance their organizational learning. It is too soon to determine which strategy is most appropriate, but it is certain that companies ignore this trend at their own peril.

Notes

1. Learning can occur at a number of different levels, but most researchers distinguish between learning that occurs within an individual and learning that occurs among a group of individuals. The latter is usually called organizational learning. In this study, when we refer to learning, we mean organizational learning unless otherwise denoted.

2. For more discussion of the role of perception in enacting a firm's environment in the context of the Japanese MNC, see chapter 12.

3. For more discussion of the notion of tacitness in the Japanese MNC, see chapter 5.

4. It is possible to establish a parent-subsidiary relationship that is content-oriented. Likely, this would be under a multidomestic strategy. It is also possible to have a dual-channel integrated approach without establishing a research facility. A long-term comprehensive cross-licensing agreement with a stable set of partners is an example. A potential candidate would be the alliance between IBM, Toshiba, and Seimens to develop the 256 M DRAM.

5. It is possible to set up a parent-subsidiary relationship that is single-channel and targets content and process R & D knowledge. This would occur in the case of a firm sending researchers over for postdoctoral research at a university.

References

Argyris, C., & Schön, D. 1978. *Organizational Learning*. London: Addison-Wesley.

Brown, J. S., & Duguid, P. 1991. "Organizational Learning and Communities-of-Practice: Toward a Unified View of Working, Learning, and Innovation." *Organization Science*. 2 (1): 40–57.

Cohen, W., & Levinthal, D. 1990. "Absorptive Capacity: A New Perspective on Learning and Innovation." *Administrative Science Quarterly*. March. 128–52.

Cole, R. 1989. *Strategies for Learning: Small-Group Activities in American, Japanese, and Swedish Industry*. University of California Press, Berkeley.

Cole, R. 1995. "Reflections on Organizational Learning in U.S. and Japanese Industry." In Liker, J., Ettlie, J., and Campbell, J. (eds.), *Managing Technology Through Organizations: U.S. and Japanese Approaches*. New York: Oxford University Press. 365–379.

Corisini, R. 1987. *Concise Encyclopedia of Psychology*. New York: Wiley.

Dierickx, I., & Cool, K. 1989 "Asset Stock Accumulation and Sustainability of Competitive Advantage." *Management Science*. 35: 1504–1511.

Dodgson, M. 1993. "Organizational Learning: A Review of Some Literatures." *Organization Studies*. 14 (3): 375–396.

Garratt, R. 1987. *The Learning Organization*. London: Fontana/Collis.

Ghoshal, S. 1987. "Global Strategy: An Organizing Framework." *Strategic Management Journal*. 8: 425–440.

Hedberg, B. 1981. "How Organizations Learn and Unlearn." In Nystrom, P., and Starbuck, W. (eds.), *Handbook of Organizational Design*. London: Oxford University Press, 3–27.

Henderson R., & Cockburn, I. 1994. *Measuring Core Competence? Evidence from the Pharmaceutical Industry*. MIT working paper, January.

Imai, K., Nonaka, I., & Takeuchi, H. 1985. "How Japanese Companies Learn and Unlearn." Clark, K., Hayes, R., & Lorenz, C. (eds.), *The Uneasy Alliance: Managing the Productivity-Technology Dilemma*. Cambridge, MA: Harvard University Press. 337–375.

Levitt, B., & March, J. 1988. "Organizational Learning." *Annual Review of Sociology*. 14: 319–340.

Methé, D. T. 1995. "Basic Research in Japanese Electronic Companies: An Attempt at Establishing New Organizational Routines." In Liker, J., Ettlie, J., & Campbell, J., (eds.), *Managing Technology Through Organizations: U.S. and Japanese Approaches*. New York: Oxford University Press. 17–39.

Methé, D. T., Mitchell, W., & Swaminathan, A. 1996. "The Underemphasized Role of Established Firms as the Source of Major Innovations." *Industrial and Corporate Change*. 5 (4, Second Special Issue on Telecommunication Policy and Strategy).

Methé, D. T. 1997. "Living on the Edge: Basic Research and Knowledge Creation in Japanese Electronics Companies." In McIntyre, J. R. (ed.), *Japan's Technical Standards: Implications for Global Trade and Competitiveness*. Westport, CT: Quorum Books. 47–64.

Nelson, R., & Winter, S. 1982. *An Evolutionary Theory of Economic Change*. Cambridge, MA: Belknap Press.

Nevis, E. C., DiBella, A. J., & Gould, J. M. 1995. "Understanding Organizations as Learning Systems." *Sloan Management Review*. Winter: 73–85.

Nonaka, I. 1991. "The Knowledge-Creating Company." *Harvard Business Review*. 69 (6): 96–104.

Nonaka, I., and Takeuchi, H. 1995. *The Knowledge Creating Company*. New York: Oxford University Press.

Penner-Hahn, J. D. 1995. *The Internationalization of Research and Development: A Firm Level Study*. Unpublished doctoral dissertation, University of Michigan, Ann Arbor.

Peteraf, M. A. 1993. "The Cornerstones of Competitive Advantage: A Resource-based view." *Strategic Management Journal*. 14 (3): 179–192.

Pisano, G. P. 1990. "The R&D Boundaries of the Firm: An Empirical Analysis." *Administrative Science Quarterly*. March: 153–176.

Pucik, V. 1988. "Strategic Alliances, Organizational Learning, and Competitive Advantage: The HRM Agenda." *Human Resource Management*. 27 (1): 77–93.

Schein, E. 1985. *Organizational Culture and Leadership*. San Francisco: Jossey-Bass.

Senge, P. 1990. "The Leader's New Work: Building Learning Organizations." *Sloan Management Review*. 32 (1): 7–23.

Simon, H. A. 1991. "Bounded Rationality and Organizationl Learning." *Organization Science*. 2 (1): 125–131.

Teece, D. J., Pisano, G., & Shuen, A. 1997. "Dynamic Capabilities and Strategic Management." *Strategic Management Journal*. 18 (7): 509–533.

Wernerfelt, B. 1984. "A Resource Based Theory of the Firm." *Strategic Management Journal*. 5: 171–180.

11

JOHN KIDD

Working Together, But How?

The Need for Intercultural Awareness

There is little doubt that major overseas capital investments in the future will be placed by firms and institutions within the triad nations—that is, in North America (represented by the North American Free Trade Area [NAFTA]), in the European Union [EU], and in Asia (which does not yet have a formal economic union). Most investments will be between firms in the developed regions, but more and more will be invested in Asia (which may be said to be developing) by a firm, that itself may be represented globally or in more than one triad region. Generally, these firms retain many aspects of their original national culture bias in their global dealings. Hence, we may look forward to ever more cross-cultural exchanges as investors and potential recipients strive to reach agreements that are, first, understandable and, second, meaningful to both negotiators.

In this chapter I consider some of the factors that may hinder investments through a lack of awareness of the other's cultural heritage. By this I mean those natural habits that may identify one as belonging to a specific nation or region but may infuriate those with whom we negotiate, or work. For instance, when the issues under discussion are not urgent, we may be indulgent of each other's foibles. But if the situation is serious, and many are, we must have learned first about the others before we can proceed. As Sun Zhu has suggested (Cleary, 1988: 48), "Assess the advantage in taking advice, then structure your forces accordingly, to supplement extraordinary tactics. Forces are to be structured strategically, based on what is advantageous."

This chapter reviews how people, in general, differ on several constructs—their use of time or space, and how well informed they wish to be with respect to the context of the issues that surround them. The chapter also discusses how individuals may be brought together as in a team to manage a project, as this relates to the globalization of investment, planning, and fulfillment. If these plans, conceived by persons of like mind from a monoculture, cannot be fulfilled when negotiated across cultures, then perhaps there is a need to be more culturally aware. Finally I review how well Italian-Japanese production firms were managed from the viewpoint of being learning organizations.

Often this chapter assumes that the participants in the negotiation and learning processes are Japanese persons working with North American or European persons. This assumption is a convenience to limit the chapter's scope since many other nations also impress their culture upon others, for instance:

> Many years ago the English, Dutch and French colonized the Caribbean and established their customs and practices. Yet Stuart Hall [a well-known British literary commentator] recently confessed that he, though having been born in Jamaica and educated in an upper class English school in Kingston, never thought of himself as British. But a peer, he suggested, living in nearby Martinique would think of himself as French, and if working there as a civil servant would be automatically granted Home Leave to *return* to Paris from time to time! Once in Paris the person from Martinique, exercising his rights through his received model of French bureaucracy, would be shocked to be described as "a 'black' from Africa." (Open University interview, BBC TV, March 1997; emphasis added)

Time, Space, and the Context in Which We Work

Hall (1959) as well as Hall and Hall (1987) discuss their models of how people deal with time and with the events taking place round them. Some persons are monochronic (M-time): they work as though time is linear. Others believe time is multistranded: they work in a parallel processing mode, so are called polychronic (P-time). Inbetweeners sometimes work in one mode or sometimes the other mode (typified by many French persons, see Platt, 1994). The M-time and the P-time persons represent the extreme poles of an organizing framework.

These notions are confounded by the degree to which individuals need supporting data to enact their life. This is not a simple question, as in a statistical test where more data lead to a stronger validation. Rather, we must realize that some persons wish to live and work in a flux of continuously ebbing and flowing information, whereas others do not wish to be confused by that form of environment.

So how can the Japanese, who are typically polychronic, work with the Americans and northern Europeans, who are basically monochronic? And, in turn, how can the Europeans themselves work together when under the umbrella of a Japanese organization? As we will see, other national characteristics indicate that Europeans are strongly differentiated country by country (see chapter 3).

The Historical Development of Time Frames

Hall (1976: 17) argues that the most natural time frame of all humans accords with nature, according to the rise and fall of the sun and to weather patterns. Indeed, most farmers must still work like this; crops are seasonal, and their gathering is intimately connected with weather patterns. Hall's argument suggests that the Industrial Revolution, initially in England, is to blame for the development of monochronic persons. Yet it was not the first wave of preindustrial persons who became monochronic because these persons, having been drafted (and enticed) from the villages and fields used to return home for a while, once they thought they had done enough work to feed themselves. It was their children who were impressionable. They grew up in and subsequently worked in the factories: they became the "changed ones," having grown up in accord with the factory whistle. They worked according to a schedule and further imprinted this mode on their own children. Thus, the Industrial Revolution created its own human solution to keep the mill wheels turning. Hall suggests the linear time person, the M-time person, is in fact trained to be so, while the P-time person has a more natural lifestyle. We suggest the majority of managers and the workforce in the European/North American regions, working in M-time, are grounded in their heredity and traditions. These create psychological tensions since they do not accord with their body clocks, or the clocks of those with whom they may work— if they are from a different culture, working in P-time.

Only now through the use of technology are some Western persons (the *northern* European and Americans) able to break out of this linear schedule tied to time, space, and institution. The "follower" nations in the terminology of macroeconomics, such as Japan, have managed to jump the long formative years of the Industrial Revolution. Persons of these nations seem to maintain a holistic view of their world including an ability to retain their concepts of space-encompassing emptiness, as well as the presence of objects. They have managed also to minimize the pressures to conform to M-time.

No one is a perfect representation of a given aspect of a model—we all are variants, and we also learn to modify behavior to fit certain situations. However, we should note that the monochronic person emphasizes schedules, segmentation of activities, and promptness. M-time is almost "real"—it is said that "time may be wasted/lost/saved" as though it were a real commodity. Thus, M-time people do not like to be interrupted in their task sequences, which often include a list of things to do today. This effectively seals off external interactions, which, by definition, must detract from the completion of today's task list. The M-person will compartmentalize his or her life and accept the schedule as sacred and unalterable, yielding to an ordered lifestyle with clear priorities.

The polychronic persons are rather different, often at the center of many simultaneous events and greatly involved with people. They focus strongly on the completion of human transactions, regardless of any ongoing schedules (such as they are). P-time is *experienced* as being much less tangible than M-time: in this sense it cannot be lost. Time for the P-time person has referents to points on a checkerboard that represents possible actions and plausible paths through life. The P-time person can jump from one point to another in a seemingly random way, rather than accepting time as a road along which the person travels without deviation.

The Japanese support a combination of both time systems. For dealings with overseas persons (Occidentals), they are monochronic, but in their own interpersonal relationships and in their own culture, they are polychronic. For the convenience of the traveler we accept that travel timetables must be monochronic, otherwise no one would be able to meet or circumvent the globe. However, the Japanese have been known to utilize the shift between M- and P-time for their own benefit against Americans' resistance to change. The Japanese arrange changes of plans at the last minute, quite natural for the polychronic, but the Americans are fixated upon their previously arranged flight plans and do not wish to deviate from their schedule. But why should a flight not be rescheduled if something important occurs? This would be a learned skill for M-persons in dealing with P-persons.

High- and Low-Context Persons: Their Joint Confusion

Hall (1976: 83) discusses the nature of *context*. He suggests that one function of culture is to provide a selective screen between humans and the outside world. This screen protects the nervous system from information overload, which when transgressed can lead to many disorders ranging from cognitive dissonance to full mental breakdowns. People handle some of these overloads by delegation, while organizations employ methods whereby they increase the mass and complexity of the system and hopefully the reactivity of the organization. Ashby (1956) in his Law of Requisite Variety ruled that "only variety can overcome complexity—so more complex systems need more complex solutions to remain viable." This is carried forward into modern systems thinking (see Beer, 1972; Espejo & Harnden, 1989). Here we accept that individuals obtain their formative learning from their home, school(s), and work. They have constructed their own model of the world, which, in soft systems modeling is called their W, that is, their Weltanshaung, or worldview. In order to cope with complexity, or employment in a different world, Hall suggests one resolution is to "preprogram" individuals through "contexting," since events are usually more complex than the language used to describe them. In other words, rather like an actor, a person should learn to recognize a complex yet novel situation and thus have internalized methods to cope with this complexity. Discussion with a mentor would be an example of how one might learn to deal with context overload.

High-context (HC) messages are those in which most of the information is in the historical physical context internalized in the person, while little is in the coded, explicitly transmitted part of the message. Thus, an HC message is one in which most of the information is already held by the recipient, so the message itself can be brief: it carries a highly condensed transmission. A low-context (LC) message is more explicit, and in order to support the information invested in the message, it has to be relatively verbose. Twins, for instance, usually use brief, coded HC messages. Having grown up together, they can be very economical. Lawyers in a courtroom tend to use LC messages so as to pass detailed information to all and sundry, especially the judge and jury, so they in turn can reformulate the evidence according to their personal needs—to match their personal worldviews—and come to a personal judgment.

Another example relates to an everyday aspect of our life that we expect others to understand, such as *being a pedestrian waiting to cross a street at the traffic lights*. This phrase has high context since many readers of this chapter will accept it at face value with little thought. Indeed, the activity seems quite reasonable, until one sees Germans, Austrians, or Japanese *waiting* in the middle of the night to cross when there has been no vehicular traffic for hours! One may ask why, since some other nationals would have no hesitation at crossing the street, at any point, at any hour—those having visited China, will no doubt recall the nature of the Chinese, who cross the busiest of streets without a glance at the oncoming traffic. Hall suggests that the more we take actions for granted (the higher their contexts), the less we talk, discuss, or think about them. That is, unless we actively deconstruct their bases to find a meaning, there will be a truth for only one group of people. Others will find this totally bizarre, quaint, or simply foreign.

In conducting business we should note that the Japanese, Arabs, and the Mediterranean persons in Europe (Latins in general) all have large family networks having close personal relationships—they are HC. They do not expect much background information to be passed in normal conversations since they understand their contexts. They keep themselves informed through their network. In contrast, American, British, and Swiss persons are LC (as are most northern European persons). LC persons compartmentalize their personal relationships, their work, and their day-to-day life, as a consequence, in their interactions, they need to be much more verbose in their exchange of information. Americans in many business situations will often need a full briefing from their team, demanding contextual information from them. Much time passes before making a decision (as they are LC), but HC persons can make personal decisions rapidly because they are networked and well briefed. There are other difficult interactions. HC persons are impatient if given lots of information by LC persons; in turn, LC persons are at a loss when not told anything by the HC person. Thus, the hesitation of the LC person when out of context can be seen as obstructionist by an HC person. We can also see subtle shifts in the coded messages between two persons as one changes from HC to LC. This signifies a change in status, for instance, in "talking down" to someone. One person gives too much information, more than is required by the recipient, so it may be seen as a form of status maintenance, or as a reprimand.

Some of this confusion existed in the 1980s in the Japanese production subsidiaries in the United Kingdom, whose staffs said it took them as much as five years to become more comfortable working with their Japanese seniors. Now this time span has shortened to about three years due perhaps to a wider accessibility of information (to both sides) about how the other works and about their expectations (Kidd & Teramoto, 1995). This aspect relates to the difficulties of LC persons (in this instance, the managers in the United Kingdom) working with HC persons (their Japanese seniors). Thus, it is not surprising that the information flow in a European subsidiary of a Japanese firm may appear fractured and intermittent to both the Japanese and the European staffs because of their mixtures of HC/LC and their mono/polychronicity. This delays the joint understanding of the "other" because of poor perceptions jointly of their context.

In a fully LC situation, we understand that the advisors to the CEO are important. They are gatekeepers, since they not only filter information but do so according to their personal model, though this may not conform to the CEO's model, or the vision of the organization, or the model of the supplicant attempting to make a case to the CEO. Furthermore, an LC CEO sees only the LC persons relevant to his or her day's work, all of whom must be on the appointment schedule. We see modern management methods forcing everyone into an LC situation in an attempt to make all facts and aspects of a situation completely explicit and transparent. There is little acceptance of that which the people involved already know. Later in this chapter this will be noted as the difficulty in moving from understanding the explicit to learning about the tacit in the organizational learning paradigm. In creating solutions to management issues, few consultants will take the time to become fully contexted in the deep complexity of the business (nor will their clients pay for this time). On the other side of this argument, very little credibility is given to the implementation of a complex solution. Solutions have to be self-evident, simple, and thus LC in the LC world.

Office and Personal Space

The marking-out of territory is a basic mammalian custom. We humans are no different—we do this with our office space. Space in an office helps protect the LC person and it may also communicate power. In the United States a corner office is more powerful, and the bigger and the higher up the building the better. The executive office in Germany is seen as a refuge for the manager—who is also an LC individual—but he needs to proclaim his status by displaying his name with all his qualifications on the door. His door remains closed, so it functions as a screen to protect his LC employees, who themselves do not wish to be continually supervised. Leaning toward HC, French managers, on the other hand, like to be in the center of the action, surrounded by their subordinates, that is, centrally positioned in a network.

The office correlates with body space. North Europeans (including Americans) have quite a large "no-go" zone, or bubble. In the United States, touching another person by accident evokes a verbalized "sorry," and generally getting too close in these countries causes the other person to back away. The Latins have a small zone and may bodily touch. In Paris, for instance, this may be observed as a French driver engages in virtual-space parking, physically bouncing other cars away to create enough space for the vehicle. We find the Arabian businessman wishes to sit close, to be able to smell one's breath (so as to be able to judge the inner person and thus the potential of the new business partner). This naturally causes considerable alarm for "big-bubble" persons (Elashmawi & Harris, 1993).

The Use of Humor

The language of the narrator and his or her body actions must be modified for any given presentation. However, jokes do not translate well. They may be offensive, and they probably cause difficulties for the translator. We have all heard of the Japanese audience that laughed uproariously at an American's joke in translation. The American man was dumbfounded at the response, yet unknown to the American the translator had told the audience in Japanese to "laugh now, please!"

It is also understood that humor increases stress, leads to broken marriages, and makes people die sooner (Zif, 1995). Zif says people with humor are seen as aggressive and they use their skill aggressively. Initially the jokers are popular among colleagues, but it is the quieter person who becomes the more liked within their peer group. Thus, the popular American person who is always on a first-name basis with everyone, who puts his arm around his host's back, and who makes jokes will not be liked in many cultures—even his own. He will not be considered to be a person of any great strength, nor be trusted to conduct business. However, the dour German image is not too acceptable, and the Asian who laughs may be misinterpreted as being happy rather than unsettled, yet may be petrified of the potential to lose face.

Playing to One's Strengths

In this section I consider personal role-preferences models and a discuss inferences derived from stereotypic data on populations. The first type of measures purport to be an aid for the design of teams for projects and for general management. I suggest that well-designed teams should perform better than a random collection of people.

Individual Role Preferences

A psychometric test developed by Belbin Associates (Belbin, 1993) is widely used by employment agencies in the United Kingdom to "fit round pegs to round holes," so assuring the employer that the potential candidate(s) are the one(s) most suitable for a particular niche in the intended organization. The Belbin test was derived from the Cattell 16PF test and the Watson Glaser test of critical thinking. The latter tests involved the candidate in a full afternoon of question answering, plus a long counseling session following an expert's evaluation of the results. In contrast, the new test may be completed in about 30 minutes and the results immediately printed from a personal computer. It is not so precise a tool as the full test battery, but it is more accessible to the generalist user.

Unfortunately, while intuitively appealing, the Belbin test has not been subject to wide replication and critical evaluation. This has led to certain negative criticisms (cf. Furnham, Steele, & Pendleton, 1993; Kidd & Stray, 1996). Notwithstanding these research findings, the test instrument continues to be used to assign individuals to project teams, aiming to create balanced managerial abilities, with chairpersons, ideas persons, evaluators, completers, and so on. This approach is quite acceptable in an LC culture, where a team must quickly learn to communicate (at length) with each other upon their task and its goals. Generally, HC persons will be happier in cultivating ties to create a family team rather than expect an outsider to understand the issues, or to communicate deeply with the family members. We find Japanese tradition refutes the ideas underpinning team design and assessment by merit but upholds their own cultural norms. Indeed, they often exclude all but Japanese persons in discussions.

I know of an internal appointment in one Japanese subsidiary in the United Kingdom that was blocked by the Japanese seniors in Japan saying, "The U.K. applicant was too young to be placed at that level in the firm," whereas the personnel managers in the United Kingdom had looked to the suitability of the applicant's skills, finding them quite satisfactory. The appointment was finally approved but after a delay of two years. Sadly, during this time the firm's trade spiraled downward under the control of a Japanese person who was older but perceived by the seniors in Japan to be more suited to that level of appointment in the United Kingdom.

Population Stereotypes

We find very few tests that measure culture. One outstanding study (now based on 110,000 respondents in over 50 countries) has been undertaken by Hofstede (1980, 1991), with partial replications undertaken by Hoppe (1993), and McGrath and colleagues (1992).

Initially Hofstede derived four indices that characterize cultural stereotypes. In his 1980 book he said his data came from only one firm, which, given the data were collected on a global scale, controlled many at-work variables, leaving only cultural differences as the cause of population differences. Later, in 1991, he admitted he collected data worldwide from IBM personnel and went on to describe research that led to a fifth index, including the following:

1. *Power distance* (PDI): Some societies like hierarchies, and others wish all to be as equal as possible. There is also an aspect of interpersonal independence in this measure, in which a tall hierarchy will be said to maintain a high PDI.
2. *Uncertainty avoidance* (UAI): Some societies prefer few rules, less stable careers, less fixed patterns of life, that is, more uncertainty and risk than others would like.
3. *Individualism* (IND): Some societies like to see individuals express themselves, while others wish for collectivism, having close relationships that even extend to permitting the firm to look after one and in return expect one's loyalty.
4. *Masculinity* (MAS): The more masculine a society, the more it values assertiveness and materialism. It cares less for the quality of life or concern about other people, that is, the more caring or feminine aspects.
5. *Confucianism* (CD): This dimension relates to the long- or short-term outlook of the society. A long-term person can be thought of as being persistent and thrifty, who orders relationships by status and seeks to maintain this order.

All persons of a given country may not be typified by one set of characteristics, yet Hofstede's research offers powerful comparisons which, in turn, lead to interesting conclusions about the ways in which *individuals* may or may not work with each other. Figure 11.1 maps a selection of countries on the two Hofstede dimensions that characterize organizational aspects.

The Hoppe data derive from studies of executives rather than the "general worker class" that Hofstede used and so may more readily link to the discussions in this chapter. The McGrath study relates to entrepreneurs. The latter found that the usual indicators of the entrepreneur were magnified when cultural differences were taken into account. Thus, the international entrepreneur has to be somewhat larger than life. However, in firms entering a period of stability it is natural they should look to less flamboyant characters. But this denies the forces of change, which demand that the firm, if globalizing, should be searching for excellence, novel ideas, and so forth, and thus be in continuous flux. In other words, there is a natural barrier between the staid worker class who looks for stability and the outward-looking entrepreneur.

Uncertainty Avoidance

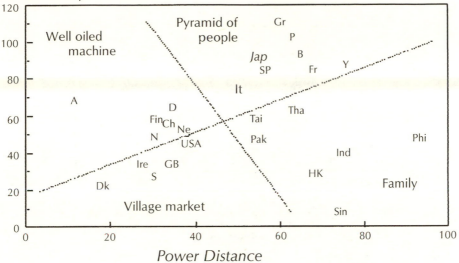

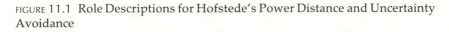

FIGURE 11.1 Role Descriptions for Hofstede's Power Distance and Uncertainty Avoidance

The descriptions derived from within figure 11.1 typify how organizations in different nations work: in one they work as a *family* unit where the head is old and revered, in another as a *well-oiled machine* where many rules account for most situations and thus the more senior persons are not bothered by general queries. People from other nations prefer a logic of hierarchy, so we find they prefer to work with a *pyramid of people* in their organization. Through the work of Hofstede, Hoppe, and others we see that attempts to merge firms with differing modes of operation may cause angst, if not actual revolt, especially if the merger is seen as a direct order from some distant owner based in a different culture (see chapter 3).

A partial set of Hofstede's data is shown in table 11.1. Assuming an individual carries the general traits and role preferences of his or her home population, one sees that the Japanese person, having the highest score on the masculinity index, will work uneasily with persons from The Netherlands or Sweden, who have low scores. In this one considers only the propensity to be hard and materialistic rather than soft and caring about relationships. The PD index implies that in France and the Latin countries their hierarchies would be tall (like that in Japan), with the ideal boss being a benevolent democrat. Collectivism may be inferred from the IND index (Japan and the Asians are all more collective than the Occidentals), while Sweden and the United Kingdom are more relaxed and are happy with fewer rules, which may well be observed through their sense of fair play and their pragmatic approach to change. The results for Singapore are anomalous, maybe stemming from the data sample of like-minded persons, who would work for firms like IBM within the strictures of Singaporean society, rather than representatives of that population in general.

TABLE 11.1 Selected Country Index Values

Country	PDI	UAI	IND	MAS	CD
Japan	54	92	46	95	80
U.S.	40	46	91	62	29
U.K.	35	35	89	66	25
Spain	57	86	51	42	*
Italy	50	75	76	70	*
Sweden	31	29	71	5	33
Singapore	74	8	20	48	48
France	68	86	71	43	*
Germany	35	65	67	66	31
Netherlands	38	53	80	14	44

Source: Hofstede, 1991.

*Data not yet collected.
PDI = power distance index. UAI = uncertainty avoidance index. IND = individualism index. MAS = masculinity index. CD = Confucianism index. See page 218 for definitions of these terms.

Finally, we note the time-horizon index, called Confucianism by Hofstede, because it relates to many Oriental attitudes such as patience, the respect of elders, and upholding the family. In this sample data set, only Japan has a high score, though one should note that China scores the maximum 100. In contrast, the United Kingdom and the United States both have low CD scores (short time frames), implying a need for instant action and, in a financial sense, looking to short-term returns on investment. Once again there is a clear impression of the potential for Oriental/Occidental conflict at many levels within these indices.

Organizational Learning

Weick and Westley (1996) have written at length on organizational learning, noting that "to learn" is to disorganize and increase variety, while "to organize" is to forget and to reduce variety. Hence, they say these two processes are essentially antithetical, and thus the phrase qualifies as an oxymoron. Nevertheless, they have produced a very good review. I note here a baseline to this construct derived from Argyris and Schön (1978). They think people might learn how to perform better in day-by-day situations if they work toward being organizationally better. I suggest this may follow different routes:

1. *Bureaucratic control system.* Here the person learns to work better and better, but within tight guidelines. For instance, I think the global pressure to achieve accreditation in ISO 9000 is one such instance. Obtaining accreditation does not guarantee high quality, only that an audit trail is available within the paperwork or electronic data flows. Individuals will learn how to maintain the audit trail only because they have to, not because they aspire to higher quality.

2. *Entrepreneurial.* In these cases the individuals get on a "high" through break-ing new ground, exploring, and developing novel ideas, sometimes in conjunction with others. There is little bureaucratic control, so audit trails do not exist for quality, nor for their embryo financial systems. Many case studies on entrepreneurs indicate their downturn follows the imposition of financial control that changes their early learning, but for the worse.

3. *The middle route.* There are two aspects here. In one case senior managers oscillate between demanding creativity or demanding tight control. Thus, the average worker finally becomes confused and so works just hard enough to remain employed. In the second case the senior managers sup-port a questioning workforce, which looks to reevaluate how they do things day by day. Even though this seems to create a semblance of anarchy, there is a core of well-understood procedures known to be good. There is intense activity around the periphery as new and better ideas are developed. This is the situation that Argyris and Schön call deutero learning.

These ideas were further developed by Kanda (1994) in his conceptualization of the "Four Knows" of learning in an organization. The following list indicates what all persons in an organization should be able to learn if that organization is to pros-per. I consider these stages as applicable to all levels of the workforce from the CEO to the most junior operator. The entry level is "knowing how:"

1. *Knowing how*—being trained in the best way to use the best tools of one's trade, be it a machine on the shop floor, a telephone, or a personal computer.

2. *Knowing what*—to understand the need to deliver on time, first time with the right quality, using the best tools, according to the needs of the customer.

3. *Knowing why*—to understand deeply the reason for one's tasks and how they fit with the overall mission of the firm and its strategic intent.

4. *Knowing who*—to be able to communicate one's ideas or one's worries so as to enhance one's own skills and those of others through the exchange of data to a peer group, or even more widely, for the good of the firm.

Individuals have differing propensities to learn; they generally commence work in a firm at differing times from differing backgrounds, unlike the traditional Japa-nese salaryman, who passes through a strongly structured education system (at school and university) and who joins a single year's cohort to be given strong in-house train-ing and enculturation. In the enlightened firm in the United States or United King-dom, one might see the staff learning by following Kanda (1994), as portrayed in fig-ure 11.2. An individual does not achieve a perfect roundness of skills, and, en masse, not all of the staff will achieve a perfect set of skills, at one instant in time—some will be naïve, others well developed. Yet all individuals are presumed by some organization theories to be able to converse and communicate well. This is not true in practice, especially if the staff are from differing cultural backgrounds. They will differ in how they communicate and share knowledge.

Nonaka (1991, 1994) postulated a dynamic pattern of organizational learning wherein an individual's learning is merged with that of others. He names four modes of knowledge conversion:

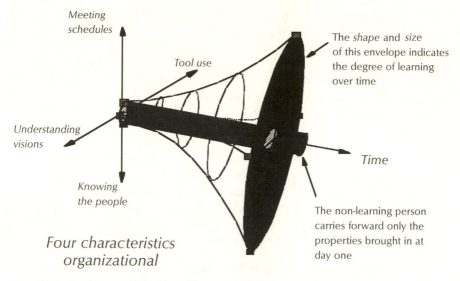

FIGURE 11.2 An Image of the Four Knows in Practice

- From tacit to tacit (*socialization*, or sympathized knowledge)
- From tacit to explicit (*externalization*, or conceptual knowledge)
- From explicit to explicit (*combination*, or systemic knowledge)
- From explicit to tacit (*internalization*, or operational knowledge)

His model is complementary to that of Kanda, though Nonaka describes his time base as a spiral, cycling through the four modes continuously. In an attempt to review the applicability of his theory, I have retrospectively analyzed data from a study of Japanese-Italian production subsidiaries. One analysis relating to the corporate governance in these firms was reported by Songini et al. (1993). They found the management styles of the companies were significantly related to the company size and to capital structure.

The following analysis takes a different route as it superimposes the work of Nonaka and Takeuchi (1995) upon the data. Specifically, I wished to see if their thesis could be upheld when the organizations were not "pure," given the enterprises were managed jointly by Japanese and Italian managers. The continuous dialogue between staff in a joint venture firm may be expected to be less than seamless, given the differences in natural languages, the norms of business culture, and the different contexts in which business is conducted in Italy and in Japan.

A Brief Consideration of Knowledge Creation

Core Competence.   Many persons accept that a firm's advantage stems from its unique knowledge—one might talk of "core competence" (Prahalad & Hamel, 1991). Few would disagree that the culture of the firm is often distinct and palpable. Just walk through the entrance halls of major organizations, even those competing in the same economic or technology sector, and one "feels" the differences, yet these are difficult to measure. It is the same with the creation of knowledge. In general, the successful firm effectively transforms inputs to outputs employing unique competence. While so doing, it also generates new knowledge about novel combinations and processes; thus, the organization is said to learn. It has also been suggested that organizational learning is under the managers' control, and this has been the focus of many researchers (Hirschhorn, 1984; Kagono et al., 1985; Nonaka, 1991, 1994; Nonaka & Takeuchi, 1995).

Knowledge: objective and tacit.   Much is made of the notion of the rationality of science, which seeks to eliminate the sources of bias, yet it may be argued that knowledge is socially constructed, simply that we are the product of our initial nurturing at home, our early learning, the socialization in schools and colleges, and our learning at work (Cook & Yanow, 1993). Further, there is no strictly private knowledge: knowledge gradually becomes evident through language and communication; thus, we accept the definition of tacit knowledge as "that which we know, but can't tell fully."

Polanyi (1958) drew a distinction between objective and tacit knowledge, the former being abstract and independent of the knower, while the latter is subjective and intimately tied to the knower's experience. It would seem that effortlessness is one characteristic of tacit knowledge. Polanyi refers to riding a bicycle; the knower cannot exactly say what the body has learned, but the tacit knowledge is in fact displayed quite effortlessly. Tacit knowledge also has a collective component, which can be likened to the narratives of troubadours or to the constant repetition of folklore lest it be forgotten. In these cases one does not really know what one knows. In this sense it is argued that organizations retain their knowledge in "organizational routines," which no single person fully understands (Nelson & Winter, 1982). Furthermore, we find this collective experience occurs in the swapping of war stories, which may form the base for emergent good practice or the expression of clarity on some organizational issue that has previously defeated institutional rules (Brown & Duguid, 1991).

Formalization of contexts.   One of the difficulties in sharing tacit knowledge is the need for formalization, the generation of a community of practice that may be seen in the workplace, in apprenticeships, and even in the structuring of academic papers. If the context and layout become unusual, knowledge exchange does not occur (Wertsch, 1985). Scribner et al. (1991) have suggested that much of the expertise in the workplace lies in being able to formulate problems in ways that are embedded in understandable contexts. Thus, tacit knowledge may become formalized and articulated. This notion is in accord with the dynamic model of knowledge creation proposed by Nonaka.

The Italian Survey

The aim of the research was to explore the relationships and beliefs held by chief executive officers (CEOs) in Italian-Japanese joint ventures. The research program was initiated by a long postal questionnaire sent to all Japanese manufacturing companies in Italy (47 in spring 1993), with a sample of follow-up interviews with CEOs. The questionnaire either elicited factual data on turnover, numbers of employees, and so on or asked for subjective data. In the latter case a 5-point Likert scale occasionally allowed free-form expression for the response. Even so, grounded in our own backgrounds and learned methodologies, my colleagues and I found we adopted a positivist approach to the questionnaire design; we inclined toward limiting the outcomes in any given question, even if we offered "other" as a catch-all response on a multipoint scale.

Due to time, distance, and calendar restrictions, interviews were restricted to 13 companies, although more firms returned the questionnaire (a total of 18 replies, yielding a 38% return rate; see table 11.2). Generally, the interviews were triggered by the early return of completed questionnaires. We took their return as a tacit acceptance of further involvement on the part of the management of the firms, and thus scheduled them into our calendar with their consent.

The questionnaire was offered in Italian and in English. The interviews were conducted usually in English but occasionally in Italian or Japanese according to the respondent's need to explain a point in detail. The interviews were relatively unstructured, although a reminder fax was sent to the CEOs highlighting points to be covered. Generally, the researchers asked questions freely and followed leads as and when the CEO offered new data or avenues of exploration. We could, in this situation, be sensitive toward the contexts in which we and the CEOs found ourselves. Potentially, the verbal responses of the CEOs were interpreted differently by the researchers because they were variously born and schooled in Italy, Japan, and the United Kingdom. Each person carried a set of overlapping cultural norms that, at the edge, remained a mystery to others, so naturally these may have affected their judgment (see Hall & Hall, 1989).

The Nonaka Model in a European Context

Argyris & Schön (1978), and Huber (1991) to some extent, postulate learning to be at the level of the individual, and organizational learning may be achieved only if individuals transcend their individuality and look for organizationwide data. Nonaka (1991, 1994), however, has defined a dynamic pattern of organizational learning wherein an individual's learning is merged with that of others, over time, in a dynamic spiral. He suggests four stages in the knowledge conversion process linking

TABLE 11.2 Firms Interviewed by Sector and Market Position

Sector	Upstream	Downstream
Electronic & electrical		A, J, M, H
Light vehicles		D, E, G, L
Heavy vehicles		F, I
Chemical processing	C, B, K	

Letters refer to the 13 companies interviewed in order from A to L.

one person to another, and thus capable of raising the learning within the firm (see figure 11.3):

Stage 1—socialization: from tacit to tacit (sympathized knowledge).   Here basic knowledge exchange is obtained by direct appreciation—being an apprentice is a good example. Knowledge is acquired from the master, not through abstract language but by observation, imitation, and practice. Nonaka notes meetings held by Japanese firms in Japan, often outside the premises, to undertake brainstorming. There is a sharing of the realities of life: drinking, eating, chatting, and experiencing communal bathing in a hot spring. It gives a throw-back appreciation of the one-time good life in Japan; the situation relaxes everyone and allows deeper communion. Bartlett & Ghoshal (1989) have also stated firmly that a firm wishing to move into the global phase (to their transnational type) must allow its staff to participate in a great deal of socialization.

Stage 2—externalization: from tacit to explicit (conceptual knowledge).   This mode relies upon analogies, metaphors, hypotheses, and models expressed through articulated language. Frequently there are gaps between the expressed knowledge and the worldview of the perceiver. This may be emphasized when a model is inadequate and a metaphor has to be employed. This should lead an individual to reflect on the potential reasons for the gaps by searching for something in terms of something else. Donnellon, Gray, and Bourgon (1986) suggest the metaphor creates a novel interpretation of experience. The metaphor, based on an intuition, may be further

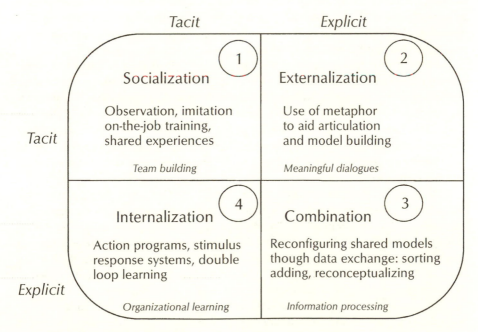

FIGURE 11.3 **Nonaka's Four Stages of Learning**

refined by the use of analogy where logic or analytical models may be employed to give the ideas more substance. Walsham (1993) also develops this argument.

It has been said the Japanese use a great deal of intuition, inferring much from what is said or not said, from the state of a room or from a business layout. They view their world holistically, which can lead to better externalization of their internal knowledge base. On the other hand, Europeans inherit a system of learning based on reductionist logic. They abhor intuition since it cannot be justified. Supposedly a French engineer was heard to say on studying a new machine while it was in operation, "That's all very well—but logically it will not work!" The Italians are no exception to this rule.

Stage 3—combination: from explicit to explicit (systemic knowledge).   This mode involves many channels of communication: face-to-face talking (socialization), using the written language (having aspects of externalization), as well as using the telephone, TV conferencing or electronic networking (E-mail). The receiving person will be able to reconfigure the data on a topic just as a computer reconfigures a database on command.

Middle management should exhibit a strong role model in this process. For instance, senior managers in Japan express their "vision" statements in quite ambiguous terms, utilizing oblique language (Kidd & Teramoto, 1995; Shenkar & Zeira, 1992). Interpretation rests with the middle managers. The decomposition-recombination process is well supported in Japanese firms by the single-year cadre, who, even if dispersed around the world in their subsidiaries, will discuss intensely the meaning of the "data" with respect to the organizations' intention. Members of this cadre have learned to respect each other and to support each other as they garner organizational learning year by year. As they become more senior, these managers may be dispersed to subsidiaries at home or abroad, or may even become managers in Keiretsu subcontractors. Nevertheless, they will actively cooperate to promote their self-perceived managerial role of "combination" to better guide their more junior staff.

Although the Italian cadre of managers is organized in family units, they receive quite direct visionary statements from their CEOs. The seniors have to be clear in the delivery of their mission statements, since their middle managers, while leaders, are not the thinkers and combiners of concépts and data as are their peers in Japan. Furthermore, the process of combination in Japanese firms is by preference a face-to-face process, while the more individualistic Occidental persons tend to use their technological support and look to electronic mail to pass messages quickly to their colleagues.

Elsewhere, in the United Kingdom, Kanda and Kidd (1994) have found that vertical relationships are more important than horizontal ones in the middle-management learning process. They found that direct vertical, upward, and downward monitoring of long-term planning enhances learning, but indirect vertical, horizontal, and external reviews statistically have no effect on learning. Wider vertical monitoring of the firm's plans as a secondary phase also enhances the learning. Thus, combinations aligned to the organizational hierarchy are more important to a manager's learning than horizontal or external networking. Managers therefore have to build learning loops, at first with direct superiors and subordinates, and then with higher superiors and lower subordinates along the hierarchy. Only after strengthening those loops can they fortify them by linkages with other departments and linkages outside the company. These findings conflict with the norm of Japanese middle management and may contradict the expectations of a Japanese senior expatriate manager who confronts managers in the United Kingdom.

It may be hypothesized that managers in northern Europe, the United Kingdom, and the United States will all behave similarly in this respect because of their monochronic use of context (LC), and because they have several of the Hofstede characteristics in common (especially those in the United Kingdom and the United States). Thus, the Japanese manager who works in one of these countries, or even the senior managers in Japan in reflecting on interpersonal behavior in their Anglo/ U.S. subsidiaries, may have some difficulty in persuading predominantly LC, M-time persons to accept the Japanese way. Thus, the combination phase may fail.

Stage 4—internalization: from explicit to tacit (operational knowledge).   Nonaka suggests this mode is close to "learning by doing." He says only by absorbing and sharing the prior stages of socialization, externalization, and combination can an individual develop his or her own internal assets, and thus bring them to bear upon the context and aims of the company. Furthermore, Nonaka suggests these internalizations are aided by the use of documentation, the creation of manuals, and by oral traditions. He suggests the knowledge spiral may commence again following this stage as an individual revises his or her worldview, so leading to a new spiral of learning, commencing once more with new learning by doing, but at a more informed level.

In the Occidental firm, time after time when a project is finished, the team simply disbands, the members disperse, and their accumulated knowledge is lost. Documentation may not be created, nor the manuals written. Generally the oral tradition remaining on site is weak. In effect, LC cultures do not see the need for context development, except as it may directly affect an individual (and maybe his résumé for the next job).

However, there is an oral tradition in the Western firm (see Brown & Duguid, 1991; Nelson & Winter, 1982) but it is not widely researched, nor is it a way of life as expressed in the Japanese firm. For instance, so-called war stories relate how individuals have found ways to make their organizational lives easier. Orr (1990) reviews the stories that repairmen used to exchange during meal breaks: he found they operated a cohesive "community of practice" that went far beyond the formal training given on the design and operation of the machines they were repairing. Internalization through such informal action programs develops organizational learning that combines, at this fourth stage, to uplift the organization along the spiral to the next phase of reexamining the tacit knowledge base.

The knowledge spiral.   Nonaka does not comment on the time to complete one cycle of the knowledge spiral, but clearly it is long. Naturally he has relied on the maintenance of the historic expectation of the job for life that was the tradition in Japan, with staff promotion and interfirm exchanges well organized so the juniors may see new parts of the organization. In many Japanese firms the well-organized personnel program, traditionally for life, would ensure that knowledge diffusion and acquisition take place in a planned fashion.

In many countries of Europe, prior to the great demise of their iron, coal, and ship-building firms, there was a tradition of jobs for life and even longer (!) as sons succeeded fathers at the same enterprise. But there was no tradition and thus no support of the learning systems portrayed by Nonaka. Japanese managers in the United Kingdom, for instance, have expressed surprise at the wealth of hidden skills at shop floor levels, yet also are horrified at the lack of networking or camaraderie that is normal in Japan when juniors and seniors stay after-hours to work and to socialize. It has been shown recently in the United Kingdom that if innovation is directed toward cost cutting, and if benefits fall to the individual from teamwork, then a Kaizen-like atmosphere can be created (see Lewis, 1995). But in Japan the staff still works generously for the firm, while Lewis finds continuous improvements in the United Kingdom occur only if individuals perceive a benefit. This is also likely to be the case in Italy (but for different reasons) as Italians first look to benefit themselves, then their city, and finally their nation (Trompenaars, 1993). Here again are differences between LC/HC and the mono/polychronic persons, between the Italians and the Japanese. The "generosity" of the Japanese workforce is made very clear in discussions on the third and fourth levels of keiretsu subcontractors in Miyashita and Russell (1994).

General Results

Not surprisingly, the dialogues between the Japanese managers and the Italian managers were fraught with difficulty as each party attempted to learn about the verbal and nonverbal exchanges that constitute their conversations. In entering a new market or country, a company has to be adaptive to deal with everyday problems that arise in unfamiliar contexts. According to Hall and Hall (1990), there is a high chance in these circumstances that the culture-bound interactions of each party in a joint venture may cause a bewildering breakdown of goodwill as each person looks unfavorably on the demands of the other. Yet interactions between individuals who often are very different in terms of culture, education, and language can lead to new ideas or to new conceptualizations of what one of the parties already understands in their own culture paradigm. Such transfers take time. For instance, in one Japanese-Italian joint venture company, according to the Japanese management, "the firm was not yet ready" to implement small-group activities within their factories, even though the company had operated in Italy since 1974. Similarly, while lean production and total quality concepts have long been promoted in Italy (typically in accord with Monden, 1994), the significant aspects of these innovations were not quickly understood, absorbed, and thus implemented by Italian managers.

The management of organization learning in Italy.   Knowledge creation in Italy is influenced by three factors: (1) the degree of local decision-making responsibility; (2) the presence of specific organizational mechanisms, both Japanese and Italian; and (3) the clarity of the company objectives. The degree of local decision-making responsibility determines the capacity to generate and maintain autonomous knowledge-creating structures such as project teams, quality circles, and organized small-group activity in keeping with the staff's perception of the Italian way. Thus, the objectives of the Italian-Japanese alliance are fundamental in defining the presence and the possibility of supporting knowledge creation. If the company objective is simply to manufacture industrial products based on an imported process (at worst, the assembly of a kit of parts as a screwdriver operation), it is difficult to see how new ideas and new knowledge may come out of these activities, be recognized as such, and be appreciated as a resource by the management team.

All companies declared their focus was on good productivity and the need to improve it through training and incentive systems. There should therefore be a mechanism to motivate and involve people, especially local employees. If the intent is to copy the Japanese processes, the short cut is to send newly hired people to Japan to a factory of the mother company so when they return home they would be able to apply what they learned. They could train their colleagues who stayed at home. Tacit and explicit knowledge exchanges are acknowledged by some Italian managers, but only one declared, "We have learnt much from the Japanese, yet we are still independent in terms of technology and products." At another site, the top Italian manager declared, "As for creativity, the Italians are better, but for technical programs the Japanese are better, because they are precise, thanks to their different education." But another Italian manager suggested that "there is too much individualism in Italy, and the 'orchestra' requires too much attention to maintain harmony," which seems to imply that Italians will not spend the time needed to learn on a voluntary basis, only if pushed and guided by the CEO.

Only three firms seemed to perform well over all four stages along the lines suggested by Nonaka. They are firms managed strongly by Italian CEOs. The Japanese partners there work in conjunction, but in the background, offering technology, techniques, and important financial support. In return, the Japanese partners receive the benefits of strong product support in a "happy" organizational environment. One may say the Italian managers themselves have initially absorbed some Japanese-ness and retranslated it to the Italian context for the benefit of their staff's learning. In these cases international contextual conflicts seem to have been contained (to at least boardroom discussions). They are not apparent to the middle and lower management levels where Italian elitism, creativity, and flair are controlled and guided by a respected Italian parent figure who is clearly seen to be the boss.

In lesser firms (in a Nonaka sense, though sometimes performing less well according to commercial economic indicators), there was more interference by the Japanese managers—allowing conflicts to arise from divided loyalties. The Japanese perceive the Italians to be too "theoretical" and not aligned to the practicalities of management. In turn, the Italians perceive the joint venture to be managed remotely from Japan, so they become strongly Italian—hierarchical, inward-looking, and apparently unhelpful. Their local workforce follows suit.

I am not saying that the Japanese ventures in Italy are a failure in 1993. Far from it. Most of the firms were financially sound (notwithstanding the general difficulties with the lira and the European recession). I am suggesting that there is a very strong culture and context clash, which makes Japanese hands-on management quite problematical in Italy. But when there is a little freedom left for the Italian manager, better results have been achieved.

The applicability of Nonaka's model.   The categorization of the Italian production firms according to their responses to the questionnaire and according to the knowledge gained during the informal interviews suggests that it is possible to use Nonaka's model as a monitoring tool. It allows insights to be made of the modus operandi of the firms. That being so, I suggest his model has wider applicability than solely in Japanese firms with highly motivated workforces. It may be applicable to other Japanese alliances outside Italy, and even to non-Japanese firms.

However, there are some limitations to this conclusion. The review presented here is based on a small sample of firms; it is based upon Italian firms inclined to work with the Japanese in joint ventures; and it was subjective since there was no test instrument applied to measure consistently how well the firms met the criteria of each stage. To the extent that knowledge creation has been observed in a cultural setting outside Japan, we might accept that Nonaka's model may be generalizable and that it may offer a base by which firms can be compared.

Conclusions

In Europe many ethnic and cultural effects operate more vigorously than in the United States. In the United States there is a regular discussion on the number of ethnic groups and languages in constant use during each working day, yet at the bottom line, most of the workers believe they are *American* since generally they have passed through the U.S. schooling system. In contrast, in Europe, there is no such leavening effect. In the EU (which is still a developing phenomenon) each nation state has a different primary language, educational pedagogy, and fundamental belief system. Politicians attend the European parliament saying to their local electorate, "I will do my best for us," meaning his or her nation. There is a palpable different "feel" between East-West, and North-South. Hofstede rules!

These differences have been the focus of several researchers, leading in one case to a statement about an emergent European management model. In essence, Calori and de Woot (1994) have discerned strong differences in management styles across Europe, somewhat corelated in the United Kingdom to the United States, and in Germany to Japan. This model is summarized in figure 11.4, where I indicate certain key differences between the triad of major models: the model of the United Kingdom, that of southern Europe (which earlier we called Latin), and the Germanic model.

When Japanese managers initiated joint ventures in Europe, they found stronger cultural differences than they expected. Historically their organizational experience was developed in the United States from their 1960s investment wave. The early expatriate managers, now in more senior positions in Japan, pressed their younger expatriates operating in Europe to believe that Europe is a subsidiary of the United States—working in the English language and having other attributes and tendencies similar to their remembered experience in the United States. This would be supported by the Hofstede data, but only in the case of the United Kingdom and the United States. The other European countries differ sufficiently in many of their attributes for their inconstancies to be clearly apparent, certainly to local managers. The Japanese managers operating in Europe know and experience these

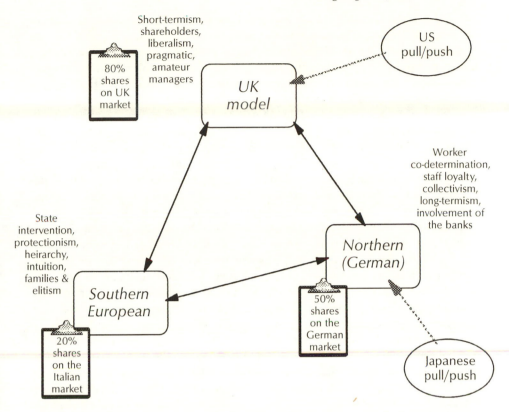

FIGURE 11.4 The Triad of European Management

differences and are at pains to point out their dilemmas to their seniors. But they suffer from the Japanese management syndrome—they may not overtly contradict their senior manager!

Discussion about European managerial differences do not depend on the origin of the inward-investing firm—Japanese, Korean, or American. The differences are indigenous to the Europeans. They have their own difficulties in working together. They are split north/south in their use of time and space (cf. Hall & Hall, 1989); they have strongly differing cultural differences (cf. Hofstede, 1991). All imply subtle, though sometimes overt management style differences country by country. These may be difficult to merge within a dynamic multinational firm trying to operate in several Europeans countries and relying on local management skills and styles. Perhaps one skill of the Japanese, since they have operated in the expatriate mode far longer and with greater intensity than other Asian nationals, is in utilizing the strengths of their opponents: a judo management style!

Consider first the U.S. case. Pascale (1990) suggested that Honda (U.S.) may be one of the world's best-managed firms through their use of controlled aggression, or more politely, creative tension. The U.S. management style may be characterized as confrontational, with the boss often shouting down the subordinate. In Honda

(U.S.), the workforce is able to make suggestions, to enter a Kaizen scheme (without this being defined as a Japanese process), and to have their natural aggression managed for the good of the enterprise. Second, in the United Kingdom, the Japanese have found the local pragmatic approach of the population curious. Local management believes the regulations may be rethought at each occasion. In this the Japanese have found, even at the highest levels of government, that a process similar to *nemawashi* promotes a solution often in favor of the Japanese firm. Third, in France, the Japanese find the Cartesian logic of the French engineer in accord with the Japanese love of minute perfection, of not rushing into a manufacturing process until all designs are ready. And fourth, in Italy, an autocratic head of the firm is naturally acceptable to the Japanese firm. And so on. Thus, by careful observation of the Japanese in different countries, one may surmise they have learned to be very adaptive, but only on a one-to-one basis, not in a pluralist sense (as in a general meeting comprising many nationalities where European-ness becomes more problematic to the Japanese CEO as the Europeans openly recall old battles and demarcations).

Meetings help us understand other viewpoints, especially if we maintain an open, learning attitude about what works in one country and accepting that it does not necessarily work in another, at least without modification to take into account differing habits, assumptions, and customs. This is vital to learn, since even modest-sized firms may have supply chains operating on a global base. Such mental restructuring assumes the power of information technology but above all demands *real* communication between each person in the firm. Individuals have to be willing to share information and be willing to help others, even before the intervention and support of coordinator managers. We therefore must learn and absorb the mental maps of others. Hamel and Prahalad (1994) said that "a world class firm must have 'the strategic intent' which fires the imagination of all concerned. This vision must be broadly shared, and this can only be through full communication and through an understanding of others needs, assumptions and habits."

References

Argyris, C., & Schön, D. A. 1978. *Organizational Learning: A Theory of Action Perspective*. Reading, MA: Addison-Wesley.

Ashby, W. R. 1956. *An Introduction to Cybernetics*. London: Chapman & Hall.

Bartlett, C. A., & Ghoshal, S. 1989. *Managing Across Borders: The Transnational Solution*. London: Century Business.

Beer, S. 1972. *The Brain of the Firm*. London: Allen Lane.

Belbin, M. 1993. *Team Roles at Work*. Oxford: Butterworth.

Brown, J. S., & Duguid, P. 1991. "Organisational Learning and Communities-of-Practice: Towards a Unified View of Working, Learning, and Innovation." *Organisational Science*. 2: 40–57.

Calori, R., & de Woot, P. A. 1994. *European Management Model: Beyond Diversity*. New York: Prentice Hall.

Cleary, T. 1988. *Sun Tzu "The Art of War."* London: Shambhala Press.

Cook, S. D. N., & Yanow, D. 1993. Culture and Organisational learning. *Journal of Management Inquiry*. 2: 373–390.

Donnellon, A., Gray, B., & Bougon, M. G. 1986. "Communication, Meaning, and Organized Action." *Administrative Science Quarterly.* 1: 3–16.

Elashmawi, F., & Harris, P. R. 1993. *Multicultural Management: New Skills for Global Success.* Houston, TX: Gulf Publishing.

Espejo, R., & Harnden, R. 1989. *The Viable Systems Model.* Chichester, England: Wiley.

Furnham, A., Steele, H., & Pendleton, D. 1993. "A Psychometric Assessment of the Belbin Team-Role Self-Perception Inventory." *Journal of Occupational and Organisational Psychology.* 66: 245–257.

Hall, E. T. 1959. *The Silent Language.* New York: Doubleday.

Hall, E. T. 1976. *Beyond Culture.* New York: Doubleday.

Hall, E. T., & Hall, M. R. 1987. *Hidden Differences: Doing Business with the Japanese.* New York: Doubleday.

Hall, E. T., & Hall, M. R. 1990. *Understanding Cultural Differences: Germans, French and Americans.* Yarmouth, ME: Intercultural Press.

Hirschhorn, L. 1984. *Beyond Mechanization: Work and Technology in a Postindustrial Age.* Cambridge, MA: MIT Press.

Hofstede, G. 1980. *Culture's Consequences.* Newbury Park, CA: Sage.

Hofstede, G. 1991. *Cultures and Organisations: Software of the Mind.* London: McGraw-Hill.

Hoppe, H. M. 1993. "The Effects of National Culture on the Theory and Practice of Managing R & D Professionals Abroad." *R&D Management.* 23: 313–325.

Huber, G. P. 1991. "Organizational learning: The Contributing Processes and the Literatures," *Organizational Science.* 2: 88–115.

Kagono, T., Nonaka, I., Sakakibara, K., & Okamura, A. 1985. *Strategic vs Evolutionary Management: A U.S.-Japan Comparison of Strategy and Organisation.* Amsterdam: North-Holland.

Kanda, M., & Kidd, J. B. 1994. *Educating Managers to Learn Strategically on the Job: Lessons from British Managers.* Presentation to Euro-Asian Management Studies Association, November 1994, University Utara, Kedah, Malaysia.

Kidd, J. B., & Stray, S. J. 1996. *The Team-Role Awareness of Project Group Members Based on a Psychometric Test.* Working paper, Aston University, Birmingham, U.K.

Kidd, J. B., & Teramoto, Y. 1995. "The Learning Organisations: The Case of the Japanese RHQs in Europe." *Management International Review.* 35 (2): 39–56.

Lewis, K. C. E. 1995. *Kaizen: The Right Approach to Continuous Improvement.* Kempston, England: IFS International.

McGrath, R. G., MacMillan, I. C., & Scheinberg, S. 1992. "Elitists, Risk-Takers, and Rugged Individualists? An Exploratory Analysis of Cultural Differences Between Entrepreneurs and Non-entrepreneurs." *Journal of Business Venturing.* 17: 117–135.

Miyashita, K., & Russell, D. W. 1994. *Keiretsu: Inside the Hidden Japanese Conglomerates.* New York: McGraw-Hill.

Monden, Y. 1994. *Toyota Production System: An Integrated Approach to Just-in-Time*, 2nd ed. London: Chapman & Hall.

Nelson, R. R., & Winter, S. G. 1982. *An Evolutionary Theory of Economic Change.* Cambridge, MA: Belknap Press.

Nonaka, I. 1991. "The Knowledge-Creating Company." *Harvard Business Review.* Dec: 96–104.

Nonaka, I. 1994. "A Dynamic Theory of Organisational Knowledge Creation." *Organisation Science.* 5: 14–37.

Nonaka, I., & Takeuchi, H. 1995. *The Knowledge-Creating Company.* New York: Oxford University Press.

Orr, J. E. 1990. *Sharing Knowledge, Celebrating Identity.* In Middleton, D. S., & Edwards, D. (eds.), *Collective Remembering.* Newbury Park, CA: Sage.

Pascale, R. 1990. *Managing on the Edge: How Successful Companies Use Conflict to Stay Ahead.* London: Penguin Books.

Platt, P. 1994. *French or Foe: Getting the Most Out of Living and Working in France.* London: Culture Crossings.

Polanyi, M. 1958. *The Tacit Dimension.* London: Routledge.

Prahalad, C. K., & Hamel, G. 1991. "The Core Competence of the Corporation." *Harvard Business Review.* 68: 79–91.

Scribner, S., Di Bello, L., Kindred, J., & Zazanis, E. 1991. *Co-ordinating Two Knowledge Systems: A Case Study.* New York: CUNY, Laboratory for Cognitive Studies of Work.

Shenkar, O., & Zeira, Y. 1992. "Role Conflict and Role Ambiguity of Chief Executive Officers in International Joint Ventures." *Journal of International Business Studies.* 23: 55–75.

Songini, L., Gnan, L., Inumaru, K., Kidd, J. B., Termaoto, Y., & Piciozzi, F. 1993. *Global Study on Management Issues in Italian-Japanese Subsidiaries.* Presentation to Euro-Asia Management Studies Association, Nürnberg, Germany.

Trompenaars, F. 1993. *Riding the Waves of Culture: Understanding Cultural Diversity in Business.* London: Economist Books.

Walsham, G. 1993. *Interpreting Information Systems in Organisations.* Chichester, England: Wiley.

Weick, K. E., & Westley, F. 1996. "Organisational Learning: Affirming an Oxymoron." In Clegg, S. R., Hardy, C., Nord, W. R. (eds.): *Handbook of Organisation Studies.* London: Sage.

Wertsch, J. V. 1985. *Vygotsky and the Social Formation of Mind.* Cambridge, MA: Harvard University Press.

Zif, A. 1995. *Humour and Stress.* Presentation to 13th *International Humour Conference,* Aston University, Birmingham, England.

12

ALLAN BIRD, SULLY TAYLOR,
& SCHON BEECHLER

Organizational Learning
in Japanese Overseas Affiliates

Any organization setting up a new operation must also establish new systems for managing that operation (Rosenzweig & Singh, 1991). These events present an occasion for organizational learning. In the case of newly established operations in the same country, the determination and implementation of those systems is usually straightforward—a simple replication of systems currently in effect at existing operations—and the learning minimal. However, because foreign operations are commonly associated with higher levels of uncertainty as a result of differing environmental contexts and influences, the question of what systems to implement overseas becomes more problematic. Consequently, these types of events provide many challenges but also significant opportunities for learning.

Our interest is in how Japanese firms learn from their overseas operations. Specifically, we are interested in what they learn with regard to their management systems. We focus on the management system for several reasons. First, of the various activities a foreign affiliate engages in, the management of people appears to be the one most sensitive to variations in environmental conditions and factors. It also appears to be the most complex and uncertain. Second, as national barriers to the flow of capital and technology continue to fall, the importance of the human factor in the value-added activities of the firm rises, further emphasizing the importance of effectively managing its human resources (Pfeffer, 1994). Third, as firms strive for true globalization, the greatest barrier appears to be the ability of the firm to adequately and equitably manage all of its employees throughout the world. Fourth, when compared to their U.S. and European counterparts, Japanese firms are often perceived as relying far more extensively on management systems as a means of achieving competitive advantage (Abo, 1994). Finally, with the simultaneous rise in the value of the yen, the longest Japanese recession in the postwar era, and keen competition globally, the overseas operations of Japanese MNCs (JMNCs) have become critical to firm survival. Consequently, the future of JMNCs hinges on their ability to learn from their overseas affiliates.

In approaching the subject of how JMNCs learn from their management activities, we have focused on three issues. First, we are interested in the content of the learning, both within the affiliate and within the larger organization, including the philosophy underlying a management system, the specific policies implemented, and the actual practices that evolve, for example. Second, we are interested in the volume of learning at both the affiliate and corporate level. Some companies learned more than others. Most important, however, we are interested in the process by which the learning takes place. Our sense is that, ultimately, what is learned, how much is learned, and who learns are determined by the particulars of the learning process itself. This is the central focus of our study.

Our analysis proceeds in the following manner. The next section describes our research methodology, outlining the reasoning behind our approach. The subsequent section presents the theoretical foundation of our inquiry, delineating a model of learning that best fits the phenomena we observed, as well as describing factors identified as influential in the process. A generalized description follows of the archetypal patterns of decisions that the firms we studied pursued. Our analysis of decision patterns at the firm level suggests four learning types among the JMNCs we studied. The fifth section of our chapter considers the similarities and contrasts among the four types. In the concluding section we consider the implications of our findings for how JMNCs should approach learning in their foreign operations. We also address the import of our findings for non-Japanese MNCs.

Methodology

Over the past five years, we have designed a series of studies to explore how JMNCs manage human resources in their overseas affiliates. Employing questionnaire surveys and semistructured, open-ended interviews conducted in person as well as over the telephone, we collected data as part of a comprehensive, multimethod project to understand the nature of management systems—philosophies, policies and practices—in Japanese overseas affiliates. Our goal was to track how management philosophies were transferred from parent companies, how policies were developed and implemented, and what the effects of specific practices were on affiliate performance in terms of a variety of outcomes (cf. Bird & Beechler, 1995). Given the preponderance of writers who have argued that Japanese corporations have a "Japanese style of management" (cf. Abo, 1994), we judged that a tangential benefit of the research would be to establish the degree to which JMNCs actually do approach the management of human resources in a similar fashion (Beechler & Bird, 1994).

The project began in 1989 with a questionnaire survey of 64 senior American personnel managers and their immediate Japanese superiors in U.S.-based affiliates. The sample included roughly equal numbers of manufacturing and service firms distributed evenly across the East Coast, Midwest, and West Coast. Executives in 30 of these firms participated in follow-up interviews conducted either in person or over the telephone. Simultaneous to the U.S. study, a parallel study of four Japanese maquiladoras was carried out in Mexico. Interview and survey data from the four Mexico-based firms were pooled with that of the U.S. study. We also included data from interview surveys in 1987 with 26 Japanese affiliates located in five countries in Southeast Asia. In 1991, interviews and a limited questionnaire survey of 38 additional Japanese affiliates based in the United States was carried out. This was followed in 1992 by field interviews with Japanese affiliates in Europe—eight in the United Kingdom and seven in Spain. A total of 147 Japanese affiliates provide the database from which our observations are drawn.

The questionnaire survey contained items measuring demographic and background information on the affiliate and parent company, as well as characteristics of affiliate employees, both local and Japanese. Additional items explored the types and extent of policies in the affiliate about the general functional areas of human resources management (HRM), including planning, staffing, training, compensation, and performance appraisal.

Each manager participating in the study was interviewed for 90 minutes to two hours on the types of policies in place in the affiliate and how these policies were actually carried out in practice. We then asked participants to discuss the process surrounding the establishment of the affiliate and the manner in which the HRM department or various HRM operations had been established. Finally, each participant was asked to discuss a key policy event, that is, how a particular HRM policy originated. For example, in fall 1990, several managers discussed their organization's creation of a policy to deal with employees who were members of the U.S. military reserve called up as part of the Desert Storm operation in Kuwait and Iraq. As there is no military reserve system in Japan, none of the companies had preexisting policies to cope with the sudden leave of absence of several or more key personnel, so there was a need to develop a policy quickly.

The interviews were taped, and notes were taken as well. The majority of the interviews were conducted by one researcher, although in some cases two researchers were present (interview notes were reviewed by both). The interviews were conducted in the mother tongue of the interviewee (English, Japanese, or Spanish), except in Southeast Asia, where they were carried out in English or Japanese.

Our analysis employed a "grounded research" approach in which we examined notes from earlier rounds of interviews to guide us in the development of questions for subsequent rounds of data collection. As part of this iterative process, we induced "working theories," which were explored and tested as we moved forward. Working theories were developed using a two-step approach. First, they were tested for internal consistency by applying them against data from earlier rounds of interviews to determine if, indeed, they could be logically induced from those observations. The second step involved a "negative case analysis" approach (Kidder, 1981) in which new observations were sought against which the working theories could be applied and, as necessary, modified.

Theoretical Foundation: Adaptation and Adjustment as Learning

What is organizational learning? As Hedberg (1981) points out, organizations are not individuals; hence, organizational learning must differ from individual learning, not simply constitute an aggregate of individual learning. More than 30 years ago Cyert and March (1963) addressed this issue by noting that organization routines, standard operating procedures, and policies change over time in response to changes in the environment. They argued that these changes, in and of themselves, constituted "stimulus-response" learning by the organization. This perspective frames learning as an adaptive-manipulative response by a system to its environment: "[L]earning results when organizations interact with their environments: each action adds information and strengthens or weakens linkages between stimuli and responses" (Hedberg, 1981: 9).

This model of learning is predicated on Campbell's (1959) suggested mechanism of *variation → selection → retention*. Changes in the environment provide the variation stimuli perceived by the organization, which then assembles responses to match the perceived stimuli. If the organization concludes that a particular response assembly matches perceived stimuli, then that assembly is retained for future use; that is, a change is made in the organization's routines.

Weick (1969), however, noted that it is not the variation of environmental stimuli per se to which organizations react, but rather organizations' perceptions of stimuli. Stimuli pass through perceptual filters so that an organization responds not to what is but to what is perceived. In this sense, organizations *enact* their environments. Consequently, the organizational learning mechanism is more accurately portrayed as *enactment → selection → retention*.

The distinction is particularly important with regard to establishing management systems within overseas affiliates. MNCs have preexisting routines and theories of how the world works, which serve as perceptual filters enacting the overseas environment. Management and other operating systems within the overseas affiliates may be viewed as *selected* response assemblies, which, if perceived to match stimuli, will be *retained*.

Our position is consistent with that of Cyert & March (1963) and Campbell (1965) in that we believe that the very process of establishing a management system in the overseas affiliate and then making adjustments to the system—fine-tuning or overhauling—constitute the initiation and continuance of an ongoing organizational learning process. The process of organizational learning pertinent to the management system in the overseas affiliate is presented in figure 12.1. It is initiated with the decision by the parent firm to establish an overseas affiliate. At that time, the parent enacts a picture of reality that includes an interpretation of the local environment in the host country and its own capabilities and assesses how well extant systems fit. Drawing either upon internal or external sources, the parent organizes appropriate systems, or components of systems, to create a management system for the overseas affiliate. To the extent that the newly installed system or some of its parts suit the local environment, they are retained in the affiliate and become institutionalized in the ongoing system. Information about what is retained feeds back to influence subsequent perceptions of the local environment and firm capabilities. Meanwhile, those aspects of the system that did not suit local conditions serve as stimuli in the enactment phase of the subsequent cycle.

It is important to note that the learning process transcends two levels of the organization and involves two sets of actors. The process is initiated by the parent firm

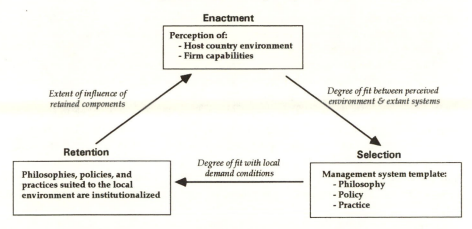

FIGURE 12.1 A Basic Process Model of the Japanese MNC Parent-Affiliate Management Learning Cycle

through decisions made by headquarters personnel, but directly involves the overseas affiliate and its personnel as the process moves forward into selection. Retention then takes place at the affiliate level, but feedback subsequently influences both affiliate and parent perceptions.

Imprinting and the Start of Learning

If organizational learning is an ongoing, cyclical process consisting of phases of enactment, selection, and retention, then it is prudent to identify at what point the learning begins. In the case of JMNCs and their overseas affiliates, we concluded that learning begins with the selection and implementation of the affiliate's management template. At this point the *nature* of the parent meets the *nurture* of the local environment and, through that interaction, both affiliate and parent learn lessons about what works and what does not. Attributes imprinted at the founding of an organization shape its subsequent trajectory of development (Stinchcombe, 1965). As outgrowths of an existing organization, affiliates are born possessing predilections and orientations. At the same time, they encounter specific conditions and chronologies in the host country not previously experienced by the parent, which may impose new constraints and apply unanticipated pressures. The imprinting of the affiliate—both genetically and environmentally—signals the start of the learning process.

Selecting Management Templates

The genetic code of the affiliate is located in the philosophies, policies, and practices of its various operating systems. Our specific interest is in the management system, by which we mean those aspects of the operating system directly related to the treatment of human resources. This definition extends beyond the notion of HRM as focused solely on planning, staffing, training, compensation, and performance appraisal by including other activities such as the supervision of workers on the shop floor and the direction of administrative personnel.

To guide them in the development of an affiliate's management system, parent firms often employ a template, a pattern or mold on which the new system can be modeled. A critical decision, then, involves the selection of the basic template to be used in guiding subsequent decision making about the specifics of the affiliate's management system. Variation in template selection occurs along two lines: the origin of the template and the level at which the template is established. The first dimension involves choosing between two possibilities. On the one hand, the parent may adopt an internal template, choosing to pattern the affiliate's system on that of the parent and making minor adjustments to accommodate local variances. The second is to opt for an external, host country template, which often requires major adjustments.

The second aspect of the template decision involves the level at which the template is established. The template can operate at any of three levels: philosophy, policy, or practice. A philosophy is a set of beliefs about how the world works. In the case of a management system, beliefs pertain to the best way to allocate, enhance, and use the human resources of an organization. Policies can be thought of as the decision rules designed to guide actions in a manner consistent with beliefs about how the world works. In short, they are procedures that organization members are expected to follow based on a belief that following them will lead to success. Practices, on the other hand, are members' responses to policy and can be thought of as the actual decisions taken and behaviors engaged in.

The relationship between philosophy, policy, and practice is analogous to the distinction Schein (1965) makes regarding culture as operating at the level of assumptions, values, and artifacts. As a template, a philosophy serves as a "theory-in-use" (Argyris, 1976) that the parent employs in constructing the affiliate's management system. If, for example, the parent uses its home country philosophy as a template, it does not necessarily make a commitment to transferring specific sets of home country policies. Rather, it leaves itself open to examining the suitability of specific home country policies for the host country environment as well as to considering the possibility that some widely accepted policies in the host country may also be congruent with its chosen philosophy. The basic mold into which policies will fit is defined by the philosophy. For example, a widely accepted Japanese management philosophy is resource accumulation (Beechler & Bird, 1994; Kagono, et al., 1986; Schuler, 1989). Predicated on a belief that successful organizations endure over time as a result of their ability to exploit human capital, such a philosophy would emphasize building maximum involvement and a pool of skilled workers by providing ongoing training and development that develops members' latent potential. Policies consistent with such a philosophy need not necessarily be drawn solely from those already in effect in Japan.

In contrast, when the parent seeks to apply a policy template, in addition to a particular philosophy, it also intends to implement specific sets of policies. In such cases, the belief is that particular policies represent the best possible fit to a philosophy. Building on the example above, a JMNC may employ an accumulator philosophy and then select parent policies with the best fit. For example, when Kyocera announced the opening of its San Diego facility in the mid-1980s, it also announced a policy of no layoffs. In doing so, Kyocera imposed a policy template, applying not only a resource accumulation philosophy, but also a specific employment policy adopted from its Japanese operations deemed consistent with that philosophy.

Finally, a practice template focuses on eliciting specific behaviors. The concern of a practice template is on actual behaviors, not necessarily attitude or intention. A firm adopting a parent practice template is interested in having host country employees behave in ways similar to Japanese employees back home. The philosophy and specific policies of the affiliate are less important than whether host country employees act in a desired fashion. When a chemical processing facility in North Carolina paid its employees overtime to stay after hours to work in quality control circles (QCs), its primary concern was in having U.S. workers engage in the same sort of small-group activities as its Japanese employees in Osaka. The fact that Japanese employees stayed after work voluntarily, without pay, reflected differing policies and differing philosophies between the two sites. A critical point here is that similarity with respect to some practices (QCs) could be achieved only through differences in other practices (compensation), thus drawing attention to the parent's assessment of certain *practices* as being essential to the effective operation of the affiliate.

Japanese Management as a Template

In subsequent discussion of management systems in Japanese overseas affiliates, we invoke generalizations regarding parent company templates and Japanese management as a general system. We recognize wide variation among firms within Japan (Beechler & Bird, 1994). Nevertheless, as a whole, the JMNCs we studied exhibited commonality in their Japan-based systems with regard to work organization, labor relations, and employee development. Therefore, when we refer to Japanese management, we are designating a system possessing an underlying philosophy of resource accumulation and development characterized by the following types of policies and practices. Japanese work organization is team-based and relies on a sense of unity and a sharing of information. Job classifications are few and job descriptions ambiguous. Wages are person-centered (Abo, 1994), focused on personal criteria such as tenure, work experience, etc. Staffing is from within and promotions are predicated in large measure on years of service. Training takes place through job rotations and ongoing educational activities both on and off the job. Loyalty to the organization is valued.

In recent years much debate has arisen over the extent to which these attributes remain typical of Japanese firms. Incidents of increases in labor mobility rates, corporate downsizings, and organizational restructurings have been cited as evidence that the Japanese management system is in a state of transition. We believe that such a conclusion is premature. Whether such actions constitute a fundamental, lasting shift or a short-term response to economic exigencies remains unclear (see also chapter 8 in this volume). Consequently, our discussion of the Japanese management system adopts the stance that it is still possible to talk about a Japanese style of management.

A Decision Tree and Four Learning Archetypes

The outcome of our extensive research on Japanese affiliates overseas was the identification of a typology of learning patterns experienced by Japanese firms in the establishment and ongoing management of their affiliates' management systems. This typology contains four distinct archetypes, each of which followed a different path in its development, presented in figure 12.2 in the context of a decision tree diagram that describes the specific sequence of decisions and set of influencing factors that characterize each of the four types.

   In the following subsections we describe the starting point common to all of the types and discuss the factors leading to differentiation into each of the archetypes. Then we compare the four types.

Tactical Decisions and Emergent Learning Strategies

The decision to set up an overseas affiliate creates, in turn, the need to make many other decisions, most of them tactical. (For our purposes here, "tactical" is defined as concerned with the act of implementing a strategy—in this case, a specific strategy for setting up operations overseas.) The first of these decisions is how to staff the new affiliate. In the case of greenfield investments, for example, most of the employees were hired locally, but key managerial positions were filled by Japanese personnel. In our studies, the actual number of Japanese expatriates installed in new overseas affiliates ranged from a low of 3% to a high of 30%. Although constraints of space do not allow for elaboration (see Beechler & Bird, 1994, for a more thorough discussion of the main sample set), initial staffing decisions were guided by preferences in ownership structure, method of establishment (greenfield, joint venture, takeover, etc.), whether the company saw Japanese management as one of its core competencies, and by the overarching corporate strategy (Taylor, Beechler, & Napier, 1996).

   The most important tactical decision involved the selection of a basic template to be used in guiding subsequent decision making about the specifics of the affiliate's management system. Some firms in our study sought to transfer the parent template at the level of management philosophy. That is, they endeavored to transfer an underlying set of values to be used in defining what policies to establish and how. For example, one firm had a well-defined corporate philosophy that valued both the development of human capital and a long-term relationship between employee and company. At the time it established its first overseas affiliate in the United States, it emphasized these values in delineating specific HRM policies. By contrast, other firms sought to implement a template at the policy level, spelling out in great detail the specific procedures to be followed. For instance, one consumer electronics firm sought to transfer the entire parent company template to its U.S. operations. To do so, it had its entire set of work rules and personnel manuals translated into English and then made modifications required by the U.S. legal system. Finally, a third set of firms was less concerned with philosophy or policy, but instead focused specifically on how they wanted employees to behave. These firms sought to establish a template at the practice level, seeking a specific behavior. Typical of this type of affiliate was a copy machine manufacturer in southern California that provided employees at each

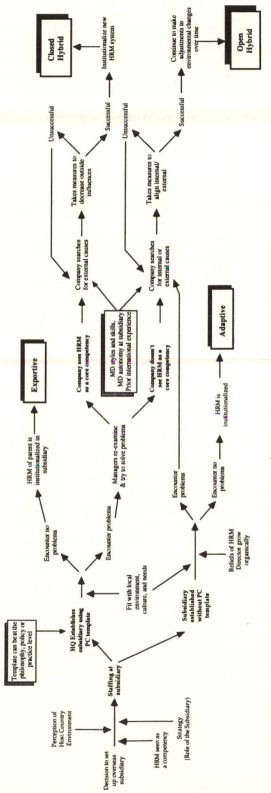

FIGURE 12.2 Diagram of Tactical Decisions and Influences in the Development of Subsidiary HRM System

work station with a sequence of instant photographs detailing each step of that station's task in lieu of on-the-job training or other methods of employee training and development. The essential behavior was the "correct" sequence of steps, even though a supervisor admitted that at some stations the task could be completed by following a different order, "but this is the way it is done in Japan."

We found that decisions by JMNCs about whether to adopt a parent or host country template and the level at which the template was to be applied were strongly influenced by two factors: the company's perception of management as a core competency and the perception that the parent's management system fit with the host country environment. In instances where management was seen as a core competence or the parent system's fit with the local environment was perceived as high, JMNCs were more inclined to select a fully elaborated parent template that included philosophy, policy, and practice. At the least, they employed a philosophy and policy template based on the parent.

The role of the affiliate in the JMNC's overall strategy also appeared to exert some influence on the choice of template. Beechler, Bird, and Raghuram (1993) theorize that the need for fit between a firm's overall business strategy and its HRM system may create pressures for consistency between parent and affiliate HRM systems. This is reflected in a preference for imposing a parent company template. Interview data from managers in the U.S.–based set of affiliates supported this thesis. One HRM manager in a New Jersey–based affiliate producing copy machine subassemblies confessed that he had little control over policy decisions because they were often dictated from Tokyo due to the affiliate's tight linkages with Japan-based facilities.

As affiliates moved forward with the implementation of their chosen template, they usually found it necessary to make adjustments in their management system. The types of adjustments they made were guided by (1) their perceptions as to the cause of problems inevitable in any implementation, (2) the degree of autonomy granted them by the parent, and (3) the amount of international experience key personnel possessed (Kobrin, 1992). For some firms the adjustments were straightforward and easily made. Typical was a photochemical processing firm that, in an effort to adapt to U.S. labor norms, had decided not to ask local employees to wear company uniforms, even though Japanese expatriates wore them on the shop floor. Local workers expressed discomfort at being treated differently than their bosses and their counterparts back in Japan. This being the company's first overseas facility, corporate planners in Osaka had assumed that the Americans would not want to wear uniforms and had instructed the U.S. plant manager not to issue them. However, once the manager became aware of local employee concerns, he instituted a policy requiring that uniforms be worn in the plant and morale improved immediately.

For others, the adjustments followed an iterative, experimental process whereby managers would try first one solution then another. For example, a copier manufacturer in the United Kingdom sustained levels of turnover higher than any local firm. Believing that turnover was due to low wage rates, the company implemented a pay increase for line workers. When turnover rates remained high, QC circles were established and a team-based bonus system was installed. When turnover still remained high, the company shifted attention away from manipulations in the compensation system and undertook a more rigorous selection procedure designed to eliminate candidates with career profiles similar to those who had quit.

It is important to point out that not all problems were resolved and that the process of adjustment was ongoing. Changes in the local environment, as well as shifts in strategy and fluctuations in parent operations, required that the affiliate management system undergo continual adaptation. In the case of another affiliate based in the United Kingdom, for example, a no layoff policy became problematic when one of the two products it assembled was discontinued. Layoffs were avoided, but only as a result of revamping work schedules and redefining a full work week in terms of fewer hours.

Though each affiliate's experiences were unique, common themes and patterns recurred as our sample of firms grew. As figure 12.2 reflects, we were eventually able to classify each affiliate's learning process into one of four types.

The Exportive Model

In establishing the overseas affiliate's HRM policies and practices, some Japanese firms seek a wholesale transplant of the management template from the parent company in Japan. In figure 12.2, this approach is labeled "exportive" because of its implicit assumption that parent company ways of doing things are inherently more appropriate than, if not superior to, other approaches. Hence, the parent exports its way of doing things to the new site. Firms following this model were inclined to view their management of human resources as a core competency that was a source of competitive advantage and, hence, were also inclined to see it as something universally applicable. Firms also saw the gap between local environmental conditions and those back home in Japan as relatively small, subsequently concluding that significant modification of the parent template was not required.

What distinguishes the exportive model from the other learning types on this particular branch of the decision tree is that, indeed, the management system did seem to work reasonably well, and on the first try. Japanese firms in the exportive category were characterized by successful management systems that closely mirrored the philosophy and policies of the parent. We were initially inclined to think that firms adopting this model would experience significant difficulty in establishing effective HRM policies and practices in their overseas affiliates, but such a sweeping conclusion proved inaccurate. The exportive model seemed to work reasonably well when affiliates were located in countries that were legally and socioculturally similar to Japan. Consequently, only minor adjustments in the parent template were necessary. The most successful examples of this type were found among affiliates in Southeast Asian countries, such as Singapore and Thailand.

Figure 12.3 indicates how the exportive learning type varies around the basic model. The affiliate enacts by perceiving the host environment as similar to Japan's and also perceives its own capabilities in management as a core competency. Given the perceived match between home and host country environments and the perceived strength of its existing management system, it selects a parent management template in the overseas affiliate. The selected template roughly suits the local environment

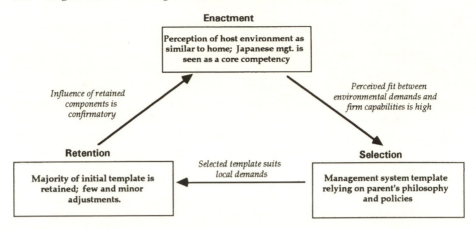

FIGURE 12.3 A Process Model of the Japanese MNC Parent-Affiliate Management Learning Cycle for Exportive Firms

so that only minor adjustments are required for it to work well there. Early on, the affiliate concludes that its experience with the parent template is successful and so it is retained. This is viewed by both the affiliate and the JMNC as a confirmation of the parent template as an appropriate way to manage the affiliate's HRM function. Consequently, learning for both the affiliate and the parent is in the form of a confirmation of the original assumption. Hedberg (1981) points out that learning derived from success often focuses on fine-tuning the existing system. We found this to be true for the Japanese firms in our study, which were convinced of the correctness of their systems as well as their systems' widespread applicability. Moreover, since the experience confirmed what was already believed, there was little attempt by the parent at disseminating this particular affiliate's experiences to its other foreign affiliates. Any minor adjustments made to the template were seen as idiosyncratic to the host country and therefore irrelevant to both the parent and to other affiliates.

The Closed Hybrid Model

A second group of firms adopted a variant of the learning model that we call closed hybrid. As was the case with exportive learners, this type was characterized by the affiliate's reliance on a parent company template in the development of the initial management system. However, early on, the affiliate encountered problems indicating that the fit was not good and that substantive changes were required. At this point, if the affiliate and the parent had strong beliefs in their management as a core competency, modifications to the system were based on a belief that the cause of problems was external. Perhaps the local workers were poorly trained or had a bad attitude, local competitors were able to pay higher wages, or government regulations interfered with management policies. Consequently, modifications to the system moved in the direction of buffering it from outside influences. Our earlier example of the affiliate experiencing high turnover in the United Kingdom falls into this type. When several adjustments designed to adapt policies to local conditions failed to achieve the desired decrease in turnover, it moved to a highly selective hiring process aimed at protecting the rest of the management system by screening out potential quitters. In other words, selection would buffer the exported system from the "failure" of the local environment to produce loyal, motivated workers.

Figure 12.4 shows how the closed hybrid learning type varies around the basic learning model. The affiliate perceives the host environment as similar to Japan's, and it perceives its own capabilities in management as a core competency. Given the perceived match between home and host country environments and the perceived strength of its existing management system, it opts for a parent template in the overseas affiliate. The closed hybrid differentiated itself from the exportive type as a result of its initial lack of success in adapting and functioning effectively in the local environment. Hedberg (1981) notes that failure often encourages a reevaluation of assumptions and beliefs. As illustrated in figure 12.4, closed hybrid firms, faced with failure, recognized that the parent template did not fit the local environment. However, because they held strong beliefs about the efficacy of their own approaches, their problem search was externally directed, as was their learning. They acquired more information about the local environment, recognized how their system needed to be modified to function well within it, and made changes accordingly. Dissemination of what they learned, however, was limited. Due to a perception that local conditions were exceptional, the parent learned very little, judging suitable adjustments for this affiliate inapplicable to other settings. This is why we label these firms closed hybrid learners: experience led to the creation of a hybrid system, but learning was closed off from the larger organization.

The Adaptive Model

In contrast to an approach that assumes the superiority and efficacy of Japanese parent company ways of managing, some firms focused on adapting as much as possible to

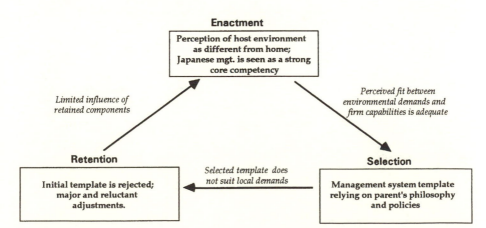

FIGURE 12.4 A Process Model of the Japanese MNC Parent-Affiliate Management Learning Cycle for Closed Hybrid Firms

the local situation, using parent company approaches only in limited areas. Because this approach led to a relatively disparate set of policies and practices across overseas affiliates, we call this the adaptive learning type. Firms employing this model downplayed the importance of the HRM function in their overseas operations. They held the position that human resources ought to be managed as effectively as possible and that, although they might possess considerable expertise in this area, parent company policies should not be imposed on overseas affiliates, which face considerably different conditions.

When these firms confronted problems in the course of establishing HRM policies, their inclination was to search for the cause of the problem internally, seeking to discern how their approach or the actions that flowed from that approach were flawed. One consequence was that these firms learned a great deal not only about the local environment and local actors, but also about themselves. Unfortunately, because of their beliefs that local conditions were so different, they also believed that what they learned could not be extended beyond their affiliate's own situation. Instead, their perception was that each affiliate had to learn on its own, with little if any transfer between them or between the affiliate and parent.

These characteristics are reflected in figure 12.5, which describes the adaptive version of the learning cycle. Perceiving a host environment dramatically different from Japan's and possessing no strong attachment to the parent's management system, the overseas affiliate begins with a template customized to fit the demands of the local environment. Because the template fits reasonably well, few adjustments are made and the system is viewed as successful in terms of its responsiveness to local demands. Again, the success of the initial implementation effort, in conjunction with a perceived misfit with the parent management system, discourages attempts to share what is learned beyond those individuals associated with fine-tuning the process. Viewed in this way, both the affiliate and the parent are inclined to conclude that learning is not easily transferred, so diffusion is limited.

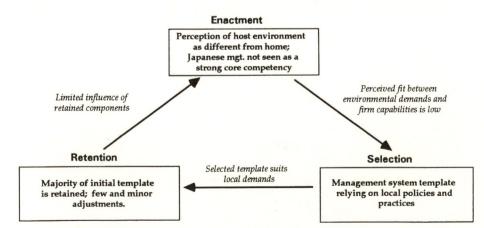

FIGURE 12.5 A Process Model of the Japanese MNC Parent-Affiliate Management Learning Cycle for Adaptive Firms

The Open Hybrid Model

The final type, what we call the open hybrid learning model, encompasses firms that approached the development of a management system for their overseas affiliates from a variety of starting points. Firms adopting this model may or may not have originally begun with a parent company template as the basis for their system. However, unlike those in the other three types, they tended to move very quickly to a position that sought a duality in outlook—a simultaneous emphasis on parent and local perspectives. Almost invariably this shift was the result of problems greater than anticipated, causing them to reevaluate their initial assumptions and beliefs. As a side note, only firms not strongly wedded to a belief in management as one of their core competencies seemed able to undergo such transformations. One consumer electronics sales operation in the United Kingdom typified this type best. The initial managing director had sought to create a bridge between the parent's strong corporate culture and the British work ethic. After nearly a year of struggle with bad morale and low productivity, nearly the entire system was jettisoned and a new one developed. Changes addressed both internal and external factors. For example, greater time was spent in socializing new local hires into corporate and Japanese ways of doing and thinking. At the same time, several of the policies relating to compensation and work assignments deemed most objectionable by British employees were modified to conform more closely to the norms in effect among British competitors.

Figure 12.6 illustrates the learning cycle as experienced by open hybrid learners. Firms in this category view the host environment as substantially different from Japan's and do not see their corporate strength or competitive advantage as lying in the management of their human resources. (This is not to suggest that they did not believe they did a good job in this area.) They subsequently initiate their affiliate management system using a customized template—modified from the parent or local models—and open themselves up to change once they encounter difficulties. They make revisions to the template involving both adjustment to local conditions and modifications from parent positions. They closely monitor the application of adjustments and are cautious in the acceptance of success. This is not to suggest that they were timid in identifying what was working—quite the opposite. When they discovered successes, they were inclined to disseminate them quickly and widely within the company. Rather, they recognized that the system required continual adjustment. They were humble regarding what they knew and, hence, made themselves open to learning. Moreover, they sought ways to connect what they were learning locally with applications to other situations in the larger organization.

The greater flexibility of the open hybrid, brought about as a result of a dual focus and a willingness to relax assumptions about the superiority of the parent company's management system, enabled these JMNCs to search for the source of problems both internally and externally. One consequence of this was that firms in this group tended to identify problems more quickly, while problems were still in gestation and before they had time to develop into fully grown crises. Change was incremental and continuous.

The orientation of open hybrids toward change was also highly proactive, characterized by a constant tinkering with the system. Open hybrid firms exhibited a will-

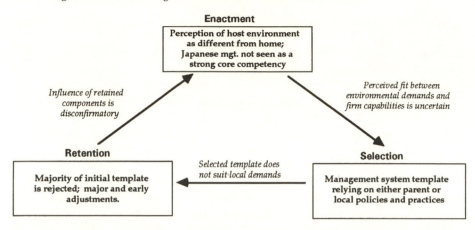

FIGURE 12.6 A Process Model of the Japanese MNC Parent-Affiliate Management Learning Cycle for Open Hybrid Firms

ingness to learn from local sources *or* from other parties within the organization. In similar fashion, they were often enthusiastic about sharing what they had learned with others in the local community, but more frequently with the parent company and with other affiliates within the organization. One affiliate in the United Kingdom in our study demonstrated this through its active membership in a local business association that met monthly to share insights about HRM issues and how to resolve various management problems. Within the larger organization, they met quarterly with HRM managers from other affiliates in Europe, again using the occasion to share information and trade insights.

The openness of affiliates in this grouping was also reflected in their interviews with us. Often interviewees sought our observations and evaluations regarding the policies they had developed. They seemed genuinely interested in exploring such events from different perspectives so as to better understand what had happened and to learn from them.

Comparing the Four Learning Types

A consideration of the similarities and differences among the four archetypes highlights several important distinctions between them. Contrasts across the models are presented in table 12.1 in terms of the three stages of the learning cycle: enactment, selection, and retention.

Enactment. The most critical decision point in the process of establishing the Japanese overseas affiliate's management system was that of the initial template to be used. This choice set the direction and tone of subsequent decisions. Exportive and closed hybrid firms opted for a parent management template, thereby establishing what would subsequently become barriers to locally responsive adaptations. By contrast, adaptive and open hybrid firms emphasized host country responsiveness and

TABLE 12.1 A Comparison of Four Learning Cycle Models

	Exportive	Closed Hybrid	Adaptive	Open Hybrid
Enactment	Parent Template	Parent Template	Local Template	Customized, temporary template
Selection	Minor adjustments	Major adjustment	Minor adjustment	Major adjustment
Retention	Verification of fit; fine-tuning	Identification of success consistent with self-image	Local success	Cautious success

put in place local templates. The template decision was influenced by a variety of organizational factors mentioned previously, most particularly their perception of the gap the between host country and Japan, as well as the belief that their management was a core competency. Just as critical as these, however, was the staffing decision, that is, who was selected to install the template. Specifically, the general manager of the affiliate served as the primary "carrier" of the template. In the case of exportive and closed hybrid models, the carrier was a Japanese expatriate from headquarters, quite often working in close connection with staff in the parent company. In contrast, adaptive and open hybrid firms were more likely to use a host country national. When the affiliate general manager of adaptive and open hybrid firms was a Japanese national, then it was common to find that the executive responsible for HRM was a local person who had been given substantial autonomy in the design of the management system.

A second distinction between the exportive/closed hybrid types and the adaptive/open hybrid firms was the level of template selected. The former were much more inclined to establish a parent template that included management philosophy and policies. Although adaptive/open hybrid firms selected a local or highly customized template, with rare exception it were predicated upon a management philosophy borrowed from the parent. Typical of this was a U.S. affiliate of a copier company that we classified as open hybrid. The U.S. manager responsible for designing the management system was given free reign. His choice was to visit the parent company in Tokyo and spend several months talking with headquarters personnel to discover why they did things the way they did. On his return he set about developing a U.S. version of the parent philosophy and then elaborated a set of policies, many of which on the surface bore little similarity to those back as the parent company. Nevertheless, the underlying aim of the policies was consistent with the values of the parent.

Selection.   The defining difference between the four learning types in the selection stage centered on the extent of adjustments required. Both open and closed hybrid types experienced substantial difficulties early on in the development process. These difficulties forced firms to reevaluate their initial assumptions about the system and develop new ways of doing things. However, closed hybrids refused to consider that problems might be caused by internal factors and assumed the difficulties arose from an improper interpretation of the host country environment. In contrast, open hybrid firms were willing to consider themselves as the cause of some problems and, hence, willing to look for internal adjustments.

Exportive and adaptive types were characterized by rather minor changes. That is, the initial templates fit reasonably so that only minor revisions were called for. Our follow-up interviews revealed that this was not always true in the long term. In several instances, firms *chose* to perceive only minor problems when, in reality, the misalignment with local requirements was great. For example, a photochemical company based in the southern United States felt comfortable with its management system after two years of being in operation. "Yes, there are problems," one U.S. manager told us, "but they'll be resolved over time." Our follow-up telephone interview nine months later revealed that the problems had worsened.

This raises another important point. Because learning is ongoing, firms occasionally moved from one type to another. This was most often the case with exportive and adaptive types. Over time, management systems that had seemed to work well occasionally experienced major difficulties. Sometimes this was due to an initial bad fit that had been glossed over. At other times it was the result of shifting conditions in the host country or a change in the affiliate's strategic role within the larger organization. Usually, such shifts caught the affiliate off guard, making the subsequent adjustment traumatic.

Retention.   The final stage of the learning cycle, where the four types diverged, involves retaining lessons from what did or did not work in the past. What exportive firms seemed to learn was that the parent template worked in the new setting. In other words, learning came in the form of a confirmation that initial assessments were correct. In concert with this learning was the perception that transference of the parent template primarily required fine-tuning. The parent could thus believe that its management template was "universal." Meanwhile, within the affiliate there was little inclination to question this belief nor much attention directed at monitoring local conditions closely.

Closed hybrid firms learned, albeit often reluctantly, that the parent template did not fit the local environment well. Given their belief that management constituted a core competency of the parent, they predicated other learning from the experience on maintaining a consistent self-image. That is, firms in this group learned that the pressures of the host country environment required buffering the management system in various ways. Consequently, much of the learning centered on how to protect the system from local pressures. Not surprisingly, at the parent level little effort was made to absorb what had been learned locally.

Adaptive types learned about the local environment and what was required to succeed there. This knowledge, often embedded in the affiliate managers themselves, included how to accommodate local, state, and government labor regulations. Affiliates found it hard to disseminate this context-specific knowledge beyond their own borders.

Finally, open hybrid firms acquired an understanding in three areas: (1) host country environment and what the affiliate management system needed to do to work well there; (2) the affiliate itself, its strengths and weaknesses; and (3) how the affiliate's experiences fit within the larger organization and what it could teach others and what it could learn from them. In a sense, such firms had a fundamentally different mindset oriented to looking for connections between experiences in ways that downplayed host country distinctiveness in favor of pursuing possible similarities with other areas of the organization.

In the next section, we address more specifically various aspects of learning that grow out of the overseas affiliate's efforts at establishing a management system. We approach the learning implications first in terms of differences among the four types.

Implications for Learning

The identification of four types of learning organizations led us to consider the various effects and implications for learning. Several issues are addressed in the following section. Then we step back from the firms in this study and reflect upon the larger implications of learning in large complex MNCs.

Implications of the Four Models

Type of learning.   Argyris and Schön (1978) make a distinction between *single-loop* and *double-loop learning*. Single-loop learning is characterized as "an ability to detect and correct error in relation to a given set of operating norms" (Morgan, 1986: 88). By contrast, double-loop learning is described as an ability "to take a 'double-look' at the situation by questioning the relevance of operating norms" (Morgan, 1986: 88). Of the four learning types identified in our study, only the open hybrid exhibited comprehensive double-loop learning capabilities (see table 12.2.) Exportive firms and adaptive firms were convinced of the correctness of operating norms; consequently, their only concern was making minor adjustments to conform to norms. Closed hybrid firms, in the face of evidence that operating norms were not effective, chose instead to focus on ways to preserve norms rather than change them. This is one facet of the label "closed." These firms may have experienced double-loop learning in the affiliate, but it stopped there.

Transferability of learning.   A second aspect of learning is the extent to which it can be transmitted to others, or its transferability (see also chapter 5). Nonaka (1991) points out that knowledge comes in two varieties: explicit and tacit. Explicit knowledge is

TABLE 12.2 Implications of the Four Models for Parent and Affiliate Learning

	Exportive	Closed hybrid	Adaptive	Open hybrid
Type of learning	Single-loop	Single-loop	Single-loop	Double-loop
Transferability of learning	Explicit	Tacit	Tacit	Tacit and explicit
Sharing of learning	Widespread; confirms original template	Limited; maintains self-image	Limited; focused on local knowledge	Widespread; multi-directional; connective

just that, easily explained or transmitted to others. Tacit knowledge, difficult to state or explain, is embedded in understandings that cannot be easily codified. Much of the learning that adaptive and closed hybrid firms experienced was tacit. It could not easily be explained or transmitted outside the affiliate. Often it was embedded in the experiences of individual managers, who understood how things were done locally but saw neither the need nor the way to explain it to the parent. "Things are simply done different here; headquarters doesn't understand," said one manager in characterizing this learning in his firm.

Exportive firms acquired explicit, albeit shallow, knowledge. Many of the changes to policies they made were straightforward and transparent, for example, an overtime policy that needed to be modified to conform to host county regulations.

Open hybrid affiliates acquired both explicit and tacit knowledge. Because they experienced double-loop learning, the tacit knowledge was both about how the affiliate could be effective locally as well as how different policies fit together or coincided with the management philosophy. Explicit learning also focused on two aspects of learning: (1) specific policies and the ways in which they worked within the affiliate, and (2) how they would work in other settings. Quite often the latter type of explicit knowledge was developed through parent-designed workshops that brought together personnel managers from different affiliates within a region.

Sharing of learning.   The preceding discussion shows that knowledge may be more or less difficult to transfer. Whether it actually is transferred is another question. Our final concern centered on the extent to which learning at the affiliate level was shared within the larger organization. For exportive firms, sharing was widespread, but superficial. Adaptive and closed hybrid affiliates engaged in only limited sharing. In contrast, open hybrid firms shared widely in a give-and-take fashion. They sought opportunities to pass on what they had learned to other units. In addition, they also actively sought input on what they were doing. Perhaps the most distinctive attribute of the open hybrid type was its openness to learning.

Larger Implications

The vast complexity of large MNCs, their institutional qualities, and the ambiguity of working across national and cultural boundaries raises a myriad of concerns. Although we cannot hope to address all of them, several are particularly cogent to our work with JMNCs and their overseas affiliates.

Learning when the cycle is incomplete.   Our discussion in the previous sections was predicated on the assumption that learning cycles are complete. Hedberg (1981) suggests that complex, highly unstable environments (typical of the international arena) may create situations wherein the learning cycle is short-circuited or remains incomplete. This was certainly true of the Japanese firms we studied. Key managers were transferred, objectives changed, and parent constraints prevented revisions to the existing system. In such instances, two types of outcomes were prevalent. In the first, the affiliate found itself repeating the mistakes of a previous administration as new managers acted on the basis of their own understandings, which were naive and not contextually grounded. This often led to a deterioration of morale among local employees and the exit of persons possessing the appropriate knowledge to help the new manager correct errors. In the second, new adjustments were made before the efficacy of prior adjustments could be determined. Consequently, the affiliate seemed to be always in a state of flux, never stable long enough to confirm that difficulties had been properly diagnosed and remedied. This, in turn, developed into a downward spiral of morale and performance in which problems grew faster than responses could handle them.

Unlearning to learn.   Parent organizations, no matter how neutral or objective they attempt to be, introduce perspectives and procedures predicated on prior learning. In this sense, learning in the Japanese overseas affiliate actually consisted of two different activities: learning and unlearning. This may be most easily understood if brought down to the level of the individual general manager. Japanese expatriates we interviewed found it necessary to *unlearn* the Japanese parent's management system before they were able to *learn* local ways of doing things. This was also true for host country managers, who needed to unlearn local management approaches before they could comprehend the parent's system. Though this is certainly not a new observation, what was striking to us was the extent to which this consistently surfaced as a problematic issue, particularly in the case of Japanese parent managers, who appeared to have a very difficult time envisioning non-Japanese approaches. Indeed, we were drawn to the stimulus-response model of learning precisely because it reflected the way in which Japanese firms often had to fail before they would then become flexible and willing to try something new.

   This suggests that humility and patience are essential qualities to be a successful affiliate manager and to operate a successful affiliate. Humility is required in terms of being willing to let go of preferred or accepted ways of doing things and in terms of being open to new approaches and ideas. Patience is required because the process of unlearning and learning takes time. A similar assessment can be made of the requirements for parent companies.

Learning what is essential.   Part of the successful development of the affiliate's management system and the subsequent effective dissemination of learning within the larger organization was the ability to identify the essential elements of the initial template as well as the essential elements of subsequent adjustments. This is clearly an area where many Japanese firms have struggled. Indeed, the past five years have witnessed an earnest and collective attempt by many Japanese companies and business associations to identify the essential aspects of the general Japanese management system. Typical of this effort was a 1992 report by the Japan Federation of Employers (Keizai Doyukai, 1992) that broke down managerial practices into two categories—practices having positive benefit and practices having uncertain benefit—which were, in turn, broken down into two classes each. Practices having certain benefit were separated into those that ought to be strongly promoted in overseas operations and those that ought to be maintained domestically and applied overseas where possible. Practices having uncertain benefit were broken down into those that should be applied only in Japan and those that ought to be eliminated even in Japan.

The strategic dimension of tactical decisions in learning.   We began our discussion of organizational learning in Japanese affiliates by noting the variety of tactical decisions associated with setting up operations overseas. While we have no desire to blur the distinction between "tactical" and "strategic," our findings suggest that what many JMNCs perceived as tactical decisions were in actuality strategic. Indeed, when it came to the establishment of a new system within the overseas affiliate, prudence seemed to point toward viewing most of the decisions as strategic. Foremost among those tactical decisions that had a powerful strategic dimension was selecting a general manager and related personnel to staff the new operation. These were the individuals responsible for determining the template to be applied and then applying it. It was not unusual for them to imbue the template and its application with a unique and personal flavor. In many instances it may well have been the case that success or failure of the template hinged more on the idiosyncratic character of the implementors / administrators of the system than on the system itself.

During our interviews we were impressed with the frequency with which a managing director, plant manager, or key personnel executive was referred to as the key to the affiliate's success or failure. Indeed, we concluded that the single most important decision that a Japanese firm may make in setting up its overseas affiliates is the selection of the person responsible for managing it.

Conclusions

In this chapter we have introduced a typology of organization learning models that we used to compare JMNCs on how they learn and the levels at which they learn. The typology and its application to JMNCs have a number of valuable implications for practitioners, as well as for international management researchers.

For practitioners, the typology and the examination of its effects on organization learning offers useful guidance in the design of management systems for overseas affiliates. As with any improvement, in product or process, the first step is understanding the present product or process. For managers in MNCs, the typology offered in this chapter is unique in its identification of the component parts of the managerial systems that operate in foreign affiliates, from selection of a template, to the level at which it is applied, to what guides adjustments in the template. This disaggregation of the managerial system into its essential elements provides a framework that may be useful in understanding the degree to which other managerial systems contribute to organizational learning.

As the final section of this chapter shows, this understanding is important. These organizational learning types have an important influence on the firm's ability to learn at a higher-order level than its competitors. In addition to the type of learning that occurs, managers must examine whether it is occurring at all and, if so, what mechanisms are being used to achieve the transfer of knowledge. As the resource-based view of the firm indicates (Barney, 1986; Grant, 1991), to the degree that firms can outperform competitors in these areas, they can create a "learning organization" in which they have the capability to integrate knowledge flexibly within the organization, a capability that can be a source of enduring competitive advantage in some industries (Hamel & Prahalad, 1994; Henderson & Cockburn, 1994; Senge, 1990).

For management theorists, this chapter contributes important refinements and extensions of previous theory in the areas of organizational learning and international management. Drawing on the seminal work of Cyert and March (1963), Weick (1969), and Campbell (1965), we have applied the enactment/selection/retention model to an important problem facing MNCs: the design of the firm's managerial systems. One of the critical tasks facing MNCs is how to design managerial systems to balance integration and localization (Bartlett & Ghoshal, 1989; Taylor, Beechler, & Napier, 1996). The four types of organizational learning presented in this chapter represent approaches to the integration-localization problem that show *intermediate* points along the continuum, thus further challenging the bipolar conceptualization of the problem. Moreover, the typology is dynamic, showing how systems can evolve over time from one approach to another. The dynamic evolution of systems and their contribution to firm competitiveness are acquiring increasing importance (Collis, 1994).

Future research should first begin by testing the robustness of the typology offered here. A second major goal must be the examination of the effect of industry on the choice among the four types of organizational learning models. Industry may affect the need for increased organizational learning (Henderson & Cockburn, 1994), which in turn will lead firms within a particular industry to choose a particular organizational learning type. By studying MNCs within a particular industry, researchers may identify the organizational learning types that high-performing MNCs in that industry adopt and the organizational consequences for firms that adopt other organizational learning types.

Several other results of the study presented in this chapter should be noted by international management theorists. First, the finding that perceived cultural distance may be as important as real cultural distance may have considerable import for researchers in the areas of cross-cultural management, as well as international strategy. That is, whereas absolute differences based on such frameworks of cultural values as Hofstede's (1980) have been utilized routinely by theorists, the analysis in this chapter points to the possibility that the perceptions of cultural distance of those in decision-making positions may actually affect the design of management systems or of international strategies. A second important result should be noted by those involved in international HRM, particularly in the selection of expatriates. The key role that the general manager seems to play in selection of a template for design of the organizational system has received minor research attention (e.g., Black, Mendenhall, & Oddou, 1991). The research reported here offers a framework by which to conceive of the different roles expatriates play in the development of an organizational learning type within an MNC, which may have important implications for international selection and performance appraisal.

Finally, there is no reason to assume that these four learning archetypes are characteristic only of JMNCs. The framework presented in this chapter provides a useful starting point for examining the process of organizational learning in other non-Japanese MNCs. An important area of research with implications for both academics and practitioners would be the similarities and differences in learning approaches of Japanese and non-Japanese MNCs and their implications for organizational competitiveness.

As we stand back from countless hours in the field talking with managers from all over the world and take stock of what we have learned as researchers from our observations, we are certain of a few points.

First, past is prologue. Even de novo affiliates set up thousands of miles from home are a reflection of past learning cycles experienced by their firm. Second, although we, like many others, have found many similarities across Japanese firms, our overwhelming conclusion is that it is just as absurd to talk about "the Japanese firm" as it would be to describe "the American firm." Finally, there is nothing mystical or magical about Japanese management. Just like everyone else, Japanese managers begin with a set of assumptions and perceptions, try out those ideas in new contexts, and adjust them based on feedback regarding sources of failure. How this process evolves, as we have seen in this chapter, is not monolithic but most certainly will help differentiate the winners from the losers in the global economic arena for years to come.

References

Abo, T. 1994. Hybrid Factory: *The Japanese Production System in the United States*. New York: Oxford University Press.

Argyris, C. 1976. "Leadership, Learning, and Changing the Status Quo." *Organizational Dynamics*. 4 (Winter): 29–43.

Argyris, C., & Schön, D. 1978. *Organizational Learning: A Theory of Action Perspective*. Reading, MA: Addison-Wesley.

Barney, J. 1986. "Types of Competition and the Theory of Strategy: Toward an Integrative Framework." *Academy of Management Review*. 11: 791–800.

Bartlett, C., & Ghoshal, S. 1989. *Managing Across Borders*. Boston: Harvard Business School Press.

Beechler, S., & Bird, A. 1994. "The Best of Both Worlds? An Exploratory Study of Human Resource Management Practices in U.S.-Based Japanese Affiliates." In Campbell, N. (ed.), *The Global Kaisha*. London: Blackwell.

Beechler, S., Bird, A., & Raghuram, S. 1993. "Linking Business Strategy and Transnational Human Resource Management Practices." *Advances in International and Comparative Management*. 8: 199–215.

Bird, A. & Beechler, S. 1995. "Links Between Business Strategy and Human Resource Management Strategies in U.S.-Based Japanese Subsidiaries: An Empirical Investigation." *Journal of International Business Studies*. 26: 23–45.

Black, J. S., Mendenhall, M. E., & Oddou, G. 1991. "Toward a Comprehensive Model of International Adjustment: An Integration of Multiple Theoretical Perspectives." *Academy of Management Review*. 16: 291–317.

Campbell, D. T. 1959. "Methodological Suggestions from a Comparative Psychology of Knowledge Processes." *Inquiry*. 2: 152–182.

Campbell, D. T. 1965. "Variation and Selective Retention in Socio-cultural Evolution." In Barringer, H. R., Blanksten, G. I., & Mack, R. W. (eds.), *Social Change in Developing Areas*. Cambridge, MA: Schenkman. 19–49.

Collis, D. 1994. "How Valuable are Organizational Capabilities?" *Strategic Management Journal*. 15: 143–152.

Cyert, R., & March, J. 1963. *A Behavioral Theory of the Firm.* Englewood Cliffs, NJ: Prentice Hall.

Grant, R. 1991. "The Resource-Based Theory of Competitive Advantage: Implications for Strategy Formulation." *California Management Review.* Spring: 114–135.

Hamel, G., & Prahalad, C. 1994. *Competing for the Future.* Boston: Harvard Business School Press.

Hedberg, B. 1981. "How Organizations Learn and Unlearn." In Nystrom, P. C., & Starbuck, W. H. (eds.), *Handbook of Organizational Design.* Vol. 1. New York: Oxford University Press. 3–27.

Henderson, R., & Cockburn, I. 1994. "Measuring Competence? Exploring Firm Effects in Pharmaceutical Research." *Strategic Management Journal.* 15: 63–84.

Hofstede, G. 1980. *Culture's Consequences.* Newbury Park, CA: Sage.

Kagono, T, Nonaka, I., Sakakibara, H., & Okumura, A. 1986. *Strategic Versus Evolutionary Management.* Amsterdam: North-Holland.

Keizai Doyakai. 1992. *Oopun shisutemu e no kigyo kakushin (Enterprise Reform for an Open System).* Tokyo: Keizai Doyukai.

Kidder, L. H. 1981. *Sellitz, Wrightsman & Cook's Research Methods in Social Relations.* New York: Holt, Rinehart & Winston.

Kobrin, S. J. 1992. *Multinational Strategy and International Human Resource Management Policy.* Working paper no. 92–14, Reginald H. Jones Center, The Wharton School, University of Pennsylvania, Philadelphia.

Morgan, G. 1986. *Images of Organization.* Beverly Hills, CA: Sage.

Nonaka, I. 1991. "The Knowledge-Creating Company." *Harvard Business Review.* 69 (6): 96–104.

Pfeffer, J. 1994. *Competitive Advantage Through People.* Boston: Harvard Business School Press.

Rosenzweig, P. M., & Singh, J. V. 1991. "Organizational Environments and the Multinational Enterprise." *Academy of Management Review.* 16: 340–361.

Schein, E. 1985. *Organizational Culture and Leadership.* San Francisco: Jossey-Bass.

Schuler, R. S. 1989. "Strategic Human Resource Management and Industrial Relations." *Human Relations.* 42: 157–184.

Senge, P. 1990. "The Leader's New Work: Building Learning Organizations." *Sloan Management Review.* 32: 7–23.

Stinchcombe, A. L. 1965. "Social Structure and Organizations." In March, J. G. (ed.), *Handbook of Organizations.* Chicago: Rand McNally. 142–193.

Taylor, S., Beechler, S., & Napier, N. 1996. "Toward an Integrative Theory of Strategic International Human Resource Management." *Academy of Management Review.* 214: 959–985.

Weick, K. 1969. *The Social Psychology of Organizing.* Reading, MA: Addison-Wesley.

Index